Dance, Human Rights, and Social Justice

Dignity in Motion

Edited by Naomi Jackson
and Toni Shapiro-Phim

To Melanie with love — Naomi Jackson

THE SCARECROW PRESS, INC.

Lanham, Maryland • Toronto • Plymouth, UK

2008

SCARECROW PRESS, INC.

Published in the United States of America
by Scarecrow Press, Inc.
A wholly owned subsidary of
The Rowman & Littlefield Publishing Group, Inc.
4501 Forbes Boulevard, Suite 200, Lanham, Maryland 20706
www.scarecrowpress.com

Estover Road
Plymouth PL6 7PY
United Kingdom

British Library Cataloguing in Publication Information Available

Library of Congress Cataloging-in-Publication Data
Dance, human rights, and social justice : dignity in motion / edited by Naomi Jackson
and Toni Shapiro-Phim.   p. cm.
    Includes bibliographical references and index.
    ISBN-13: 978-0-8108-6149-7 (pbk. : alk. paper)
    ISBN-10: 0-8108-6149-6 (pbk. : alk. paper)
    eISBN-13: 978-0-8108-6218-0
    eISBN-10: 0-8108-6218-2
    1. Dance—Sociological aspects. 2. Dance—Social aspects. 3. Dance—Political aspects.
4. Human rights. 5. Social justice. I. Jackson, Naomi M. II. Phim, Toni Shapiro.
    GV1588.6D3734 2008
    306.4'846—dc22   2008022471

∞™   The paper used in this publication meets the minimum requirements of
American National Standard for Information Sciences—Permanence of Paper
for Printed Library Materials, ANSI/NISO Z39.48-1992.
Manufactured in the United States of America.

To Nalani Mehra,
and to Sarah and Anthony Jackson,
for their commitment to democracy and socially responsible art

"Few rational human beings anywhere, regardless of their race, religion, or culture, would deny the supreme value of peace, justice, and freedom in their positive, vigorous aspects. It is now widely seen that peace should be more than mere absence of war; it should be a positive force that counters violence as a means of resolving the problems of human society. Justice should not only aim at controlling the negative traits in human nature. It should work to promote a sense of fairness, compassion, and universal brotherhood. Freedom should be more than a lack of shackles. It should mean an environment where the right to develop one's own potential, without curbing that of others, can be exercised without fear."

—Aung San Suu Kyi (Burmese dissident and Nobel Peace Prize laureate), message to the International Conference on Universal Human Rights and Human Values, 2000

Contents

Preface

Naomi Jackson

The inspiration for this book emanated from my involvement with an Afghani refugee family that I befriended as a volunteer in the summer of 2000. In the process of helping them acclimate to their newly acquired American culture, I became a privileged witness to the resiliency of the human spirit. The openness, enthusiasm, and warmth of this mother and three children for their new life, and the fulfillment I experienced in assisting them navigate their new world, led me to seek pathways to bridge my humanitarian and scholarly interests. I began to research who was working locally and internationally in the arena of dance as it related to a variety of humanitarian concerns, conducted my own examination of the possible links between dance and human rights issues, and planned projects and publications that would address this field of enquiry.

One of the first manifestations of these efforts was the design and implementation of a study between 2002 and 2004, which focused on the question of how movement and dance might be employed as a healing modality for women refugees primarily from Afghanistan, Iraq, and Syria. The project engaged a colleague, dancer/choreographer Melissa Rolnick, along with graduate and undergraduate students from Arizona State University's Department of Dance, and local community organizations, including the Phoenix Arizona Survivors of Torture program (PAST), Refugee Women United for Progress, and the Arizona Refugee Community Center. As a team we designed weekly movement sessions that drew on exercise, play, yoga, massage, and indigenous dance forms, as well as ideas and practices from western modern dance, as a way of increasing well-being for women from the PAST program.[1] The camaraderie, exuberance, and humor that became hallmarks of these sessions surpassed our expectations, and demonstrated the need for both this kind of programming as a form of participatory justice, and more scholarly research to fully understand how it should, and does, achieve beneficial results.

Meanwhile, I began gathering research and commissioning articles on the intersection of dance and human rights in preparation for an ambitiously inclusive international anthology. As the work began to flow in from across the world, the opportunity presented itself for the publication of a smaller, more focused volume on dance, human rights, and cultural rights, within the Canadian context—*Right to Dance: Dancing for Rights* (Banff Centre Press, 2004), and the organization of an international Congress on Research on Dance (CORD) conference on Dance and Human Rights, which took place in Montreal at the University of Quebec (UQAM), Tangente, and Montréal Arts Interculturels (MAI), in November 2005. These two landmark events brought significant attention to the intensely moving, often overlooked ways in which dance and dancers participate in acts of abuse and humiliation, as well as in efforts to fight oppression and create a more just world. Recognition grew that dance and human rights are not such unrelated spheres, but intimately and actively engage along a continuum of exchange from the most harrowing experiences in which dancing is banned, and dancers tortured, to the ways in which dancers can be degraded in rehearsals.

Through these efforts, and following advice from colleagues, the need to reorganize and refine the planned international volume became evident. I invited Toni Shapiro-Phim, an expert on dance in war-torn zones and specifically Cambodian dance, to be coeditor of the anthology, and she graciously accepted. We then worked extensively on the table of contents as well as individual articles over the next couple of years. It is as a result of our combined efforts that the present volume exists, with its aim to be at once as geographically representative as well as issue sensitive as possible within the scope of a single book. We also strove for a balance between celebrated and lesser-known authors, and between more scholarly and intimate "voices" within the text, to give a sense of just how sweeping and ever-present this topic is.

My hope with the completion of this book is that all readers will find in it something that stimulates them to new thought, behavior in their chosen field, and social action—whether it be dancers recognizing their role in shaping a society that accepts the ideals of freedom, justice, and peace, or whether it be activists acknowledging the remarkable place of the arts in their efforts. I especially look forward to the many ways in which individuals are inspired to reach out to each other, and find ways, through dance, to promote ideals of freedom, justice, and peace. This book is a tribute to the complexity, frictions, and problematics associated with such an endeavor, as well as the positive impact and sense of fulfillment that can accompany it. Eight years after moving to the United States, the oldest Afghani daughter, Yasameen Aboozar, has this to say about the project of building a more peaceful and just world:

> Serving the survivors of war who are trying hard to restore their shattered dreams while grieving for their vanished spirits, is a fine alley in building a more peaceful and just world. Praising their power of survival, lifting up their hopes for new lives, helping them to move on after experiencing the darkest of times, are simply done by planting in their hearts the seeds of happiness and anticipation for a better future. Therefore, building a more peaceful and just world is far more than supplying and providing monetary support to the victims of violence.[2]

NOTES

1. Melissa Rolnick, "Working with Women Refugees from Afghanistan to Iraq: A Final Report," unpublished paper, 2004.
2. Personal communication, February 9, 2008.

Acknowledgments

We would like to first and foremost thank Anthony Jackson for his generous editorial assistance, and Sarah Seaver for so graciously helping to format the final manuscript. Graduate assistants Emily Wright and Lisa Thorngren were instrumental in helping with research and tying up loose ends. Lynn Garafola and Jennifer Fisher provided much valued editorial guidance at various stages of preparation.

Individuals whose research informed this publication, and to whom we are most grateful, include Andrea Blankstein, Iris Bräuninger, Ramsay Burt, Deena Burton, Barbara Cohen-Stratyner, Margaux Delotte-Bennett, Lisa Doolittle, Anne Flynn, Sylvia Glasser, Cecilia Gudmundsson and Lisbeth Hansson, Rosa Lina Lima de Jesus, Lynn Maners, Andrew Needhammer, Brian Obernauf, Melissa Rolnick, Eluza Santos, Iro Tembeck, and Sonia Tsai.

We would also like to express our thanks to the following people whose assistance and support have helped make this book a reality: Agnes Allgäuer, Jobi and Ed Brown, JoAnn Carmin, Peg Connor and Alan Shapiro, Lynn and Dale Delsing, Sharon Friedler, Emi Hasegawa and Tom Shapiro, Germaine Ingram, Tim Jackson, Roko Kawai, Debora Kodish, Mario Martinez, Claire and Jerry McBride, Moeun Bun Thy, Sam Sathya, John Shapiro, Karen and Tim Shapiro, Lorraine Shaw, Judy Van Zile, and Margaret Walker. Thank you also to Renée Camus at Scarecrow Press for recognizing the value of this manuscript and being so supportive during its publication.

We would like to acknowledge the Herberger College of the Arts, and the Joan and David Lincoln Center for Applied Ethics, at Arizona State University for assisting with institutional support.

Finally, we would like to thank the authors included in this volume for their patience and generosity in trusting us with their work, and the wealth of expertise they bring to the topic of dance, human rights, and social justice.

Introduction

Naomi Jackson and Toni Shapiro-Phim

This volume is a collection of international writings on the subjects of dance, human rights, and a range of social justice concerns in the twentieth and twenty-first centuries. The book illuminates and analyzes dance in contexts of oppression and its subversion, healing from human rights abuses, and promoting access to the arts. The scope is broad, yet richly conceived, to demonstrate the multifaceted ways in which these historically disparate fields intersect. Dance is shown to be both a force in human rights abuses and an important player in countering tyranny and advancing a just society.

The anthology explores a number of interconnected themes. It looks, for example, at ways in which dance has been used repeatedly, at different periods in history and in many parts of the world, to promote strict adherence to repressive ideologies. Dance and dancers are also recognized in these pages as being subject to artistic restrictions or worse through laws, bans, and other means. In addition, we examine dance as a powerful vehicle for revealing, resisting, and rectifying differing forms of abuse and injustice, both through intentionally choreographed work and as part of broader social movements that engage in wider struggles for justice. Further, articles in this book illustrate how dance bridges diverse communities, provides avenues for cultural expression, and, through specific treatment modalities such as dance movement therapy, helps heal the wounds of torture and trauma and build a more humane society. Throughout, we delve into the daily struggles and accomplishments of those who devote themselves to this art.

The book takes into account, on the one hand, how dance intersects with extreme human rights abuses such as genocide, slavery, forced displacement, terrorism, and other forms of violence. It also considers how dance has been a vehicle for commentary on systemic poverty and homelessness, as well as other types of manipulation and/or discrimination based on age, gender, sexual orientation, ethnicity, disability, criminal record, and nationality. It pays attention, as well, to the proactive use of dance by individuals and groups to promote ideals such as equality, freedom from want and fear, and peace. The emphasis is on action and the need to take steps to ensure that all human beings are treated fairly and with dignity.

The concept of human rights referred to here dates from the Universal Declaration of Human Rights, which, although having antecedents, was first proclaimed by an international body in 1948 by the General Assembly of the United Nations.[1] That document outlined a specific set of civil, political, economic, social, and cultural rights, which have been regarded by supporters as universal, inherent, and inalienable. Since that time six international human rights treaties have elaborated various aspects of the initial declaration in more detail, including treaties devoted to children's rights, women's rights, racial discrimination, and a convention against torture and other cruel, inhuman, or degrading treatment or punishment.[2]

The related and, in some ways, overlapping concept of social justice describes what kinds of respect, recognition, and rights are due to people because of their membership in a particular society. The focus is on the fair allocation of and access to goods and resources, as well as how best to address situations and acts that violate such distribution.[3] Anthropologist and human rights expert Sally Engle Merry discusses how "human rights have become the major global approach to social justice."[4] In this way she indicates the extent to which the discourse of human rights provides the ground from which many people argue for social justice. Similarly, the contributors to this book contemplate rights and justice as they examine dance's role in claiming the visibility of, bearing witness to, and/or scrutinizing racism, violence against women, homophobia, environmental degradation, and other assaults on dignity, self-determination, and equity.

We, the editors, recognize that debates exist about the concept of human rights and their "universal" application, and about the principle of social justice. While this book takes as its premise the importance of human rights and social justice in creating a world that offers individuals and communities circumstances within which to thrive, it also considers that detailed, local interpretations and analyses of particular peoples and their situations and practices will yield the clearest insight into realizing individual and collective dignity, whether it be through time-honored or innovative means.[5]

The articles collected here are intended to provide expert insight while encouraging dialogue and debate over these multifaceted issues. The authors

Yoko Ando in William Forsythe's installation *Human Writes*, 2005, in which the performers inscribe text drawn from the Universal Declaration of Human Rights but must do so through some physical constraint. Courtesy of the photographer, Dominik Mentzos.

African American women form a conga line as they dance around "sleep-out" demonstrators preparing to spend a second night bedded down on a street in Selma, Alabama, March 11, 1965. Courtesy of the Library of Congress.

are choreographers, dancers, scholars, critics, therapists, and educators—many assuming a combination of these roles. They are sensitive to the complexities and ironies, as well as joys and hopes that their analyses convey, and they are aware of the need to contextualize and ground their remarks in specific circumstances. Whereas the majority of the essays directly implicate acute human rights concerns, some instead highlight issues of dignity, freedom, and hypocrisy for professional dancers within economic, legal, and pedagogical systems the authors deem unjust. They are included because of the broad societal implications drawn from an analysis of specific conditions and practices.

At the same time, the geographic scope of the essays indicates the relevance of dance in relation to human rights and social justice in all corners of the globe, including North and South America and the Caribbean, Europe, Asia and the Pacific, Africa, and the Middle East, while focusing on particular areas that have experienced, or continue to experience, extreme upheaval. Such places include Cambodia, Chile, Germany, Haiti, Rwanda, Serbia, the West Bank, and Zaire (the Democratic Republic of Congo), as well as others. The book also has a number of essays on the United States, allowing readers to draw both diachronic connections, for instance, between slavery and present-day discriminatory practices, and synchronic relationships, between certain questionable practices within American society related to, say, exotic dancers, and blatant human rights violations in other countries. The contributors offer a range of cultural understandings of justice and rights, and of their violation, along with diverse paths to address wrongdoing.

Even with this broad sweep of geography and approach, the collection, taken as a whole, presents the connection between dance, rights, and justice as a very intimate one. Two vivid examples capture this intimacy. In one, a gun is trained at an African American man as he is ordered to dance.[6] In that moment lies an entire story about the way that dance can be found at the heart of some of the worst human rights offenses, as the ultimate insult that allows the profoundest of humiliations to occur. It is the moment when dancing, which so often in everyday life occurs as a spontaneous expression of the ecstasy of existence, is turned on its head, and made into its barbaric opposite—a puppet-like entertainment for another, with the victim fearing for his or her life, all sense of human dignity eradicated.

In a second example, a torture victim is finally able to fully move her arm and shoulder again, through months of careful work with a movement therapist.[7] In that moment an entire story emerges about the way that dance is often located at the most uplifting of times, when memories lodged in the body, beyond the easy grasp of consciousness and cognition, are accessed, and safety is restored to the body, along with a capacity to experience joy and well-being.

This anthology elaborates the multilayered power of dance, and how that force can find itself used to uphold the dignity of individuals and their civil, political, economic, and cultural rights, or to assist in destroying that dignity. Dance holds the power to create a sense of community and shared perspective, displays sensuality and sexuality, embodies memories in a tangible medium, sustains and communicates cultural values that are held dear to a group, and expresses deeply felt emotions, including the agony of loss and the exuberance of life and/or transcendence of spirit. The reminiscences and scholarly accounts within these pages appear in overwhelming fashion to remind those in the dance field and beyond of the moral imperative to keep an eye on the implications of their efforts involving this potent medium.[8] As Marion Kant points out in her essay on dance during the Holocaust (this volume), it is in the "small spaces" (of the classroom, studio, and workplace) that human rights violations take root.[9]

Since the early 1990s, the field of dance studies has seen a flurry of publications that have investigated the relationship of dance to forces of power.[10] This book participates in and extends these efforts by focusing closely on the ways in which dance appears at the heart of the most abusive as well as very best exercises of power in society, between individuals and groups. Considering dance through the lens of human rights and social justice brings to light specific research on this evocative topic, and the incredible amount of international work being done in this area that heretofore has been undocumented. This is especially true in relation to the exploitation and persecution of dancers under particular regimes, the use of movement and dancing as a means of healing victims of abuse, and the attempts of dancers and choreographers to fight for individual and collective rights.[11] By placing these efforts next to analyses of choreographic work, the book also creates an important link between staged art dance that strives to change society by revealing and challenging injustice, and other kinds of activities in the broader society that share similar aims. An often-overlooked connection is thereby made between choreographic insurgency in the theatre, and in the refugee camp, the courtroom, and the street.

Authors of individual essays in this book also recognize another connection—that between the Universal Declaration and related documents and concerns about movement, the body, and art and artists. As the writings in this anthology demonstrate, the Universal Declaration's thirty articles address a number of issues that impact these spheres. This is because they deal with the freedom of individuals to control their own bodies, and freedom from slavery or torture. The Declaration also recognizes the place of culture in the sphere of

Dancers picketing outside American Ballet Theatre's offices in Manhattan during the 1979 lockout. Courtesy of the photographer, Andrew Savulich.

human rights, including the arts, and as such creates a space where dancing and dancers can be represented and valued.[12] In this sense, the *Declaration* considers cultural rights as everything from working conditions of artists, to the protection of the moral and material interests resulting from any artistic production of which the person is the author.[13] Important, as well, is the insistence that everyone, as a member of society, is entitled to the "realization, through national effort and international co-operation and in accordance with the organization and resources of each State, of the . . . cultural rights indispensable for his dignity and the free development of his personality" (Article 22).[14]

Radiating outward from how specific concerns around bodily freedom, access to the arts, and freedom of expression are signaled in the human rights literature, a critical point for discussions found in the following essays is that, as the Human Rights Watch website states, "economic, social, and cultural rights are an integral part of the body of international human rights law, with the same character and standing as civil and political rights."[15] Enforcement of human rights is meant to rectify assaults on human dignity in any and all these spheres. Dance, as both a source for learning about and for impacting/changing our social, cultural, political, and economic worlds, deserves to be "heard" in any arena in which rights and justice concerns are raised.

Indeed, dance and dancers, though figuring centrally (for the most part, as victims) in some of the twentieth century's most sweeping atrocities, have only occasionally had their roles researched and documented in depth—something so important to recognizing larger patterns of how the arts figure into human rights discussions. During the Cultural Revolution in China, for example, countless dancers, along with other performing artists, intellectuals, and professionals, were targeted for persecution, and in many cases, murdered,[16] because what they practiced—what they symbolized and taught—mattered. They were deemed a significant threat to the revolution. Tactics for persecuting artists were perfected with particular cruelty by the Nazis, who banned Jewish dancers from studios and the stage, then commanded them to perform in the concentration camps in concerts and revues before sending them to the gas chambers. They also forced Jewish musicians to accompany the march of fellow prisoners to those chambers of death.[17]

The importance of documentation and analysis is not, however, taken lightly. The Nazis staged (and stole) the beauty of Jewish artistry, even as they killed the individual artists involved. We have struggled alongside the books' authors through the tension-laden terrain of taking responsibility for communicating, as anthropologist E. Valentine Daniel does, "some part of the passion and the pain of violence in its brutal immediacy . . . [along with related] demands for justice, revenge, freedom, and relief." And we have taken to heart his concern about the ease with which "beauty is wrung out of terror."

"For," he warns us, "before tuning our ears, lifting our eyes, and opening our hearts to terror turned beauty so as to find therein final redemption and repose, we—the survivors and those among us who find comfort in their recovery into culture—need to ride our consolations between two echoes," taking care not to lose sight of both the importance of giving voice to suffering, and of the perils of "aestheticiz[ing] at the expense of the fallen."[18] Recognizing the dangers of exoticizing or romanticizing the barbaric as well as the beautiful, we have tried to find a balance that respects the potential and the limits of representation and interpretation of abuse and injustice, and the art and artists working to counter them.

Given this background and its broad context, the collection is designed to highlight writings in four core areas: 1) regulation and exploitation of dance activity and dancers by governments and other groups with authority, as well as abusive treatment of dancers within the dance profession; 2) choreography involving human rights as a central theme; 3) the engagement of dance as a means of healing victims of trauma, societal exclusion, and human rights abuses; and 4) broad-scale social/political movements and smaller-scale local practices in which dance plays a powerful role in providing people agency in fighting oppression. Each section contains a grouping of scholarly articles along with personal testimonials, carefully chosen to mine the richness of the given topic. The sections are as follows:

Part one, "Regulatory Moves," considers how national and local governments and other institutions regulate, denounce, exploit, and harness dance to legitimize their control, and contain or even eradicate opposition. It also considers how such moves impact dancers, personally and collectively, and communities and cultures as a whole. Rafeedie's visceral "Roadblock," about trying to get to a Palestinian children's dance class in a refugee camp, sets the mood by illuminating just how effective and devastating military aggression can be in silencing cultural expression through controlling the movement of bodies in public space. Marion Kant's essay, "Practical Imperative: German Dance, Dancers, and Nazi Politics," then brings readers back to the period of the Second World War, one of the most infamous examples of genocide in modern times, and to the international reaction that led to the drafting of the Universal Declaration of Human Rights. Her piece argues that Nazi ideology was easily embraced by many German modern dancers because of their shared views related to submission of the self to a greater ideal. She raises compelling questions about possible parallels between submission to authoritarian political systems, individual dancers' devotion to choreographers, and the body's submission to specific dance techniques.

Elizabeth Aldrich's "Plunge Not into the Mire of Worldly Folly: Nineteenth-Century and Early Twentieth-Century Religious Objections to

Social Dance in the United States" points to another historically repressive force in history, namely, organized religion. As many have observed, Christian views toward the body, hand in hand with western notions of "civilized" behavior, have led to the devastation of many native and aboriginal cultures, including those aspects involving performance and dance.[19] In her article, Aldrich focuses on American Christian "antidance" literature from the late nineteenth and early twentieth centuries, and prevalent arguments against social dance. She shows how these views were based on a strict interpretation of the Bible, a belief that social dancing led to a weakened body (especially in women), and arguments that Christians should find better use of their leisure time.

The next two articles shift to exemplify how dance can be highly effective in propaganda campaigns of ideological indoctrination and the galvanizing of group feeling in favor of a particular individual or community.[20] "Dancing Chinese Nationalism and Anticommunism: The *Minzu Wudao* Movement in 1950s Taiwan," by Ya-ping Chen, is an analysis of a dance form imposed by the Chinese Nationalist Government on Taiwanese society. Joan Huckstep's "*Animation Politique*: The Embodiment of Nationalism in Zaire [Democratic Republic of Congo]" examines a daily nationwide compulsory jubilance involving dance to enforce both President Mobutu Sese Seko's ideology and the adoration of him as an individual.

The final four papers of this section continue considering the ways in which religion and governments, and the dance field itself, repress and degrade those engaging in dance, with explorations of a range of responses to such repression and degradation. Examples are given that turn the commandeering of the symbolic power of dance to promote and communicate specific ideological and nationalistic messages, as seen in Taiwan and Zaire, on its head. In some situations, those with authority seek to contain dance's potency for fear of its disruptive potential. The essays include stories of those who choose to go underground, to pursue litigation, to challenge traditional pedagogical approaches and practices, or to find new, more liberating contexts in which to dance.

"Dance and Human Rights in the Middle East, North Africa, and Central Asia," by Anthony Shay, examines the role of dance in places where it is widely perceived as a negative, ambiguous, and sometimes disreputable behavior that nonetheless contains within it the potential for expressing joy and resistance. Judith Lynne Hanna's "Right to Dance: Exotic Dancing in the United States" discusses exotic dance litigation and how local and state governments, often in response to pressure from the Christian Right, use the coercive power of regulations to force the adult entertainment of exotic dance out of existence.[21] "The Hidden Authoritarian Roots in Western Concert

Dance," by Robin Lakes, challenges certain teaching and rehearsing practices of modern dance and ballet, seeing them as both physically and psychologically abusive of dancers. Finally, in her piece, "Human Rights and Dance through an Artist's Eyes," Yunyu Wang reminiscences about her upbringing in Taiwan following the White Terror, and her experience as a dancer for the military, as well as for the modern dance company, Cloud Gate Dance Theatre, led by choreographer Lin Hwai Min.

Part two, "Choreographing Human Rights," picks up this last thread, and addresses more closely the ways in which specific choreographers have chosen to address human rights themes in their work. In the context of dance as a theatrical art, choreographers have long created works that represent and recreate a sense of the horror, suffering, and courage of the victims of human rights abuses, as well as the brutality of the victimizers. They also have created works that problematize or deconstruct the ways in which violence can become a part of everyday life, and search for ways to make visible the horror of injustice.[22] Choreographers achieve this through a variety of techniques, including parody and satire, metaphor and allegory, and by representing/recreating the somatic experience of trauma, from uncontrollable shaking to severe immobility, which can be staged to powerful effect.

Several of the most celebrated of these pieces within Europe and North America include: *The Green Table* by Kurt Jooss (1932) about the horrors of war, *Dreams* (1961) by Anna Sokolow about the Nazi concentration camps, *Soweto* (1977) by Mats Ek about apartheid in South Africa, *Ghost Dances* (1983) by Christopher Bruce, about the Chilean military coup, William Forsythe's installation, *Human Writes* (2005), which creates a space in which dancers and audience alike bring the words of the Universal Declaration of Human Rights into being, and Liz Lerman's *Small Dances about Big Ideas* (2005), reflecting on genocide and the Nuremberg Trials following World War II. No doubt there are many other works, familiar to audiences in specific communities, and deserving of broad recognition and analysis, which have not yet enjoyed international exposure.

The choreographers/companies included in this particular collection were chosen because they have had an ongoing commitment to the subject, they have had an important impact nationally and internationally, and strong writing exists on their work.[23] Several of the essays here are written about specific choreographers and choreography by scholars and performers; others are written by the choreographers themselves. For example, Cecilia Olsson and Linda Frye Burnham discuss, respectively, Swedish choreographers Birgit Cullberg and Mats Ek, and American choreographer Liz Lerman, who have created work related to a range of social justice and human rights issues throughout their careers. César Delgado Martínez explores the work of the

Small Dances about Big Ideas by Liz Lerman, 2006, a piece on genocide and the Nuremberg Trials. Copyright the photographer, Enoch Chan.

Mexican-based company Barro Rojo Arte Escénico, an ensemble long concentrating on human rights abuses in Latin America, while Sal Murgiyanto writes about renowned Indonesian choreographer Sardono W. Kusumo, who has developed a relationship with indigenous peoples in the face of foreign logging companies that are destroying their ecosystem.

Space is also opened in this section for choreographers to voice their complex perceptions of pieces and projects that range in topic from genocide and apartheid, to women's and aboriginal rights. Senegalese choreographer Germaine Acogny, for instance, asks her dancers what it is like to be both a victim and a victimizer, as she reflects on creating the dance work *Fagaala*, inspired by the genocide in Rwanda. African American choreographer Ralph Lemon strives to align his own perceptions of slavery and racism with the reality he encountered as he traveled in the American Deep South. During this trip, Lemon performed "counter-memorials" in acknowledgment of the "unfinished memorial process" and desire to "guarantee the life of memory" of racist acts.[24]

In very different ways, Sophiline Cheam Shapiro, a Cambodian choreographer and survivor of Pol Pot's killing fields, and Ananya Chatterjea, an Indian classical dancer and scholar, both engage with traditional dance forms and ways of telling stories in a contemporary context, to confront injustice. Samoan choreographer Lemi Ponifasio addresses the tension between mourning and hope as he reflects on his monumental work *Requiem.* "Adib's Dance," by Israeli theatre director and dance critic Gaby Aldor, concludes this section, with its intimate glimpse into a rehearsal during the creation of a new work. Aldor's memory evokes the fraught nature of finding reconciliation between warring factions, and points to the desire to navigate, through dance and a compassionate community, a path forward to peace.

Part three, "Healing, Access, and the Experience of Youth," illuminates the emancipatory and healing nature of dance especially as related to advocating cultural rights—providing access to the arts within a community, and promoting participatory and restorative justice—opportunities for social participation, recognition of dignity, and citizenship. The authors offer convincing evidence that whether the forms are traditional in nature or more avant-garde, indigenous or foreign, within the context of a therapy session, or part of a theatrical performance, participation in dancing within a nurturing context can provide people the means to live more fully and self-reliantly, as productive members of a society.

The collection of essays in this section, concerning work in healing and the accessibility of the arts more broadly, are heavily influenced by sacred/ritual-based performance traditions (like Vodou), dance/movement therapy, and the community arts movement. Within the United States, the pioneering efforts of individuals such as Katherine Dunham, Marian Chace, and Anna Halprin, to name just a few, have focused awareness on the vital link among access, communities, and well-being.[25] However, it is clear that there exists a global effort in this realm.[26] Indeed, extensive international work related to children and teens uses the arts as a way of promoting ideals of freedom, justice, and peace for future generations.[27]

The section opens with Judith Kajiwara's account of her use of the Japanese American internment experience as a theme for movement healing workshops and choreography in "Japanese Butoh and My Right to Heal." The next three articles focus on the healing aspects of dance exhibited in settings of extreme suffering, as overseen by trained therapists and those directly engaged in recovery work from trauma. "Dancing in our Blood: Dance/Movement Therapy with Street Children and Victims of Organized Violence in Haiti," by Amber Elizabeth Lynn Gray, considers the value of both indigenous and western approaches as healing modalities for her ongoing work with children who suffer from multiple forms of violence and abuse in Haiti. Allison Jane Singer's "Interactions between Movement and Dance, Visual Images, *Etno*, and Physical Environments: Psychosocial Work with War-Affected Refugee and Internally Displaced Children and Adults (Serbia 2001–2002)" discusses the use of movement, image, and space in developmental work with survivors of war. Dance/movement therapist David Alan Harris, in "Sudanese Youth: Dance as

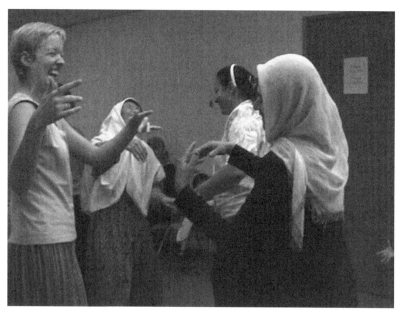

Movement session with refugee women, participants of the Phoenix Arizona Survivors of Torture (PAST) program, 2003. Courtesy of the photographer, Heidi Shikles Beier.

Mobilization in the Aftermath of War," describes an afternoon dancing with southern Sudanese youth in a Pennsylvania village. The author illuminates the importance of traditional dance in rebuilding community for these youth who, as children, had been ripped from their homes and families and forced to relocate numerous times before eventually resettling in America.

The final three articles in this section consider community-based dance initiatives led by professional dancers and choreographers within the United States. "Community Dance: Dance Arizona Repertory Theatre as a Vehicle for Cultural Emancipation," by Mary Fitzgerald, offers a brief history of community art movements, and observations on community-based collaborative choreographic projects as a means of empowering the participating partners. A case study is made of the work of the community dance company housed in the Department of Dance at Arizona State University, which partners with the Sylvestre Herrera School, a school with a large minority population, and the Thomas J. Pappas School for Homeless and Migrant Youth. Janice Ross's "Doing Time: Dance in Prison," is an analysis of three separate prison programs headed by dancers Ehud Krauss, Rhodessa Jones, and Pat Graney. Ross examines the ironic juxtaposition of the restrictive prison environment and the practice of dance that hones tools of autonomy and physical and emotional control. Wyatt Bessing's "Balance and Freedom: Dancing in from the Margins of Disability" offers a poignant ending to this section, as he reflects on the liberating effects of a class involving disabled individuals that the author, who suffers from spina bifida, took with AXIS Dance Company near San Francisco.

The final section of the anthology, titled "Kinetic Transgressions," shifts to consider how broad-scale social and political movements, as well as smaller-scale local practices, engage dance to fight discrimination and injustice. The emphasis here is not so much on individual choreographic work or projects, as on how dance brings visibility and bears witness in situations in which people are often made invisible; through dance—through acts of making and doing—people strive to reclaim their humanity. As the director Peter Sellars has observed, this is a courageous and often ambivalent exercise, a mixture of sadness, pride, and protest. He recognized this in 1989 while watching a group of youth perform a jig at the Festival of Pacific Arts. Sellars writes:

> I learned two nights later [that] in the 1860s, three whaling vessels pulled up next to this little island in the Northern Marianas, and the crews disembarked and slaughtered every male on the island and took the women as their wives and taught them this jig. And for those people, the presentation of this jig at a Festival of Pacific Dance was a statement that their race will never be exterminated, that they will continue to live, and they hate those people, but those people are also their fathers now, and so they are not allowed to hate them. So the tone with which this jig is executed—not spirited, not sad, just perfectly poised—is the key to their own sense of continuity in their own lives. That dance was the most courageous thing they could think of to present at a Festival of Pacific Dance. Two nights later . . . you saw the same dance, and, of course, you were weeping.[28]

In this section of the book, the tone is set with Nicholas Rowe's "Exposure and Concealment," which uses a particular incident of sniper fire following a rehearsal in the West Bank to reflect on the politics of visibility and invisibility. Marjorie Agosín's "The Dance of Life: Women and Human Rights in Chile" follows, with an analysis of the *cueca sola* performed by female members of the Association of the Detained and Disappeared in Chile as a form of protest against human rights atrocities in South America. The *cueca sola*, traditionally a dance for couples, is performed as a solo, with photographs or men's shirts symbolizing the women's missing partners who were "disappeared."

Toni Shapiro-Phim's article, "Mediating Cambodian History, the Sacred, and the Earth," also examines how dance is linked to memory and survival, this time in relation to displaced Cambodians living in refugee camps. Her essay explores the logic of loss that invites a need to replace and regain, and the logic of chaos that invites a need to establish appropriate or distinctive order, through ritual and through dance, during and in the aftermath of war. A people with a profound attachment to the spirit of the land that constitutes their country, the Khmer (Cambodians) carry that spirit with and within them, thereby partially transcending geographical and cultural displacement through embodiment of their culture.

The following three articles consider in turn how dance features in social, economic, and political movements related to care for the elderly, disabled, and people with AIDS in North America. The first of these, "No More Starving in the Attic: Senior Dance Artists Advocate a Canadian Artists' Heritage Resource Centre" by Carol Anderson, addresses economic and artistic matters affecting aging dancers, and the ageism that seems endemic to dance. "Dance and Disability," by Alito Alessi with Sara Zolbrod, recalls the day on March 10, 1987, when Alessi and his partner held their first contact improvisation workshop for people with and without disabilities, and how this transformative event led to the formation of Joint Forces Dance Company/DanceAbility. "Monuments and Insurgencies in the Age of AIDS," by David Gere, analyzes the unfurling of the NAMES Project AIDS Quilt on the Washington Mall as an act of resistance to homo- and AIDS-phobic oppression. Once again, memory, visibility, choreography, and insurgency are linked as part of an expansive movement for change.

Finally, in "*If I Survive*: Yehudit Arnon's Story," choreographer Yehudit Arnon reflects on how her love of dance helped her survive the brutality of the Nazi concentration camps. It is a sobering survival, in which the ending of the story finds her silently eating food hastily abandoned by a German family fleeing liberation forces. Eventually, Arnon founded the Kibbutz Contemporary Dance Company in Israel, an achievement that testifies to many of the ideals addressed in this book. Yet it is in that overwhelming silence as she partakes of another's intended sustenance that many questions ferment regarding the compatibility of art practices with ethical considerations.

How can socially committed artists impact their communities, yet avoid becoming dogmatic, programmatic, or self-righteous? How can an artist really know whether the rights and freedoms he or she fights for will in fact result in positive benefits for those with much at stake? How can choreography be aesthetically engaging *and* an effective means of political, social, and economic change? How can technical and artistic excellence be achieved as a dancer without suffering under or resorting to practices that undermine the dignity of the individual performer? How can dance professionals, who specialize in their own discipline, become conversant in human rights and social justice issues? How can we who write, choreograph, or perform about or within contexts of oppression remind the world about what possibilities just might lie at the other end of the struggle, and about how dance figures into this complex picture?

These and other questions raised by the anthology invite continued consideration and study by readers. This exchange, we believe, will constitute an opening for the integral inclusion of dance into discussions of human rights and social justice issues. It will also, we hope, bring human rights and social justice awareness more fully into the dance world, so that dancers, as well as scholars of movement and performance, can benefit from the insights of those fields.

NOTES

1. While there is debate as to the origins of the notion of human rights, the western tradition traces it to ethical and philosophical ideas evolved by the Greeks, and in the Torah and New Testament. In terms of modern thought, the notion has existed under several names since the thirteenth century and the Magna Carta. During the eighteenth and nineteenth centuries, several European philosophers, the most influential of whom was John Locke, proposed the concept of "natural rights." Such rights belonged to a person by nature and because he was a human being endowed with reason (and by implication knew right from wrong). Locke formulated the classic trinity of these natural rights as life, liberty, and property. In the late 1700s the American Declaration of Independence and the French Declaration of the Rights of Man and of the Citizen drew heavily on Locke's notion. While the idea of natural rights became increasingly challenged along philosophical lines, certain humanitarian organizations took hold in the 1800s, keeping the basic concept alive. These organizations grew up in relation to a number of important social movements in the United States, including the abolitionist movement, the women's suffrage movement, and the labor movement, which addressed issues such as brutal working conditions, starvation wages, and child labor. Following World War II, human rights were promoted as universally relevant. See Micheline R. Ishay, *The History of Human Rights: From Ancient Times to the Globalization Era* (Berkeley: University of California Press, 2004).

2. The other two are the International Covenant on Civil and Political Rights, and the International Covenant on Economic, Social and Cultural Rights—both of which were ratified in 1976.

3. Social justice, because it considers the rights due to citizens in such a broadly conceived manner, usually encompasses politics, economics, and gender concerns, and may also address racial, environmental, historical, and intergenerational justice.

4. One of the examples she cites involves the New Territories of Hong Kong, where "women were denied the right to inherit property under a law passed by the British colonial government and legitimated as ancient Chinese custom. The international human rights language of women's rights and sex discrimination proved critical to overturning this legislation." *Human Rights and Gender Violence* (Chicago: University of Chicago Press, 2006), 2.

5. Sally Engel Merry addresses "the processes of transplantation and translation" that help close the gap between universal human rights principles and local cultural, social, and political contexts, *Human Rights and Gender Violence*, 103.

6. See Ralph Lemon's article, this volume, for a description of a white man or-dering a black man at gunpoint to dance for the amusement of himself and his white friends. For more on slavery and dance, see P. Sterling Stuckey, "Christian Conver-sion and the Challenge of Dance," in *Dancing Many Drums*, ed. Thomas F. DeFrantz (Madison: University of Wisconsin Press, 2002), 39–58. This episode resonates with many others in history in which people have been forced to dance under threat of violence. Such episodes appear in recent Human Rights Watch literature, as in a 2002 report on Russian abuses in Chechnya when four nurses were "stripped naked and forced to dance in front of the soldiers," "Russian Federation: Serious Violations of Women's Human Rights in Chechnya," *Human Rights Watch World Report 2002*, at hrw.org/backgrounder/eca/chechnya_women.htm; and Amnesty International, as in a report on mistreatment of detainees at the United States detention camp at Guantánamo Bay when a male prisoner was forced to dance with a male interrogator while wearing a towel on his head "like a burka," "USA: Guantánamo—Torture and Other Ill-Treatment" (AMR 51/189/2006), at asiapacific.amnesty.org/library/Index/ENGAMR511892006?open&of=ENG-USA.

7. See the case study described by Amber Gray in "The Body Remembers: Dance/Movement Therapy with an Adult Survivor of Torture," *American Journal of Dance Therapy* 23, no. 1 (March 2001): 29–43.

8. How "dance" is conceived by any particular community also clearly affects its potency; within a single community certain kinds of "dancing" may be acceptable within some contexts, and not within others. This is articulated by Anthony Shay in his article in this book, as well as in his *Choreophobia: Solo Improvised Dance in the Iranian World*, Bibliotheca Iranica No. 4 (Costa Mesa, Calif.: Mazda Publishers, 1999).

9. See also Marion Kant and Lilian Karina, *Hitler's Dancers: German Modern Dance and the Third Reich* (New York: Berghahn Books, 2003). Dance scholar Brenda Dixon Gottschild, during her keynote address, "Recovering the Phoenix: Dance, Education, Society & the Politics of Race" (Black Britons and Dance conference, De Montfort University, U.K., June 2007), also emphasized the importance of taking responsibility, in her case, for reversing the established invisibilization of and discrimination against those considered "other." "Just as those 'bad seeds' [racist concepts] were sowed in another place and time, so you have the power to plant the seeds of change. . . . [T]he only place to begin is at the beginning—namely, with myself—with yourself. Where does the bigot live in *me*? Whether by commission or omission, how do I perpetuate the status quo and obfuscate the efflorescence of heretofore invisibilized histories? How, and when, do my personal, private biases and limitations hinder my movement forward as an effective professional in the [dance] field?" at danceadvance.org/03archives/gottschild02/index.html.

10. Examples of such books include: Ann Cooper Albright, *Choreographing Difference: The Body and Identity in Contemporary Dance* (Middletown, Conn.: Wesleyan University Press, 1997); Barbara Browning, *Samba: Resistance in Motion* (Bloomington: Indiana University Press, 1995); Ananya Chatterjea, *Butting Out: Reading Resistive Choreographies through Works by Jawole Willa Jo Zollar and Chandralekha* (Middletown, Conn.: Wesleyan University Press, 2004); Thomas F. DeFrantz, ed., *Dancing Many Drums: Excavations in African American Dance* (Madison: University of Wisconsin Press, 2002); Jane Desmond,

ed., *Dancing Desires: Choreographing Sexualities on and off the Stage* (Madison: University of Wisconsin Press, 2001); Brenda Dixon Gottschild, *The Black Dancing Body: A Geography from Coon to Cool* (New York: Palgrave Macmillan, 2003); Ellen Graff, *Stepping Left: Dance and Politics in New York City, 1928–1942* (Durham, N.C.: Duke University Press, 1997); and Robert Farris Thompson, *Tango: The Art History of Love* (New York: Pantheon Books, 2005). There are, of course, examples reaching back to the early twentieth century as well. Listed here is only a sampling of recent relevant publications.

11. Numerous recent examples exist of ballet and modern dancers organizing for greater rights. Several examples from the United States are as follows: Labor disputes resulted in lockouts at American Ballet Theater in 1979 and 1982, and, ultimately, gains in wages and working conditions. In the early 1990s, ballet dancers from American Ballet Theater, the New York City Ballet, Dance Theater of Harlem, and the Joffrey Ballet filed a class-action suit against the American Guild of Musical Artists demanding better benefits. Dancers at Dance Theatre of Harlem struck in 1997 over health and safety concerns. In 2006, dancers at the Washington Ballet went on strike with questions over the artistic director's range of control especially in relation to job security. In the modern dance realm, a group of concerned dancers organized in New York to draw up a "Dancers Forum Compact," a document available as of 2002, outlining guidelines for good working relations between dancers and choreographers (available through the National Dance Education Organization website at ndeo.org/Dancers%20Forum%20Compact%204-03.pdf).

12. For detailed discussions of the inclusion of culture in the declaration, and its implications, see Johannes Morsink, *The Universal Declaration of Human Rights: Origins, Drafting, and Intent* (Philadelphia: University of Pennsylvania Press, 1999); Gudmundur Alfredsson and Asbjorn Eide, eds., *The Universal Declaration of Human Rights: A Common Standard of Achievement* (The Hague: Martinus Nijhoff Publishers, 1999); and Asbjorn Eide, Catarina Krause, and Allan Rosas, eds., *Economic, Social and Cultural Rights: A Textbook* (Dordrecht: Martinus Nijhoff Publishers, 1995).

13. While certainly an important and fascinating topic, intellectual rights as related to dance are not covered in this volume. See Anthea Kraut's work on copyright issues in the dance field: "Race-ing Choreographic Copyright: From The Black Bottom to *Kiss Me, Kate*," in *Worlding Dance*, ed. Susan Leigh Foster, series ed. Janelle Reinelt and Brian Singleton (Palgrave, forthcoming 2008); and "Dance Copyright and Migrations of Choreography," paper delivered at the Congress on Research in Dance conference, Barnard College, New York, November 2007.

14. Sections of two articles, in particular, are worth noting here. One, from Article 27, calls for the right of everyone to access the arts. It reads, "Everyone has the right freely to participate in the cultural life of the community, to enjoy the arts and to share in scientific advancement and its benefits." Another, from Article 19, concerns freedom of expression. It states, "Everyone has the right to freedom of opinion and expression; this right includes freedom to hold opinions without interference and to seek, receive and impart information and ideas through any media and regardless of frontiers" (Universal Declaration of Human Rights, at un.org/Overview/rights.html). These assertions are reiterated in two other international documents. Article 15 of the International Covenant on Economic, Social and Cultural Rights reiterates the right of

everyone to "take part in cultural life" and to "respect the freedom indispensable for scientific research and creative activity," at www.unhchr.ch/html/menu3/b/a_cescr .htm. The *Recommendation Concerning the Status of the Artist*, meanwhile, is an extremely detailed twelve-page text that recognizes the "essential role of art in the life and development of the individual and of society," and asserts that member states therefore have a duty to "protect, defend and assist artists and their freedom of creation." It goes on to provide recommendations concerning the participation of artists in decisions concerning the quality of life, the vocation and training of artists, and the employment, working, and living conditions of artists, including professional and trade union opportunities, at portal.unesco.org/en/ev.php-URL_ID=13138&URL_DO=DO_TOPIC&URL_SECTION=201.html.

15. See hrw.org/doc/?t=esc. Despite such statements, organizations such as Human Rights Watch and Amnesty International still primarily focus on political, civil, and economic rights (although Amnesty's initiatives include Artists for Amnesty and Art for Amnesty, which provide ways for artists to participate in consciousness-raising efforts). Research in how the arts intersect with the work of these organizations might assist them in more clearly defining and incorporating cultural rights as an additional focus. See Naomi Jackson, "Dance and Human Rights: Tracking Dance in the World of Amnesty International and Human Rights Watch," *Contact Quarterly* 33, no. 2 (Summer/Fall 2008): 32–35.

16. See Margaret Chan, "Negotiating Artistic Spaces: Beijing Opera and the Cultural Revolution in China," in *Right to Dance: Dancing for Rights*, ed. Naomi Jackson (Banff, Alberta: Banff Centre Press, 2004), 99–122. For the plight of dancers under another communist regime, see Toni Shapiro-Phim, "Dance, Music, and the Nature of Terror in Democratic Kampuchea," in *Annihilating Difference: The Anthropology of Genocide*, ed. Alexander Hinton (Berkeley: University of California Press, 2002), 179–93.

17. See Judith Brin Ingber, "Dancing Despite the Scourge: Jewish Dancers during the Nazi Period," paper presented at the International CORD Conference on Dance and Human Rights, Montreal, Canada, November 12–13, 2005. In one particularly tragic account, Ingber recounts the fate of a child prodigy, Miriam Dajches, who was singled out in Auschwitz for "medical experiments" performed on her remarkable dancing legs by Josef Mengele and his "doctors." Poisonous materials were poured into holes in her legs and nerves were severed, leaving her crippled for life.

18. E. Valentine Daniel in his study of terror in Sri Lanka, *Charred Lullabies: Chapters in an Anthropology of Violence* (Princeton: Princeton University Press, 1996), 153.

19. Numerous resources exist tracing the banning and exploitation of native/aboriginal dance in North America, along with acts of resistance. See, for instance, Clyde Ellis, "'There Is No Doubt . . . The Dances Should Be Curtailed': Indian Dances and Federal Policy on the Southern Plains, 1880–1930," *Pacific Historical Review* 70, no. 4 (2001): 543–69; Aaron Glass, "The Thin Edge of the Wedge: Dancing around the Potlatch Ban, 1921–1951," in *Right to Dance: Dancing for Rights*, 51–83; eds. Heather Elton, Paul Seesequasis, and Florence Belmore, *Chinook Winds: Aboriginal Dance Project* (Banff, Alberta: Banff Centre Press, 1997); and Jacqueline Shea Murphy, *The People Have Never Stopped Dancing: Native American Modern Dance Histories* (Minneapolis: University of Minnesota Press, 2007).

20. There is a long tradition, in many cultures, of dance being used to help prepare for war and celebrate victory. Well known in the West is the pyrrhic dance, which was practiced in ancient Greece to train for battle. In more recent history, traditional and folk forms have been employed by totalitarian regimes as part of their propaganda campaigns. For good examinations of the connection between nationalism and folk dance, for instance, see Anca Giurchescu, "The National Festival 'Song to Romania': Manipulation of Symbols in the Political Discourse," in *Symbols of Power: The Esthetics of Political Legitimation in the Soviet Union and Eastern Europe,* ed. Claes Arvidsson and Lars Erik Blomqvist (Stockholm, Sweden: Almqvist & Wiksell International, 1987); and Anthony Shay, *Choreographic Politics: State Folk Dance Ensembles, Representation and Power* (Middletown, Conn.: Wesleyan University Press, 2002). Today in various locations, war dances are taught alongside fighting techniques as part of recruitment strategies. See, for instance, "Abuses Committed by UNITA," section in Human Rights Watch report *Angola Unravels: The Rise and Fall of the Lusaka Peace Process*, September 1, 1999, at hrw.org/reports/1999/angola/Angl998-06.htm.

21. Judith Lynn Hanna's article connects to larger tensions that have been unfolding within American culture around government funding for the arts and specifically the "culture wars" of the period around 1990, when Senator Jesse Helms led an attack on the National Endowment for the Arts (NEA). The moral opposition to the NEA coalesced around art concerned with women, homosexuals, and minorities. In 1994, when Newt Gingrich became Speaker of the House of Representatives, the situation worsened and NEA funding plummeted. As an example, in 1980 "total NEA funding for dance was $8,631,567. By 1996 it had dropped to $2,725,000" (quoted in Shelley Masar, "The Culture Wars Are Over—For Now," The Urbana-Champaign Independent Media Center, Sept. 2001, at publici.ucimc.org/sept2001/092001_10.htm). In 1997, the House of Representatives voted to abolish the NEA by eliminating funding altogether. Fortunately, the Senate overturned the House, and funding was restored.

22. See, for instance, *Strawberry Cream and Gunpowder* (2004), by Israel-based Yasmeen Godder and the Bloody Bench Players, in which images of war omnipresent in Israel are deconstructed, according to a statement on Godder's website, "into an alternate reality, one with the same aesthetics but with new and personal connotation. The desire for this project came with the need to bring to life, resuscitate, the grotesque and disturbing images which have become inseparable from our lives, and in their repetitive nature, have brought us to numbness. A look at local imagery as local mythology, through its flat cartoon-like representation, the work attempts at bringing back these images into a three-dimensional world," at www.yasmeengodder.com/index.php?p=works&id=2&m=ABOUT.

23. Others are acknowledged as being important contributors to this subject, but unfortunately are omitted from this volume because of space constraints.

24. Statements from program notes written by James Young for Ralph Lemon's work, quoted in Anna Kisselgoff, "A Counter-Memorial on a Northern Lynching," *New York Times*, October 28, 2004, at www.nytimes.com/2004/10/28/arts/dance/28wave.html.

25. Among the many dancers and choreographers in the twentieth and twenty-first centuries who have engaged in social activism, these three women are noted here

because of their early and lifelong interest in the therapeutic attributes of dance, and making dance accessible to the broader community. See "Katherine Dunham: Global Activist," at mohistory.org/KatherineDunham/global_activist.htm; Anna Halprin, *Returning to Health: With Dance, Movement & Imagery* (Mendocino, Calif.: Liferhythm, 2002); and Marian Chace, Susan L. Sandel, Sharon Chaiklin, and Ann Lohn, *Foundations of Dance/Movement Therapy: The Life and Work of Marian Chace* (Columbia, Md.: Marian Chace Memorial Fund of the American Dance Therapy Association, 1993).

26. It is impossible within this introduction to outline the extent of the international scope of work related to dance, healing, and community access. Some helpful references include: *Dancing Our Stories: Personal Narratives from Dance Animation and Community Dance Projects in Canada* (Douglas Durand, Canada Council for the Arts, 2005); *Thinking Aloud: In Search of a Framework for Community Dance* (Leicester, U.K.: Foundation for Community Dance, 1996); Dianne Dulicai and Miriam Roskin Berger, "Global Dance/Movement Therapy Growth and Development," *The Arts in Psychotherapy* 32, no. 3 (2005): 205–16; and John M. Janzen, *Ngoma: Discourses of Healing in Central and Southern Africa* (Berkeley: University of California Press, 1992).

27. Resources on work with children include: "The Exile of Poetic Imagination: Challenges to the Use of Expressive Arts with Children in Adversity," in *Right to Dance: Dancing for Rights*, 247–68; Edward C. Green and Alcinda Honwana, "Indigenous Healing of War-Affected Children in Africa," *IK Notes*, no. 10 (July 1999), at www.worldbank.org/afr/ik/iknt10.pdf; and Iris Bräuninger, *Consideration of Children's Held Upper Body Posture as a Reaction to Stressful Events* (Master's thesis, Laban Centre for Movement & Dance, City University, London, U.K., 1994). Recent films dealing with children and dance in war zones include the 2002 documentary *Dans, Grozny, Dans* (The Damned and the Sacred), directed by Jos de Putter (Paris: Ideale Audience), which focuses on a Chechnyan youth dance group's discovery of comfort, confidence, and dignity through dance, and *War/Dance*, directed by Sean and Andrea Nix Fine (New York: ThinkFILM, 2007), which tells the story of three children whose families have been torn apart by civil war in Uganda. Large-scale projects involving global youth in relation to dance, community, and social activism include Canadian choreographer Judith Marcuse's ICE, FIRE, and EARTH, at jmprojects.ca/.

28. Peter Sellars, "The New Territory," keynote address at the Dance Critics Association conference, San Francisco, June 10, 1989. Most of the text was published as "Sellars in Criticland," in the *DCA News* (Fall 1989): 12.

Part One

REGULATORY MOVES

Roadblock

Journal Excerpt, November 26, 2001

Maysoun Rafeedie

"What?" *It was a silly question. My mind blocked. "What is your primary image of going to teach children in the refugee camp?"*

It was a question I was asked by a journalist who was writing a report about the Popular Art Centre's activities in the refugee camps of Palestine. (The Popular Art Centre is a Palestinian nongovernmental organization, established in Al-Bireh in the West Bank in 1987. With a focus on dance, the Popular Art Centre has been involved in promoting performing arts in Palestine, organizing the Palestine International Festival, providing rehearsal space for local dance groups, hosting workshops with foreign dance teachers, and administering local community outreach projects.) I had spent the last few months, since the intifada began in September 2000, teaching Palestinian folk dance (*dabke*) to children in the refugee camps of Balata, Askar, and Alain in Nablus and in the villages around Ramallah such as Biet Leqya and Kofur Neímey. We started with some games, like moving and freezing to starts and stops in the music, then began putting some steps together. It was amazing the way dance helped these kids focus for an hour, creating a *dabke* piece to traditional Palestinian rhythms while so much was happening outside—lots of shooting and screaming, lots of ambulances going around. Maybe one of those kids' friends, brothers, or cousins is shot now, yesterday, a week ago . . .

A week ago, as part of my Teaching Studies course at the Laban Centre in London, I visited a primary school to watch a demonstration dance class. It was great, as usual, for me to see children innocently jumping around and having fun. I visited their classroom, full of educational pictures about technology, mathematics, geography, and literature hanging all over the walls. I couldn't remember anything except unpainted and chipped surfaces on the bare walls in some of the classrooms in the refugee camps. Also, the dance teacher here in London can ask the kids to curl up on the dance floor of the school's practice hall. My students in Palestine couldn't do that because the room we use is simply their regular classroom, with a cold, hard floor and the desks pushed out of the way and piled up in the corner.

Back to the question: What was the primary image of going to the camps?

Maybe the road to reach them. Normally it takes only an hour to get to Nablus from Ramallah, but because of the Israeli military roadblocks and checkpoints we had to leave at 7:30 a.m. to be there by midday. Waiting and waiting for our turn. Standing in line on the dirt under the sun, my legs getting tired before the dancing even began. Hey! Here comes our turn. But you know what? The soldiers took all our IDs and made us wait for another hour because they were having their lunch. It's twelve now, and we have received several calls from the coordinator in Nablus telling us the children are waiting for us, very worried that we won't arrive.

Or maybe it is the kids welcoming us with a big smile, helping us to unload our material from the back of the van. There are so many kids this time because they've heard about the dance class from other children. Maybe there are more than two hundred.

I was happy that day because dance made some kids smile, have fun, and enjoy their time.

I didn't know what to say to the journalist and I was confused, so I just said "poverty." It was a silly answer.

· 2 ·

Practical Imperative

German Dance, Dancers, and Nazi Politics

Marion Kant

*I*n 1938, when Nazism was well established in Germany, when the Soviet Union was progressing toward an ever more dictatorial regime, when Asia was in turmoil, and shortly before World War II broke out, Eleanor Roosevelt, wife of Franklin D. Roosevelt, president of the United States, wrote, "the whole situation seems intolerable. We face today a world filled with suspicion and hatred. We look at Europe and see a civil war going on, with other nations participating not only as individual volunteers, but obviously with the help and approval of their governments. We look at the Far East and see two nations, technically not at war, killing each other in great numbers."[1]

In the twentieth century, influential political groups, primarily in European countries, had gained power and used their status to persecute other, unwanted groups or individuals who believed in a different religion, looked different, were considered economic rivals, or were simply declared enemies for convenient ideological reasons. Nazi Germany was by no means the only country in which respect for human integrity and life had been swept away. But it proved to be one of the worst offenders in the 1930s and 1940s.

This sense of witnessing a world falling apart and having to do something about it prompted Eleanor Roosevelt to become one of the advocates in the fight for the protection of human rights. Her commitment to a fairer world was, in fact, an important moment in the beginning of a political course that would recognize that human life needed to be guarded; that it needed to be defended from other human beings who had assaulted those elementary rights.

After a long and complicated process of negotiation, the Universal Declaration of Human Rights was pronounced on December 10, 1948 as a direct answer to the experiences with German Nazism, with a war that it had initiated, and the atrocities that had accompanied it. The instigation of a catalog of rights was an attempt to make sure that nothing similar happened again.

The Declaration of Human Rights saw the "recognition of the inherent dignity and . . . equal and inalienable rights of all members of the human family [as] the foundation of freedom, justice and peace in the world and understood that disregard and contempt for human rights have resulted in barbarous acts which have outraged the conscience of mankind, and the advent of a world in which human beings shall enjoy freedom of speech and belief and freedom from fear and want has been proclaimed as the highest aspiration of the common people."[2]

Right from the beginning, though, those writing the declaration were aware of an inescapable dilemma. Whereas certain rights could be proclaimed and regulated through institutions, other rights could not and depended very much on the individual to take responsibility. One of several

> difference[s] between the civil and political provisions and the economic, social, and cultural provisions is the manner in which the obligation is expected to be performed. In the case of the civil and political rights, they can in general be achieved by the enactment of appropriate legislation, enforced under effective administrative machinery. On the other hand, it is recognized that economic, social, and cultural progress and development cannot be achieved simply by the enactment of legislation and its enforcement. Private as well as public action is necessary. . . . The Commission fully recognized the importance of private as well as governmental action for the achievement of these rights.[3]

This paragraph refers to one particular and particularly horrifying aspect of Nazism: it addresses the responsibility of the single human being, so vulnerable under certain social conditions, to ensure in its own environment that human rights are respected. After all, no system can carry out assaults on other people without some kind of assistance from its citizens.

The world had been shocked by the complicity of seemingly educated and cultured people with an evil system. When the Allied armies reached the concentration camps in 1945 and the pictures of piles of dead bodies and starving inmates were shown to the public, there was not only a feeling of horror at what had taken place but some persistent questions arose: How could the German people have allowed this to happen? What made them part of the evil Nazi system? How could a civilized nation turn into a barbarous monster? What became of simple decency; what happened to courage and compassion?

Was there a national character that programmed Germans to be wicked, immoral, and destructive?

And above all: was Germany an exception or could any state, any nationality, any political system, end in a total breakdown of its civil liberties?

When the covenant spoke of the necessity of private together with governmental action to achieve human rights, it was for two reasons. Experience had shown that the state, as well as the citizens of a state, could either offend and abuse or respect and protect human rights. The Nazi state might have initiated racist legislation but it could only operate on the grand scale it had envisaged with the help of the German population. After World War II and German Nazism one thing became very clear: human and civil rights could not be taken for granted anywhere, not even in supposedly civilized western countries.

During the Weimar Republic, from 1918 through the 1920s, Germany had witnessed social upheaval and economic disaster. Moderate, social democratic, liberal, militant, and right-wing chancellors came and went. The republic, torn by political battles, destabilized and soon people cried for a "strong man" to clean up the mess left by seemingly feeble and incompetent leaders. Thus, the National Socialist German Worker's Party, Adolf Hitler's movement, gained popularity. In the elections on November 6, 1932, the party won 33.09 percent[4] of the votes, not enough to take over the government and much less than the 37.3 percent they had obtained in the elections of July 31, 1932. After negotiations between right-wing political, industrial, and bank representatives, former Chancellor Franz von Papen and members of the president's entourage managed to persuade the president of Germany, Paul von Hindenburg, to appoint Hitler as chancellor on January 30, 1933. Once in power, the Nazis quickly dismantled the Weimar parliamentary system and pushed aside the upper-class plotters who thought they had Hitler "hemmed in." When Hitler called for new elections on March 5, 1933, the NSDAP, the Nazi Party, gained more than 10 percent and secured 43.9 percent of all votes.[5] After removing their immediate enemy, the Communist Party, from the Reichstag, the German parliament, Hitler announced the *Ermächtigungsgesetz*, the Enabling Law, on March 24, 1933. The day before, on March 23, 1933, the Reichstag had decreed the law with a majority of 444 to 94 votes. With the communist delegates eliminated and locked up in prisons, the only opposition came from the Social Democratic Party, whose members were soon to be persecuted and along with their communist fellows placed in concentration camps. From now on the Third Reich fell under the total authority of Hitler. Quickly, all political enemies were removed from any influential positions; even Hitler's former coalition partners were pushed aside. Laws and decrees cleansed society of "undesired elements"; the racial state began to operate.

Where were the arts, where was dance, when Nazi policies began to take away the human rights of German citizens? Though artists could claim not to have been directly involved with the installation of the Nazis in power, they had smoothed their path in a different, indirect way. Every political system favors certain belief systems. It justifies its foundations with ideologies and uses the arts and sciences to further its course. The Nazis were masters at turning the arts into political propaganda. They took art seriously because it could be used as an ideological weapon. Artists and intellectuals were or became Nazis themselves by supplying the political movement with a thought structure; they accepted and promoted the political framework to realize their own aesthetic principles that were in themselves founded on ideological preferences. They were an essential part of the deal.

Many intellectuals and artists had been latent backers of the Nazis and the majority of Germans tolerated, if not welcomed, the new regime. Some quickly withdrew into silence after becoming disillusioned, such as the poet Gottfried Benn or the painter Oskar Schlemmer; some died before they got too entangled in Nazi cultural politics; others were explicitly rejected by the Nazis and declared "degenerate," such as the painters Paul Klee or Ludwig Kirchner, who had expressed his loyalties. The philosopher Martin Heidegger, composer Richard Strauss, conductors Wilhelm Furtwängler and Clemens Krauss, actor and director Gustav Gründgens (whose "devilish" relationship to the Nazis was portrayed in Klaus Mann's novel *Mephisto*), writer Ernst Jünger, sculptor Arno Breker, and filmmaker Leni Riefenstahl all emphatically contributed to Nazi ideas. Despite occasionally running into difficulties,[6] they remained supporters and never questioned the regime. Others, such as the composers Werner Egk and Carl Orff, conductor Herbert von Karajan, opera singer Elisabeth Schwarzkopf, actor Hans George, philosopher Hans-Georg Gadamer, and many lesser known people, also actively assisted the Nazis. The list is long and not one of them protested when their Jewish colleagues were pushed out and persecuted. When the refugees left Germany, Ilse Meudtner, a young dancer, had only one thing in mind—her own career. "I was now twenty and it was my turn."[7]

The collaborators were rewarded with official recognition, commissions, and advancement in their professional careers. The involvement in and compliance of artists with the Nazi regime took many forms. The conservative and political right-wing movements had always espoused and depended on "their" intellectuals who found it easy to identify with Nazism, at least initially before feeling appalled and insulted by the vulgar and plebeian tendencies of the Nazi movement. Ernst von Salomon's quasi novel *Der Fragebogen* or *The Questionnaire* in English translation—an account written after having been confronted with the Allied denazification forms—provides an insight into such thinking.

For him Nazism, at least at the start, was a coherent movement to which a conservative nationalist could and should contribute.

Once the Nazis had seized power, the majority of intellectuals backed the regime by sanctioning its values. One only has to look at the way in which the structures and organizations were established that enabled the cultural policies and artistic fantasies of the Nazis to be carried out. Not a single one of the Reich Culture Chambers, founded by decree as subsidiaries of the Ministry for Popular Enlightenment and Propaganda in 1933 and in existence to the bitter end in 1945, could have been run effectively without the artists' active involvement and advice. All presidents of the various chambers were or claimed to be respected artists in their field. And novelist Werner Bergengruen reminds us of the continuity:

> Nazism did not fall from the skies as a blood rain and did not explode as a magical elemental catastrophe but stands in the midst of the web of cause and effect; there were reasons why National Socialism emerged, there were initiatives, pre-histories . . . this devastating stream united many and many different brooks and not just those flowing out of murky swamps[8]

The history of Germany in the twentieth century and the rise of Nazism demonstrate how art as an ideological means assists a state in depriving its citizens of their rights. It also shows how art and artists can oppose it. Therefore, we can find the representatives of dance on both sides of the divide: some supported Nazism, at the least taking advantage of it, while others resisted the racial state ideology. Eleanor Roosevelt asked where human rights began. And she stated:

> In small places, close to home—so close and so small that they cannot be seen on any maps of the world. Yet they *are* the world of the individual person; the neighborhood he lives in; the school or college he attends; the factory, farm, or office where he works. Such are the places where every man, woman, and child seeks equal justice, equal opportunity, equal dignity without discrimination. Unless these rights have meaning there, they have little meaning anywhere. Without concerted citizen action to uphold them close to home, we shall look in vain for progress in the larger world.[9]

The small places were also the dance groups; *the schools* were also dance schools; *the workplaces* were also the theaters and studios. And it was here that human rights were violated right from the beginning of the Third Reich and without the Nazi state putting much pressure on the dancers, teachers, and their pupils. It was in *the small places*, performance sites, and rehearsal rooms that Nazi legislation took root and was put into practice. The dancers, too, belonged to the masses that made Nazism a widely acceptable and accepted movement. They were to be found at every imaginable level of the social ladder, with little or with considerable influence.

Dancers and musicians cleansed their profession when the Nazis proclaimed the Law for the Re-Establishment of the Professional Civil Service on April 7, 1933.[10] They took the new legislation and turned it against those colleagues whom they conveniently labeled "Jews" or "degenerate" or both. The legislation had been put in place by the Nazi state; it was being practiced and realized by dancers and choreographers to their own advantage. By denouncing other dancers to the Gestapo, the secret police, and drawing up blacklists, which the Nazi bureaucracy could use, human rights were being violated. German dancers were literally kicked out, threatened, and humiliated by other German dancers. Nazi ideology was being turned into an opportune instrument to abuse fundamental human rights by the very people who should have protected them. It was the Mary Wigmans and Gret Paluccas (and most of the well-known teachers and choreographers) who publicly proclaimed their adherence to racial criteria and who closed their schools to Jewish pupils. They enrolled in the *Kampfbund für Deutsche Kultur* (The Fighting League for German Culture), one of the most radical political organizations, out of free will and they—the teachers and artists—insisted on the fulfillment of the "Aryan" directives from their pupils in April 1933.[11] The Wigmans and Paluccas took up Nazi racial edicts and cleansed their schools long before the universities or other private schools were forced to do so by state authorities. It was Gret Palucca who, though herself Jewish according to Nazi racial legislation, dismissed her Jewish headmistress—Tilc Rössler—and cancelled the contract with her Jewish agent Bernstein in May and August 1933.[12] It was Rudolf von Laban as ballet master who agreed to remove Jewish children from dance instruction in the State Opera Ballet School in Berlin.[13] It was Mary Wigman who protested to the cultural administration about the "Jewish magazine" *Der Tanz* and its Jewish editor Josef Lewitan and wished him removed from the German landscape. Throughout 1934 and 1935 she waged this ideological war—with success. Lewitan was forced to sell his journal and emigrate.[14]

There are many examples of German dancers, choreographers, and dance teachers collaborating with the Nazis. Specifically relevant for our discussion is the scale and the organizational forms by which cooperation took place. The move toward right-wing political programs began before 1933 with inherently nationalist-conservative and racist concepts, concepts German modern dance had explored and nurtured throughout its evolution, or dance "revolution" as Laban and Wigman preferred to call their version of expressionist dance. After the Nazi seizure of power in 1933, the modern dance camp integrated into the Nazi cultural setting not only on its own terms, but in an orderly fashion, as an institutional takeover, for it already possessed the necessary and appropriate structures. The motives of the dance artists to close ranks with Nazism were racism and hatred of anything different from themselves, opportunism, and true conviction. They stemmed from personal choices and deeply ingrained belief systems; they had to do with upbringing, education—or the lack of it—snobbism, arrogance, fanaticism, meanness, cowardice or other character-istics; but also with historic experience and a socialization that incorporated and relied on a quasi-religious faith, the principles at the core of their idea of art as a surrogate religion.

Once Nazism was established, it proved difficult for the individual dancer to resist the inhumane policies and act against the practices, though it was never impossible. There are few examples of courageous artists who did not fall for Nazism and did not display the enthusiasm their many colleagues did. The dissenters always remained a tiny minority.[15]

Eleanor Roosevelt, the Universal Declaration of Human Rights, and the example of dance and dancers I have used point to another, very different problem. The convention speaks of the rights of the individual, but never of the rights and responsibilities of a group or a corporation. We therefore tend to judge actions by individuals as actions that have nothing or little to do with a social context that goes beyond the world of the individual citizen. Wigman or Laban believed in Nazism as a means to rescue Germany and German cul-ture from threatening dangers, the phenomenon of modernization they were witnessing, a modernization in many different incarnations. Their dance, as they understood it, had been the instrument to defy those assaults on Ger-many. Thus they were convinced that their actions promoted *the dance* per se, the only possible and acceptable dance, and protected not only its rights but much more, its existence. It would be wrong to think of them acting merely in an egotistical way; their own personal rights were not in the foreground of their thinking, though the master-personality best manifested the art itself. The problem lay in their successful mandate that the artist, the individual, identify totally with the aesthetic concept. The identification of art as a way of life, as a life philosophy or *weltanschauung*, proved a vital step in the creation of a modern dance. Dance, from the beginning of its formulation in Ascona in the 1910s onwards, became not merely a profession to secure a material existence but a guiding principle to conduct one's life. The new dance was more than a breadwinning activity; it became a conviction. The modern dancers around Laban and Wigman fiercely believed in a mission, which justified using any means to carry it out. Because Laban or Wigman asserted that they represented dance as such, they could do away with all other versions of dance and their actions were now beyond criticism. Individual dancers who were in their way—in the way of *the dance*—had to be removed, or "eliminated," in Nazi

language. Laban, Wigman, and Palucca spoke of and advocated their dance as
a higher form of living, as a higher artistic principle—above and beyond social
and political reality, which supplied them with all rights. Whatever kind of
defense, attack, or crusade they chose, it would always be in the interest of
the dance, their dance. The individual was merely a servant of a greater force.
In relation to the mission the individual appeared as an irrelevant entity. The
individual's rights disappeared before those of the group or community, which
the great masters of the new dance invented and announced. The group thus
acted as the protector of the rights of the dance. Neither this supposition nor
the dynamic between individual member of the group and the group as the
sum of all members has been challenged.

Dance, though, cannot have rights per se. It is an art with many facets
and many underlying concepts and theories. It is an idea, which is realized
through bodily movement. If the idea is proclaimed more important than the
human being who expresses it, then the foundations for totalitarian thought
and power structures are laid. Totalitarianism begins with the obliteration of
the balance between idea and its enacted practice. Whether in philosophy,
politics, or dance, such attitudes ensure that the human being turns into a slave
of the idea. According to the human rights convention, only individuals have
rights. To acquire the "freedom of speech and belief" and reach "the freedom
from fear and want"[16] was (and is) the goal of the Convention. It ignores the
complex relationship between individual and idea and individual and group.
Hence we can evaluate the behavior of the individual dancers as social beings, judge them by their actions, and accuse them of infringing civil rights—
though they would hardly adhere to such a concept. Within this context, we
can judge the individual; but we cannot discuss dance as collective activity in
relation to human rights, we cannot discuss a group of modern dancers, all
following a similar set of convictions, and the distinction between individual
rights and corporate responsibilities without changing our paradigms (by accepting the limits of enlightened thought, for instance, with all its subsequent
implications) and setting up a different historical and legal perspective.

The notion that humans as individuals actually had certain rights evolved
in the seventeenth century and above all during the Enlightenment of the
eighteenth century. Theorists through the centuries defined rights as natural
or adventitious, as perfect or imperfect, alienable or unalienable. Rights ma-
terialized with the liberty to contemplate human existence outside religious
doctrine. Philosophers of the Enlightenment envisioned man as an intelligent
and sensible creature, able to think and reflect in order to free himself from, as
the philosopher Immanuel Kant put it, his "self-incurred tutelage."[17]

Whereas the question of what constituted human rights was initially
discussed within the confines of a philosophical debate, it quickly moved

beyond metaphysics and into the sphere of politics. The Declaration of the Rights of Man and of the Citizen, approved and pronounced by the National Assembly of France, on August 26, 1789, was one such move toward the practical political application of rights. The Universal Declaration of Human Rights from 1948, which had been informed by enlightened concepts, extended them and articulated political, in addition to cultural or economic, rights. Henceforth the declaration became an instrument to question political systems, as did, for example, the Helsinki Convention of 1977, which was used by socialist dissidents to attack the Soviet Union and its satellites.

As we have seen, these declarations and the resulting discussions hardly ever address the problem of groups, of people who form corporations or communities and do not believe in individual human rights. Meanwhile, we can see that there is any amount of advice concerning homosexual rights, welfare rights, rights to smoke and rights not to have to be exposed to smoke, rights to practice a religion and the rights to separate church and state, the right of Muslim women to wear a headscarf required by Islamic law and the right of schools in Turkey to prevent female students from entering the classroom in religious dress, and so forth. There are arguments for and against more or less every conceivable notion of the "right" of a human being. No area has been left unexplored for the existence and consequent protection of rights, including dance practices. But all these interpretations of human rights are directed toward the individual and the expansion of individual rights. The puzzle remains: the focus on the individual means that the individual can certainly be protected by law from abuse or even accused of abuse. Yet at the same time, it proved and proves in principle difficult under the same legislation to make the same individual accountable for having committed offences as a member of an institution or group. It is just as difficult to define the rights of a group in order to shield individuals within the group. We are faced with a contradiction in the discussion about human rights. From the origins of the debate to the contemporary interpretation, this gray area has created confusion and, in the end, a void into which rights and their defense only too often have slipped. We also face the quandary that the Enlightenment as a historical period, together with its philosophy, could never solve the abundant irrationality of human nature. Man has not become more sensible. Quite the contrary, attempts to overcome the "self-incurred tutelage" have been answered with the search for the meaning of life beyond rational explanations and a turn to dark, obscure, and mystical answers. Even if we understand some structures of the human psyche, the subconscious, the hidden desires, drives, and fears, even if we unravel irrational behavior, mankind has not managed to make peace with itself. The notion of an enlightened human being as the core of western citizenship and rights has failed. Scientific transparency and the genetic mapping of the human being on the one hand have been accompanied by a surge of religion, from mild expressions to fanatical campaigns, on the other.

Let us return to dance under the Nazis and the question of common ground between dance and human rights. There is a set of problems involved, which is not restricted to the case of German dance, only one, if extreme, example of the conundrums. After World War II, the majority of German modern dancers claimed that their expressionist art had been misused by the Nazi system. This was, and still is, a myth, yet an exceptionally successful one. The second part of the myth contained an argument, which offered an explanation for the assumed persecution: expressionist dance was an individualistic art, one that entailed and respected the individual. The Nazis as persecutors of individuals per se could not tolerate any individualistic tendencies. Hence modern dance in its true essence had been persecuted and forbidden.

There are two sides to this assumption—a theoretical problem that arose from the lack of a clear distinction between individual and group or community, and a practical application. Both are interdependent and closely connected to each other. The creation of a myth was possible by treating an entire art form as though it were an individual person—by applying values and rights designed for individuals to the art of dance. Though dance had actually been stained by the collaboration of its agents, it could be salvaged as a whole. The construction necessarily involved casting a shroud over the history of dance under the Third Reich. That was relatively easy to achieve. Because dancers, as everyone else, had been exposed to the arbitrary violence and equally extreme bureaucratic precision of the Nazi system (elements they had praised as long as they did not interfere with their own lives and work conditions but had applied to the lives and work conditions of others), because Laban had eventually emigrated from Nazi Germany, because Wigman had finally given up her dance school to overly eager personnel, because Palucca had fallen victim—partly—to the racist Nazi jurisdiction, in their own wisdom the dance concepts they embodied consequently and logically had endured the same fate. The mechanism with which modern German dance had made its way into Nazism and secured a prominent place there functioned as its rescue from Nazism: the groups, the schools as entities serving the Nazis, and the authoritarian structures that they had all imposed on their dancers, who were disciples rather than colleagues, made that move so very smooth. German dancers acted as a group, an institution. The dancers treated German dance as a general concept and aesthetic umbrella; the Nazis accepted German dance as an organized institution with its own substructures. Consequently, German dance after the war should have been questioned as a community about its philosophy, and before a tribunal; but this is impossible, as western law rests on the enlightened principles of individual rights. Only the individual representative, the single human being, can be forced before a court hearing. According to the then-prevailing practice, only individuals, the individual German choreographer, dancer, or theorist, could have been charged with and prosecuted for collaboration. Not only did the German dancers as a group cease to exist (with the end of the Nazi regime, they, too, were shattered), but even if they had actually acted as a group and accepted the consequences and responsibilities arising from their close relationship to Nazism, there existed no techniques to hold them accountable for the community they had formed. Hence it lay in the principles of the human rights themselves that the relationship between individual, group, and concept was simply reversible. When German dance had been identified as the ideal movement for Nazism, its choreographers and dancers as an entity, as a dance community (which of course had already cleansed itself of "degenerate" elements), were automatically found suitable. Reversing the mechanism meant unraveling the tight association and separating what formerly and conceptually belonged together. The emphasis on the individual allowed German dance to claim individual human rights and distract possible critics from the question of "group responsibilities," an unwelcome and problematic thought in Germany at any time.

The irony lies in the fact that right from their birth, German modern dance ideologies had turned against the rational enlightened thought that had initiated the making of the Universal Declaration of Human Rights. German modern dance's origins were embedded in the antirational traditions that ran from the philosophy of Arthur Schopenhauer through Richard Wagner to Friedrich Nietzsche. Laban and Wigman erected their reactionary modernism[18] on anti-enlightened foundations. Their reference to, and rejection of, history, in particular dance history, is one of the important features that characterized their attitude. One corresponding aspect, the cause as well as result of such a *weltanschauung*, was the belief in corporate structures, closed group entities, a totality in which the complete life of a dancer was dominated by submission to the principles outlined by their leaders. The Nazi cultural hierarchy that saw German dance as the expression of the "master race" required an obedience, which German dancers had practiced through the 1920s. In the dance groups and summer camps, in Ascona, in Gleschendorf, in Hamburg or Berlin, in those "small places" as Eleanor Roosevelt called them, tolerance was neither studied nor experienced. The affinity to right-wing and Nazi ideology was born there and grew out of a larger German debate seeking *Kultur*, culture within communities, and denying *Gesellschaft*, art as social factor with a civic duty.[19] There the *Kulturkampf*, the battle between reason and romantic unreason, between the relationship of form and feeling, which lies at the heart of the whole struggle to define a "German," not a French or international culture, was decided and there the conditioning for a future exclusively German society—the

"*Volksgemeinschaft*"—was accomplished. The foundations of the German modern dance rested on the cult scene of the years 1900–1914 and cultivated a mythical language that promulgated nationalist ideals and thus could easily be appropriated by the Nazis. In the "small places," criticism and critics were identified as subversively "Jewish" and undesirably cerebral. Through the "language of dance," as Laban and Wigman defined it, the folkish communities were built, and the abuse of fundamental human rights began.

With the support of people like Laban, Wigman, or their disciples, the Nazis could declare entire sections of a society "degenerate" and "unfit to live." The German dancers were not prepared to reject Nazism when it claimed power because they, with their dance, belonged to Nazism. They watched, applauded, and partook in the dismantling of civil rights.

These reflections raise wider and more unsettling thoughts. Dance became "nazified" through German modern dance's adoption of right-wing ideas. That is, it had not only incorporated authoritarian habits but accepted the ultimate surrender of the dancer's personality—it exemplified artistic totalitarianism. But are not many dance groups likely to fall into similar traps? The list of great choreographers is full of figures notorious for their authoritarian attitude. Did Martha Graham not expect total acceptance and did George Balanchine not treat even his greatest, especially his greatest ballerinas, as vessels into which to pour his ideas? Did they not all break down the border between themselves and their subordinates?

To use a human being as an instrument violates the most fundamental of rights—the stipulation that a human being is always an end, never a means to an end. The enlightened philosopher Immanuel Kant prescribed, "Act so that you treat humanity, whether in your own person or in that of another, always as an end and never as a means only."[20] This "practical imperative" operates within the frame in which the Declaration of Human Rights was conceived; that is why it is quoted here. Yet dance by its nature is designed to use dancers "as means only." Then dancers as individuals are manipulated, subordinated, and subdued through dance. The essence of some of the great theatrical dances lies in the complete disappearance of individuality in the concept of a whole. Dancers become subjects of the will of the choreographer; they are subjected to the will as a force other than their own.

According to the human rights convention that is unacceptable. Modern dance in Germany solved the unavoidable contradiction between the integrity of the individual and the demands of the choreographer by evading the question and redefining the problematic relationship. As a result of banning enlightened principles from the concept of modern dance, consent between dancer and choreographer could be achieved through co-opting into the group and by brainwashing. The dancer would give up her will and recognize the outer force of the choreographer and the group as her own. She would internalize her master's or mistress's orders and hence lend not only her body but also her soul as an integral part of the choreographic enterprise. Through this measure the unity of body and mind (their separation had been regarded as one of the troubling and unacceptable aspects of Cartesian philosophy—and consequently ballet) was resumed. As soon as the dancer questioned the principles that the master had imposed on the group, she had to leave. The "free expressiveness" of modern dance concealed the dilemma. Since the dance was "free" of the traditions and restrictions of ballet, the dancer could believe she too was free and, indeed, could only be part of the group as long as she thought she was free, as long as she accepted that illusion that free dance freed the dancers as well as their form of dancing.

To mold the body was, of course, also the objective of ballet. The paradox lies in the fact that the molding in ballet followed strict but transparent rules. Ballet, though rigid and stylized, has an outer framework of rules, which creates a well-understood hierarchy of dancers and dance style. These rules might inhibit "free expression" but they provide certain external defenses for the dancer. Ballet was present at the very same time in the late eighteenth and early nineteenth centuries when the rights and duties of the free citizen were being enunciated. It reflects them in its own aesthetic structures, in the division of labor, and theatrical hierarchy. By the mid-twentieth century, dancers within the institutional theater possessed a number of rights, for instance, to join a trade union, to receive health insurance, to be paid a minimum salary or be granted annual leave, and so on. Ballet may follow authoritarian structures, but it does not devour the soul of the dancer. It subordinates dance to formal aesthetics and those formal aesthetic rules correspond to the political constitutions drawn up at the same time. They are abstract and impersonal. The dancer is the instrument to realize form and the medium to convey the meaning expressed through form.

To have freed dance of the restrictions of tradition, as the German pioneers claimed, again indicated a certain set of beliefs: first, that there was a need for liberation; and second, that the tools for this liberation provided the right method for the desired change. It also espoused the idea that abstract, impersonal, and universal rights were outdated and could not answer pressing questions. But seen in a political light and with the historical knowledge of what happened in Germany, the move away from enlightened universalism equaled the move toward a different kind of servitude. The replacement of ballet regulations by the undefined mythical dogmatism of the genius choreographer made things worse in Germany. The master choreographer was free to advance his or her ideas and follow his or her artistic callings. The modern dancers were free to follow the master, but they were not free to express their individuality against the master. In this sense they were just as much or even more slave objects to the choreographer genius as were their ballet colleagues to the ballet master. They had virtually no rights, except that of submission; ballet dancers at least had a minimum of social rights.

Is dance by its nature inevitably authoritarian? Can human rights coexist with the aims of dance, the art of the body? Or will dance be acutely bound to represent stifled individuals, their humiliation and their desire for freedom, because it is so interlinked with suppression and violation of the human body itself? And what would a democratic or a rights-based dance look like? Can such a thing exist? Would that be the ultimate anti-art, so politically correct and unprovocative, that it becomes absurdly boring?

It is not possible to answer these questions in an easy way. Only one thing can be said: No dance can have exclusive rights. Human rights begin with tolerance. Tolerance in the dance world begins in dance schools, performance groups, and on the tiniest stage. Dance can flourish in any society, whether democratic or dictatorial; human rights cannot. Dancers, choreographers, performers—they too are responsible for making a society that accepts the ideals of "freedom, justice, and peace" and takes responsibility, moral and political responsibility, for the ideas that their dances promote.

NOTES

1. Eleanor Roosevelt, *This Troubled World* (New York: Kinsey, 1938).
2. UN General Assembly, Universal Declaration of Human Rights, Resolution 217 A (III), Preamble, December 10, 1948, at un.org/Overview/rights.html (accessed January 6, 2008).
3. U.S. Department of State, *Statement on Draft Covenant on Human Rights*, Department of State Bulletin, December 31, 1951, 1059, 1064–66.
4. Compare *Statistisches Jahrbuch für das Deutsches Reich* (Statistical yearbook of the German Reich) (*StatJbDR*) 1935, 8–10, 76–78.
5. Compare *StatJbDR*, 1933, 540.
6. The debate between Furtwängler and Goebbels concerning the position of the composer Richard Strauss may serve as one example.
7. Ilse Meudtner,—*Tanzen konnte man immer noch: Erinnerungen* [—one could always dance: Memoir], ed. and with an epilogue by Dietrich Steinbeck (Berlin: Edition Hentrich, 1990), 46, 114.
8. Hrsg. von Frank-Lothar Kroll, N. Luise Hackelsberger, Sylvia Taschka, *Werner Bergengruen: Schriftstellerexistenz in der Diktatur. Aufzeichnungen und Reflexionen zu Politik, Geschichte und Kultur 1940 bis 1963* (Munich: Oldenbourg, 2005), 80. My translation.
9. Eleanor Roosevelt, "In Your Hands" (address delivered to the UN on the tenth anniversary of the Universal Declaration of Human Rights, March 27, 1958) at udhr.org/history/frbioer.htm (accessed January 10, 2008).

10. According to the legislation non-Aryans and those whose political beliefs differed from the Nazis were to be fired or forcibly "'retired'" from their civil service jobs.

11. Compare Lilian Karina and Marion Kant, *Hitler's Dancers* (New York: Berghahn Books, 2003).

12. Compare Katja Erdmann-Rajski, *Gret Palucca: Tanz und Zeiterfahrung in Deutschland im 20. Jahrhundert: Weimarer Republik, Nationalsozialismus, Deutsche Demokratische Republik*, ed. Deutsches Tanzarchiv Cologne (Hildesheim, Germany, and New York: Georg Olms, 2000), 400.

13. Compare Karina and Kant, *Hitler's Dancers*.

14. Compare Karina and Kant, *Hitler's Dancers*.

15. Several dozen dance artists managed to leave Germany and, like Kurt Jooss, Valseka Gert, Jean Weidt, Julia Marcus, Hilde Holger, emigrated on political or racial grounds. Less known are those who stayed in Germany and resisted the Nazi regime: Hanna Berger belonged to the communist underground and was imprisoned; Oda Schottmüller belonged to the Rote Kapelle resistance group, was tried and beheaded; Marianne Vogelsang withdrew in horror from group collaboration and acted in her performances against the regime with intimidating and menacing personal consequences.

16. See endnote 2.

17. Immanuel Kant, "Was ist Aufklärung?" (What Is enlightenment?") in *Foundations of the Metaphysics of Morals*, trans. and with an introduction by Lewis White Beck (Indianapolis: Bobbs-Merrill Company, 1959), 85.

18. A term coined by Jeffrey Herf in *Reactionary Modernism: Technology, Culture, and Politics in Weimar and the Third Reich* (Cambridge: Cambridge University Press, 1984).

19. On the history and debate of *Kultur* versus *Zivilisation* see Norbert Elias, *The Civilizing Process, Part I* (Oxford: Blackwell Publishing, 2000). For its relevance to dance see Inge Baxmann, *Mythos: Gemeinschaft. Körper- und Tanzkulturen in der Moderne* (Munich: Wilhelm Fink Verlag, 2000).

20. Immanuel Kant, *Foundations of the Metaphysics of Morals,* 47.

Plunge Not into the Mire of Worldly Folly

Nineteenth-Century and Early Twentieth-Century Religious Objections to Social Dance in the United States

Elizabeth Aldrich

The debate over whether dance is an expression of piety and an acceptable, even necessary, pastime in "good society," or a vice that embodies ultimate evil, is one that has a rich and long history. Starting in the sixteenth century, a body of writings appeared in Europe that has come to be classified as "anti-dance" literature, in which followers of the Christian church struggled with this question as they strove to denounce most social forms of dancing. Vehemently against any aspects of pagan ceremonies, these Reformation church leaders could not, however, deny that dance was mentioned in early biblical writings as part of festive celebrations. Moreover, sacred dancing existed to some extent within the medieval Christian church, and medieval religious visual arts often represented positive images of dance and music. At the same time, the existence of social dancing was clearly anathema to church leaders, as attested to by the multitude of church documents that condemned the practice as invariably immoral, dangerous, and uncivilized. Preachers greatly influenced the treatment of dancing in the West and conquered colonial lands, and made the "right to dance" or freely express oneself through movement extremely circumscribed.

However, the very vehemence of the attacks is ironic proof of the ongoing, enormous popularity of social dancing and raises interesting questions regarding the place of social dancing in European, and later, American society, for it to warrant such wrathful denunciation. Why, for instance, did the church condemn a practice so closely linked to class standing and maintaining a clear social hierarchy? Clearly, for the upper classes throughout Europe, condemnation of dance did not fit into the prevailing view that the ability to dance—and to dance well—was an important aspect of upper-class behavior.

If, initially, in the sixteenth and seventeenth centuries dance was integral to court etiquette and the display of political status, later, dancing was considered an appropriate exercise and an excellent venue for learning poise, an important component of the nineteenth-century middle class quest to gain upward social mobility and become "ladies" and "gentlemen."

The following article alludes to this and other broader social issues related particularly to the status of women, as it briefly surveys the antidance literature from the sixteenth to early twentieth centuries, with a special focus on nineteenth-century American writings. The reasons given in the antidance material for both accepting certain kinds of dancing, and banning others, are described, with examples drawn from a variety of different pamphlets and sermons.

EARLY HISTORY

Sixteenth-century Reformation leaders were among the first to note the connection between the Bible and dance. These early religious reformers suggested that dancing in the Bible was done by and for women and only for religious purposes. Embellishments on this theme included the suggestion that dancing in biblical times was performed in the fresh air of the outdoors during daylight hours, never in closed rooms or during the evening and night, as was the practice with current social dancing.

Consequently, while some of the early European antidance writers accepted the piety of dance as presented in the Bible, social dance was seen in a very different light. Jean Boiseul in his *Traité contre les dances,* 1606, claimed that biblical dance was "joyous and spontaneous," but seventeenth-century social dances, including the *courante, branle,* and *galliard* were regarded as immoral. Many writers concurred with Boiseul and did not condemn dance per se, but attacked the popular social dances of the day as fundamentally evil. This is the claim that grounds nineteenth-century American criticism against social dance.

By 1633 antidance sentiment in Europe was widespread among religious leaders. This is demonstrated by William Prynne's published list of Catholic and Protestant antidance writers in *Histrio-Mastix,* a diatribe of over one thousand pages that raged against the theater and dance. In this work, Prynne suggested that women who participated in court masques were of dubious character. As it happened, this proved to be a disastrous career move for Prynne, as England's Queen Anne not only supplied money for masques, but also danced in them. Consequently, the work was banned soon after its publication and Prynne eventually was tried for libel and sent to prison.

In 1685, New England's Increase Mather published *An Arrow against Profane and Promiscuous Dancing Drawn out of the Quiver of the Scriptures*. Although its contents consisted of previously published views on the subject, drawn from a number of European sources, the work is noteworthy because it represented the first antidance exposition published in the New World. Mather was the minister of New England's most respected church, Old North Church in Boston, the first president of Harvard College, and a respected statesman who was chosen to go to England in 1687 to negotiate a new royal charter for the Massachusetts Bay Colony. Thus, it can be assumed that his words carried considerable weight. On the other hand, however, there is no indication that his inflammatory words had any effect on the dancing public.

Carrying on his father's crusade, in 1700 Cotton Mather posed the question, which—in some quarters of society—continues to echo into the twenty-first century. Mather asks "whether the dancing humour, as it now prevails, and especially in balls, or in circumstances that Lead the Young People of both Sexes, unto great Liberties with one another, be not a vanity forbidden by the Rules of Christianity?"[1] As such, the early writings of New England Puritans Increase and Cotton Mather ushered in an American tradition of opposition to dancing that has "emanated from white, male, Protestant clergy and evangelists who argued from a narrow and selective interpretation of biblical passages."[2]

ANTIDANCE LITERATURE IN NINETEENTH-CENTURY AMERICA

A considerable amount of antidance literature was unleashed from the nineteenth-century publishing houses of the United States. As with earlier European writers, American antidance authors continued to compare the purity of Biblical dance with contemporary standards. For example, Jacob Ide, in two sermons given in Medway, Massachusetts, published in 1819, did not "dispute the propriety of an ancient religious ceremony, in which the people of God occasionally expressed their pious gratitude and joy, by dancing before the Lord." Ide continued, "Nor do I feel myself called upon, in this place, to attack the Shakers, who, professedly in imitation of the ancient saints, now make dancing part of their religious worship." However, he did object to balls "where the mind is necessarily dissipated; where health and property are often wantonly sacrificed; where hours, consecrated, by nature, to silence and repose, are devoted to hilarity and mirth."[3] Pastor B. M. Palmer of South Carolina claimed there were seventeen references to dance in the Bible and, in his published sermon *Social Dancing Inconsistent with a Christian Profession*, analyzes each reference, concluding—as did many other writers—that dances mentioned in the Bible were all performed by one sex, in open fields, and in broad daylight. Then again, he warned readers that those who participated in social dances were "fallen and depraved, subject to the domination of wicked passions."[4] Palmer was not alone in his stance; in fact, from the mid-nineteenth century until the outbreak of the Civil War, denunciations against dance—specifically social dance—grew increasingly shrill.

Throughout the nineteenth century, American antidance writers centered their condemnation on four themes: 1) religious censure based on a strict interpretation of the Bible; 2) health concerns that proclaimed dancing led to a weakened body, especially in women; 3) arguments that Christians should find better use of their leisure time; and 4) a myriad of attacks centering on women, either those in need of protection from the evils of the ballroom or women who tempted unsuspecting men through their revealing ball gowns and close embraces while dancing.

Religious Censure

Religious arguments centered on a strict evangelic interpretation of the Bible, because, as Rev. John F. Mesick reminded his congregation, "The Bible is the only rule for all those who wish to be saved."[5] Christians were expected to turn away from temptation and it was the duty of the clergy to inform congregations what constituted a sin and, more importantly, to warn about the consequences. The Rev. J. R. Sikes of York, Pennsylvania, declared the ballroom is where "wicked men and women seek their pleasure. Their thoughts so far as we can judge from their words and actions, are ungodly. They are not moral, and therefore they are immoral, and to be shunned by all who fear the wrath to come."[6]

These zealots also felt it obligatory to separate the "good" from the "bad" dancing described in the Bible. Good dancing was performed by women, for joyous religious purposes, who danced with "fervent piety, and a heart over flowing with gratitude."[7] "In Ex. 15:20, Miriam, the Prophetess, and her company of women, respond to the Song of Moses and the Children of Israel upon the destruction of Pharaoh's host in the Red Sea."[8] Bad dancing usually referred to Salome's dance for Herod. "It is needless to comment upon the dance of Herodias's daughter before Herod, Mat. 14:6, since the vicious character of all the parties concerned, and the detestable crime to which this dance led, are sufficient guarantee that it will not be pressed into service as a justifying precedent."[9]

A common argument was that dance broke at least one of the Ten Commandments. For some, dance represented idolatry, thus breaking the

First Commandment. For others, the Seventh Commandment, forbidding adultery, was largely in danger and, as one Kentucky minister noted, "There is no disguising the fact, that promiscuous dancing, including the Waltz and Round-dances, to which the 'square dances' naturally lead, are essentially licentious, and legitimately tend to the violation of the Seventh Commandment."[10] With similar thinking, in 1910 Don Luigi Sartori also claimed that dance might violate the Seventh Commandment, because social dance encouraged "unchaste thoughts, looks, words, jests, and whatever violates modesty and leads to impurity."[11]

Health Concerns

A second focus for these writers centered on the assumed unhealthy physical and environmental matters that were associated with dancing. An excellent example of this opinion can be found in Philadelphia Presbyterian minister George Heckman's writings. Heckman noted that dance was not a good form of exercise and that "judicious labor and regular outdoor exercise, as in play, walking, riding and gymnastics, will produce far greater ease and dignity, strength and grace of movement." He concluded that dance "is unnatural, violent, especially for women, producing unhealthful nervous excitement, quick inhalation of impure air surcharged with the dust of the floor and fine loosened particles of carpets. The body becomes heated to that degree that the temptation to seek a colder atmosphere is seldom resisted, while frequently such exposure from open doors and windows is unavoidable. The hours of dancing are generally those which Nature and science declare unfitted for exercise, permitting only gentle exertion and soon calling for entire repose." Heckman promised his readers that this would lead to "reactive prostration of the nervous system, poisoning and obstruction of the lungs and throat, often resulting in hemorrhages and consumption, palpitation and other diseases of the heart, frequent headaches, with their train of evils, and internal injuries of various kinds."[12] Condemnation was similar in England and exercise specialist Donald Walker noted that women who performed certain dances, such as the waltz, would suffer the effects of vertigo, which "produce sometimes, in women of a very irritable constitution, syncopes, spasms and other accidents which would induce them to renounce it."[13]

Indeed, the consequences of dance on women's health specifically were a chief concern for many antidance writers. Rufus W. Bailey informed women that the preservation of health "is among our first duties, and inseparable from the first law of nature which requires us to preserve our lives."[14] For the most fervent writers, death was the inevitable consequence of neglecting Bailey's perception of "duty." "Many an untimely death has been the dreadful penalty incurred by exposure [at balls] on such occasions; and the fearful blow has generally fallen among the ranks of lovely women."[15] Sikes added, "The mode of dressing for balls, the unnatural excitement, and the excessive exercise all tend to invite and develop disease. Cold is contracted, fever, rheumatism or consumption follows, and death often ensues as the result."[16] "Whiskey has slain its thousands, but the ball, the hop, the dance, its tens of thousands."[17]

Leisure Time

A third popular contention maintained that dance was a waste of valuable time. "For children to learn to dance requires a great deal of time, which they need for other and better purposes; and both private and public dancing, in after life, are a waste of precious time, of which no Christian especially should ever be guilty."[18] During the nineteenth century, America changed from a predominantly rural society to an urban culture influenced and enhanced by an Industrial Revolution that provided the growing middle class with time for leisure activities. It is not surprising that the question of *how* to spend this time became a topic of significance. George S. Weaver noted, "Half the dissipation and wickedness in civilized society grow out of ill-directed amusements; and not a little disease, despondency, and peevishness, originate in a want of proper amusements. Time, money, character, happiness, are all involved in this question."[19] Dance, as a recreational activity, is performed during one's free time and, according to some authors, leisure time should not be spent in worldly pursuits but in glorifying God, or in other accepted Christian pursuits, such as helping the poor. Mesick admitted that while the object of dancing might be the "acquisition of a graceful carriage, an easy movement, and elegant manners," its goal "did not extend beyond the success of worldly prospects." Thus, dance did not represent *true* grace and piety, and those who claimed otherwise were the "God-forgetting, pleasure-seeking multitude, [who wish] to exclude their Maker from their minds and from his own world."[20]

Vanity was often paired with misuse of leisure time and Bailey noted that a young girl who falls victim to vanity soon "has no time for anything but dress, and balls, and parties, and idle conversation with the idle."[21] Ide claimed in no uncertain terms, "Balls consume much time, which ought to be devoted to more important objects."[22]

Not only was dancing a waste of time, it symbolized wasted capital. "Extravagance of ornament and apparel is the ruin of many a fortune . . . which carries down whole families, with aching hearts, from affluence to sudden penury."[23] Indeed, substantial sums of money were required for ball dresses and, of course, for dance lessons. When Cecil B. Hartley observed, "Nothing will give ease of manner and a graceful carriage to a gentleman more surely than the knowledge of dancing,"[24] he was expressing the view of most nineteenth-century etiquette manuals. Nevertheless, dancing schools were often blamed for encouraging un-Christian use of time. The Rev. William Lyman noted that dancing schools were "branches or twigs of the general system of anti-Christianism which is, at present, demoralizing the world."[25]

Woman as Victim or Woman as Temptress

The connection between the sexual act, and a man and a woman moving together rhythmically, could not be ignored by nineteenth-century writers. "Dancing very often acts as a substitute for the natural gratification of the sexual impulse. It is note-worthy and significant that after marriage girls generally lose much of their ardor in dancing. Rhythmical movement is a stimulant to tumescence, which, uncontrolled, excites the sexual feeling."[26] Dance prevented the mind from ruling the body. "Souls should rule over the body and sensual motions and lust."[27]

Two diametrically opposed subthemes arose apropos women's participation in dance. Women were either assumed to be weak and in need of protection from the dangers of the ballroom, or were considered temptresses, enticing good Christian men into the folds of sin through the allurement of dance. Often this argument led back to Biblical prohibitions with Salome's infamous dance as "proof," or, the line of reasoning would return to breaking the Seventh Commandment, prohibiting adultery. "Dancing is used by the most wretched of females, as a mode of advertising their profession, and of inflaming the passions of their miserable victims."[28]

TARGET AUDIENCE

Antidance treatises were aimed at middle-class society—specifically women. Women, by nature of their newly defined roles that had evolved by mid-century into the guardians of family morality, were considered the obvious readership for antidance treatises, as they were believed to hold "a powerful and inextinguishable dominion over human customs and laws, over the temper and tone of civilization."[29] Until the end of the nineteenth century, the writers of antidance literature conspicuously ignored immigrant or working-class society and, in particular, they excluded women who earned their living as prostitutes—who would never be welcome among the congregations of these class-conscious churches.

CARNAL PASSIONS ARE NOT RESPECTERS OF
AGE.

Illustration from the *Immorality of Modern Dances*, New York, 1904. Courtesy of the Music Division, Library of Congress.

Dance prohibitions aside, nineteenth-century middle-class women were, nevertheless, expected to move seamlessly through polite society with grace and refinement. However, women were bombarded by two utterly opposing categories of advice. At the same time this vast amount of antidance literature was circulating, urban publishers were producing etiquette manuals for men and women in unprecedented numbers. By the 1820s etiquette manuals for women began to devote more attention to the ceremonial details of life aimed at the three areas thought to be appropriate for women: the kitchen, the dining room, and the parlor. Manuals detailed how to set a table and which foods to serve; which fork to use while eating; how to appropriately dress for every imaginable occasion; and how to organize every element of a family's entertainment, including evenings devoted to dancing. Based on a European courtesy tradition that dates to the medieval times, much of this literature focused on tenets that would pave the way—through a series of rules and regulations—to acceptance in polite society.[30] Etiquette was defined as "nothing more nor less than the law, written and unwritten, which regulates the society of civilized people, distinguishing them from the communities of barbarous tribes, whose lives are hard and their manner still harder."[31] Ironically, this same middle-class society, who strove to be well mannered, always avoiding the vulgar, was not only the target audience but, more importantly, the true enemy for antidance writers. To be polished in worldly accomplishments in order to be accepted in fashionable society went counter to the prevailing religious doctrine.

However, embedded in all etiquette and dance manuals and implicit in all the instructions surrounding dance is the fact that an evening of fashionable dancing, throughout the nineteenth century, was based on a stringent, inflexible, and strict set of conventions and structures. Some of the rules and regulations found in this literature included appropriate introductions for dancing partners—introductions that were not to be exercised outside the ballroom; the appropriate number of times married or engaged couples might dance together without causing embarrassment; rules that detailed the exact words a gentleman must use to ask a lady to dance; rules that defined appropriate topics for discussion in the ballroom; and so on. Many of these dance and etiquette manuals also offered opinions on the appropriate type of dances. For example, *The Mirror of the Graces*, an etiquette manual published in London in 1810 and 1811 and in New York in 1813, felt that the "close approximation of persons, in the attitudes, and in the motion, which ill agrees with the delicacy of woman" rendered the waltz an unsuitable social dance.[32] *The Gentleman and Lady's Book* was also critical of the waltz and its effects upon women. "The waltz is a dance of quite too loose a character, and unmarried ladies should refrain from it altogether, both in public and private."[33]

LATE NINETEENTH- AND EARLY TWENTIETH-CENTURY TRENDS

Toward the end of the nineteenth century and into the early decades of the twentieth century, virulent antidance sentiment—again aimed mostly at women—was renewed. During this period, traditional roles for women were changing. Many women left the private (and assumed "safe") sphere of the home and entered the public arena of the workplace. Other women took up civic causes such as suffrage, child labor, temperance, and prison reform. Evangelical clerics were only one class of people who felt threatened by these changes and both Faulkner's next work, *The Lure of the Dance,* and Revels A. Adams's *The Social Dance* reflected that dance was too passionate, declaring that women should not dance because, by nature, they were weak. Indeed, they continued to preach that women needed protection from dancing and from the potential lustfulness of men. (*The Lure of the Dance* even proposed that dance halls provided victims for the white slave trade.)[34] In 1921, M. C. Drumm took this fairly widespread argument one step further, claiming that as the result of dancing, "[t]here are 5,000 girls now locked behind iron bars in Chicago alone, where they are visited by 25,000 libertines. Their life lasts, under those conditions, about seven years."[35] (Drumm's comments are typical of a growing interest in statistics that offered "proof" of the evils of dance. "The chief of Police of New York City in his official Report some years since stated, that three-fourths of the abandoned girls of that city were ruined by dancing."[36])

During the latter part of the nineteenth century—a period of massive immigration to the United States from all corners of Europe that paralleled an influx of persons from the South to the urban cities of the North—it is possible to identify a substantial number of self-help and etiquette manuals published for and directed toward the new arrivals. The purpose of this literature was to inform the immigrant and newcomer regarding "civilized" ways of behavior. Publications were issued that ranged from assisting in losing one's foreign accent to the proper management of silverware to how to dress and behave in the land that was becoming the melting pot of the world. However, those expecting to be assimilated into the melting pot were instructed, largely through this literature, that no vestiges of a foreign culture would meet the requirements for acceptance into polite society. Etiquette writers no longer concentrated on white middle-class women but now took aim at *all* classes that might lack "the cultivation" through "isolation from society, the want of proper instruction, the ill effect of bad example, the advice of the prejudiced, the association with the low-bred" to fit into polite society.[37] During this time, at least two antidance authors specifically targeted the large German-speaking population of immigrants who settled the midwestern United States. To warn German Lutherans about the dangers of dance, in 1901 G. J. Pfefferkorn published *Ist tanzen sünde?* For the citizens of Chippewa Falls, Wisconsin, targeting German Catholics in Collegeville, Indiana, Don Luigi Sartori published his especially virulent attack against dance, *Die modernen tanze*. (The work also appeared the same year in English as *Modern Dances*.)

SAVAGES AND ANIMALS

For other antidance writers, dance was frequently associated with the habits of "savages," in writings that often revealed conventional racist views. In 1849 Crane noted the "savage gesticulations of the Indian warrior, when he returns from battle, bringing a goodly store of scalps and plunder." He also observed that the Children of Israel, "an imitative and not very enlightened race . . . doubtless became acquainted with [dance] during their sojourn in the house of bondage." He further postulated that "dancing yet forms a part of the religious ceremonies of the savage and the semi-civilized," a list that included India and Western Africa.[38] Ham noted that "with many tribes, dancing is [a] prelude to sexual indulgence."[39]

The 1893 World's Fair presented opportunities for many to see "savages" for the first time, and their habits were noted—albeit misinterpreted—by many antidance writers as evidence that none in polite society would consider imitating such behavior. "Savage" behavior was coupled with "animal" behavior and W. C. Wilkinson claimed the "modern manner of dancing" was unacceptable, noting that a ball was simply a "massing together of a jostling crowd of mute or merely gibbering animals."[40]

UNIQUE TACTICS AND OBJECTIONS TO DANCE MASTERS

While most of the hypotheses in antidance manuals follow predictable paths, some authors utilized novel and creative approaches to illustrate their objections. W. E. Penn's *There Is No Harm in Dancing* used trees as metaphors, noting that it was the fruit of the tree that might prove dangerous. The "fruit" on the tree of dancing included pride, lasciviousness, lying, drunkenness, embezzlement, fornication, cruelty, idolatry, prostitution, abortion, and assassination.[41] The Rev. George Davis used his training as a lawyer to present his "trial" against dance, including a "jury" composed of the public conscience and "witnesses" with names such as Mr. Round Dancing Master and Miss Chicago Barmaid.[42]

Likewise, dancing masters, who were often criticized for their lack of "prudence and modesty,"[43] often came under attack. Crane blamed Parisian dancing masters, observing that from "this elegant city, renowned for vice and moral pollution of every description, do troops of dancing-masters issue forth every year, and come upon the surrounding nations as did the locusts of the Egyptian plague." He accused dancing masters, who teach their students "to ape their model and learn, consequently, an artificial, mechanical system of manners, made up of French smirk and grimace, which produce a luxuriant growth of absurdity, when grafted upon Anglo-Saxon calmness and reserve."[44] Ham—in an unusually inspired addition to "save many young men and women from one of Satan's most fetching appeals to the lust of the flesh"—includes an attack against social dance, which he alleges to have been written by Lydia Lupokova, perhaps the most famous ballerina of the time. Lupokova is claimed to have said, "I am done with dancing. It is only a sensation, and any sensation overindulged in is harmful. I willingly drop it; for I am suffering of disgust."[45] Even economic woes were blamed on social dance and Ham quotes Stanley W. Finch, "former United States special commissioner for the suppression of the white slave traffic, now head of the National Social Welfare League" as claiming that "he has come to the conclusion that the present business depression can be blamed to some extent on the tango and the maxixe."[46]

CONCLUSION

For all antidance writers, social dance opened the door to sin and temptation. Although many of these authors proposed what might today be considered questionable arguments against the practice of social dance and oftentimes utilized language offensive to contemporary thinking, there is no question that opposition to dance, which increased significantly from the time of the Reformation, became an important moral issue, especially in nineteenth-century America. In the name of reform, these authors sought to convince social dancers that social dance would lead to unimaginable harm to both body and soul.

In the early years of the twenty-first century, antidance views are still very much part of the fabric of our way of life. As long as dance continues to function as a significant cultural expression, those who fear the imagined or authentic subversive power of a dancing body will scrutinize its practice. For example, numerous religious colleges and universities closely monitor the types of social gatherings that include dance. Efforts to control the moral fabric of those assumed to be vulnerable (adolescents and women in particular) include public outcries against raves (often called "parties") and other underground settings for contemporary social dance. Attempts to cut funding or to outright disband the National Endowment for the Arts reflect a fear not only of government-sanctioned expressions of dance, but wariness toward the body. Throughout the decades, the arguments against the practice of social dance have changed little; however, for dance historians, this literature provides an important means of understanding the place of dance in society.

NOTES

1. Cotton Mather, *A Cloud of Witnesses: Darting Out Light upon a Case, Too Unseasonably Made Seasonable to Be Discoursed On* (n.p., 1700).

2. Ann Wagner, *Adversaries of Dance: From the Puritans to the Present* (Urbana: University of Illinois Press, 1997), xiv–xv. Wagner's book is an excellent source for detailed information on this subject.

3. Jacob Ide, *The Nature and Tendency of Balls, Seriously and Candidly Considered: In Two Sermons* (Dedham, Mass.: M. & W. H. Mann, 1819), 4–5.

4. B. M. Palmer, *Social Dancing Inconsistent with a Christian Profession and Baptismal Vows* (Columbia, S.C.: Office of the South Carolinian, 1849), 21.

5. John F. Mesick, *Discourse on the Evils of Dancing* (Harrisburg, Pa.: Theo: Fenn, Printer, 1846).

6. Rev. J. R. Sikes, *A Time to Dance: A Sermon on Dancing* (York, Pa.: Office of the Teachers' Journal, 1879).

7. John G. Jones, *An Appeal to All Christians, Especially the Members of the Methodist Episcopal Church, against the Practice of Social Dancing* (St. Louis: P. M. Pinckard, 1867), 15.

8. Palmer, *Social Dancing*, 7.

9. Palmer, *Social Dancing*, 9.

10. W. W. Gardner, *Modern Dancing in the Light of Scripture and Facts* (Louis, Ky.: Baptist Book Concerns, 1893), 30–31. Gardner's discourse was apparently quite popular. First delivered as sermons in 1849 and 1866, Gardner's tract was published in 1874 and revised in 1887.

11. Although the focus of this article is on evangelical Protestant writers, antidance Catholics were also well represented, for example, Rt. Rev. Mgr. Don Luigi Sartori, *Modern Dances* (Colleg[e]ville, Ind.: St. Joseph's Printing Office, 1910), 14.

12. George C. Heckman, *Dancing as a Christian Amusement* (Philadelphia: Presbyterian Board of Publishers, 1879), 7, 17.

13. Donald Walker, *Exercises for Ladies: Calculated to Preserve and Improve Beauty, and to Prevent and Correct Personal Defects* (London: Thomas Hurst, 1836), 148–49.

14. Rev. Rufus W. Bailey, *Daughters at School: Instructed in a Series of Letters* (Philadelphia: Presbyterian Board of Publications, 1857), 151.

15. Mesick, *Discourse on the Evils of Dancing*.

16. Sikes, *A Time to Dance*.

17. W. C. Wilkinson, *The Dance of Modern Society* (New York: Oakly, Mason & Co., 1869), 41.

18. Hiram Mattison, *Popular Amusements: An Appeal to Methodists, in Regard to the Evils of Card-Playing, Billiards, Dancing, Theatre-Going, etc.* (New York: Carlgon & Porter, [1867]), 9.

19. George S. Weaver, *Hopes and Helps for the Young of Both Sexes* (New York: Fowlers & Wells, 1854), 6–7.

20. Mesick, *Discourse on the Evils of Dancing*.

21. Bailey, *Daughters at School*, 150.

22. Ide, *The Nature and Tendency of Balls*, 9.

23. Rev. Byron Sunderland, *Discourse to Young Ladies* (Washington, D.C.: Cornelius Wendell, Printer, 1857), 7.

24. Cecil B. Hartley, *The Gentleman's Book of Etiquette, and Manual of Politeness* (Boston: DeWolfe, Fiske & Co., 1873), 92.

25. William Lyman, *Modern Refinement* (East Haddan, Conn.: 1801). Quoted in Wagner, *Adversaries of Dance*, 108.

26. M. F. Ham, *The Modern Dance*, 2nd ed. (San Antonio,Tex.: San Antonio Printing Co., 1916).

27. Sartori, *Modern Dances*, 21.

28. J. Townley Crane, *An Essay on Dancing* (New York: Nelson & Phillips, [1849]), 99.

29. Sunderland, *Discourse to Young Ladies*, 7.

30. For a contextual discussion of etiquette manuals in nineteenth-century America, see Elizabeth Aldrich, *From the Ballroom to Hell: Grace and Folly in Nineteenth-Century Dance* (Evanston, Ill.: Northwestern University Press, 1991).

31. S. A. Frost, *Frost's Laws and By-Laws of American Society* (New York: Dick & Fitzgerald, 1869), 9.

32. *The Mirror of the Graces: By a Lady of Distinction* (London, 1810, 1811; New York: C. Wiley, 1813), 117.

33. Mme. Celnart, *The Gentleman and Lady's Book of Politeness and Propriety of Deportment* (Boston: Allen and Ticknor and Carter, Hendee & Co., 1833), 187. During the nineteenth century the waltz was the dance most often used as an example of the corrupt influences of the ballroom.

34. The subtext in most of these late nineteenth- and early twentieth-century antidance writings was that, because of their fragile natures, women should not venture out into the world at large, but remain in the safety of their homes, under the protection of their husbands or family. T. A. Faulkner, *The Lure of the Dance* (Los Angeles: the Author, 1916); Revels A. Adams, *The Social Dance* (Kansas City, Kan.: the Author, 1921).

35. M. C. Drumm, *The Modern Dance and What Shall Take Its Place* (Center Hall, Penn.: Center Reporter Printing Office, 1921), 21.

36. Gardner, *Modern Dancing in the Light of Scripture and Facts*, 31.

37. Frost, *Frost's Laws and By-Laws*, 7.

38. Crane, *An Essay on Dancing*, 11.

39. Ham, 26.

40. Wilkinson, *The Dance of Modern Society*, 41.

41. W. E. Penn, *There Is No Harm in Dancing, with an Introduction by Rev. J. H. Stribling* (St. Louis, Mo.: L. E. Klein, 1884), 46–57.

42. Rev. George Davis, *An Account of the Trial of Social Dance* (Roundout, N.Y.: K. Freeman Printing House, 1899), 7, 21, 25.

43. Lewis Rice, *A Discourse on Dancing Delivered in the Central Presbyterian Church* (Cincinnati, 1847), quoted in Wagner, *Adversaries of Dance,* 155.

44. Crane, *An Essay on Dancing,* 63, 72.

45. Ham, 20.

46. Ham, 27.

• 4 •

Dancing Chinese Nationalism
and Anticommunism

The Minzu Wudao *Movement in 1950s Taiwan*

YA-PING CHEN

Minzu wudao (Chinese national or ethnic dance),[1] a well-known genre of dance in Taiwan, is a subject not yet well researched by dance scholars. Many Taiwanese born before the 1980s learned and performed *minzu wudao* either at private dance studios or in public schools. Essentially a product of state nationalism and anticommunism imposed by the Chinese Nationalist Government (also known as Kuomintang, or the KMT) on Taiwanese society in the 1950s, the height of the Cold War, *minzu wudao* exemplified how dance could be used as an instrument of political warfare and how ideological indoctrination could be conducted through the physical activity of dancing, especially through the participation of hundreds or even thousands of people in the tremendously popular and widely promoted form of mass dance in the *minzu wudao* movement.

Initiated by political and military authorities in 1952, the *minzu wudao* movement was not only part of the KMT's scheme of internal control through cultural means but also an integral sector of its Sinocentric cultural policy aimed at re-Sinicizing the Taiwanese, who had just been "liberated" from five decades of Japanese colonization (1895–1945). Moreover, the dance movement was closely related to the regime's political agenda of presenting itself as the sole legitimate government representing the whole of China in the international community after 1949, the year the KMT was ousted by the Chinese communists from mainland China. Before discussing in detail the phenomenon and cultural-political implications of this state-operated dance movement, we need first to look at the island's history during the Japanese occupation and postwar years.

HISTORICAL BACKGROUND
TO THE *MINZU WUDAO* MOVEMENT

In 1895, when China lost the Sino-Japanese War, Taiwan, a large island off the southeastern shore of mainland China, was ceded to Japan as a colony. During the fifty years of occupation, while the Japanese imposed tyrannical rule over the Taiwanese and shaped the island's economy to suit its imperialist goals, they also brought modernization, including a modern educational system modeled after Japan's. It was through this colonial educational system that the form and idea of western-style creative dance were first introduced to Taiwan. Beginning in the 1930s, some Taiwanese youths, including Ts'ai Jui-yüeh, Li Ts'ai-e, and Li Shu-fen,[2] went to Japan to study dance. The dance styles they brought back in the 1940s included Duncanesque free dance, Oriental dances after Denishawn, neo-Romantic ballets in the style of Fokine, and abstract choreography inspired by German *neue tanz*.

While Taiwan ran its own course of history during the fifty years of Japanese occupation, China underwent tremendous upheavals in the first half of the twentieth century. In 1911, the Qing Dynasty was toppled by the Chinese Nationalist Party (the KMT) led by Sun Yat-sen, who founded the Republic of China (the ROC) in the next year. Ever since the ROC's founding, the country was plagued by feuding warlords and corrupt bureaucrats. To make things worse, the eight years of the Anti-Japanese War (1937–1945) further deteriorated the socioeconomic conditions, which paved the way for the rise and eventual victory of the Chinese Communist Party (the CCP).

When Japan lost the Second World War in 1945, Taiwan was retroceded to China, then the ROC, as part of the agreement reached at the Cairo Conference in 1943. Soon after the retrocession, Taiwan's natural resources and industrial materials were siphoned off to the mainland, fueling Chiang Kai-shek's war machine against the communists and causing social and economic turmoil on the island. Only less than two years after the Taiwanese had welcomed their "liberator," the traumatic "February 28th Incident"[3] occurred. Newly free of the repressive rule of the Japanese, the Taiwanese found themselves in yet another colonial relationship with an even more oppressive master—their supposed Mother-nation, China.[4] In late 1949, the KMT lost the whole mainland to the CCP and retreated to Taiwan. Earlier in the same year, a general state of siege had already been proclaimed and martial law imposed on the island. In the worldwide trend of anticommunism beginning in 1950, a tide of rampant political persecution was already under way in the so-called "Free China"[5] with the more or less tacit acquiescence of the United States, the major supplier of military and financial aid to the KMT regime during the Cold War.

From 1949 to about 1960, many liberal or left-inclined mainlanders[6] and thousands of Taiwanese, most of them social elite and intellectuals, were either executed or incarcerated by the KMT under the often-fabricated charges of sedition or spying for the communists. These brutal measures were meant to achieve two aims—to cleanse Taiwan of any possible political elements that might endanger KMT rule on the island and to eliminate the influence of existent social forces so as to take complete control of Taiwanese society. This period of intensive political persecution and social suppression was later known as the "Age of White Terror"—the background against which the *minzu wudao* movement was born.[7]

THE *MINZU WUDAO* MOVEMENT
AND THE KMT'S POLITICS OF CULTURE

After retreating to Taiwan, the KMT leadership proclaimed that it had lost the mainland through failure of morale, in other words, through both negligence of the power of the arts and incompetence in ideological warfare. Hence, as the regime consolidated its rule on the island, two measures constituted the main concern of its cultural policy. One was the policing of all products of thought through governmental censorship. The other was the development and implementation of state-sponsored cultural programs, initiated around 1950, which included founding a variety of cultural organizations and inaugurating cultural movements to promote official policy and disseminate anticommunist doctrine. As a result, a network of thought control and state-prescribed cultural production was established, turning all cultural activities into part of the state-machine of ideological indoctrination.

In 1952, Chiang Ching-kuo, the son of Chiang Kai-shek and then the director of the General Political Department in the Ministry of Defense, appointed Lieutenant General He Chih-hao to promote dance activities in the military to boost morale and provide entertainment for the 600,000 soldiers the KMT had brought from the mainland. In the same year, President Chiang Kai-shek wrote *The Amendment to the Chapters of "Education" and "Recreation" in the Principle of People's Livelihood* (*Minshen zhuyi yu le liangpian bushu*),[8] in which he not only laid out moral as well as ideological guidelines for the arts, including dance, but stated explicitly that the focal point of the official art policy was to extol national culture by making combat literature and arts (*zhandou wenyi*) the mainstream.[9] As a response to the two Chiangs' instructions, General He founded the *Minzu Wudao* Propagation Committee to carry out the task of "uniting forces to build [the society into] a strong military unit . . . through the art of dance."[10] In the article "On the Promulgation of *Minzu Wudao*," He writes,

> Our motivation is to enhance healthy recreational activities in the military to make the soldiers lead a happy life and to study a way of enabling them to sing and dance. . . . President [Chiang] said, "Good soldiers are the model of good citizens." We want to transform the pathetic dance that consumes our spirit into a healthy dance that inspires our spiritual power, thus increasing the youthful energy of the Chinese national culture. If every soldier can do *minzu wudao*, as a result of this influence, every individual in the society will have fighting spirit [against communism].[11]

Around the same time, the Ministry of Defense expanded the "Literature Movement in the Military" (*Junzhong Wenyi Yundong*) and sponsored the "National Forces' Grand Contest of Arts and Recreation" (*Guojun Wenhua Kangle Da Jingsai*). The *minzu wudao* propagation movement was essentially an offshoot of this cultural policy of "combat literature and arts" (*zhandou wenyi*) proclaimed by Chiang Kai-shek and carried out by Chiang Ching-kuo. Advocating anticommunism, patriotism, and loyalty to the KMT, *zhandou wenyi* exemplified the regime's cultural strategy, especially during the 1950s, of using the military as the vanguard in cultural movements to propagandize the population with official dogmas on the one hand and to militarize Taiwanese society for Chiang Kai-shek's ambition of retaking the mainland on the other.

Minzu wudao was a vague and loosely defined term. There were roughly five types of *minzu wudao* in terms of style and content: *gudian wu* (classical dance, including Chinese fan dance, court lamp dance, and so on); *minjian wu* (folk dance of the Han Chinese, such as lion dance and other festive dances); *bianjiang wu* (dance of ethnic minorities, for instance Mongolian dance, Tibetan dance, among others); *zhandou wu* (military dance, such as sword and spear dances); and *shandi wu* (dance of Taiwan's indigenous people). Accordingly, *minzu wudao* encompassed choreographies with pan-Chinese national themes with special emphasis on traditional motifs and ethnic representation. Furthermore, it adhered closely to Chiang Kai-shek's prescription of "Sunist realism" for the arts, which Edwin A. Winckler describes as follows: "In his main postwar discussion of cultural policy, Chiang Kai-shek prescribed the kinds of music, dance and sport he thought salutary. The basic Nationalist line, in all genres, had been Sunist realism—not just preventing heterodox statements, but promoting orthodox ones that stress the upbeat side of Taiwan's development."[12] Typical examples were dances from the 1950s with titles such as *The Laughter of Victory* (*Shengli de xiaosheng*), *Soaring Will Reaches the Clouds* (*Zhuangzhi lingyun*), *The Song of Liberty* (*Ziyou zhi ge*), among many others.[13]

With the inauguration of annual *minzu wudao* competitions in 1954, the dance movement spread rapidly from the military to every corner of Taiwanese society. Under the mandate of the Education Bureau of the Taiwan Provincial Government, all levels of schools—ranging from kindergarten to university—began training in *minzu wudao* to participate in the annual dance contests. At the same time, private dance studios across the island, seeing the opportunity to present their students and build their reputation, also avidly practiced the dance form in hope of scoring victories in the competitions. For more than two decades, the impact of *minzu wudao* competitions on Taiwan's dance scene was tremendous. Prize-winning schools got points of merit from the education bureau, which contributed to the promotion of their principals and teachers. Similarly, trophies from the contests served as the best advertisement for private dance studios, drawing students to famous teachers often by the hundreds. As a consequence, in the postwar years of severe material shortage, enormous energy and resources were devoted annually to this national ritual of dance contests, which became not only the arbiter of aesthetic standards, but also the trendsetter of popular dance styles and themes. Before long, *minzu wudao* constituted the core of most private dance studios' curricula, and by the late 1950s, this state-promoted dance form was securely established as the most important and widely practiced dance genre in Taiwan.

From the very beginning, the interference of the state and the military in the *minzu wudao* movement was both direct and immense. As part of the KMT party-state's network of ideological control, the dance movement and its accompanying annual contests were heavily endowed with political agendas. To begin with, they fulfilled one of the regime's most urgent cultural/political objectives: de-Japanizing and re-Sinicizing the Taiwanese. By making primary education universal, the government successfully imposed Mandarin Chinese as the sole official language, and implemented a Sinocentric nationalist curriculum, which placed exclusive emphasis on the history, culture, tradition, and geography of mainland China.[14] Following this ideological line, *minzu wudao*—with its infiltration of the whole educational system and its immense popularity among private dance teachers—played a significant role in teaching new generations of Taiwanese about their Chinese identity while at the same time reinforcing the mainlanders' connection with their Chinese origin. By impersonating officially sanctioned historical figures as well as embodying the images and movements of various Chinese ethnic groups through dance, the young students were bodily indoctrinated with the concept of "Chineseness" and the dogma of Sinocentric nationalism.

Secondly, *minzu wudao*, by mobilizing the masses in the collective activity of dancing, served as an ideal medium for promulgating the propaganda of anticommunism and of the importance of retaking the mainland. Chung Lei, a member of the Propagation Committee, congratulated the first annual *minzu wudao* competition with the following verse:

> *Minzu wudao* should exalt the nation's righteous morale
> To destroy the ugly and debased *Yange*. . . .[15]
> Come! Eight-million people of the Free China,
> Regardless of your sex and age, come to dance.
> To stride the grand path of anti-communism and recovering the nation,
> Incite the climax of *minzu wudao* in the first place.[16]

Not surprisingly, in that year's contest, there were quite a few dances with explicit titles such as *Anticommunist Dance* (*Fan gong wu*) and *Retaking the Mainland* (*Fangong dalu*), not to mention numerous others advocating militaristic valor and patriotic spirit.

Last and most importantly, the *minzu wudao* movement illustrated vividly the KMT regime's ideological struggle with the People's Republic of China on the mainland, in its contention for legitimacy and authority in representing China. Backed by the anticommunist United States, the ROC on Taiwan secured its status as the only legitimate Chinese government in the United Nations, even though its jurisdiction was limited to Taiwan and several surrounding small islands. In order to perpetuate this myth of being the rightful representative of the whole of China, a major concern of the KMT's cultural policy was to establish the regime as the orthodox inheritor of China's five-millennium-old heritage. Calling for the revival of China's "glorious ancient dance tradition," the *minzu wudao* movement fit perfectly into the scheme of claiming cultural authenticity and, by extension, political legitimacy. Indeed, General He, the chairman of the Propagation Committee, took great pains to trace the history of ancient Chinese dance in his many essays advocating the promotion of *minzu wudao*, which, according to him, was "to exalt the nation's traditional culture."[17] In addition to all these, the collection as well as codification in the *minzu wudao* movement of a wide array of alleged folk or ethnic dances from all over China—for instance, Mongolian dance, Tibetan dance, among many others—also helped to maintain the illusion that the Republic of China led by the KMT still governed and represented all the ethnic and geographical groups on the mainland.

MINZU WUDAO AND PEKING OPERA—
INVENTED TRADITIONS AND CULTURAL NATIONALISM

In the introduction to his book *In Theory: Classes, Nations, Literatures*, Aijaz Ahmad writes, "Used in relation to the equally problematic category of 'Third

World,' 'cultural nationalism' resonates equally frequently with 'tradition' . . . , which then opens up a space for defense of the most obscurantist positions in the name of cultural nationalism."[18] Though primarily a comment on the theory of Third World literature, Ahmad's critique of the myth of "cultural nationalism" provides a poignant framework for analyzing the interrelation between tradition, representation, and nationalism in the *minzu wudao* movement. One of the most salient features of "cultural nationalism" is "the nation/culture equation," whereby a singular cultural formation, itself often the result of "invented tradition," is upheld as representing the essence of a whole nation.[19] The *minzu wudao* created in 1950s Taiwan was an "invented tradition" of such kind, which the ROC regime used to proclaim itself as the "authentic" Chinese nation-state representing the elusive collectivity of the "Chinese nation" (*zhonghua minzu*).[20]

The material available for creating *minzu wudao* at the time was extremely limited. Except for the Confucius Dance (*Ba yi wu*) performed annually on the birthday of this great master, and certain movement vocabulary preserved in traditional theatres (*xiqu*), the tradition of Chinese classical dance had largely been neglected by the end of the Qing Dynasty.[21] To make the situation worse, the many folk or ethnic dances still vibrantly practiced on the mainland became totally inaccessible after 1949 when Taiwan was once again severed from China due to the state of war claimed between the PRC and the ROC. To resolve the problem, the *Minzu Wudao* Propagation Committee organized a demonstration performance in Taipei in 1953, seeking to define guidelines as well as to formulate performative styles for this dance form that was to represent "China," its people, history, culture, and geography. In addition to dance artists such as Ts'ai Jui-yűeh and others who were recruited to perform, several Peking Opera performers were also invited by the committee to demonstrate movements and gestures from this emblematic Chinese theatre that had earned the title *"guoju"* (*the* National Opera) in the 1920s.[22] Though primarily a theatre of acting and singing, Peking Opera, with its stylized movements, was believed to have preserved traces of Chinese classical dancing in its body language. Besides, the acrobatic martial art display in the theatre could be easily transformed into the movement vocabulary of *zhandou wu* (military dance), a major category of *minzu wudao*, which often used historical motifs to extol militarism and patriotism.[23]

According to Chou Huei-ling's account in *"Guoju*, Nationalism, and Cultural Policy," during the 1930s, Mei Lan-fang, the legendary impersonator of female roles in Peking Opera, and Chi Ju-shan, an ardent advocate of this theatre form, collaborated on developing a new style of performance that placed increasing emphasis on the element of dancing, in an effort to promote

Peking Opera in the western world as an emblem of Chinese culture. In order to compose a repertoire that suited the western eye and ear, they sometimes extracted dance scenes from traditional dramatic oeuvres, elaborated on the steps and movements, and then performed the segments as independent numbers for foreign audiences. In her analysis, Chou points out that this modified presentation was often advertised by Chi and Mei in the West as representing the "authentic" tradition of Chinese theatrical art; moreover, they sometimes alluded to the titles of ancient Chinese dances to enhance the impression of the performance's antiquity. "As a result," Chou writes, "the repertoire [the westerners] saw was, in fact, newer than the Peking Opera seen by the Chinese audience [at the time]; yet, the history of the theatre they acquired was much longer than the reality."[24]

By the mid-twentieth century, Peking Opera was securely established as *the* representative Chinese theatre. Unsurprisingly, when the *Minzu Wudao* Propagation Committee began searching for the tradition of Chinese classical dance, it turned to the theatre for inspiration. Yet, interestingly enough, it was the newly created dance style of Peking Opera by Chi and Mei only two decades before that served conveniently as the model for *minzu wudao*, especially the genre of *gudian wu* (classical dance). Through the mediation of General He, Taiwanese dance artists began learning the movement vocabulary of Peking Opera with masters such as Su Sheng-shih and Ha Yuan-chang, two of the many Peking Opera performers escaping communism to Taiwan. Throughout the 1950s, Taiwanese dance artists such as Li Shu-fen and Ts'ai Jui-yűeh learned and presented "classical dances," drawing directly upon the Peking Opera dance numbers reformulated and popularized by reformists like Mei Lan-fang. As a consequence, these modernized Peking Opera pieces not only became part of the standard repertoire of *minzu wudao*, but were also revered as the prototypes of Chinese classical dance.

For the "invented tradition" of *minzu wudao*, Peking Opera, by its own status as *guoju*, not only served as the much-desired link that connected the dance form to China's past, but also endowed it with the identity and authority of orthodox Chinese culture. In 1959, when the *Minzu Wudao* Propagation Committee proposed the formulation of a dance system called "*guowu*" (*the* National Dance) that was to be the singular and most representative dance form of the Chinese nation, the body language of Peking Opera was once again regarded as the backbone of its training method. From *minzu wudao* to *guowu*, history, tradition, culture, nation, and the state became increasingly interchangeable terms in the policy of the KMT's cultural nationalism; at the same time, the interpretation of their meaning and content also grew more and more standardized and institutionalized.

BIANJIANG WU, IMAGINATIVE GEOGRAPHY, AND PHANTASMIC NATIONALISM

Besides resorting to Peking Opera to establish continuity with China's past, thus institutionalizing *minzu wudao* as a national tradition, the *minzu wudao* movement also attempted to project an imaginary image and geography of China through dance so as to create the illusion of a unified Chinese nation on Taiwan. This phenomenon of what I call "phantasmic nationalism" was closely related to the political myth of retaking the mainland and reuniting China, a myth perpetuated by the KMT government up until the early 1980s. For decades, the existence of the myth was critical for securing the regime's survival as well as its continuing control of the island, its last holding of sovereignty. On the one hand, the myth helped consolidate the loyalty of the mainlanders, numbered between one and two million, who had escaped the communists to Taiwan between 1948 and 1950. On the other, it served as the raison d'être for the practice of martial law (1949–87) on the island by imposing an artificial state of war, which legitimized the regime's totalitarian rule over the society.

As an integral part of the KMT's Sinocentric national policy, "phantasmic nationalism" infiltrated almost every social, cultural, and educational system in post-1949 Taiwan. And nothing, perhaps, demonstrated the nature of this unique phenomenon more vividly and concretely than the *minzu wudao* movement, especially the genre of *bianjiang wu*, or ethnic minority dances. Literally meaning "dance of the bordering regions," where most of the ethnic minorities reside in China, *bianjiang wu* was in fact an invented dance style largely formulated and conventionalized in Taiwan during the 1950s. A product of the post-1949 sociopolitical conditions and the island's colonial history, the dance form offers an excellent subject for cultural studies of dance.[25]

In *The Amendment to the Chapters of "Education" and "Recreation" in the Principle of People's Livelihood*, Chiang Kai-shek ponders the function of dance as a potential tool for indoctrinating citizens in Chinese national culture and the ideology of anticommunism. After lamenting the disappearance of China's ancient dance tradition, he then proceeds to advocate the revival of the nation's dance culture: "The ancient Chinese said, 'When ceremonial rites are lost at court, seek them among the folk' (*Li shi qiou zhu ye*). In the bordering regions and various other places of our China, many ethnic groups still preserve beautiful dance traditions. We should study and develop [them] into a major subject for citizen education, and propagate [them] in the whole society."[26] As a result of Chiang's instruction, the genre of so-called *bianjiang wu* constituted, from the very beginning, an essential part of the *minzu wudao* movement. In retrospect, the development of the dance form took two closely interrelated routes. The first one was dances that originated partially on the mainland China during the Second World War, while the second type was purely invented "ethnic" dance styles that had their roots in the dance trainings the Taiwanese dance pioneers had acquired in Japan before and during the war.[27]

Between 1948 and 1950, several mainland dancers—including Kao Yen, Li Tien-min, and Liu Feng-hsueh—followed the KMT government to Taiwan, and brought with them memory and knowledge of certain ethnic minority dances they had learned or seen on the mainland. Though having different training backgrounds and objectives in dance, the three dancer/educators shared a common experience: that is, in one way or another, their knowledge about ethnic minority dances can be traced back to their contact with Dai Ailian, a pioneer in ethnic and folk dance research in China. Trained in ballet, modern dance, and Labanotation in London, Dai returned to China in 1941 to join the Anti-Japanese War (1937–45) and started her lifelong work of collecting, preserving, as well as recreating Chinese ethnic minority and folk dances.

In 1944, Kao Yen and her sister Kao Tzu, then teaching in Chongqing (China's temporary capital during the Anti-Japanese War), invited Dai Ailian to give dance lessons at a summer school for the training of local dance teachers. Inspired by Dai's work, Kao Yen briefly visited the border of Xinjiang, Chinese Turkestan in northwest China, and later Tibet to see firsthand the dances of ethnic minorities. She recalled staying in Tibet for about a week, witnessing processions of a local festival and learning dance steps on the street. In a spirit not unlike western Oriental dancers such as those with Denishawn, both Dai's and Kao's interest at the time was to collect ethnic dance movements and rearrange them into versions suitable for stage (re)presentation. A typical example was *Dance Song of Youth* (*Qingchun wuqu*), a "Xinjiang dance" taught by Dai in Chongqing. According to Kao, it was neither a reproduction nor a reinterpretation of any existing dance in Xinjiang; instead, it was essentially Dai's own choreography based on some dance movements typical of the Uigur tribe in Chinese Turkestan, for instance the trademark gestures of head and shoulders shifting horizontally either back and forth or sideways.[28] Labeled "Xinjiang dance," choreographies like *Dance Song of Youth* would later in Taiwan become not only equivalent to, but also regarded as representative of, the dance tradition in that region. In a similar spirit, Li Tien-min recalled that his knowledge about "Xinjiang dance" was gained mostly from a concert by Dai's group, which included the performance of *Dance Song of Youth* he saw in Beijing in 1947.[29] In 1948, Liu Feng-hsueh, then enrolled in the Changbai Normal College in Manchuria, also learned from Dai, in addition to Labanotation, certain Chinese ethnic minority dances.[30]

When *bianjiang wu* was established as one of the major categories of the *minzu wudao* movement and its annual dance contests, the "Xinjiang dance," "Mongolian dance," and "Tibetan dance" transplanted to Taiwan by the mainland dancers naturally served as the prototypes for emulation. In addition, between 1951 and 1956, there was a group called "Xinjiang Song and Dance Troupe" composed of men and women from Chinese Turkestan. As a patriotic gesture of supporting the KMT's policy of anticommunism and retaking the mainland, they often performed songs and dances from that region to entertain soldiers and participate in official gatherings of celebration. Interestingly enough, the person who was appointed to direct and organize the group's performance was Li Tien-min, whose only experience with "Xinjiang dance" before then was the one performance by Dai's company he had seen in Beijing.[31] A leading figure in organizing mass dances as cultural propaganda, Li later taught his own version of "Xinjiang dance" to several military-related propagandist groups in 1952, thus turning ethnic minority dance forms officially into weapons of ideological warfare.

From the very beginning, authenticity in representation had rarely been a serious concern for the advocates of *bianjiang wu*. To its audience as well as many of its creators alike, Xinjiang dance and Mongolian dance were just as foreign and exotic as Spanish dance or Indian dance. With the benefit of historical hindsight, it is clear that the prevalent attitude regarding cultural representation among dance creators at the time, as well as the actual difficulty in acquiring materials for creating ethnic minority dances, gave rise to the second type of *bianjiang wu*—the purely invented dances that drew upon visual images collected from newspapers and magazines, descriptions or hearsay gathered from mainlander students and friends, and, most important of all, the choreographers' own rich imagination.

A well-known example of such invented ethnic minority dances is Ts'ai Jui-yüeh's *Miaonu Nongbei* (Miao maidens dancing with wine cups), choreographed in 1959. From a friend of one of her students, Ts'ai learned about a simple game of playing with small Chinese wine cups allegedly practiced in the informant's home province of Hunan in southwest China. Based on a few gestures of holding two cups together between the thumb, index, and middle fingers of each hand—for instance, closing the cups repeatedly or rattling them slightly against each other to produce sounds—Ts'ai made up the dance steps for her imaginary Miao maidens to a melody she composed by elaborating on a short folk tune the informant had sung to her. Borrowing the name and costumes of the Miao tribe, a minority group inhabiting the mountainous area of southwest China, Ts'ai created one of the most widely performed works of *minzu wudao* by conjuring up an imaginary image of this remote and relatively unknown people. For at least two decades, the dance remained extremely popular among private dance studios in Taiwan. When the author began learning dance and participating in the *minzu wudao* competitions in the late 1970s, it was still taught enthusiastically by many dance teachers with the same title and to the same piece of music. In other words, *Miaonu Nongbei*, like many other similar works of *bianjiang wu*, became an "invented tradition" that was entirely fictional, while the overarching concept of *minzu wudao* endowed it with assumed "authenticity."

Comparable to the Oriental dance in the West, *bianjiang wu* was essentially a self-referential system of *idées reçues*, ideas that are "repeated, echoed and re-echoed uncritically" in representational systems such as Orientalism.[32] Many of the prototypical dances in the *bianjiang wu* genre shared the history of an endless chain of recycling and imitation, not to mention a decades-long process of distortion and degeneration. As the various dance styles of *bianjiang wu* were passed on from one dancer to another and from one generation to the next, costumes and props became more and more elaborate while dance steps grew increasingly stagnant and exaggerated. The partially authentic styles, such as Tibetan dance and Xinjiang dance, became gradually indistinguishable from the purely invented ones, for, at the end, these self-proclaimed "ethnic dances" were all defined by a few worn-out tunes, standard props, and some conventionalized eccentric postures and movements. As a second-generation Taiwanese dancer, Ts'ai Hsueh-hui, jokingly put it: "Mongolian dance equals chopsticks dance, and the one with shifting head is Xinjiang dance."[33]

There is no denying that, under the KMT's repressive control of all cultural activities during the 1950s, the initial creations of *bianjiang wu* provided the individual dance artists with an important avenue for releasing artistic creativity and imagination.[34] Yet, as a cultural phenomenon, it was also undoubtedly a product of the regime's Sinocentric cultural policy and an active ingredient in its formulation of phantasmic nationalism—the cultivation of love for an imaginary united China.

Shortly after the KMT retreated to Taiwan in 1949, the street names of Taipei were changed to carry the names of major cities on the mainland, so as to compose an imaginary map of China upon the geography of Taipei, the temporary capital of the exiled Chinese government. Similarly, in the educational system, while knowledge related to Taiwan was severely discriminated against, students were forced to learn and memorize in trifling detail the history and geography of mainland China. For decades, the social, historical, and cultural reality of Taiwan was denied and haunted by the phantom of a lost nation. In 1956, Chang Chi-yun, then the minister of education, addressed the third annual *minzu wudao* competition with the following words: "Today, we participate in this gathering of [dance] contests, as if seeing our heavenly state of [Chinese] mainland (*shenzhou dalu*), its picturesque landscape of rivers and mountains (*jinxiu heshan*)."[35] Indeed, a typical *minzu wudao* competition at the time was a compilation of images that aimed at conjuring up and piecing together the impression of an imaginary China. Dances depicting loyal characters and heroic events from ancient dynasties enacted an officially sanctioned narrative of Chinese history, while choreographies bearing the names of geographic locations on the mainland offered nostalgic imaginings of the lost Motherland. The performance on the same stage of "Xinjiang dance," "Mongolian dance," "Tibetan dance," "Miao tribe dance," as well as alleged folk dances of many other regions, not only presented the audiences with an "imaginative geography"[36] of representative figures that impersonated those remote places and peoples, but projected a much desired illusion of a unified Chinese nation with all the ethnic groups together under the leadership of the KMT.

This magic of phantasmic nationalism was brought to its fullest expression in the widely practiced form of mass dance (*tuanti wu*)[37] in the *minzu wudao* movement. In his instruction on the sociopolitical function of dance, Chiang Kai-shek points out the importance of "forging the collective will as well as cultivating the cooperative spirit" by means of mass dances.[38] Moreover, General He Chih-hao also states explicitly that, for the healthy development of *minzu wudao,* "solo dances are not as applaudible and valuable as mass dances."[39] Originating in the propagandist performances in the military, mass dances, especially those performed by school students, not only made up a major category in the *minzu wudao* competitions, but also played an indispensable role in the ceremonial gatherings that were a standard part of national holidays and official celebrations in Taiwan up until the 1980s. Participated in by hundreds, sometimes even thousands, of people, these performances were important showcases for displaying nationalism and patriotism during the martial law era. By submitting oneself to the uniform rhythm and movement of the group, the act of participating in mass dances fulfilled, for both the dancers and spectators alike, "the echoed physical [as well as psychological] realization of the imagined community."[40]

After the arrival of television in Taiwan in the 1960s, broadcasting the official ceremonies became obligatory routines for all TV stations. Thanks to the magic of modern technology and the KMT's absolute control over the media before 1987, the "imagined communion" brought about by the mass performance of *minzu wudao* was expanded to encompass the millions sitting before the television screens. Along with the images of these dances were transmitted the imaginary geography of a fantasized China, the KMT's ideology of phantasmic nationalism, and, above all, the myth of the ROC as the "truly" legitimate Chinese nation-state.

NOTES

1. The Chinese term *minzu* means nation, people, and ethnicity, and *wudao* means dance. Hence, *minzu wudao* connotes both national dance (i.e., Chinese national dance) and ethnic dances (i.e., minority dances such as Mongolian dance, Tibetan dance, and so on). To avoid confusion, I will use the original Chinese term throughout the essay.

2. All the Chinese names in the article are spelled family name first, following the convention of the Chinese language.

3. On the evening of February 27, 1947, Monopoly Bureau agents beat a woman selling cigarettes on the black market and shot a protesting bystander. The next day, angry crowds marching to the administrator-general's office building were dispersed mercilessly by armed soldiers. In the ensuing weeks, violent conflicts between the Taiwanese and mainlanders erupted; then in May, reinforcement troops sent by the KMT arrived from the mainland and opened war on the islanders, resulting in the death of thousands of people. Thomas B. Gold, *State and Society in the Taiwan Miracle* (Armond, N.Y.: M. E. Sharpe, 1986), 50–52; Peter R. Moody Jr., *Political Change on Taiwan* (New York: Praeger, 1992), 42–43.

4. In the 1990s, some historians, such as Chen Fang-ming, began to assess the experience of the "February 28th Incident" as the "re-colonization" of Taiwan, this time by the KMT Chinese regime.

5. Originally used during the Second World War for mainland areas not occupied by the Japanese, the term "Free China" was later used to indicate regions not in the communists' hands.

6. The mainlanders persecuted by the KMT included those who came before 1949 and those who arrived with the regime. Not all people who fled Red China after 1949 were supporters of the KMT. Moreover, in those chaotic years of "White Terror," even KMT loyalists could be wrongly punished since the charges of sedition or spying for the communists could sometimes serve as convenient means for getting rid of one's opponents.

7. This wave of rampant political "witch hunts" engulfed at least one Taiwanese dancer, Ts'ai Jui-yüeh. In 1949, Ts'ai's husband Lei Shih-yu, a mainlander who had come to Taiwan after the war and taught Chinese literature at the National Taiwan University, was arrested. After half a year of imprisonment, he was expelled from Taiwan and deported back to the mainland. A few months later, Ts'ai was also apprehended for her relation with Lei and eventually jailed for two years. Even after her release, her family and dance school were harassed constantly by police and special agents for several years. Ts'ai did not see her husband again until forty years later when unofficial communication across the Taiwan Straits was resumed.

8. Chiang Kai-shek, *Amendment to the Chapters of "Education" and "Recreation" in the Principle of People's Livelihood (Minshen zhuyi yu le liangpian bushu)* (Taipei: Central Documents [Zhongyang Wenwu], 1954). "The Principle of People's Livelihood" is one of the Three Principles of the People formulated by Dr. Sun Yat-sen, the founder

of the Republic of China and the KMT party. The three principles (nationalism, democracy, and people's livelihood) form the foundation of the ROC's constitution.

9. Wu Tzu-chun, ed. *Historical Documents of the National Forces' Political Warfare* (*Guojun zhengzhan shi gao*) (Taiwan: Dept. of General Political Warfare, Ministry of Defense, 1983), 727.

10. He Chih-hao, *Anthology of Essays on National Dance* (*Minzu wudao luen ji*) (Taipei: Minzu Wudao Promulgation Committee, 1959), 17.

11. He Chih-hao, "About the Promulgation of National Dance" (*Guanyu minzu wudao de yichang*) (ca. 1953), 18. From Ts'ai Jui-yüeh's personal collection of newspaper clippings.

12. Edwin A. Winckler, "Cultural Policy on Postwar Taiwan," in *Cultural Change in Postwar Taiwan,* ed. Stevan Harrell and Huang Chűn-chieh (Boulder, Colo.: Westview Press, 1994), 36. *Sunist* refers to the nationalist ideology of Sun Yat-sen, the first president of the Republic of China (1912).

13. The dance titles are taken from the program notes of the first annual *minzu wudao* competition in 1954.

14. Before the arrival of large numbers of mainlanders with the KMT around 1949, the majority of the population in Taiwan included Fulao (originally from southern Fujian), Hakka, and the Taiwanese indigenous people, each having their own dialects. Up until the 1970s, students were punished for speaking dialects, their mother tongues, in school. Policies like this were meant to erase or prevent the existence of Taiwanese consciousness considered dangerous by the KMT, in other words to de-Taiwanize the Taiwanese.

15. *Yang-ge* is a form of folk dance performed by farmers in northeastern China during the planting season. In the civil war against the Nationalists, the Chinese communists promoted it as a model for proletarian dancing and used it as an instrument for mobilizing the masses.

16. Chung Lei, "Incite the Climax of National Dance" (*Xienqi minzu wudao de gaochao*), *Young Warrior's Daily* (*Qingnian zhanshi bao*), February 16, 1954, 4.

17. He Chih-hao, "The Creation and Development of National Dance" (*Minzu wudao de chuangzao yu fazhan*), *Young Warrior's Daily* (*Qingnian zhanshi bao*), February 16, 1954, 4.

18. Aijaz Ahmad, *In Theory: Classes, Nations, Literatures* (London: Verso, 1992), 9.

19. The idea of "invented tradition" is indebted to Eric Hobsbawm's elaboration on the term in his influential essay, "Inventing Traditions and Mass-Producing Traditions: Europe, 1870–1914," in *The Invention of Tradition*, ed. Eric Hobsbawm and Terence Ranger (Cambridge: Cambridge University Press, 1983).

20. In fact, the "Chinese nation" itself is an invented concept that did not come into existence until the founding of the Republic of China in 1912. Before then, the Nationalists' revolutionary slogan for overturning the Qing court was "expelling the ferocious savages (i.e., the Manchurians) and restoring China" (*quzhu dalu, huifu zhonghua*). However, after 1912, the Nationalists' propaganda was changed to "uniting and harmonizing the five major ethnic groups" (Han Chinese, Manchurians, Mongolians, Moslems, and Tibetans) (*wuzu gonghe*) to make a great Chinese nation (*zhonghua minzu*).

21. WangKefen, *Chinese Dance: An Illustrated History* (Taipei: Wen-jing Publishers, 2002), 161–78.

22. The dance artists recruited were mostly trained originally in western styles of creative dance. But many of them sought instruction from Peking Opera masters in order to compose dances in the style of *minzu wudao*. Though this traditional Chinese theatre is known as *Jingju* on the mainland, it has been traditionally called Peking Opera in Taiwan. The Peking Opera in Taiwan before 1980 was considered more conservative in terms of style when compared to the development of its counterpart on the mainland. To maintain this distinction, I use the term *Peking Opera* rather than *Jingju* throughout this article.

23. It is interesting to note that when the PRC created the genre called Model Opera (*yangban xi*) during the Cultural Revolution to represent Red China and to propagate the message of communist revolution, Peking Opera or *Jingju* was also chosen as the form and foundation of this new theatre.

24. Chou Huei-ling, "*Guoju*, Nationalism, and Cultural Policy" (*Guoju, guojia zhuyi yu wenhua zhengce*), *Contemporary Monthly* (*Dangdai*), no. 107 (1995): 54.

25. In post-1949 China, the creation/development of ethnic minority dances for stage presentation was also closely related to the construction of Chinese nationhood on the mainland. However, due to the state of war proclaimed between the PRC and the ROC, this similar approach to "nation-building" through dance developed independently on the two sides.

26. Chiang Kai-shek, *Amendment to the Chapters of "Education" and "Recreation,"* 83.

27. In my view, the dance trainings contributing to the creation of *bianjiang wu* included so-called "creative dance," a form of modern dance originating in Japan, which mixed the style of Duncanesque free dance, the creative method of Émile Jaques-Dalcroze's eurhythmics and certain concepts of German *neue tanz*, Oriental dance, and Japanese folk dance that the Taiwanese dance pioneers had learned in Japan.

28. Personal interview with Kao Yen, August 22, 1997.

29. Personal interview with Li Tien-min, September 1, 1997.

30. In 1955, Liu choreographed a "Mongolian dance," *Menggu Zhujie Wu* (Mongolian Dance of Victory Celebration), for that year's *Minzu Wudao* Competition (program notes of 1955's *Minzu Wudao* Competition). However, suspicious of the nature of the *minzu wudao* movement in general and disappointed at the limitation imposed by the competitions, Liu not only withdrew from participating in the annual dance contests after 1956, but stopped choreographing any dances under the title of *minzu wudao* from that time onward.

31. See Li Tien-min's memoir "Wu Tuo" in *Proceedings of the Conference on Taiwan's Dance History* (Taipei: Council for Cultural Development, ROC, 1995), 69–70. The information is also based on the interview with Mr. Li.

32. Edward Said, *Orientalism* (New York: Vintage Books, 1979). Said makes the following observation about the Western system of representing the Orient: "[The Orient] is . . . circumscribed by a series of attitudes and judgments that send the Western mind, not first to Oriental sources for correction and verification, but rather to other Orientalist works" (67). The result, according to Said, is the production and reiteration of *idées reçues* (116).

33. Personal interview with Ts'ai Hsueh-hui, September 5, 1996.

34. Coexistent with *minzu wudao* at the time were ballet and "creative dance." Relatively free from the ideology of the KMT and hence without any support from the government, the choreography of ballet and creative dance allowed more space for the expression of the individual artists' creativity. Many dance teachers strove hard to have annual concerts for their students, even though they were not allowed to sell tickets to the public and had to take great financial risks. These concerts featured not only *minzu wudao* but also ballet and creative dance pieces. The works presented, like all other cultural products at the time, had to be examined by the government's strict censorship, which checked for "improper" themes and styles.

35. He Chih-hao, *Anthology of Essays on National Dance*, 2.

36. The concept of "imaginative geography" used here is indebted to Edward Said's critique of Orientalism: "*Imaginative geography* . . . legitimates a vocabulary, a universe of representative discourse peculiar to the discussion and understanding of Islam and of the Orient. . . . Underlying all the different units of Orientalist discourse . . . is a set of *representative figures*, or tropes. These figures are to the actual Orient . . . as stylized costumes are to characters in a play." Said, *Orientalism,* 71 (emphasis added).

37. I choose "mass dance," rather than "group dance," to translate the term *tuanti wu* because I intend to emphasize certain characteristics of *tuanti wu* as manifested not only in the *minzu wudao* competitions but also in the dances staged for official ceremonies on national holidays. First of all, *tuanti wu* often involved hundreds, or even thousands, of people. Secondly, the focal point of all *tuanti wu* was placed less on the creative innovation in movement and choreographic structure, and more on the composition of group formations and floor patterns. As a result, uniformity and order became the highest values in the performance, while individual expression was totally subsumed under the flow of mass movement. In my opinion, group dance is closer to the Chinese term *qun wu,* in which people dance together as individuals rather than as anonymous parts of a gigantic collective.

38. Chiang Kai-shek, *Amendment to the Chapters of "Education" and "Recreation,"* 83.

39. He Chih-hao, *Anthology of Essays on National Dance,* 64.

40. Benedict Anderson talks about the creation of "contemporaneous community," or the selfless immersion in the experience of "unisonance," by such symbolic action as singing the national anthem. *Imagined Communities: Reflections on the Origin and Spread of Nationalism* (London: Verso, 1983), 132. The mass dances in the *minzu wudao* movement achieved the same effect.

• 5 •

Animation Politique

The Embodiment of Nationalism in Zaire

Joan Huckstep

On the African continent, the embodiment of one's social, cultural, and political worlds through dance is such an elemental aspect of being that many traditional languages do not have a discrete word for dance or for dancing.[1] For example, in Bapende initiation dances in Zaire/Congo, through which men become accepted members of the tribe, initiates are not "dancing," they are *mingajei*—spiritually preparing the body for physical initiation ordeals. Danced embodiment—as in the expression of social or political relations, and of spiritual belief, through dance—ubiquitous in Congolese culture, took on new significance during the era of President Mobutu Sese Seko (1965–1997), in what was then Zaire, because of its coercion by the state.[2] In a place where dance floats through every aspect of life, where every social interaction can be danced, and where dance has long been an agent of multiple sociopolitical and religious ends on individual and communal levels, dance was harnessed for nationalist purposes in the late twentieth century through the Congolese (Zairian) political dance phenomenon, *animation politique*. Though dance was intimately related to the political landscape across continental Africa, *animation politique*, because of its forced nature, and the dire consequences suffered by those who did not participate as required, became a unique example of how dance tied an African society to the contemporaneous sociopolitical environment.

Animation politique was a nationally observed, compulsory activity in Zaire during Mobutu's rule, one of the core objectives of which was to inculcate citizens with notions of Zairian national identity through the dancing, singing, and chanting of praises to Mobutu, his family, his ancestral village, or to some aspect of his political agenda. *Animation* was a tool used to develop and to educate people in the ideology of the new state, a means of mass and rapid political enculturation. On its face, *animation politique* drew upon the use of dance from ancient traditions in ways that forged an African/Congolese/national identity matching the jubilance the people felt as they abandoned European, particularly Belgian, cultural conventions following independence. However, the practice of *animation politique* had a corrosive effect as well. It became state-mandated jubilance—the repressive state control of the body and mind.

This essay presents an analysis of expatriate Zairians' interpretations and memories of danced politics, in particular, their experiences with *animation politique,* the danced embodiment of the Zairian cultural politics of President Mobutu Sese Seko.[3] The individuals interviewed are professional and semi-professional dancers/musicians, some of whom were professional *animateurs/animatrices* during the Mobutu era, while others merely engaged in the obligatory *animation*. Mufulu Kingambo Gilonda, educator (B.Sc. in social science and pedagogy, University of Kinshasa; M.A. in education/reading, Lincoln University in Pennsylvania), and a member of Mobutu's folkloric company with administrative responsibilities, is the primary voice in this essay. Gilonda is the only individual who elected to use his name; all other interviewees elected to remain anonymous; thus, their names in this essay are fictitious.

A scarcity of corroborating documentary evidence (to date) supporting the fact that participation in *animation politique* was state mandated limits the reach of this study.[4] As is often the case in instances in which the state is intolerant of anyone opposing or defying its core organizing ideology, punishment for such actions is not written into the rule of law, though it is reported in oral histories and interviews. Moreover, this is particularly true in a repressive state built upon personalism—ideology and governance based on the personality cult of one individual. *Animation politique* was a function of political education to forge the new man—the authentic *citoyen/citoyenne*. Further, the Mobutu state was based in clientism whereby culling favor of the state and its agents, from the national to the neighborhood echelons, was a major factor in securing basic necessities such as employment.[5] Punishment for refusing to participate in *animation politique* or participating in a mocking manner could be reported to a state agent by one's neighbor. That agent meted out the punishment he or she deemed appropriate.

The stories of the people interviewed are consistent; the newspaper articles announcing formations of animation cadres, videotapes of regional performances, popular art of the day,[6] and Mobutu's writings[7] all serve to reinforce my contention that political animation was a kind of forced embodied nationalism. In examining people's recollections of *animation politique*, I document and explore one way in which dance played a central political role in early postcolonial Zaire.[8]

In the many cultures of Zaire, as well as in African cultures in general, multiple core social, political, and religious elements are embodied in dance phenomena. In the second half of the twentieth century, the numerous forms of dance in Zaire had distinct characteristics and functions. In addition to dances that celebrated weddings, births, deaths, and the comings and goings of friends and relatives, among other occasions, dance was also found in popular (urban club) and professional contexts. Dancers in regional folkloric dance companies performed works that preserved (for the stage) traditional dances or works that were creative expressions of national or universal themes, such as harvest times and community celebrations. There were also regional dance companies that performed ballets melding traditional forms to tell a story. Another category of professional dancer was traditional or *matanga,* usually more commercial in commitment. *Matanga* performances were generally improvised, based in traditional dance conventions, and infused with popular dance. *Matanga* dancers, or traditional dancers-for-hire, were often engaged by families on occasions marking significant family events, such as the celebration of a deceased family member. "End-of-mourning funeral parties (*matanga*) [were] . . . increasingly commonplace in recent years, but . . . can also be present at marriages or in urban forms of traditional healing."[9]

The *matanga* dancer, while concerned with the artistic quality of the work (there were established touring ensembles), was equally engaged with the viability of the dance as enterprise.[10] Dance was also interwoven with popular music performance. Within the broad dance landscape in Zaire, only political animation dance existed solely to promote state ideology; only political animation was compulsory, carrying the risk of punishment for lack of participation.

At its core, political animation was a lynchpin of nation-building in Zaire. Benedict Anderson posits that ". . . nation-ness, as well as nationalism . . . [are] cultural artifacts of a particular kind . . . [that] command . . . profound emotional legitimacy."[11] Political animation, although coercive, tapped into the emotional affinities with individual ethnicities and the popular ideal of Patrice Lumumba's vision at the dawn of Congolese independence. Lumumba, the first prime minister following independence, made a declaration to the world of a uniquely Congolese modern nation-state: "We have absolutely no intention of letting ourselves be guided by any ideology whatsoever. We have our own ideology, a strong, noble ideology which is the affirmation of the African personality."[12]

Mobutu's vision was perhaps an appropriation of that of Lumumba. Mobutu's "imagined" state had to represent a Congolese reality to the world as well as to individual citizens. Anderson's definition of the nation (and nationalism) as "an imagined political community imagined as both inherently limited and sovereign" is relevant here. "The nation is imagined as *limited* because even the largest of them, encompassing perhaps a billion living human beings, has finite, if elastic, boundaries beyond which lie other nations."[13]

Animation was an integral component of Mobutu's efforts to forge a new citizen of Zaire. In a nation the size of Zaire, covering an area of more than 900,000 square miles, with more than two hundred ethnic groups, languages, and traditional indigenous polities, it was a challenge to indoctrinate all citizens, urban and rural, educated and illiterate, and to know when and in what manner each individual participated in animation. It was essential that the restatement of the theme of the utopian state occur on a constant, daily basis, and that it reach all sectors of the population in that vast country. Daily political animation mirrored daily radio broadcasts of political education in different languages.[14]

Mobutu's Zaire had to be simultaneously a unified nation with a Pan Congolese national character, and a national culture in the international Pan African arena in which newly independent nations of Africa were trying to distinguish themselves as recognizably "African," as opposed to, most especially, "European." These two constructs did not always complement each other. There was seemingly a tension between the contemporary notions of nation-state, contemporary permutations of traditional Congolese governance systems, and the perceived need to forge a macro-level Pan Africanism.

The oppressive militaristic brutality of colonial occupation was Mobutu's only experience of the contemporary nation-state. Crawford Young and Thomas Turner describe this circumstance:

> In colonial times an especially powerful instrument of alien hegemony was constructed in Zaire. . . . A profoundly revealing metaphor is embodied in the term Bula Matari (or Bula Matadi) by which the colonial state was widely known. . . . The expression means, literally, "he who breaks rocks"; by metaphorical extension it came to convey the image of force which crushes all resistance.[15]

This political animation, practiced daily by both Zairian citizens and foreign residents, preceded all public events, those that were overtly political, as well as those that could be superficially labeled nonpolitical such as popular music concerts and daily television news broadcasts.[16] President Mobutu himself described "animation" in the following terms:

> The "animation" is at the same time a dance show, a procession, a choreographed parade and a lesson in political science. In practice, no anniversary,

congress or popular assembly ever takes place without such an event, and each region, every village even, takes competitive pride in presenting its own. Here we are touching upon one of the most promising phenomena of Zairese art: the ability to draw on tradition to create modern forms. For one must not underestimate the influence of the traditional dances. These still exist, but deprived of their former social and religious context, they have lost a lot of their meaning, at least in the towns. One must go to the village festivals to admire them and to appreciate their purity and their emotional force, still intact. Intore and Bapende dancers still perform today; one can also admire the Munsonge dance or the Ekonda dance. Certainly, they have been to some degree secularized, reduced to a single function as preserves of tradition, but on the other hand they retain a genuine vitality in the adaptations for animations.[17]

While in office Mobutu was, in addition to president of the Zairian state, the minister of defense and the president of the sole political party, Mouvement Populaire de la Revolution (MPR). Although structurally there was a post of prime minister, the prime minister was under the direct authority of Mobutu and served at his pleasure, as did those in the various ministerial posts and the entire government. In the capacity of minister of defense, Mobutu maintained control over the military, including special forces, intelligence, and his personal elite unit of bodyguards.

Mobutu had created MPR and appointed himself president of it. It was through MPR that Mobutu was able to penetrate the farthest corners of the nation. MPR was the government in action in the daily lives of the people. The means of disseminating information from the top to the individual Zairian citizen (and monitoring outward response to policies) was through *Mobilisation Propaganda et Animation Politique (MOPAP)*.[18]

Directly under the president of MPR (Mobutu) was the secretary general of MPR; directly under the secretary general was a director of the regional ballet companies. (The term *ballet* in a troupe's title did not imply the practice of Western dance. It was used as a kind of official, formal marker in this nation that had recently declared independence from Belgium.) Recruitment of dancers for regional, national, and presidential (Ballet Kaké, that traveled exclusively with Mobutu) dance companies generally occurred through several channels related to already-established formal organizations, such as educational institutions, businesses, neighborhood-level MPR cadres,[19] and the youth wing of the MPR. Recruitment also occurred through word-of-mouth as special favors, or, as one informant indicated, as a special favor for the female interest of a political official.[20] Businesses hired personnel to run their mandatory animation unit who in turn hired other colleagues. In the beginning, there was also direct recruitment through the press.[21]

For organizations and businesses with large animation units, daily re-hearsal schedules were maintained and expanded as necessary. For example, yearly competitions among companies or the occasion of a visit from an important political official might be the impetus for coming up with new routines and costumes. Ideas for new material would come from the artistic directors of the regional ballet companies, which had to maintain their own separate animation units. Source material was often popular song and dance; indirectly, the source was traditional song and dance as many of the popular genres were based on traditional repertoire.

Political animation had roots in more traditional esoteric conventions that dealt with the passing on and entrenchment of political power. Gilonda explains how the passing on of ritual power for the Pende (the ethnic group to which he belongs) involved dance: "Before you become chief, everybody from all over is going to come and [each person will] teach you everything he knows [about ritual power] . . . that way you will have all the power when you become chief"; with some of the power being transmitted through a danced ritual.[22] The notion of dance as an agent of power (or as a mode for the transmission of power) was apparently a foundational cultural concept/construct that found a new kind of contemporary expression in the Zairian state. On numerous occasions informants spoke of how the practice of political animation gave Mobutu power from all the cultures throughout the nation. Further, many observed that when political animation was no longer manda-tory (in the late 1980s), Mobutu rapidly declined in power.

Animation and its official dancers were firmly within the state's net-work of control over the population. There were official professional and semiprofessional (those who danced but had other professions) performers called *animateurs* and *animatrices*. According to all the interviewees, *animateurs* and *animatrices* performed at every official public gathering (large or small): they performed before every public social/entertainment event. The mean-ing of the presidential dance company's name, Ballet Kaké, is quite revealing in this regard. The translation of the word *kaké,* according to Gilonda, is the act of having the ability to ritually summon the power of thunder to strike down or terrorize one's enemies at will. Ballet Kaké, then, held symbolic and perhaps actual power to summon something akin to thunder to domi-nate or oppress enemies.

Almost everyone danced throughout the country, "animating" the politi-cal vision of the nation promoted by the Mobutu government each morning while the flag was raised. People who could not physically dance had to clap in time with the music and appear joyous. Dance was similar to an embodied pledge of allegiance with the addition that it was necessary to show enthusi-asm; to energize (animate) the good of the state. Accounts of nondancers show

how the act of political animation was a personal and cultural violation. A high school principal, Gregoire Batodisa, recalls that every morning when he was in elementary school, the first fifteen minutes were dedicated to dancing and shouting the name of the president. "We had to recite one party, one country, one father, Mobutu, Mobutu. . . . It was ridiculous. You knew it but you could not do anything about it. Not to sing and dance was to commit suicide. You just went along with it."[23]

Political animation was a reflective practice whereby the citizen was both participant and audience. Fellow citizens spied on their neighbors, reporting to the government those individuals who did not carry out animation with the appropriate spirit. Gilonda described an incident involving a family friend:

> My brother came to get me in Kinshasa saying I had to come home right away because the police had picked up (my close friend) Jean-Claude. He had been reported as laughing during animation. A week later, he was arrested. I went to the police, showed them my Ballet Lipopo [an officially recognized dance ensemble] identification and explained that he was my brother and talked them into releasing him to me. I told them he had been hired to work in the company in Kinshasa; that he was just joking about the dancers in Kikwit. I told them he was happy about going to Kinshasa. When they let him go, I told him he had to leave the city, because he was in a lot of trouble.[24]

Moreover, professional *animateurs/animatrices*, by virtue of their governmental affiliation, had personal power. This power carried over into the daily life of the dancers. Gilonda relates an incident in which he was detained at a military checkpoint of questionable legitimacy.[25] When he was asked for his identification he said,

> Do you know who I am? Do you know who you are talking to? (That man, he started to get nervous.) I said are you sure you want my papers? If I give you my papers you are going to have a problem, you might get in trouble. (That man, he really started to think, but, he wanted me to show him the papers anyway; the other soldiers were standing behind him.) When I showed him my papers, he really got scared. He told the others that I was MOPAP (*Mobilisation Propaganda et Animation Politique*), that I was an *animateur* with Lipopo.[26] He kept apologizing; the others, they ran away. Nobody messed with *animateurs* and *animatrices*. They would get in big trouble. *Animateurs* had power.[27]

Characteristics common to all political animation were the use of gesture to pantomime pro-Mobutu lyrics and the use of traditional music and dance. Gesture-based choreography can be both easy to learn and remember, and adaptable to any size space. It is, therefore, accessible to nearly everyone regardless of dance prowess. It could fit on a stage in a classroom, a stadium, or in a small office, important for a dance that every citizen and resident had to perform at least once a day. Gestures accompanying lyrics provided reciprocal mnemonic devices for the dances and the songs. This type of choreography served to embed the political education of the Mobutu government into people's being.

Additionally, political animation involved the appropriation and cooptation of sacred movement (and sacred music)[28] across the many Zairian cultures and of the immensely pleasurable popular dance conventions. Appropriation and transmutation of sacred movement was neither an unusual occurrence in African (and African Diasporan) cultures nor was it, on its face, offensive. For example, dance scholar Kariamu Welsh Asante has identified "epic memory" as one of the core senses in an African dance aesthetic, senses being "qualities that make up the integral composition of [a] dance."[29] Epic memory refers to ancestral memories and connections. "The story behind the dance is not so important as who danced it, before whom was it danced, and is it now being danced well."[30] Reflecting on the work of J. H. Kwabena Nketia, Welsh Asante notes that the context in which a dance is (or should be) performed is dictated by tradition. Nketia, in *Music in African Cultures*, discusses the importance of the "concrete realization of a tradition in a way and manner acceptable to a traditional audience, . . . which may show the extent of the performer's correctness of memory and fidelity to tradition as well as the creative imagination he brings into it. . . . It cannot be overemphasized that in traditional society a great premium is placed on the renewal of experience."[31] The choreographic conventions in political animation in no way precluded the improvisation or innovation of traditional forms, both of which are part of dance traditions in the Congo.[32] But it helps us recognize that when Zairian citizens were told to dance in contexts unacceptable to tradition, this kind of "renewal of experience" and its inherent pleasure, meaning, and value, were ruptured.

According to Gilonda, Mobutu insisted on the use of traditional dance and music at the provincial and village level because those dances and songs held deep (and often ritual/spiritual) meaning.[33] *Animateurs/animatrices* appropriated aspects of traditional dance, combining elements across ethnicities into one piece. This was a use of traditional dance similar to that of national dance companies throughout the continent. Dance then became an agent in establishing Mobutu's notion of national unity.[34] When *animateurs* performed a dance of one ethnicity in its entirety, the lyrics accompanying the dance replaced the name of the person traditionally honored by the song and dance with Mobutu's name. Therefore, the accomplishments and important people within a culture's history were made invisible as part of state propaganda.

Gilonda also maintains that Mobutu's insistence on appropriating traditional dance/songs was to access the ritual power embedded in them.

Political animation lyrics related directly to the accomplishments, ideology, and aspirations of the Mobutu government. The refrain of *Mobutu Aye* serves to illustrate this:

> Mobutu has come
> People clap your hands, be happy
> Mobutu is the father of the MPR
> He changed the country from Congo to Zaire
> Zairian Money
> Zairian Country
> Zairian River
> We live in the epoch of three "Zs"[35]

These and other political animation lyrics, for the most part, were appropriations and adaptations of traditional songs.

The dance *Mobutu Aye*, as performed by Ballet Kaké, involved mainly actions and movement that did not travel through space, with motions imitating honorific gestures shown to leaders by their subjects.[36] The movement conveyed the excitement about Mobutu and about the "fortune" of being a Zairian citizen. Dancers began in a three-column format with a column of men in the middle flanked by columns of women. All the women had hair parted in sections and fashioned into spires with tufts differing slightly at the tips. The costumes for men and women consisted of a green (seemingly wax print) fabric bearing Mobutu's image and a map of Africa with Zaire highlighted. Women wore two-piece dresses with short flared sleeves on a square-neck bodice. The bottom consisted of fabric wrapped tightly around the body allowing freedom of movement for one moderately long step. A wide thick band of fabric formed a belt that covered the waist and pelvic area, accentuating pelvic rotations and contractions. The men wore short-sleeved collarless shirts, and matching visor caps reminiscent of some military uniform headwear.

The dance begins during the percussion introduction with everyone marking time shifting their weight from one foot to the other (women) or with a slight lifting of the knee or front knee kick while transferring weight (men). Shallow pelvic and torso contractions accompany the footwork; the arms bend gently, swinging side to side across the body. The singer begins the first verse without accompaniment for the first two measures until the instrumental music joins in. The women's movement is stationary with both arms extending out to the right then bending in to touch the chest. The head inclines towards the direction of the arms; the gaze follows. The motif repeats twice in succession on each side and alternates right and left.

In motif/verse, two men and women perform the same movement in unison with only a slight variation in level with women in a deeper knee bend. The motif is stationary, knees bent sufficiently to allow freedom of the spine and pelvis for torso contraction and pelvis rotation. The arms pump up and down four times per measure at the sides of the body in a cutting motion; the feet mark time, the knees bounce with body, arms, and feet in quarter notes. In part two of this motif, the arms, gently bent, move right to left in half notes while the pelvis rotates accented by a single forward pelvic contraction on the upbeat forming sixteenth (and grace) notes of each measure. The chorus motif repeats for a twelve-measure bridge.

Ballet Kaké's political animation performance blended popular dance and ritual gesture. The basic movement patterns were from popular dance while the gesture described above as the arms extended above the head swinging (or with some dancers, palms framing the face), were from traditional dances. The dancers wore costumes that reflected Mobutu's *authenticité* initiative.[37] Women wore neo-traditional wrapped long skirts with a *zigita*; men wore the new national dress decreed by the state to replace the European suit called an *abacost*—a collarless suit, worn without shirt or tie.[38]

In rural areas, and in the regional dance companies, the instrumentation for animation was almost exclusively traditional. The songs were sung closer to their original forms accompanied by the acoustic percussion and melodic instruments of each culture. This meant that the instrumentalists were important cultural repositories and transmitters of sacred cosmologies, histories, and rites. These instrumentalists were those who would have accompanied (and often did accompany) sacred ceremonies such as initiations, and other important individual and communal rites.[39]

In Kinshasa, the urban hub of Zaire, the same traditional songs were arranged to fit the instrumentation of Zairian popular music. Music still provided a degree of continuity with tradition as it did in rural areas. Although urban dwellers (those born and raised in urban areas) did not have the same acculturation from within their own traditions as did rural dwellers, people still had strong ties to ethnicity, clan, and traditional polities (kingdoms). It was common for a family to send their children to the rural areas for initiation.[40] It was also common for urbanites to attend ritual observances and to vacation in the village. Using traditional songs in political animation, therefore, served the same aims of continuity and change, but with an added element.

While the traditional songs were well known to urban dwellers, they were not as influential in their daily lives as were the songs of popular music. Marrying popular music with traditional music through specific instrumentation and arrangement and changing the lyrics to fit Mobutu's agenda had another effect. This aesthetic marriage was a trope for the national narrative of progress.

Unlike other dance performance (staged popular dance and folkloric dance) in Zaire, the basic formation of professional political animation performance resembled a military column. At some point in all the dances studied for this essay, the dancers were in three box-shaped groups (or columns), one male group in the center flanked by two female groups, as described above. In front of the column was a singer/exhorter who led the songs and chanted political slogans. He was independent of the dancers, moving back and forth in front of them. The three columns of *animateurs* behind him sang (or shouted slogans) in response to his calls with accompanying choreographed unison movements. *Animateurs* and their leader faced the instrumentalists and the audience of political elites and their guests. Regular citizens were spectators but were not the audience to whom the *animateurs* directed their focus. This performance staging gave the dance a paramilitary nature.

The overall relationship between Mobutu and the nation appears in another aspect of political animation aesthetic conventions. Robert Farris Thompson's observation about the sociopolitical meaning of call-and-response in African dance and music is relevant here. In his eighth aesthetic canon of fine form, "Call-and-Response: The Politics of Perfection," Thompson writes:

> Call-and-response goes to the very heart of the notion of good government, of popular response to the actions of the ideal leader. . . . There are proverbs galore to warn the ruler . . . that he can be replaced, should he prove despotic. Herein another telling point of connection between life and art. Between call-and-response, and the phenomenon of master-and-entourage in the urban states of traditional West Africa. . . . Thus, call-and-response and solo-and-circle, far from solely constituting matters of structure, are in actuality levels of perfected social interaction. The canon is a danced judgment of qualities of social integration and cohesion.[41]

Political animation might be interpreted here as the "call-and-response" between the leader and the people. Mobutu imparted his vision of Zaire; the people performed the desired response. However, congruity with Thompson's explication, based on extensive studies of West Africa, departs at the level of broad comparison. It is my contention that Zaire was an entity constructed by Mobutu and that political animation was not, for those I interviewed, an embodiment of open dialogue between the ruler and the people. The responses were forced, rather than being a popular reply "to the actions of the ideal leader." For the people whose narratives informed the basis of this essay, this kind of dance served to try to imprint and reinforce state doctrine. Almost all said they detested the reinterpretation of dances and songs. In addition, the threat of punishment for nonparticipation took away from any desire to praise the leader, even though traditional praise songs and dances were common throughout Zaire.

Political animation provided the nation and Mobutu with a reflection of the "imagined" response by the people to his ideal of Zaire, but it did not match the reality for many. As one informant stated, "It was really like being raped. I wept when I saw my father being forced to dance on the podium, it was painful to see him so humiliated."[42] His outrage went beyond observing his father forcibly dancing, embodying an ideology and political praxis with which he fundamentally and morally disagreed. In his tradition, given his social status, his father would not have danced publicly for others; others would have danced for his father.[43]

According to all my interviewees, the Zairian state used dance as a tool of subjugation of the individual, as a demonstration of dominance of the nation over traditional polities, and as a mode of demonstrating or bringing to life individual support for the ideals of the state. The rape referred to above was an invasion of the body in the same spirit as the more common sense of the word—a violent sexual act. In this "rape," the state forced people to participate in an activity of the body that is usually pleasurable and, in some instances, sacred. Further, the enforcement of political animation not only imposed subservience to the state, but delegitimized traditional authority.[44] Mandatory animation was then an embodied ideological rape that in a perverse way served to potentially equalize everyone as a servant to the state.

NOTES

1. During my fieldwork, when I asked continental African participants for phraseology in their traditional languages for "let's dance, party, throw-down" (African American slang for "dance intensely"), the responses indicated the name of a specific dance or the act of dancing rather than a word for dance as a separate category of activity. Scholars of African music often note this practice. See John Miller Chernoff, *African Rhythm and Sensibility: Aesthetics and Social Action in African Musical Idioms* (Chicago: University of Chicago Press, 1979); Bob Whitman White, "Modernity's Spiral: Popular Culture, Mastery, and the Politics of Dance Music in Congo-Kinshasa" (PhD dissertation Montreal, Canada: McGill University, 1998), forthcoming as *Rumba Rules: The Politics of Dance Music in Mobutu's Zaire* (Durham, N.C.: Duke University Press, 2008).

2. The coercive nature of the Mobutu government in general and *animation politique* in particular as an aspect of his government is alluded to in Mobutu's writings and speeches. Mobutu Sese Seko, *Mobutu Discours, Allocutions et Messages 1965–1975*,

2 vols. (Paris: Éditions J.A., 1975); Mobutu Sese Seko, "Discours de Président-Foundateur du Mouvement Populaire de la Révolution, Président de la République, le Citoyen Mobutu Sese Seko," *Authenticité et Développement: Actes de Colloque National Sur L'Authenticité* (Carnot, Dakar, Senegal: Présence Africaine, 1982), 53.

3. I conducted research among immigrants from Zaire/Congo living in Pennsylvania, Ohio, and the Washington, D.C., area, as well as with two visitors to the U.S. from the Democratic Republic of Congo (DRC, formerly Zaire) in 2001 and 2002. The latter are members of regional dance companies in the DRC. Most interviewees based in the U.S. were and/or are dancers. Others included an engineer, school teacher, public administrator, and so on. I interviewed both women and men, from urban and rural backgrounds. This brief study in no way attempts to interpret the experiences of the majority of Congolese, in the U.S. or in their homeland. It is an analysis of a select group of narratives focused on one element of the interviewees' lives that kept surfacing in my conversations with them—that is, political animation. Nearly four million people have perished as a result of ongoing war in the DRC since 1998. The danger and devastation led many to seek refuge abroad, including those interviewed as part of my research.

4. The state archives from the Mobutu period are extremely uneven and rare. Paper traces of decrees are currently limited to Mobutu's speeches, published by the government in three volumes. See endnote 2.

5. Among employed Zairians, actual payment of salaries was unpredictable. People engaged in numerous enterprises to meet their living costs, including collecting fees from individuals for performing the work they were "hired" to do. For a thorough explanation see Janet MacGaffey, Bwakyanakazi Mukohya, Rukarangira waa Nkera, Brooke Grundfest Schoepf, Makwala ma Mavambu ye Beda, Walu Engundu, *The Real Economy of Zaire: The Contribution of Smuggling and Other Unofficial Activities to National Wealth* (Philadelphia: University of Pennsylvania Press, 1991).

6. Johannes Fabian, *Remembering the Present: Painting and Popular History in Zaire* (Berkeley: University of California Press, 1996).

7. See note 2 for Mobutu's writings.

8. President Mobutu Sese Seko renamed his country—which had most recently been called the Belgian Congo—Zaire. Following Mobutu's ouster in 1997, it became the Democratic Republic of the Congo. The country gained independence in 1960.

9. White, "Modernity's Spiral, in Congo-Kinshasa," 122 [citing Corin, 1976].

10. Many of the dancers in the Philadelphia-based dance troupe, Eteko Bonyoma/Lisanga Ya Bana Kin, whom I interviewed as part of this research, were former members of such dance ensembles in Zaire/Congo. During the course of my work with the dancers the company split into the concert- and education-focused Lisanga Ya Bana Kin; Eteko Bonyoma retained its structure and focus as an ensemble concerned only with performance. Some of Eteko Bonyoma's members shunned teaching their dances to others because of the possibility of creating competition for their work. Costumes were highly individual and distinguished each dancer as a separate persona who was also for hire as a soloist.

11. Benedict Anderson, *Imagined Communities: Reflections on the Origin and Spread of Nationalism* (New York: Verso Press, 1991), 4.

12. P. Olisanwuche Esedebe, *Pan-Africanism: The Idea and Movement 1776–1991* (Washington, D.C.: Howard University Press, 1994), 177, quoting Patrice Lumumba in *The African Reader: Independent Africa*, ed. Wilfred Cartey and Martin Kilson (New York: Vintage Books, 1970), 87–89.

13. Anderson, *Imagined Communities*, 6–7; 4.

14. The radio programs were listed on a daily basis in *Salongo*, the state newspaper, giving times for each broadcast in Lingala, French, KiKongo, and so on.

15. Crawford Young and Thomas Turner, *The Rise and Decline of the Zairian State* (Madison: University of Wisconsin Press, 1985), 30–31.

16. The convention of performing praise dances to open public events in itself is not unique to Zaire and is a cultural practice commonplace throughout the continent dating back to precolonial antiquity. Again, what is unique is the way in which Mobutu coercively co-opted this practice to enforce his political vision.

17. Jean-Louis Remilleux, *Dignity for Africa: Mobutu Interviews with Jean-Louis Remilleux* (Paris: Albin Michel, 1989), 148–49.

18. *Mobilisation Propaganda et Animation Politique (MOPAP)* was the propaganda division of the Mobutu government. Its central office was in the capital, Kinshasa, with official offices within each province. MOPAP had an extensive network of "unofficial" offices that allowed a presence in almost all aspects of Zairian life. Everyone was conscious of being under the possible gaze of MOPAP personnel. Moreover, MOPAP was the central training arena for everyone working in the Mobutu government, from the highest official to relatively minor provincial workers. MOPAP designed the training that taught people how to carry out the tenets of MPR.

19. "Confirmation de la tenue d'un conclave du Bureau politique." *Solongo*, Saturday, May 31 and Sunday, June 1, 1980. This article indicated that the MPR was stratified down to the neighborhood level.

20. Young and Turner (*The Rise and Decline of the Zairian State*, 124) allude to the social/sexual nature of political animation. This is the only time they mention political animation in that text.

21. "Lingwla Cloture du seminaire des animateurs." *Solongo*, October 2, 1972, 10. This newspaper article demonstrates that participants were recruited from the youth wing of the MPR, JMPR. "Ouverture d'un séminaire d'animation en présence du commissaire de region." *Solongo*, Wednesday, July 4, 1973. This article discusses the gathering of the youth wings of the Shaba region for an animation seminar.

22. Mufulu Kingambo Gilonda, interview, January 2002, Philadelphia. Gilonda is now a resident of the U.S. where he has received recognition as an outstanding artist by being awarded a prestigious Pew Fellowship in the Arts in 2004.

23. Howard W. French, "Anatomy of an Autocracy: Mobutu's 32-Year Reign," *New York Times*, May 17, 1997, at diversityjobmarket.com/library/world/africa/051797zaire-mobutu.html.

24. Mufulu Kingambo Gilonda, interview, Philadelphia, 2001.

25. According to Gilonda, the military and the police would sometimes detain people for the purpose of robbing them.

26. Ballet Lipopo was Mobutu's strictly traditional dance company.

27. Mufulu Kingambo Gilonda, taped interview, Philadelphia, 2001.

28. The late scholar Kapalanga Gazungil Sang'Amin provides a thorough description and analysis of traditional dance throughout Zaire and its use in *animation politique*. (Kapalanga Gazungil Sang'Amin, *Les Spectacles d'Animation Politique en République du Zaire: Analyse des Mécanismes de Reprise, d'Actualisation et de Politisation des Formes Culturelles Africaines dans les Créations Spectaculaires Modernes* [Louvain-la-Nueve, Belgium: Cahiers Théâtre Louvain, 1989]).

29. Kariamu Welsh, "Commonalities in African Dance: An Aesthetic Foundation," in *African Culture: The Rhythms of Unity,* ed. Molefi Kete Asante and Kariamu Welsh Asante (Trenton, N.J.: Africa World Press, 1993), 71.

30. Kariamu Welsh Asante, ed., *African Dance: An Artistic, Historical and Philosophical Inquiry* (Trenton, N.J: Africa World Press, 1996), 213–14.

31. Welsh Asante, *African Dance*, 213–14, citing J. H. Kwabena Nketia*, Music in African Cultures: A Review of the Meaning and Significance of Traditional African Music* ([Legon]: Institute of African Studies, University of Ghana, 1966), 48.

32. See Z. S. Strother's article on Zairian masquerade/dance: "Invention and Reinvention in the Traditional Arts," in *Moving History/Dancing Cultures*, ed. Ann Dils and Ann Cooper Albright (Middletown, Conn.: Wesleyan University Press, 2001), 152–64.

33. Gilonda, perhaps, has this perception because in his traditional Pende culture, a boy receives the dance(s) of power he will perform throughout his life during his initiation period. Another informant also spoke of inheriting his ability to dance with fire from his grandfather and learned this dance during his initiation.

34. See Anthony Shay, *Choreographic Politics: State Folk Dance Companies, Representation, and Power* (Middletown, Conn.: Wesleyan University Press, 2002), on the development of national folk dance troupes around the world.

35. "Mobutu Aye," MOPAP videocassette tape (Zaire, now Democratic Republic of Congo: MAAVAS, producer).

36. The following discussion of Ballet Kaké's version of *Mobutu Aye* comes from a videotape, recorded by the national television station, now in the private collection of Mufulu Kingambo Gilonda. Gilonda obtained a copy of the tape from another Congolese immigrant in the United States. Gilonda dates the animation dances on the tape to the mid-1980s by noting certain people on the tape and the years of their passing.

37. Theater and performance studies scholar Dieudonne-Christophe Mbala Nkanga observes that "*Authenticité* was a kind of cult ideology developed around Mobutu, his ideas, actions, indeed, everything he did. Formally, *authenticité* pushed for the rediscovery of what could be claimed as 'African' within the former Belgian colony, but in practice it meant enhancing the status of Mobutu as the 'guide' for all Zairians." See "An Interview with Dieudonne-Christophe Mbala Nkanga: Performance and Politics in Africa," *Journal of the International Institute* 6, no. 3 (Summer 1999), at quod.lib .umich.edu/cgi/t/text/text-idx?c=jii;cc=jii;q1=4750978.0006.3%2A;rgn=main;view =text;idno=4750978.0006.305.

38. Young and Turner, "Zaire in the Mobutu Years: An Overview, 1965–1980," in *The Rise and Decline of the Zairian State,* 117.

39. According to Gilonda and other interviewees, in the rural areas, only specific people learned to drum. In Gilonda's culture, who would learn music, dance, and so

forth, was usually determined during the first stage (seven years old) or at the very early stages (by ten years old) of initiation.

40. From a conversation with a young Pende woman in Pittsburgh (2001) who was too young to be considered for a formal interview on political animation but who was willing to explain aspects of Pende female initiation. Although she was an urban dweller, she was taken for initiation to her family village at different intervals as a child.

41. Robert Farris Thompson, *African Art in Motion: Icon and Act* (Berkeley: University of California Press, 1974), 27–28.

42. Tape-recorded interview with Congolese expatriate who wished to remain anonymous, September 9, 2002, Philadelphia.

43. Interview with Congolese expatriate requesting anonymity, Philadelphia, September 8, 2001.

44. Paul Connerton, *How Societies Remember* (New York: Cambridge University Press, 1989). Connerton discusses the use of delegitimization of the old order to create a new political reality during the French Revolution.

· 6 ·

Dance and Human Rights in the Middle East, North Africa, and Central Asia

Anthony Shay

*W*hile presently dance, in many western eyes, generally constitutes a refined art form, a stage entertainment, or a social pastime, in the Middle East dance is widely perceived as a negative, ambiguous, and sometimes disreputable symbol of behavior that contains within it, in the view of large segments of the population, the potential for social disruption (*fitnah*).[1] At the same time, dance is also enjoyed as a social activity and an important means of expressing joy and happiness in socially approved contexts. Individuals in various regions of the Middle East sometimes put themselves at considerable risk of severe punishment and fines, and even death, to dance, since expressing joy at weddings, for example, constitutes an important societal value.

Given these radically differing perceptions, dance in some Middle Eastern societies intersects, sometimes violently, with issues of politics, ethnicity and gender, and thus can constitute a space for political resistance. The term *choreophobia*, which I coined to describe this ambiguity, helps us to understand this phenomenon. Any social action that can raise such powerful negative reactions that periodic attempts are made to ban it in its various forms can be viewed as an activity that is also saturated with potential subversive power.[2] In this context, dance provides a unique lens through which to analyze the dynamics of societal values and attitudes.

In order to understand the relationship of dance and human rights in the Middle East, North Africa, and Central Asia, the first step is to recognize that it is both complex and many-layered. Dance and its relation to human rights, especially regarding women, manifests itself in multivalent forms and does not lend itself to easy explanations. This essay therefore addresses complex issues of the local and the transnational, Islam and fundamentalism, and the myriad forms in which dance is manifest in both public and private presentation and representation, ultimately attempting a fuller understanding of how dance forms a lightning rod for fundamentalist attacks in some Muslim regions.

The forms that these attacks take and the targets that they focus on vary from Algeria to Egypt, Turkey to Iran, Afghanistan to Pakistan and into Central Asia to the borders of China. Not only do government officials and organs such as the Taliban in Afghanistan, until their defeat in October 2001, and the Islamic Republic of Iran mount attacks against dance as a public performance activity, but they also often launch assaults against dance as a private social activity that happens behind closed doors. This is most frequently done through the use of zealous vigilantes. Consequently, these attacks constitute an assault against the rights of individuals to freely perform dancing and express their joy; in fact, to freely use their bodies. In Egypt, Iran, and previously in Afghanistan, official and quasi-official goon squads, known as the *pasdaran* and *basij*, would regularly patrol the streets listening for the sounds of dance music, native or western, not hesitating to break into people's homes to arrest and physically assault people whom they would find dancing. These attacks assume different guises and, moreover, have had different goals in different places. For example, in Egypt, individual members of Muslim brotherhoods, who are not associated with the government, attempt to threaten and intimidate individual targets, such as merchants who sell videos with dance scenes, or families who are planning to hold a wedding.[3] The government officials in Egypt fear the potential power of these groups and through passive behavior encourage Islamists to attempt to curtail other people's rights.[4]

Newspapers and other news media continue to offer evidence of the phenomenon of banning dance or punishing those who perform it in the Middle East; but ultimately, because the individual western writer/reporter often does not possess a comprehensive overview of how dance intersects with existing and historical perceptions of dancing, and other societal activities, such as feminist struggles in its myriad contexts, their accounts remain partial, and ultimately unsatisfying. Nor do these brief news accounts interrogate the specific interdictions against dancing, or the underlying reasons given by the authorities who enforce them in a particular city or country; rather, the popular media provide only specific, discrete instances of the clash of human rights and dancing, omitting the necessary historical and contextual information to elucidate its causes.[5]

This lack of understanding was displayed in the many conflicting accounts of the arrest, detention, and trial of an Iranian American male dancer, Mohammad Khordadian, which was widely reported and commented on in the American press throughout the summer and fall of 2002. While in Iran,

Khordadian was formally charged with corrupting the morals of youth for teaching dance classes in the United States in the Iranian American community. After spending a short time in prison, he was given a stiff fine of $25,000 and "a suspended ten-year jail term. He was also barred from leaving Iran for a decade and from giving dance classes for the rest of his life. He will be jailed if he violates the ban."[6] He subsequently escaped to the West and is reported to be performing for the large Iranian community in Dubai.[7]

In this essay, Islam itself is first examined in order to determine how individual Muslims justify to themselves and to others the banning of dancing in various contexts. Following a brief discussion of Islam as it relates to dance, some of the myriad dance genres and contexts found in the Middle East, North Africa, and Central Asia are discussed. Finally, I consider the many ways in which many Muslims perceive dance, and then describe and analyze the local reactions to dancing in its complexity. This approach elucidates multiple meanings that create a pattern of behavior within specific cultural contexts.

ESSENTIALIZATION

I use the term *essentialization* as a stereotyping and characterizing of all the individuals of a culture or society as thinking and acting alike, and holding the same views and attitudes. There is a strong tendency among some western scholars, as well as the general public, to essentialize the Middle East and Islam, to portray the *Dar-al-Islam* (House of Islam, i.e., the Islamic world) as a place of unity. Several negative symbols of the Middle East still loom large in various western media and in the popular imagination—the wild-eyed religious fanatic, the bomb-carrying terrorist, the sexy belly dancer, the dangerous and over-sexed sheik of Arabia, along with mosques, minarets, and oil fields.

Another aspect of essentializing is the belief that the entire population behaves in a lock-step fashion in regard to its belief in Islam, that all Muslims think and act alike. Just as in the West, the gamut of religious observance and belief varies widely; so, too, among Muslims one can find a wide variety of beliefs and commitments to Islam ranging from intensely fervent belief to atheism. It is important to grasp that in countries with large Muslim majorities, everyone who is not a member of a religious minority is considered a Muslim, whether or not that person is a practicing Muslim.

Contributing to this essentializing tendency is the way in which historians present the history of Islam and Muslim civilization in both the East and the West. For example, both in Iran and in the West, books and essays about Iranian history and art, as well as university courses on Iranian history, are invariably divided into two parts: "Before Islam" and "After Islam." This artificial division creates the notion that in AD 610 Islam arrived when the first verses of the Qur'an were revealed to the Prophet Muhammad, the lights went out, and the next day everyone awoke to an "Islamic" world. In fact, the formation of a specific Islamic civilization and art took three to four centuries to develop and it was not uniform throughout the Islamic world. The westerner must also put aside his or her often-cherished idea of wild-eyed fanatic Muslim hordes spreading Islam through fire and massacre, so beloved of Hollywood filmmakers:

> The Muslim takeover largely occurred without physical destruction and without massacres, and one can point out only a small number of instances of major population movements within the conquered area. As a result the sum total of the art and the material culture of the pre-Islamic world remained as such with the functions, purposes, and associations it had before. But there is more to it than simply forms and meanings attached to forms. Islam also inherited an immensely complex set of collective memories, legends, and myths. This all means that the point of departure of Islamic art does not lie merely in a physical or aesthetic reaction to another art—but in the actual utilization by the Muslim world of the material, aesthetic, and emotional order of the conquered territories.[8]

In order to understand the ambiguous symbol that dance constitutes in many Middle Eastern societies, and how political attacks against dance are constituted, one must look at the basic tenets of Islam and the other Islamic sources upon which such attacks are often based. Issues regarding the propriety of and attitudes toward performing dance and music are considerably different in the Islamic Far East than they are in the Middle East. In Java, for example, dance is a highly esteemed form of cultural expression with a classical dance tradition associated with court culture. Thus, this essay does not deal with dance and human rights in a pan-Islamic context, but rather with that large contiguous geographic area comprising the Middle East, North Africa, and Central Asia.[9]

Many negative and ambiguous attitudes toward dance, as they are widely held in the Middle East, are in all likelihood not originally Islamic in origin, but were widely held in pre-Islamic times. C. E. Bosworth, a scholar of the Medieval Islamic period, includes entertainers, a class of individuals who danced, as among those who were considered by their contemporaries as members of the *Banu Sasan*, the name for associates of the underworld.[10]

It is important to note that dance and reactions to it are dynamic and contingent, as I hope to make clear with examples from Iran, which, due to the fascination of the western press with the Islamic Republic, is better documented than other areas. In addition, the private and public attitudes and reactions to various genres of dance stand in sharp contrast to one another. For example, Attaollah Mohajerani, the minister of culture of Iran from 1997 to 2000, "plainly stated that 'dance is neither futile nor frivolous.' In fact, he praises Iran's folk-dance tradition and hopes to see it revived," a far cry from Ayatollah Ruhollah Khomeini's edict, issued twenty years earlier, against all dance as "frivolous."[11]

ISLAM

Members of the Muslim clergy are the individuals whose pronouncements most often incite governments and populations to prevent or ban dance activities. However, they by no means form a unified body. Since the start of the Iraq War in 2003, many individuals in the West now realize that there exist at least two major divisions of Islam: Shi'ism and Sunnism. There are actually many more.[12]

Within all divisions of Islam there is little hierarchy such as that found in Christianity in which positions suggest a formal order of decision-making. Rather, for the most part, local religious leaders, whose opinions and pronouncements are known as *fatwas* when formally promulgated, gain local prominence because of their perceived scholarship. As an individual cleric achieves fame, his (never her) attitudes assume greater importance, while also coming into competition with other rising or established clergy who create diverse, often mutually hostile, groups of followers. I cannot emphasize enough that these legal opinions are not lightly considered; most Islamic scholars issue *fatwas* only after intensive study and deep consideration of the topic, weighing through all the evidence.[13]

Religion and religious differences and opinions garner the same heat, financial backing, and intense emotions that both politics and entertainment evoke for many westerners. "From top to bottom, Islam provided the central drama of urban social life."[14] This contentious environment remains a feature of Islam in contemporary Iranian life and constitutes one of the reasons why attitudes toward music and dance may be seen as potentially dynamic.[15]

Along with this diversity come certain basic tenets held in common by Muslims. All Muslims who are true believers consider that the Qur'an is the divinely revealed book of God, as revealed to the Prophet Muhammad in Arabic. Also, devout Muslims follow the five basic actions, sometimes known as the five pillars of Islam: 1) *shahada*, the profession of faith; 2) *namaz*, prayer five times a day; 3) *zakat*, the giving of alms to the needy; 4) *sawm* or *ruzeh*, fasting during the month of Ramadan; and 5) undertaking the *hajj*, the pilgrimage to Mecca.[16]

In searching for the sources that members of the Muslim clergy use for their edicts, including those related to dance, one must look at the hierarchy of sources for law in the Islamic world. First, there is the Qur'an. The Qur'an remains silent on the topics of music or dance, as well as the visual arts. Had the Qur'an openly opposed dance and music, quite simply, dance and music would not exist in Islamic societies. This fact is important for those writers and scholars who make the problematic claim that Islam is hostile to dance and music.[17]

Having established that the Qur'an is silent on this topic, I rehearse the other basic elements individuals and governments frequently invoke to justify their attacks. First, apart from such violent crimes as murder, rape, and theft, for all believing Muslims, the Qur'an mentions three prohibitions: 1) Surah 31, verse 6 prohibits the telling of frivolous tales or jokes; 2) Surah 5, verses 1–4 prohibit the consuming of animals that are already dead (as opposed to after the proper ritual slaughter); and 3) Surah 5, verse 92 prohibits the drinking of wine, games of chance, and idolatry.[18] When Khomeini issued a *fatwa* prohibiting dancing, he called on Surah 31.[19]

Second in importance to the Qur'an in providing guidance for the proper conduct of life to Islamic communities are the *hadith*. The hadith constitute a body of observations devoted to the sayings and actions, personally witnessed by individuals, of the Prophet Muhammad. These sayings and actions of the prophet serve as a model of proper behavior for a Muslim.[20]

Finally, in addition to the Qur'an and the hadith, respected scholars utilize the precedent of existing laws and judgments, which are extended to new situations. Thus, Khomeini and his government immediately banned dance and most music after the Islamic Revolution on the basis that it was "frivolous." This was a term that he likely took from the precedent of the prohibition against "frivolous tales" or jokes and extended the meaning of the verse to include dance and other forms of entertainment such as theatre. Khomeini stated plainly that "there is no fun in Islam."[21]

In general, music, dance, and entertainment have created an enormous and heated discourse in the Islamic world, each cleric weighing in on this issue:

> In the interminable debate about the *sama'* [musical and movement practices of the dervishes], legalists, theologians, spiritual leaders, custodians of morality in the cities, the *literati* and Sufi leaders all participated. The debate elicited views that varied from complete negation to full admittance of all musical forms and means, even dance. Between these two extremes we can find all possible nuances—some, for instance, tolerate a rudimentary form of cantillation and functional song, but ban all instruments; others permit

cantillation and add the frame-drum but without discs, of course forbidding all other instruments and all forms of dance, and so on. The mystic orders, for whom music and dance were an essential part of their spiritual and ecstatic exercises, were seriously concerned with the debate and participated ardently in the polemics. As a result, the controversy touches on a wide range of musical topics sometimes with a view to refuting them and at other times attempting to justify their adoption.[22]

A century ago, when cities were smaller and communications primitive and limited, the locally produced *fatwas* carried considerably less impact than edicts pronounced in this transnational age. The modern edicts carry influence across wide swaths of territory in North Africa, the Middle East, and Central Asia where millions can hear them on cassettes, the Internet, and other electronic media.[23]

Movement away from the local to the transnational, or "deterritorialization," as cultural studies scholar Arjun Appadurai stresses, "whether of Hindus, Sikhs, Palestinians, or Ukrainians, is now at the core of a variety of global fundamentalisms, including Islamic and Hindu fundamentalism."[24] I predict that we will see more prominent individuals pronounce against dance and that their words will be transnational, spoken across many borders, no longer affecting only the local contexts.

THE IMPORTANCE OF CONTEXT

In many cases the crux of the issue is not so much dance, per se, as dancing in the wrong context. For example, a woman dancing in a social event attended by other women occurs frequently in Saudi Arabia,[25] but dancing at a private party in which men are present can result in severe punishment. While rarely ending in death, public floggings and imprisonment are common.[26] Islam regards the human body, both male and female, as the site of intense sexual emotions and longings. This is seen as natural and right, but because these emotions are so powerful it is regarded as necessary to maintain sexual relations within the proper legal context of marriage. All other sexual acts have the potential of *fitnah*, which I translate as the tearing apart of the social fabric or social chaos.[27]

For this reason, Muslim society attempts to contain these emotions by the segregation of the sexes so that women do not appear in improper garb in front of men who are not in close kinship with them (father, husband, brother, uncle, cousin, son, etc.). Professional female dancers are regarded as invading male space and raising unlawful passions through their dancing. However, domestic dancing, while forbidden in Iran and Afghanistan, is both legal and popular in Saudi Arabia. Professional female dancers do not exist in Saudi Arabia. That is why in conservative Muslim states such as Saudi Arabia and Yemen, dancing is often a principal and approved entertainment and activity in women's quarters and also among men in segregated settings in which women dance for women and men perform for men, although as Adra notes, dance was banned for a period in Yemen by a hard-line cleric.[28]

DANCE

Every investigator of dance in the Middle East is soon confronted with the ambiguous and negative attitudes toward dance that I have described above. In an earlier essay[29] I stressed the importance for scholars and students of dance in the Middle East to exercise care in labeling movement activities as "dance" that are, in fact, forms of martial arts, such as sword and shield displays in Turkey, Lebanon, Iran, and the Arabian peninsula and the *zurkhaneh* exercises of Iran, Afghanistan, and Azerbaijan; or of a spiritual nature such as the patterned movements of the Mevlevi dervishes in Konya, Turkey, or the Shi'i religious processions of *ashura* and *tasu'a* in Iran. There is a word for dance, *raqs*, which is found throughout the region, and I follow native usage in determining which activities constitute dance and which constitute non-dance. This is crucial in a Middle Eastern context because whereas dance may be a disreputable or unlawful activity, other forms of patterned movement activity are not illegal and may even be highly regarded by significant elements of the population.[30]

There are two main types of dance in the Middle East: regional folk dances, associated largely with the countryside and performed in villages and by tribal groups, and solo improvised dance, which is performed by the urban population. That having been said, one can see solo improvised dances in the Egyptian countryside where a domestic form of belly dancing constitutes one of the main dance genres for young and old, male and female, and one may see group folk dances in the towns. In some cities such as Tehran and Cairo, solo improvised dance is the only genre that is, or was, widely performed in domestic spaces, as well as in public.

Solo Improvised Dance in Context

Dance scholars have subjected the topic of solo improvised dance in the Middle East to much misinterpretation and neglect. The overt perceived sexuality, its frequent association with striptease dance, and its status as a form of popular culture are among the reasons for the scholarly avoidance. The *Oxford Encyclopedia of Dance* omitted the term *belly dance*, the best known form of solo improvised dance in the West, in favor of the presumably more polite French term *danse du ventre*.[31] This dance genre might be best conceptualized as a complex of movement practices that extends from the Atlantic Ocean in North Africa and the Balkans in the west to the western areas of China, Central Asia, and the western portions of the Indian subcontinent in the east. In each of these areas, the dance is characterized by improvised articulations of the torso, hands, arms, head, and facial features such as the eyebrows and mouth. In domestic settings dance skills range from professional levels of performance to individuals who are only able to sketch one or two movements.

The professional dancer of the highest level is able to perform technically dazzling articulations of the body.[32] Thus, throughout many of these regions of the Islamic world there are always both professional dancers and the general urban population for whom this genre is their principal expressive form of dance. It constitutes at once a social, folk, professional, and, more recently, classicized dance.

Performances of belly dance in the Egyptian cinema from the 1930s to the present and solo improvised dance in the Iranian cinema from the 1950s to the 1970s reinforced the negative attitudes toward solo improvised dance by frequently depicting professional dancers as fallen women who inhabit male-centered night clubs and improperly display their bodies by performing sexually suggestive movements in revealing costumes. The negative attitudes toward dance are more often directed at solo improvised dancing as performed by professional dancers, both male and female, who are widely viewed as sexually available, than people dancing in domestic contexts. And, many individuals who descry the lax morals of professional dancers happily perform the domestic version of this dance at weddings and parties as an appropriate sign of joy.

In addition to the complexity of traditional performance contexts and environments, several new genres of dance have been created and performed under the impact of westernization. Turkey, Iran, and Egypt have all had professional classical western ballet companies, and, except for Iran, still maintain them. Turkey boasts several modern dance companies. Western dance traditions do not arouse feelings of choreophobia among the majority of Middle Easterners as their own solo improvised dance forms do, because dance genres such as classical ballet carry the cachet of an elite western form of art. However, couple dances, such as tango and waltz, shock the vast majority of Middle Easterners because of the physical proximity and intimacy between the partners. In addition, several of these nation-states, such as Iran, Egypt,

Tunisia, and Saudi Arabia, created national dance companies to perform the-atricalized "traditional" regional folk dances and/or solo improvised dance in the framework of highly sophisticated western choreographic strategies.[33]

DANCE AND HUMAN RIGHTS

Bans and Punishments

In Iran, as soon as the Islamic Republic was established in 1979, as one of his first acts, Khomeini banished all forms of dance. The classical ballet company, the national folk dance ensemble (known as the Mahalli Dancers in the West), and all other forms of dance (traditional and westernized, ballet, regional folk dances and domestic and professional solo improvised dance) were banned as "frivolous" and a sin. The professional dance concerts and rehearsals consti-tuted performances in which unrelated men and women danced together and for mixed audiences. In my opinion, however, this ban was more a result of the ubiquitous sleazy cinematic portrayals of dance and its popularity in the red-light district and working-class nightclubs, where prostitutes entertained customers by performing solo improvised dancing.

The Iranian press widely publicizes each infraction of the law against dancing in an attempt to intimidate the populace. The free use of one's body comes with a high price in these societies, and the power of dance and its bodily discourse are shown in the regime's desperate attempts to stamp it out in all its manifestations. "The Islamic Republic routinely violates private spaces if there are suspicions of drinking, dancing, or gatherings of unrelated men and women."[34] Conservatives in Iran find the concept of dance so threatening that images of Degas' famous depictions of ballerinas in his painting *Dancers Practicing at the Bar* were airbrushed out of an art book, and scenes of dance in the film *Mary Poppins* were cut out by Iranian censors.[35] In such an environment of ram-pant choreophobia, it is a wonder that people still find the fortitude to dance.

I have interviewed dozens of Iranians and western scholars who return to visit Iran on a regular basis, and all of them, as well as several media reports, comment that people pay heavy bribes to guards in order to dance at weddings and parties. As *New York Times* reporter Stephen Kinzer observes, "Squads of policemen and religious vigilantes patrol the streets at night listening for the forbidden sound of Western music."[36] In fact, according to informants, the goon squads listen for westernized popular music recorded in the United States in the thriving Iranian music business in Los Angeles, and Persian dance music as well.

"'We live a double life in this country,' said a middle-aged mother who voted for then-president Mr. Khatami. 'My children know that when their schoolteachers ask whether we drink at home, they have to say no. If they are asked whether we dance or play cards, they have to say no. But the fact is that we do drink, dance and play cards, and the kids know it. So they are growing up as liars. . . . That's a terrible thing, and I want it to change.'"[37]

After the death of Ayatollah Khomeini in 1989, reports began to circulate in the Iranian American community that dance was once again permitted in public space in Iran. However, these reports were the results of oversimplification. Only one form of dance has been permitted, in carefully segregated contexts, and that is regional folk dances. Men are now permitted to dance regional folk dances in front of all-male audiences. The government even permitted, if not encouraged, the video recording of these dances (*raqs-ha-ye mahalli-ye Iran*). While the minister of culture cited above stated that dance is not a frivolity and that he would like to see folk dancing revived, he remained silent on the topic of solo improvised dance. He clearly did not feel obligated to follow Khomeini's blanket *fatwa*.

This governmental policy, or perhaps attitude, closely followed the way in which the performance of traditional folk music was first permitted in public performance a few years after the revolution, before public performances of western and Iranian classical music, and even some types of Iranian popular music, which now occur regularly. One of the principal reasons for the permission given for public performances of folk music, after an initial ban on all music and dance, was a result of the performers' ability to legitimize the new Islamic regime through altering their song texts to praise the regime. In the same way, folk dances that were associated with this music, and the native male performers of these dances with their emphasis on athletic prowess and displays of masculine strength, were not viewed as potentially transgressive in their performances, in contrast to the way that solo improvised dance is perceived by many devout Muslims to contain the potential for *fitnah*, societal disruption.[38]

Permission to perform solo improvised dance still does not exist. Although regularly performed by men, urban solo improvised dance is largely viewed as a primary site of female performance. By way of contrast, reports have been circulating that women can openly learn solo improvised dancing in classes.[39] However, other reports indicate that these classes might be better characterized as quasi-open secrets.[40] These classes used to be held underground in strict secrecy, and there was always the fear that either the police or *basij* militia and the *pasdaran*, the quasi-official local goon squads, would break in and arrest and/or beat the participants.[41]

Journalist Camelia Entekhabi-Fard reports that Farzaneh Kaboli, one of the lead dancers with the former state folk ensemble, the Mahalli Dancers, gave a concert in the summer of 1998. According to the article it was the "first public performance of contemporary dance to be performed in Iran in two decades."[42] Nevertheless, the concert was called "A Performance of Harmonious Motions"; the dreaded name *dance* could not be used. A later concert in December 2003 was closed down, and twenty-four dancers and Kaboli were jailed and shortly thereafter released.[43]

In Afghanistan, a total ban on all music and dance existed from 1996 under Taliban rule, until the United States and its allies overthrew the Taliban regime in the autumn of 2001. So strict was the surveillance that

> although women are the main victims of the "virtue and vice" teams, men are not immune. In an incident this summer, Mr. Qalamuddin's men hid on the roof of a house in the center of Kabul, waiting until men in an adjoining house began watching a video of an Indian dance movie, a popular genre in this part of Asia. According to a neighbor, one of the men seized by the Taliban, a 25-year-old welder who had been deaf since birth, died in custody within 48 hours.[44]

Attempts to ban dancing are not only contemporary phenomena, but have deep historical roots. In Egypt, Iran, Yemen, Turkey, and other areas, historical attempts to ban dance performances are well attested.[45]

In the present, increasingly over the past three decades in Egypt, the pressure of private fundamentalists to prevent dance has been intense. The government sometimes bows to the pressure, for example, banning belly dance performances to be shown on television, except in old films. Islamic brotherhoods attempt to bring pressure to bear on whole neighborhoods as well as individuals, and they are not hesitant to use violence to gain their ends:

> In Cairo, a few neighborhoods are effectively controlled by Islamic fundamentalists. They manage to keep unwanted female entertainers out of their areas. Islamic fundamentalists occasionally disturb weddings, break the musicians' instruments, and chase the female performers from the stage. This sometimes leads to fights with party goers, who defend the entertainers' and their right to merriment.[46]

As if in league with the Islamists, Hosni Mubarak, the Egyptian president, blamed civil unrest in Cairo neighborhoods in the 1990s not on the Islamic fundamentalists, but on "Bellydancers [sic], (and) drummers from the slums."[47]

Dancers also face social pressure to leave their profession. In Egypt, as Van Nieuwkerk and personal interviews have pointed out, the very term *dancer* or *entertainer* constitutes a deadly insult. One dancer in Egypt told me that she left dancing, a profession she enjoyed, because she could not bear the taunts of "son of a dancer" that her son endured.[48]

In Turkey, the government ban on the Mevlevi dervish order practicing its patterned movement rituals is still largely in effect except as a theatrical tourist attraction. This ban was passed in 1926 when Ataturk was consolidating his political control over Turkey and felt the need to suppress the dervish groups because of their powerful hold on the people that he perceived the dervish orders had.[49] Unlike many of the other groups I have surveyed here, the Turks have a passionate love of their traditional regional folk dances that has been abetted by the Turkish government, which regards regional group folk dances as a visual icon of Turkish identity.[50]

Dance as a Space of Resistance

At the same time, these laws and prohibitions, which attempt to banish dance from public discourse, and the disbanding of these dance companies, have also had the unintended effect of creating a space for resistance to regimes. Radio Seda-ye Iran (September 5, 1995) reported that a group of Iranian women exiles performed solo improvised dance at the International Women's Conference in

In the security of a family basement in Afghanistan, relatives of a couple to be married dance, men and women together, with the women uncovered—behavior that would be punished on the street. This photo was taken just before the fall of the Taliban. Photo by Lynsey Addaro.

Beijing to taunt the official Islamic Republic's delegation. In another example, during a highly publicized soccer game held in Tehran between Iran and Australia in 1997, from which women were banned, a large number of women burst into the stadium and danced in the bleachers, while thousands more danced in the streets. The footage was shown on local Iranian television stations.[51] The YouTube Internet site is filled with many examples of Iranians dancing in public and private spaces, in defiance of the ban on dance.

Quiet and small rebellious acts of dancing also exist throughout the country:

> "I'm tired of high prices. I'm tired of all of this unemployment. I'm tired of someone telling me I can't dance or can't read this book or watch that movie. It's gone too far and I'm ready to fight back," said Ali, a defiant 18-year-old with long, meticulously coifed black hair and blazing blue eyes. Ali, it should be noted, is from South Tehran, site of Iran's teeming slums and the *mostazafin* (the oppressed), in whose name the revolution was fought. But today, Ali and his South Tehran friends just want the right to dance . . . and invited giggling girls to dance with them.
>
> Finally, one brave young girl, her brown scarf displaying dangerously large amounts of her chestnut-colored hair, accepted Ali's exhortations and joined the circle of boys dancing. It was a defiant moment, its importance not underestimated by the crowd, who gave the girl a rousing cheer for her courage. After all, Iran's morals police, the *komiteh*, could punish the offending dancers harshly for the sin of dancing in public and mixing with members of the opposite sex.[52]

Individuals, like the pseudonymous Ali above, who are frustrated with the restrictions, continue to defy the law against dance.[53] People throughout the vast region of the Middle East, Central Asia, and North Africa dance in the face of severe punishments and even death and continue to exercise their human rights, to own their own bodies and dance if, where, and when they choose. Dance will not only remain a negative symbol for some inhabitants of the Middle East, but increasingly it will constitute a symbol of joy and political resistance to repressive regimes like the Islamic Republic of Iran and the former Taliban regime in Afghanistan (1996–2001). Newspaper accounts of the fall of the Taliban were accompanied by numerous photographs of men dancing for joy and exercising the human right to dance after a long dark night of political and religious repression.[54] Dance, after frequent bans by zealous clerics and Islamist elements of the population, always manages to return, as it did in Afghanistan, and somewhat in Iran, where serious articles on dance are beginning to appear in Persian scholarly journals.[55] Hopefully these small steps provide potential proof of yet another renaissance of dance in the Islamic

Middle East. And with it, the right for human beings to possess the legitimate use of their own (dancing) bodies.

NOTES

1. For brevity, in this essay the entire region of the Middle East, North Africa, and Central Asia is referred to as the "Middle East."

2. Anthony Shay, *Choreophobia: Solo Improvised Dance in the Iranian World* (Costa Mesa, Calif.: Mazda Publishers, 1999).

3. Personal interviews in Cairo, January 19–20, 2000.

4. Anthony Shay, "Dance and Jurisprudence in the Islamic Middle East" in *Belly Dance: Orientalism, Transnationalism and Harem Fantasy*, ed. Anthony Shay and Barbara Sellers-Young (Costa Mesa, Calif.: Mazda Publishers, 2005), 110.

5. A *New York Times* story demonstrates this problem: "With their [Taliban] rule comes their rules: no music, no dancing, no mingling between unrelated men and women, according to their stern version of Islam," "An Afghan City Where Taliban Keep Grip Loose to Keep Power," International Section, July 1, 2001, 7. The (unnamed) reporter, while alluding to ethnicity, like most casual reports, failed to note that under the veneer of the Taliban as a fundamentalist Islamic movement, much more importantly, there exists a titanic ethnic struggle between the Pashtun majority on the one hand, and the large Persian (known as Dari in Afghanistan) and Turkic-speaking minorities in the north and west on the other. Because the media has focused on issues of Islam, they have largely failed to fathom the ethnic divide, which has resulted in terrible massacres.

6. Sandra Marquez, "Dancer's Detention Alarming to Emigres," *Los Angeles Times*, July 26, 2002, D4. This news was not, however, widely or extensively reported in Iran. The reluctance to publish this story may have been occasioned by the fact that Khordadian holds American citizenship and there is much behind-the-scenes diplomatic activity occurring between Iran and the United States. His sentence, compared to others who have been charged with dancing, was extremely light. Generally, those people found dancing are publicly flogged. The entire affair was widely discussed and commented on through the media in the Iranian American community.

7. Jamal, personal interview, June 19, 2007.

8. Oleg Grabar, *Formation of Islamic Art,* revised and enlarged ed. (New Haven: Yale University Press [1973], 1987), 41.

9. I do not wish to create the notion that the Middle East is the only region of the world in which dance is attacked and attempts made to ban its performances. Fundamentalist Christian groups in the United States have attempted to ban dancing activity since the sixteenth century, and many still rail against it. The emphasis in the United States, however, as Ann Wagner points out in her study, *Adversaries of Dance: From the Puritans to the Present* (Urbana and Chicago: University of Illinois Press, 1997), was to prevent men and women from dancing together on a social basis. In the Middle East, dancing was already segregated and dances do not exist in which a man takes a woman

into his arms, such as the waltz or fox trot. (See also Elizabeth Aldrich's essay, "Plunge Not into the Mire of Worldly Folly: Nineteenth-Century and Early Twentieth-Century Religious Objections to Social Dance in the United States" in this volume.) In the Middle East the attacks are made upon dancers and/or dance events in which there is an improper presence of specific individuals, such as females dancing in front of males who are not in proper kinship relationship to them.

10. Clifford Edmond Bosworth, *Mediaeval Islamic Underworld: The Banu Sasan in Arabic Society and Literature* (Leiden, The Netherlands: E. J. Brill, 1976), 1.

11. Canadian Broadcast Company, "Dance Isn't Frivolous, Says Iran's Culture Minister," *CBC Infoculture*, August 23, 1999.

12. "It would also be misleading to assume a uniformity of Muslim identity. The Shi'a, the Alevis, the Muwahhidun (the Wahhabiyya) of Saudi Arabia, the Ibadiyya, the Isma'iliyya, the Zaydis, the Sunnis, and so on, all possess—at least on the basis of self-assertion—a Muslim identity." Dale F. Eickelman and James Piscatori, "Social Theory in the Study of Muslim Societies," in *Muslim Travellers: Pilgrimage, Migration, and the Religious Imagination,* ed. Dale F. Eickelman and James Piscatori (Berkeley and Los Angeles: University of California Press, 1990), 16.

13. It is crucial to grasp that all Muslims are not bound to follow edicts promulgated by a specific clerical figure (such as Ayatollah Khomeini's famous *fatwa* against Salman Rushdie). Rather, individual Muslims have the choice of which individual cleric he or she most esteems and chooses to follow. Indeed, it should be pointed out that much of the travel that occurred in the Islamic world before the twentieth century was religiously and spiritually motivated through the visiting of shrines and seeking audiences with learned clerics and religious scholars whose fame had spread beyond the local.

14. Richard W. Bulliet, *Islam: The View from the Edge* (New York: Columbia University Press, 1994), 98.

15. "Iran is still engaged in a battle over interpretations of Islam. The struggle is not only between Shiites and Sunnis but within Shiism itself. Contrary to perception outside Iran that religious truth is monolithic and that dissent is not tolerated, one of the defining traits of Shiism is its emphasis on argument. Clerics are encouraged and expected to challenge interpretations of the Koran, even those of the most learned ayatollahs, in the hope that new and better interpretations may emerge. It is a concept little grasped in the West." Elaine Sciolino, *Persian Mirrors: The Elusive Face of Iran* (New York: Free Press, 2000), 39.

16. In addition, the believing "true" Muslim should also participate in *jihad*, a concept that is poorly understood in the West. Jihad can take several forms in an Islamic context, ranging from an individual's single struggle not to eat during the fasting period (Ramadan), fighting local oppression, or participating in wide holy wars, such as the Crusades, for the protection of Islam.

17. See for example: Metin And, *Dances of Anatolian Turkey* (Brooklyn: Dance Perspectives 3, 1959); Hormoz Farhat, "Dastgah Concept in Persian Music," (PhD dissertation, UCLA, 1965); La Meri (Russel Merriweather Hughes), "Learning the Danse Du Ventre," in *Curious and Wonderful Gymnastic* (Brooklyn: Dance Perspectives 10, 1961), 43–44.

18. M. L. Roy Choudhury, "Music in Islam," *Journal of the Asiatic Society* 23, no. 2, Letters (1957): 43–102.

19. *Glorious Qur'an*, text and explanatory translation by Mohammad M. Pickthall (Des Plaines, Ill.: Library of Islam, 1994).

20. The study of hadith, each accompanied by *esnad*, a list of the chain of individuals who passed the observation of the saying and/or action of the prophet to others, has constituted a major area of study in the field of *figh*, Islamic jurisprudence. Because the hadith were passed down in chains of oral communications through the centuries, numerous scholars devoted their lives to separating the correct (*sahih*) hadith, from the weak or outright false (*da'if*) ones. Schools (Maleki, Shafii, Ash'ari, Ja'fari, Hanbali, Hanafi to name some of the most famous) formed around those scholars who were deemed as the most knowledgeable individuals to discern the true from the false hadith upon which the Muslim community depended for authoritative legal decisions. Clearly, there are many false hadith, and the different schools of interpretation differ as to which ones are accurate. For the interested reader, Choudhury's essay (*Music in Islam*, 1957) provides an excellent in-depth study of how the Qur'an, the hadith, and other sources have been interpreted in regard to music, and by extension dance, by Muslim scholars over the centuries. Unfortunately, terms such as *singing girls* and *dancing girls* are used interchangeably, but as I explained above, until well into the twentieth century, entertainers danced, sang, played instruments, acted, and performed acrobatic feats. This has resulted in confusion in modern terminology.

21. Sciolino, *Persian Mirrors*, 1; see also, Corporal Punishment Archive, "Flogging Sentences in Iran," *Reuters*, March 18, 1999.

22. Amnon Shiloah, *Music in the World of Islam: A Socio-Cultural Study* (Detroit: Wayne State University Press, 1995), 31.

23. These religious figures do not, as is widely thought, turn their back on everything western. Without western technology their programs would not be possible. It was precisely through the manipulation of modern western technology that Ayatollah Khomeini triumphed over the Pahlavi regime and established the Islamic Republic. Advanced spying technology also enables the governments of Iran and Afghanistan to ferret out and punish those individuals who would defy their bans on dancing.

24. Arjun Appurdai, "Global Ethnoscapes: Notes and Queries for a Transnational Anthropology," in *Recapturing Anthropology: Working in the Present*, ed. Richard G. Fox (Santa Fe, N.M.: School of American Research Press, 1991), 193.

25. Sherri Deaver, "Concealment vs. Display: The Modern Saudi Woman," *Dance Research Journal*, Summer 1978: 14–18; Saleem, personal interview, July 14, 2007.

26. "20 Sentenced for Attending Party," *Los Angeles Times*, February 5, 2007, A7.

27. Fatimah Mernissi, *Beyond the Veil: Male-Female Dynamics in a Modern Muslim Society* (New York: John Wiley & Sons, 1975).

28. Najwa Adra, "Tribal Dancing and Yemeni Nationalism," *Revue du Monde Musulman et de la Méditerranée* 67, no. 1 (1993): 161–68; Deaver, "Concealment vs. Display," 1978.

29. Anthony Shay, "Dance and Non-Dance: Patterned Movement in Iran and Islam," *Iranian Studies* 28, no. 1–2 (Winter/Spring 1995): 61–78.

30. Middle East dance scholar Najwa Adra points out that in Yemen the *bar'a*, which she calls a dance, is, through its naming and conception in the popular Yemeni mind, not considered *raqs* or *li'ba* (game). "When *li'ba* and the playing of musical instruments were banned on religious grounds by the Hamid al-Din Imams (who ruled Yemen in the first half of the twentieth century), *bar'a* was not included in the ban." Adra, "Concept of Tribe in Rural Yemen," in *Arab Society: Social Science Perspectives*, ed. Saad Eddin Ibrahim and Nicholas S. Hopkins (Cairo: American University in Cairo Press, 1985), 282.

31. Anthony Shay, "Danse du Ventre," *International Encyclopedia of Dance*, vol. 2 (New York [u.a.]: Oxford University Press, 1998), 344.

32. Anthony Shay and Barbara Sellers-Young, "Introduction," in *Belly Dance: Orientalism, Transnationalism and Harem Fantasy*, ed. Anthony Shay and Barbara Sellers-Young (Costa Mesa, Calif.: Mazda Publishers, 2005), 1–27.

33. Anthony Shay, *Choreographic Politics: State Folk Dance Ensembles, Representation and Power* (Middletown, Conn.: Wesleyan University Press, 2002).

34. Sciolino, *Persian Mirrors*, 98.

35. Azar Nafisi, "Veiled Threat," *Nation*, TNR Online, February 22, 1999, 1–2.

36. Stephen Kinzer, "Beating the System, with Bribes and the Big Lie," *New York Times*, May 27, 1997.

37. Kinzer, "Beating the System."

38. Shay, *Choreophobia*; and "Dance and Jurisprudence."

39. Mohammad Nejad, musician, personal interview, July 19, 2001.

40. Azardokht Ameri, dance and music scholar who lives in Iran, personal interview, June 23, 2006.

41. Farzaneh Kaboli, former soloist with and member of the Mahalli Dancers, personal interview, September 4, 1994.

42. Camelia Entekhabi-Fard, "Behind the Veil," *Mother Jones*, July/August 2001, 69. In the article Entekhabi-Fard quotes Kaboli as saying, "Next time we will see you in Roudaki Hall." The reference to the old prerevolution name of the main Tehran concert hall, which is now called Vahdat (unity) Hall, was possibly more revolutionary than the dance performance itself, and perhaps caused the concert to be closed.

43. *New York Times*, December 26, 2003, A4.

44. John F. Burns, "Sex and the Afghan Woman: Islam's Straitjacket," *New York Times*, August 29, 1997. Nevertheless, as in Iran, people risked the Taliban's goon squads to dance at weddings; see: "An Afghan City Where Taliban Keep Grip Loose to Keep Power," *New York Times*, July 1, 2001, 7; Naim Majrooh, "Talibans have Banned All Music in Afghanistan" (paper presented at the 1st World Conference on Music and Censorship, Copenhagen, November 20–22, 1998).

45. Adra, "Concept of Tribe in Rural Yemen," 282; And, *Dances of Anatolian Turkey*, 30–31; and Karen Van Nieuwkirk, *Trade Like Any Other: Female Singers and Dancers in Egypt* (Austin: University of Texas Press, 1995), 32.

46. Van Nieuwkirk, *Trade Like Any Other*, 64.

47. *Egyptian Gazette*, 115th issue, no. 35,519, January 25, 1995, 1.

48. Personal interview, January 20, 2000.

49. In all likelihood the Sufis did not refer to their movement practices as dance, sometimes joining the hard-line Muslims in the condemnation of dance as entertainment (See And, *Dances of Anatolian Turkey*, 13–14.) Orthodox Muslims, however, called the Sufis' movements dance and often persecuted them for it.

50. Melissa Cefkin, "Choreographing Culture: Dance, Folklore and the Politics of Identity in Turkey," (PhD dissertation, Rice University, 1993).

51. Nafisi, "Veiled Threat," 12.

52. Afshin Molavi, "Letter from Iran," *Nation*, July 19, 1999.

53. *Kayhan,* a Tehran daily, reported that forty-two men and women received thirty-five lashes in the City of Shiraz for dancing at a party (March 1, 2001). Reuters reported that six Iranians celebrating *chahrshanbeh suri*, an evening celebration before the advent of Now Ruz, the Persian New year, were seized on the outskirts of the holy city of Mashhad for dancing and "goading passers-by to dance." They each received 228 lashes and eighteen months in jail. According to Amnesty International, the ultimate sentence of death was meted to Sheyda Khoramzadeh Esfahani after being convicted of "organizing 'corrupt gatherings' with prostitutes, alcohol, drugs, music and dance." Amnesty International: *Iran Bulletin*, Sheyda Khoramzadeh Esfahani (f), January 29, 1997.

54. John Hendren, "Night of Firsts for Afghans and Their U.S. Party Guests," *Los Angeles Times*, August 23, 2002, A1, 8.

55. Azardokht 'Ameri, *"Raqs-e 'amianeh-ye shahri va raqs-e mowsum be klasik: barrasi-ye tatbiqi dar howze-ye Tehran,"* *Mahour Music Quarterly*, no. 20 (Summer 2003): 24–28. This article, "Iranian Urban Popular Social Dance and So-Called Classical Dance: A Comparative Investigation in the District of Tehran," is translated in *Dance Research Journal*, 38 (Summer & Winter 2006): 163–79. Anthony Shay, *"Raqs-e Irani: moruri daneshvaraneh bar mas'ael-e pazhuheshi,"* [Iranian Dance: A Scholarly Overview of Research Issues], *Mahoor Music Quarterly* 7, no. 28 (Summer 2005): 9–26; and Anthony Shay, *"Tarahi-ye raqs-e 'persha': Baznama'i va sharqimo'bi dar sahneh'i kardan va tarahi-ye raqs-e Irani"* [Choreographing Persia: Representation and Orientalism in Staging and Choreographing Iranian Dance], *Mahoor Music Quarterly* 8, no. 30 (Winter 2006): 11–34.

· 7 ·

Right to Dance

Exotic Dancing in the United States

JUDITH LYNNE HANNA

I began my research on exotic dance adult entertainment in 1995 when I was asked to be an expert court witness in a First Amendment case.[1] I was contacted by an expert on the location and effects of exotic dance from the American Institute of Certified Planners and a lawyer representing dancers and owners of exotic dance clubs in Seattle, Washington, because they had discovered my anthropological research on dance as nonverbal communication through *Books in Print.*[2] They asked me to apply to exotic dance the semiotic, sociolinguistic paradigm I had used to study dance in Africa, on school playgrounds, and in American theaters. Since then, I have worked with fifty-five attorneys in regard to 117 legal cases in twenty-six states and the District of Columbia, and in the process I have observed and interviewed dancers (in more than 140 clubs), as well as members of their communities, including those in city and county council meetings and courtrooms.[3]

The Supreme Court of the United States recognizes artistic dance as protected expressive behavior, as a kind of "speech" that therefore falls under the First Amendment to the U.S. Constitution. (See Appendix 1.) As I will explain, it follows that the same protection should apply to exotic dance (also called striptease, stripping or erotic, topless, nude, table, couch, lap, go-go, juice bar, sports bar, and "gentleman's club" dance). Civil libertarians believe that exotic dancers, like other performers, should have the freedom to control their own artistic communication without state interference, police harassment, or the attacks of community members who try to impose their version of morality on everyone.

Despite the "protected expressive behavior" and "speech" connection, hundreds of local and state governments nationwide use the coercive power of regulations to limit exotic dance, to force it out of existence, or to prevent new exotic dance clubs from opening.[4] Laws against adult clubs include banning nudity or partial nudity, "simulated nudity," "simulated sex," touching another person or self-touch, and "obscene" and "lewd" behavior—terms that are, of course, open to wide interpretation. Some laws have placed restrictions on direct tipping or require bright lighting, specific hours of operation, and licensing of dancers. Fighting such laws is costly, and not all clubs or dancers can afford to litigate them.

It is significant to note that some anti-exotic-dance laws are so broad they could easily be applied to other dance styles in different contexts. Nudity, touching another person or self-touch, "simulated nudity," and "simulated sex" occur in choreography shown in mainstream theaters. Had censorship succeeded, such past shockers and present classics as Maud Allan's *Dance of Salomé*, Michel Fokine's *Schéhérazade*, Isadora Duncan's modern dance, George Balanchine's *Prodigal Son* and *Bugaku*, Jerome Robbins's *The Cage*, Martha Graham's *Phaedra*, Anna Halprin's *Parades and Changes*, Glen Tetley and Hans van Manen's *Mutations*, or Rudi van Dantzig's *Monument for a Dead Boy* would have been lost.[5]

Ironically, these restrictive laws are not applied to social dancing in public, so that performers in licensed adult businesses could be arrested for dancing the way couples in many nightclubs do, or the way kids routinely dance at school dances today. Although some schools have banned so-called "freak dancing," it is still common to see young people perform variations of social dance that are called booty dancing, da butt, doggy dancing, front piggybacking, and hot salsa. These variants include moments when pelvises touch and rotate, upper torsos meet, and thighs entwine. Females often bend over until their hands are on the floor, then press and grind their buttocks against a male's thighs and crotch, much like adults engaged in lap dancing.

Especially when compared to tolerance for sexuality and nudity in stage dance, the targeted attacks on exotic dance can be seen as class related; that is, different standards are applied to dance not considered "high art"—dance not taught in schools and not privileged by the dance community or the general public. But the enforcement of anti-exotic-dance laws sets a problematic precedent for censorship in general, in that these laws might eventually be applied to other forms of dance and art, forcing them out of existence. The wider principle is the infringement upon the civil liberties of all people in the United States.

In the following article, I will discuss the myths and realities of exotic dance as I have discovered them through my research. Included will be reports of performers' attitudes toward their work, legal treatment of exotic dance, and the tactics and reasoning used by adversaries of exotic dance. I will explain why their objections are ultimately limited and why all of this matters in the realm of dance and democracy.

EXOTIC DANCE IS DANCE

Exotic dance shares with virtually all dance genres the fact that it is a purposeful, intentionally rhythmical, culturally patterned, nonverbal, body movement communication in time and space, using effort and having its own criteria for excellence.[6] Like other kinds of dance, exotic dance conveys meaning by the use of space, touch, proximity to an observer, nudity, stillness, and specific body movements.[7] To use a ballet example, recall any number of versions of *Romeo and Juliet*, where the dancers' bodies are barely draped, and love is shown by touching hands, stroking a face, arching backward or falling into each other's arms. When Juliet's parents are urging her to marry Paris against her will, there's a moment when standing near him, her eyes coolly survey him from toe to head. Then her eyes turn away, and, rising on pointe, she briskly travels away from him.

In exotic dance, a performer might also emphasize lines of the body and use stroking and arching, eye contact, and proximity to a patron, but in this genre usually to indicate a more explicitly sexual way in which love is expressed, equally recognizable and also requiring choreographic creativity. Exotic dance also conveys a multitude of meanings, such as health, nature, beauty of the body, and feminine power. The meanings conveyed in contemporary exotic dance may be erotic, but erotic expression certainly does not exclude artistry. Indeed, some outstanding exotic dancers have attended performing arts high schools and performed in ballet companies and on Broadway. The excellent pole dancers have often trained in gymnastics.

All forms of dance have a range of amateur to professional, and an excellent performance can arouse emotions or suggest ideas for audience members. "Artistry," according to many dictionaries and choreographers, refers to the quality found in a performance that has creative imagination and knowledge and skill acquired by experience, study or observation, and communication. Dance writer Walter Sorell referred to artistry as "bringing dynamics and responsiveness to the craftsmanship."[8] These levels of mastery pertain to exotic dance. Artistic merit in exotic dance is recognized according to specific criteria applied in competitions, as well as when patrons remunerate dancers with individual tips and fees during performances. These criteria include talent, individual creativity, personality, appearance and costume, musicality, athletic strength and flexibility, and audience appeal.

In the course of studying many exotic dance performances, I could see that there was/is often more going on than sexual fantasy. One aspect that relates to the criteria for artistic expression is parody, when a dancer makes fun of the pretext of clothing, such as a police uniform or a cowboy outfit, and gender identity, female stereotypes, or femininity by exaggerating them. As adult theatrical entertainment, exotic dance involves play, fantasy, and acting; by definition it is supposed to be risqué, disclosing more of the body and kinds of movements than seen in public. We see minimal breast coverings and thongs that expose much of the body in public swimming areas, and sexually suggestive movements on MTV and social dance floors. These forms of dress and behavior are not policed in the same way exotic dancing often is, nor are many stage performers in so-called legitimate theatre harassed the way adult entertainment participants are.

Exotic dance, also like other dance forms, has its own history. Its roots can be seen in various styles of shimmying and hip-rotating Middle Eastern dance, especially in its incarnation as belly dance, which has also been called *danse du ventre, danse orientale,* hootchy-kootchy, or cooch. After Egyptian dancers were a sensation at the 1893 Chicago World's Columbian Exposition, aspects of this kind of dancing, previously a folk form in the Middle East, were appropriated widely.[9] It influenced not only many amateurs and pioneers of modern dance such as Maud Allen and Ruth St. Denis, but performers on the stages of American burlesque theaters. While many dancers tried to distance themselves from the sexual aspects of belly dance by emphasizing spiritual and artistic associations, exotic dancers developed their own forms in strip clubs, until their decline after World War II. Exotic dance began to flourish anew in the 1980s as upscale "gentlemen's clubs," managed by businesspeople and corporations, increasingly supplanted the old-style strip bars. This transformation was like going from greasy spoons to four-star gourmet restaurants. Indeed, some clubs serve excellent food.

Contemporary exotic dance has also been influenced by many important twentieth-century artistic developments, such as African American social dance forms, nudity in mainstream theater, and dance showcases. The development of exotic dance can be seen as part of a western art aesthetic mandate to explore what has been deemed off limits, such as gay themes, to find new objects to look at, such as multi-media productions, and new ways to look at familiar ones, such as Pilobolus dancers appearing as moving fungi. Pole dancing and lap dancing (extending the tradition of taxi dancing) are recent exotic dance innovations.

Exotic dance usually has two sequential parts. First, a dancer performs onstage for the audience as a whole to entertain and then to showcase herself for the second part of the dance. Generally, nudity climaxes the last of a three-song performance in which the dancer appears on stage clothed for the first song, partially removes her clothes during the second, and strips to nudity at the end. The dance varies depending on the dancer, club, and locality. Performed in six- to eight-inch heels, the movements derive from belly dance, burlesque, popular dance, Broadway theater, music videos, jazz, hip-hop, cheerleading, and gymnastics. The common pole onstage serves as a prop and permits athletic stunts. Demi Moore's dance in *Striptease* is illustrative of some of this type of dancing. Dancers commonly gyrate hips and torso, thrust hips back and forth and rotate them ("bump & grind"), rotate hips into a squat (like a screw), undulate body or body parts, shimmy breasts, and bend torso to peek through one's legs.

The following is a description of a performer pole dancing to the music in a club in Albany, New York. First Song: Dancer walks onstage. Wipes mirror with cloth to best reflect her image. Twirls on her own axis while circling around the pole. Holds pole with right hand as support to twirl around pole, right thigh lifted. Places back to pole and extends right leg. Turns around, grabs pole and shimmies up, right leg extended outward, leans back, straightens up, leans back with legs outward horizontally, brings them up to chest. Flips body upside down on pole, extends legs in a split, slides to floor. Hooks right leg around pole as support to twirl around pole. Sits down, arches backward, unfastens hair tie to let hair flow with movement. Twirls around pole, shimmies up pole with both legs, hangs upside down by legs. Slides to knees, extends torso forward, legs bent outward. Stands with back to pole, arches head back. Swings up pole with one foot on stage rail, one hand on ceiling hook. Descends to floor, knees swivel toward and away from each other. Leans back against the mirror, extends hands upward, turns around, moves hands down body, faces mirror, twirls, creating self images twirling along mirror to right and then reversing direction. Sits down, flips head back. Walks to pole, twirls around it with right foot up. Lifts body onto pole with hands, flipping legs back and out. Hangs by one leg, the other extended outward, splits legs, descends to floor head first. Places hand modestly over pubic area. Shimmies up pole, turns upside down holding on with thighs, bounces buttocks sliding down. Twirls about pole, bends backward, one leg bent at knee. Shimmies up pole, moves body toward and away from pole, splits legs. Descends and twirls around pole; music accelerates as does movement. Slides back against pole, hands go up side of torso. Moves to edge of stage for patron to reward her performance by putting bill in her garter.

Second Song: Wipes mirror. Walks to pole, twirls about it, leg hooked. Shimmies up pole, turns upside down holding with one leg hooked around pole, the other in bent shape extends outward. Stands with back to pole and removes her top. Shimmies up pole, spins in backbend, brushes her hair, upside down splits legs, extends them vertically and together, grasps pole. Descends to floor, flips hair back and forth, on hands and knees bounces buttocks, kneels, stands. Twirls about pole.

Third Song: Takes thong off. Backs up to mirror, creates S shape, slides to seated position, opens and closes legs. Walks to pole, hooks leg and twirls around pole, tosses head back, shakes hair. Descends pole into split, then rises with legs vertical to floor, buttocks first with torso bent forward, stands upright, tosses hair. Leans against pole, swings up with hands, body flung outward, and then legs grab pole. Vibrates legs in descent to floor. Circles pole. As foot pushes off from stage rail and one hand grasps a ceiling hook, swings up pole. Descends to floor with one, then another leg. Leans against pole, twirls, head arched backward. Shimmies up pole, splits legs outward, extends arms outward as thighs grip pole. Descends. Receives tips. Walks offstage.

In the second part of exotic dance, for a fee a performer dances for individual patrons next to where they are seated (or in lap dancing a performer dances on, straddling, or between a patron's legs). The dancer "says" through body and facial movement, proximity, and touch, the fantasy of "I am interested in you, I understand you, you're special and important to me." The patron's purchased "commodity" is a license to dream.

In many ways, the performance venues for exotic dance parallel those of mainstream dance forms. Gentlemen's clubs are theaters with an entrance fee that provides access to a place where professionals perform on a raised stage with special lighting, a commercial music system, and a master of ceremonies and/or disc jockey. Similar to mainstream dinner theaters, tables and chairs for audience members are arranged in areas where exotic dancers also perform. "Ushers" (floor managers or doormen) seat patrons, answer questions, and ensure proper audience behavior. As has traditionally been a feature of many major opera houses, clubs often have a special "VIP" room for audience members who pay for special ambience, alcoholic beverages, and attention. Backstage, there is a dressing area for performers.

Currently, there are approximately 4,000 clubs where exotic dance is performed, and the industry is estimated to be a multibillion-dollar concern, with clubs on the NASDAQ Stock Exchange (National Association of Securities Dealers Automated) and the American Stock Exchange. Annual individual club revenues may reach five million dollars, and clubs pay substantial local and state taxes. The industry boasts a host of organizations, schools, publications, and national trade expositions. Among the patrons are businessmen and women who frequent exotic dance clubs to put their clients in the mood to close commercial deals. Onstage, performers include those who are also college students, lawyers, accountants, stockbrokers, artists, athletes, single moms, married women, ballet and modern dancers, and high-school dropouts. What they all share is that they are all professionals, all earning income, all doing a job.

EXOTIC DANCERS' PERCEPTIONS OF THEIR WORK

My interviews with hundreds of exotic dancers since 1995 reveal multiple reasons for choosing to perform. Earning money from this legitimate work is key. Some women become dancers through serendipity, meeting someone who does it or who knows a dancer. Being an exotic dancer offers women the opportunity to work fewer hours and earn more income than they would in doing many other jobs. Choosing their own schedules gives them time to attend college or bring up children.

While the exotic dance industry, like many other businesses, has its share of good bosses and bad bosses, and of illegal behavior, it has no monopoly. Most dancers in the clubs I have visited (and others who have written about their experiences) assert that they are independent subjects creating art, not submissive objects. They feel empowered by the financial independence they achieve and talk about the increased self-confidence and self-esteem gained from successfully facing strangers and winning their appreciation. Many identify themselves as feminists and think that dancers should be the ones to decide if, when, and under what circumstances they feel oppressed. A number of exotic dance supporters consider that the dancer's choice to place her body within a financial transaction does not reduce her to a commodity any more than a model, actor, or athlete would be by choosing their respective professions. Conversations with dancers and audience members alike have revealed an awareness that exotic dance merely taps into contemporary attitudes toward the body as something to be cultivated, used, and presented.

Dancers say the biggest problem they face is the stigma attributed to exotic dance. Doors held by employers who are biased against exotic dance may be closed to those who have had a career in this industry. The dancers may not only be stigmatized as instigators of crime when government regulations have been imposed on their industry, but their civil liberties are also threatened and their freedom of speech curtailed by their inability to speak about their work widely without fear of prejudice. Stigmatization of dancers can easily bleed into their private lives as well. It has proved to be a negative factor in cases of child custody or rape, for example, and in being denied access to housing. As a result of the stigma, many dancers feel compelled to perform incognito, not only using stage names, wearing heavy make-up and wigs, but also changing their contact lens color and way of speaking. For some women, exotic dance is an alternative path to success, but it is paved with the pain of public misperception. Yet from my research, I could see that performing in exotic dance clubs is far from a one-way trip to hell.

THE LAW: MORALS, OBSCENITY, AND ADVERSE EFFECTS

The U.S. Constitution, Supreme Court decisions, and subsequent case law provide constraints for regulating exotic dance.[10] Although the Supreme Court has recognized exotic dance as expression, or "speech," with First Amendment protection, in 1991, a fractured Supreme Court allowed exotic dance regulation on moral grounds (*Barnes v. Glen Theatre*). But that "morality" justification has since fallen by the wayside. An expression-restricting law based on public morality reflects a political consensus among a majority of elected representatives, not necessarily the moral preferences of a majority of citizens. In the more recent case of *City of Erie v. Pap's A.M.* (2000), the Supreme Court held that government could regulate adult-entertainment clubs if the aim is to prevent crime, property depreciation, and sexually transmitted disease—the legal doctrine of "adverse secondary effects." Content neutral (not impinging upon meaning) time, place, and manner regulations of exotic dance were permitted, the amount of regulatory control dependent upon whether or not alcohol was sold. In general, speech that aims to reconcile the individual's and society's interests must be justified by evidence that expression creates a clear, present danger, or that it is "obscene" under the difficult three-pronged "Miller test" (*Miller v. California,* 1973),[11] or that the restrictions otherwise further a compelling government interest. Furthermore, restrictions on speech generally must combat the danger by the least restrictive means.

Up until at least 2002, the federal, state, and local courts did not question local and state legislatures' specified intentions for regulations to deal with the "negative" effects of exotic dance. However, *Pap's, City of Los Angeles v. Alameda Books* (2002), and subsequent cases now allow the merit of a government's evidence for the need to control exotic dance to be challenged in court. "Shoddy" evidence or reasoning does not suffice, the Supreme Court said. Consequently, exotic dance clubs and associations have commissioned social scientists not only to critique "studies" that localities previously had been permitted to rely upon to justify their legislation, but also to conduct new research.

Social scientists in the twenty-first century have critiqued the "studies" that governments have relied on as evidence to justify regulations that strangle exotic dance.[12] The "studies" typically include these faults: most do not follow professional standards of inquiry or meet the basic requirements for acceptance of scientific evidence. No control site is matched with an exotic dance cabaret site to ascertain if the latter is different regarding negative behavior, such as crime. No determination is made as to what exists before and what exists after a cabaret is opened in a particular location. No data are collected over several years to distinguish a relatively unstable or a one-time blip from what is usually the case. Studies conducted over a single time period and at a specific site are not applied to gentlemen's clubs located in adjacent counties and in other places. Studies focused on concentrations of a combination of different kinds of adult businesses, such as bookstores, peep shows, and massage parlors, are not necessarily applicable to cabarets. And there have been no studies examining the impact of a particular type of dance or kind of expression (whether nudity, semi-nudity, simulated nudity, stage design, or dancer-patron interaction) taking place inside an adult business.

Although adult entertainment cabarets in poor neighborhoods have more crime than businesses in other neighborhoods, this does not prove that the clubs cause crime (correlation is not causation). Change in police surveillance may also account for crime rates. Police calls by a cabaret may not indicate a troublesome business, but rather its commitment to maintain a safe and lawful establishment. Some police reports are proven false in court or do not reflect convictions. Charges for prostitution are at times merely based on the perception of "sexy" dancing or "come-on" fantasy talk. Opinions of appraisers constitute speculation, not empirical evidence of a valid relationship between exotic dance cabarets and their actual impact on property values. A "potential" negative impact is not a real impact. People presume nightclubs in general also cause noise, drunkenness, and litter. However, despite the intuitive appeal of these assumptions, there is a surprising absence of proof.

Most importantly, recent valid and reliable research has disproved the adverse secondary effects of exotic dance.[13] Of course, clubs may have crime, but not disproportionate to other businesses that are public places of assembly, and clubs often have positive effects. Clubs frequently benefit communities by attracting new business, providing employment, and paying taxes.

Typically, government regulates every exotic dance club the same way, regardless of their differences in operational character or their economic contribution to the community. Zoning is the first line of government control of adult entertainment. Areas are often set aside for clubs and distances from school and churches specified. Yet there is no evidence that it makes a difference if clubs are clustered or dispersed. Clubs may be eliminated through eminent domain, which is the government purchase of land for the public interest.

In general, the courts have tended to be unaware of how dance conveys content symbolically and thus have permitted problematic "content-neutral" regulations. Some judges who recognize exotic dance as "speech" or "artistic expression" view it as less important than political speech in the hierarchy of First Amendment protection. Again, the problem is lack of knowledge about dance in general and exotic dance in particular, as well as the reigning supremacy of the verbal over the nonverbal.

ADVERSARIES OF EXOTIC DANCE

To begin my research in preparation for testifying in my first exotic dance court case, I had to break through demonstrators to get inside an exotic dance club. Adults and children who were picketing the club held banners that screamed, "Washington Together against Pornography!" I could see that a particular strain of Christian church was behind the opposition to adult entertainment, and I learned more about such hostility as I went along.

My research enabled me to prepare study reports, affidavits, and testimony to prevent the enactment of laws or to challenge laws that infringe upon the First Amendment of the U.S. Constitution (freedom of expression), the Fifth Amendment (due process related to arrests without warrants and regulatory and court proceedings) and/or Fourteenth Amendment (discrimination by singling out one kind of dance, nightclub, or business for regulation), or to defend dancers against charges of prostitution, lewdness, indecency, or obscenity. In every case, a pastor or church group was also involved, spearheading efforts to wipe out exotic dance. At first it seemed that these Protestant churches were acting independently in the tradition of local control; but eventually I realized they were part of a web of connection in a powerful Christian Right political alliance. I began to study these groups.[14]

In 1973, the politically active Christian Right was a small group of people with a grand design for the nation. Since then, a thirty-year effort using dynamic organizational momentum has led to religious conservatives gaining office at the local, state, and Supreme Court levels, to their taking control of Congress for the first time in forty years, and the elevation of George W. Bush, a born-again evangelical, to the White House. One of the major players I repeatedly saw in courtrooms across the country was attorney Scott Bergthold, who had been a member of several Christian Right political organizations, such as the Alliance Defense Fund, which are devoted to fighting adult entertainment. Now he carries on the fight through his own firm.[15]

Through an organizational network fueled by money, lawyers, and technology, an emboldened division of the Christian Right fights adult entertainment as part of a political religious movement called Dominionism. Its goals are to supplant constitutional democracy with a bible-based Christian-governing theocratic elite.[16] Fights against exotic dance occur on merely one front in a broader culture war,[17] with other battles concentrating on abortion and prayer in the schools, for instance. Composed of evangelical traditionalists, centrists, and modernists, Christian Right divisions fight to have their voice and ideology prevail. My focus here is on the segment of political activists who have a thirst for eliminating the separation of church and state in order to create a scripture-guided nation, not the other divisions that concentrate on social welfare and global warming. However, if there are differences of opinion within the Christian Right regarding some "hot-button" issues, it is doubtful that they extend to exotic dance, which is broadly demonized.

Attempts to ban dance, of course, are not new.[18] The current rhetoric of the Christian Right echoes some past objections to dance based on the perceived threat it is seen to pose, in that the instrument of dance and sexuality are one and the same, namely, the human body. Eroticism has unleashed passions that have defied the dictates of many religious and political groups. As with theater, dance has been the object of suppression not only because of its perceived sexual nature, but because it has been associated with what is seen as "deceit and pretense," which is interpreted as "bearing false witness." In some religious interpretations, mimesis is linked to sin and blasphemy, in that it mocks nature and God. In other words, theatrical spectacle calls into question the very nature of truth by exaggerating it. Moreover, dance is considered to dissipate God's gift of time and money, because it is thought to serve no Christian purpose and to be poor preparation for death and eternity.

Moral crusades against dance are part of America's heritage, especially when dancers reveal evermore flesh and experiment with movement in ways that seem to flaunt traditional notions of modesty. Even ballet, perhaps the quintessential conception of high art dance today, was widely considered disreputable in the nineteenth century, because it publicly displayed the female body and provided a venue for rich gentlemen to pick up mistresses.[19] The current objections of the Christian Right repeat much of the anti-dance religious rhetoric of the past, in that Biblical injunctions concerning the use of the body and modesty recur,[20] and there is an emphasis on patriarchy, male-female polarity, and the belief that men have an inherently uncontrollable nature.[21]

Believing that people are tempted by sin and cannot be trusted with liberty, the Christian Right targets the publicly expressive body. Broadly speaking, white middle-class evangelical Christians who are socially, theologically, and economically conservative believe that a woman's place is in the home and only the husband should see the wife's nude body. They express outrage when a woman goes into the workplace and strips.

While many of these arguments may sound familiar, today's anti-exotic-dance brigade is different from those in the past because of the Christian Right's grasp of government policy and use of modern technology. A segment of the Christian Right is determined to reorganize American life more broadly.[22] Civil liberties constrain the movement's use of government to ban exotic dance outright; therefore, in the name of the "public good" and "protecting our children," which the Christian Right proclaims in public hearings and in legislative preambles, some members become legislators or enlist legislators to enact regulations that censor key elements of exotic dance, harm the business by eating away at its essence, and trample many people's civil liberties.

Wittingly or unwittingly, members of the Christian Right are joined by some feminists and the American Planning Association (APA) in the attempt to strip the First Amendment, corset the exotic dancer, and dismantle the industry. Concerned with protecting women, they consider exotic dancers to be objects of the "degrading" male gaze, said to hurt all women whether they know it or not. In this scheme, exotic dancers are infantilized by being characterized as hapless, exploited victims of patriarchy and unbridled male control, lust, and avarice. Yet my research indicates that most dancers are savvy entrepreneurs and, if they are subjects of the erotic gaze, they return that gaze in order to assess the monetary spending potential of patrons.[23] The female adversaries do not seem to recognize that male legislators who try to control exotic dance might be attempting to control women to reinforce patriarchy. In the economic realm, some businesses and property owners ally themselves with the moralists, fearing exotic dance in their neighborhoods would jeopardize safety and depreciate property values. Again, there is no scientific evidence to justify these fears.

Many people may join the anti-exotic-dance bandwagon in good faith, because they believe conservative propaganda and the stereotypes perpetuated by the media, or because they might remember past allegations that "strip joints" were run by organized crime and are unfamiliar with today's modern, well-run gentlemen's clubs. Easy to demonize because it is misunderstood, exotic dance adult entertainment is a lightning rod for culture conflicts in America and an easy scapegoat for fear of change in society. Exotic dance easily provokes public denunciation and governmental suppression for "the public good." Historically, those who perceive dance as a threat have responded in ways that have led to abuses of American and Fourth Geneva Convention human rights of autonomy, dignity, and justice. These abuses have challenged women's choice of work, freedom from exploitation and control, and choice of artistic expression. The NIMBY (not-in-my-backyard) issue also pits segments of the community against exotic dance stakeholders (dancers, pa-trons, club owners, and personnel).

TACTICS USED AGAINST EXOTIC DANCE

Strategies to promote the anti-exotic-dance agenda include the APA provid-ing local governments with faulty, biased, outdated studies that claim exotic dance clubs cause harm.[24] One of their publications appears to call on the resources of academic experts, but, in fact, is inaccurate and misleading.[25] In addition, the APA files amicus curiae or friend-of-the-court briefs (namely, information provided on points of law or other aspects of a case to assist a court in its decision) against the adult industry.

More dire tactics against exotic dancers, including death threats and ha-rassment of exotic dance stakeholders, are similar to those used against abor-tion service providers. The Christian Right also uses agitprop tactics by mo-bilizing the forces of highly organized church groups who respond to calls for massive letter-writing campaigns and become more visible though its media empire.[26] Not only do they attack exotic dance, but they assault the National Endowment for the Arts' existence and funding, disapproving of some grant-ees' work on moral grounds.

To help in these crusades, a number of religious conservative political ac-tion groups provide a model for anti-exotic-dance legislation[27] and other legal services to local governments. For example, the Community Defense Counsel (CDC) was set up by members of the Christian Right specifically to fight adult businesses and has offered national legal conferences, training seminars for prosecutors or city attorneys, drafting services for statutes or ordinances and testimonies, trial assistance, and appellate and amicus curiae briefs. It also provides a law library with "studies of secondary effects," a legal manual, model city ordinances, and workshops for church members held around the country to teach people how to keep adult businesses out of neighborhoods. The organization has been training a thousand attorneys to develop "secure cities" to improve the "the quality of life" in their communities. The CDC publishes articles in law journals and the popular media and puts out slick mul-ticolored flyers that feature statements such as "We can help you draw the line for decency," "How can I get involved?" "You call this victimless?" "How to keep sex businesses out of your neighborhood," and "There's no place like home . . . for pornography?" (The Christian Right confounds exotic dance with pornography.)

The Christian Right also seeks to impose its views through lobbying, voter guides, and organizational structures, such as prayer-action groups that become political action committees. Christian Right stay-at-home women have become available platoons to further the conservative agenda.

In addition, the Christian Right pressures and also participates in government. A tactic against exotic dance clubs is for governments to require clubs to hire police for security, more expensive than private guards. Jurisdictions may turn to discriminatory licensing of exotic dancers (but not other dancers), clubs, and managers. Licensing, often expensive and cumbersome to the licensee, enables a locality to refuse, suspend, or revoke a license, often at a government official's discretion and without equitable appeal procedures. There may be special entertainment taxes ("sin" taxes) on adult clubs.

Criminal "obscenity," "public indecency," and "lewd conduct" laws tie the noose tighter. Governments may set hours of operation and require specific configurations of stage and seating. Some localities mandate bright lighting and patron-dancer distance requirements "to facilitate law enforcement against drugs and prostitution" and further impede dancers' creativity by specifying costumes, dictating what body parts can be exposed, and determining exotic dance styles, movements, the use of self-touch, and the manner in which patrons may tip dancers. Adversaries attempt to ban simulated nudity and simulated sex even though they do not define them.

Another tactic is to change the rules as soon as exotic clubs comply with a regulation ordinance and still thrive or the court overturns a restrictive law. If during a court hearing a government realizes a challenge to its ordinance will most likely succeed, it amends the restriction to render the court case moot and to avoid paying the challenger's attorney's fees. Fearful of losing in court and paying costs and damages, some local governments are becoming cautious about passing anti-exotic-dance ordinances. They may require adversarial church groups to first create a legal defense fund of one hundred thousand dollars to cover the expected cost of club challenges to the ordinances.

Law enforcement may root out, prosecute, and render stiff penalties for violations of adult business regulations.[28] Asking inspectors from fire, health, building, alcohol, or public works agencies and the Internal Revenue Service or state tax authority to find any kind of code violation is another form of harassment. Club Exstasy in Prince Georges County, Maryland, experienced four raids in thirty days in 2006, and customers received citations for jaywalking and not parking between a private parking lot's lines. Intimidating threats of undercover operations and vice-squad raids exert control. In some localities, law enforcement has prevented entry into a club and deterred patrons under the pretext of protecting demonstrators against the club, at the same time permitting the demonstrators to trespass. A Kansas law mandates a grand jury investigation if enough names (3,300 signatures) can be gathered through a petition process. Thus the Christian Right in several cities forced grand jury investigations of sexually oriented businesses. However, grand juries refused to issue indictments in most cases.

Tactics against exotic dance also include a kind of psychological assault on specific exotic dancers and patrons and on the reputation of the exotic dance industry in general. At public hearings, on websites, and in publications, Christian Right talk show hosts, writers, and organizers often characterize the exotic dance world as dangerous, suggesting along the way that the rights women have gained through the feminist movement and 1960s sexual revolution are causing their lives to fall apart. Former strippers who are "born-again" Christians commonly tell dark tales, which, even if true, serve mostly to exaggerate outsider fears, the way much stereotyping does.

Along with picketing exotic dance clubs, members of the Christian Right note patrons' license plate numbers and phone their families and employers. One Christian group sent a letter to parents living within three blocks of a club, alerting them to the recently opened business and making negative allegations against the owners and their wives; this led to club owners' children being harassed in school. Club customers have received postcards mailed by a church group. The text read, "Observed you in the neighborhood. Didn't know if you were aware there is a church in the area." Patrons were sent photos of their cars parked outside the club and had their faces and license plate numbers photographed by picketers posted on a website called "seewhosthere." A group called People Advocating Decency videotaped patrons entering a club. "We just wanted to make people think twice before they go in," a spokesperson said. "They might think, 'I don't want the world to know about this.'"

Going even further, the Carolina Family Alliance used patrons' car tags to track their identity and contact them by phone or mail to encourage them to seek professional help. They also notified their family and friends about the potential "danger" the clubs pose to loved ones. Protesters have used bullhorns on a club's property. The Family Coalition protested outside a club for over a year with a billboard that read, "Pornography Breeds Rapists," although exotic dance is not pornography; nor is there evidence it causes rape.[29] Anti-club protesters also engage in assaults on property and physical threats. Some slash tires in club parking lots. A club called Delilah's Gone Platinum was vandalized twice. Vandals made sledgehammer-sized holes throughout the building; substantially smashed block-glass windows, mirrors, ceramic statues and the stereo system; flooded several hallways and rooms with an inch of water; and tore up the dance stage floor.[30] In another case in upstate New York, a couple that owned a club under attack sent their daughter to live with relatives for safety after threats to her life.

Stigmatization of dancers is yet another means of assaulting an industry. Groups trying to "save" dancers are stigmatizing them, assassinating their characters as independent decision-making women, and re-sowing false myths. When governments require a six-foot buffer zone between the dancer and her audience—or even a clear unbreakable glass or Plexiglas wall prohibiting physical contact between the entertainer and her audience—this dehumanizes the dancer and sends patrons the message that she is like an infectious patient in a hospital isolation ward, or a prisoner or caged animal in a zoo. The rights of patrons are also affected when draconian laws prevail; when direct tipping is banned, they cannot say thank-you to the dancer and express their opinions about the merit of the performance. The impact of the ordinance is like a salesperson not being able to hand a customer a receipt or a maître d' not being able to receive a tip.

DEFENDERS

People who challenge the religious, feminist, economic interest, social, and governmental assaults on exotic dance include equally passionate liberal feminists and civil rights activists. Many citizens object to singling out exotic dance clubs for special regulations because these regulations not only infringe on civil liberties, but they cost taxpayer money to develop, enact, enforce, and defend. Government jurisdictions have spent millions of dollars in litigation and damages, and the exotic dance regulations divert needed resources from real problems and cut the local government tax income. After all, the clubs pay taxes, employ people, support legitimate businesses through purchasing a range of goods and services, and attract new businesses to their neighborhoods, including upscale women's dress stores. As well, there are some businessmen who do not like the idea of government micromanaging any business.

Exotic dancers and clubs have fought opponents with the help of members of the First Amendment Lawyers Association, Association of Club Executives National Trade Association, American Civil Liberties Union, other civil liberties organizations, as well as Dance USA among arts groups.[31] In countering attacks on their businesses, exotic dance clubs take offensive and defensive action in the courts of public opinion and law. Lobbying, presentations to local councils and state committees, as well as support for open-minded political candidates, are preemptive efforts to halt the passage of restrictive ordinances. Some club owners and dancers run for political office. Clubs have organized successful referenda against club regulations in California, Washington, and Arizona. Litigation over exotic dance is ongoing in local, state, and federal courts with wins and losses.[32] However, the highly organized, religiously motivated adversaries of exotic dance are persistent and dangerous, requiring equal persistence in efforts to uphold the U.S. Constitution.

IMPLICATIONS

The Christian Right, viewing exotic dance as a cancer to be eliminated as part of creating a scripture-based society, acts against it with much muscle. Adversaries of exotic dance try to keep it out of their neighborhoods on the basis of a widespread mythology that recently has been shown to be false. In the conflict, antagonists infringe on the First Amendment and other civil liberties of the exotic dance stakeholders. When local governments single out exotic dancers to be licensed, without requiring licenses for other kinds of dancers, the governments discriminate against exotic dancers and violate their Fourteenth Amendment rights. Planners and legislatures mandate distance requirements, including raised platforms, between dancers and patrons on the presumption that it will prevent illegal behavior. Yet by using the logic that planners and legislatures apply to exotic dance for monitoring misbehavior, there should be similar requirements to separate children and priests and pastors in church or teachers at school, because the adults might sexually molest the children. In fact there is substantial evidence of clerical sexual abuse of children and adults, with convictions and churches paying billions of dollars in settlements, whereas no such evidence has been produced regarding the dangers of exotic dance.

Inherent in the debate over exotic dancing is a class and social status issue, in that so-called "high art" dance is not similarly controlled and censored. To cite just one example, on January 31, 1978, April 28, 1982, and January 25, 1992, the community of theater-goers in Roanoke, Virginia, accepted nudity in the touring Broadway show *Oh! Calcutta,* with male and female nude bodies touching. But in 1997 a Roanoke jury did not accept nude female soloists in the exotic dance club Girls, Girls, Girls, and charged them with obscenity. As well, there is a contradiction in terms of regulation when it comes to social dancing; while exotic dancers are censored or harassed, there is relative acceptance of adults or teenagers who are similarly attired and engaged in sexually explicit dancing.

Various kinds of government-imposed burdensome regulations diminish the multifaceted messages of exotic dance and constrain the free market. This effectively denies both dancers and audience members access to free artistic expression. The restrictions imposed on exotic dance have the potential to impact other dance and performing arts, and, indeed, all Americans. Had dance been successfully censored in the past, many dance forms and masterworks recognized today would have been lost.[33] Throughout history, battles have been waged over the shock of unconventional sexuality, miscegenation, bodily disclosure, touching, and homosexuality in ballet, modern, postmodern, and performance art dance. A censorship assault on any form of dance, even the stigmatized exotic dance, harms all art. For example, the Christian Right's intimidation causes some choreographers to self-censor and shrinks public and private dance funding for "controversial" work.

Moreover, the art of dance develops with inspiration from, and porous boundaries between, various kinds of dance, especially if they are sexual and shocking. Jerome Robbins directed and choreographed the Broadway show *Gypsy* in 1959 based on the life of stripper Gypsy Rose Lee; modern dancer Mark Morris choreographed *Striptease*; renowned choreographer and founder of the New York City Ballet George Balanchine featured a striptease dancer in *Slaughter on Tenth Avenue*. Broadway star Bob Fosse produced renditions of exotic dance in Broadway musicals (the comic "Hernando's Hideaway" in *The Pajama Game* and "Whatever Lola Wants" in *Damn Yankees*) and the film *All That Jazz* (a suggestive ballet). Jawole Willa Jo Zollar, a modern dancer based in New York City and head of the Urban Bush Women company, has spoken of the influence of the strippers she saw in her childhood on her dances.

Assaults against dance eerily recall tactics by fascist and totalitarian governments whose legislation gradually eats away at human rights. The banning of dance in Afghanistan by the Taliban was only one of the most recent examples of how human rights are curtailed. It only takes one look at anti-dance rhetoric of the past to see the dangers. A famous man once wrote that "our whole public life today is like a hothouse for sexual ideas and stimulations. Theater, art, literature, cinema, press, posters, and window displays must be cleaned of all manifestations of our rotting world and placed in the service of a moral, political, and cultural idea." The man was Adolf Hitler.[34]

In sum, the opprobrium targeted at exotic dance threatens all dance, and more importantly, places everyone's civil liberties at risk. Nadine Strossen, New York University law professor and president of the American Civil Liberties Union, said, "Once we cede to the government the power to violate one right for one person, or group, then no right is safe for any person or group."[35]

APPENDIX 1: PROTECTION UNDER THE CONSTITUTION OF THE UNITED STATES OF AMERICA

Amendment I

Congress shall make no law respecting an establishment of religion, or prohibiting the free exercise thereof; or abridging the freedom of speech, or of the press, or the right of the people peaceably to assemble, and to petition the Government for a redress of grievances.

Amendment V

No person shall be held to answer for a capital, or otherwise infamous crime, unless on a presentment or indictment of a Grand Jury, except in cases arising in the land or naval forces, or in the Militia, when in actual service in time of War or public danger; nor shall any person be subject for the same offence to be twice put in jeopardy of life or limb, nor shall be compelled in any criminal case to be a witness against himself, nor be deprived of life, liberty, or property, without due process of law; nor shall private property be taken for public use without just compensation.

Amendment XIV

Section 1. All persons born or naturalized in the United States and subject to the jurisdiction thereof, are citizens of the United States and of the State wherein they reside. No state shall make or enforce any law which shall abridge the privileges or immunities of citizens of the United States; nor shall any State deprive any person of life, liberty, or property, without due process of law; nor deny to any person within its jurisdiction the equal protection of the laws.

NOTES

1. I wish to acknowledge the helpful comments of Pamela Squires, Naomi Jackson, Toni Shapiro-Phim, and Jennifer Fisher on this article. All arguments and interpretations are, ultimately, mine. This essay is biased in favor of the U.S. Constitution—free speech, due process of the law, and nondiscrimination—and evidence over misperception and myth.

2. Judith Lynne Hanna, *To Dance Is Human: A Theory of Nonverbal Communication* (Chicago: University of Chicago Press, 1987); *Dance, Sex, and Gender: Signs of Identity, Dominance, Defiance and Desire* (Chicago: University of Chicago Press, 1988); *Disruptive School Behavior: Class, Race and Culture* (New York: Holmes & Meier, 1988); *The Performer-Audience Connection: Emotion to Metaphor in Dance and Society* (Austin: University of Texas Press, 1983); and a 1988 preliminary version of *Dancing for Health: Conquering and Preventing Stress* (Lanham, Md., AltaMira Press, 2006). Since 1995, I have continued my work on dance as nonverbal communication: *Partnering Dance and Education: Intelligent Moves for Changing Times* (Champaign, Ill.: Human Kinetics, 1999); "The Language of Dance," *JOPERD* 72, no. 4 (2001): 40–45, 53; numerous peer-reviewed articles and nearly one hundred fifty articles for dance magazines (see www.judithhanna.com).

3. A listing of most of the forty-four cases in which a court swore me in as expert court witness appears in Hanna, "Adult Entertainment Exotic Dance: A Guide for

Planners and Policy Makers" (CPL [Council of Planning Librarians] Bibliography 375), *Journal of Planning Literature* 20, no. 2 (2005): 116–34. I also gave presentations at public hearings and regulatory boards and wrote reports for cases that precluded a lawsuit or were settled.

4. Since 1995, I have come across more than four hundred jurisdictions fighting exotic dance, and often more than once. Angelina Spencer, National Executive Director of the Association of Club Executives, reported that two hundred state legislative bills were leveled at the industry in 2007.

5. Poseyville and New Harmony, Indiana, for instance, have passed ordinances that ban nudity in "performances," including any play, motion picture, dance, or other exhibition or presentation, whether it is pictured, animated, or live, performed before an audience of one or more. This means libraries, museums, and movie theaters could all be breaking the law.

6. Hanna, "Undressing the First Amendment and Corsetting the Striptease Dancer," *The Drama Review* 42, no. 2 (Summer 1998): 38–69; Hanna, "Toying with the Striptease Dancer and the First Amendment," in *Play and Culture Studies, Vol. 2*, ed. Stuart Reifel (Greenwich, Conn.: Ablex, 1999), 37–55. Over the past six decades, numerous dancers have written about their lives as strippers, there are how-to books, journalists have given us reports, scholarly articles abound, and recently revised dissertations, some by former exotic dancers, have appeared: Katherine Frank, *G-Strings and Sympathy: Strip Club Regulars and Male Desire* (Raleigh, N.C.: Duke University Press, 2002); Katherine Liepe-Levinson, *Strip Show: Performances of Gender and Desire* (New York: Routledge, 2002); Christine Bruckert, *Taking It Off, Putting It On: Women in the Strip Trade* (Toronto: Women's Press, 2002); R. Danielle Egan, *Dancing for Dollars and Paying for Love* (New York: Palgrave Macmillan, 2006); Bernadette Barton, *Stripped: Inside the Lives of Exotic Dancers* (New York: New York University Press, 2006); and Catherine M. Roach, *Stripping, Sex, and Popular Culture* (New York: Berg, 2007).

7. Hanna, "The Language of Dance," *JOPERD* 72, no. 4 (2001): 40–45, 53; Hanna, "Body Language and Learning: Insights for K–12 Education," in *Dance: Current Selected Research, Vol. 5*, ed. Lynnette Y. Overby and Billie Lepczyk (New York: AMS Press, 2005), 203–20.

8. Valerie Preston-Dunlop, compiler, *Dance Words* (Chur, Switzerland: Harwood Academic Publishers, 1995), 139.

9. See Anthony Shay and Barbara Sellers-Young, eds., *Belly Dance: Orientalism, Transnationalism, and Harem Fantasy*, Biblioteca Iranica: Performing Arts Series, 6 (Costa Mesa, Calif.: Mazda Publishers, 2005).

10. For a listing of such cases, see Hanna, "Adult Entertainment Exotic Dance: A Guide for Planners and Policy Makers" (CPL [Council of Planning Librarians] Bibliography 375), *Journal of Planning Literature* 20, no. 2 (2005): 116–34.

11. All three prongs of the definition must be satisfied for a work to be constitutionally obscene: 1) whether the average person, applying contemporary community standards, would find that the work, taken as a whole, appeals to the prurient interest; 2) whether the work depicts, or describes in a patently offensive way, sexual conduct specifically defined by the applicable state law; and 3) whether the work, taken as a whole, lacks serious literary, artistic, political, or scientific value.

12. Bryant Paul, Daniel Linz, and Bradley J. Shafer, "Government Regulation of Adult Businesses through Zoning and Anti-Nudity Ordinances: Debunking the Legal Myth of Negative Secondary Effects," *Communication Law and Policy* 6, no. 2 (2001): 355–91.

13. For example, Hanna, "Reality and Myth: What Neighbors Say about Exotic Dance Clubs: A Case Study on Charlotte, North Carolina," (Charlotte, N.C.: Tarheel Entertainment Association, 2001), submitted to the City of Charlotte Zoning Board; Roger Enriquez, Jeffrey Cancino, and Sean Varano, "A Legal and Empirical Perspective on Crime and Adult Establishments: A Secondary Effects Study in San Antonio, Texas," *American University Journal of Gender, Social Policy and the Law* 15, no. 1 (2006): 1–41; Jeffrey Cancino, "Assessing the Effects of Human Display Establishments on Property Values: An Empirical Study in San Antonio, Texas" (2004); Kenneth C. Land, Jay R. Williams, Michael E. Ezell, Bryant Paul, and Daniel Linz, "An Examination of the Assumption That Adult Businesses Are Associated with Crime in Surrounding Areas: A Secondary Effects Study in Charlotte, North Carolina," *Law and Society Review* 38, no. 1 (2004): 69–103; J. R. Greenwood, "A Public Health Analysis of Rancho Cordova," submitted to Rancho Cordova concerning its proposed adult business ordinance number 22-2004, 2004.

14. Hanna, "'Toxic' Strip Clubs: The Intersection of Religion, Law and Fantasy," and "Naked Truth: A Christian Right, Strip Clubs and Democracy" (under publication review).

15. See www.sbergthold@adultbusinesslaw.com.

16. See Paul Apostolidis, *Stations of the Cross: Adorno and Christian Right Radio* (Durham, N.C.: Duke University Press, 2000); Robert Atkins and Svetlana Mintcheva, *Censoring Culture: Contemporary Threats to Free Expression* (New York: New Press, 2006); Randall Balmer, *Thy Kingdom Come: How the Religious Right Distorts the Faith and Threatens America; An Evangelical's Lament* (New York: Perseus Books, 2006); Judy Brink and Joan Mencher, *Mixed Blessings: Gender and Religious Fundamentalism Cross Culturally* (New York: Routledge, 1997), Paula Cooey, *Religious Imagination and the Body: A Feminist Analysis* (New York: Oxford University Press, 1994); Catherine Crier, *Contempt: How the Right Is Wronging American Justice* (New York: Rugged Land Books, 2005); Marie R. Griffith, *Born Again Bodies: Flesh and Spirit in American Christianity* (Berkeley: University of California Press, 2004); Marci A. Hamilton, *God vs. the Gavel: Religion and the Rule of Law* (Cambridge and New York: Cambridge University Press, 2005); Susan Friend Harding, *The Book of Jerry Falwell: Fundamentalist Language and Politics* (Princeton, N.J.: Princeton University Press, 2000); Chris Hedges, *American Fascists: The Christian Right and the War on America* (New York: Simon & Schuster, 2006); Catherine Clark Kroeger and James R. Beck, eds., *Women, Abuse, and the Bible: How Scripture Can Be Used to Hurt or Heal* (Grand Rapids, Mich.: Baker Books, 1996); David Kuo, *Tempting Faith: An Inside Story of Political Seduction* (New York: Free Press, 2006); Tim LaHaye, *How to Be Happy Though Married* (Wheaton, Ill.: Tyndale House, 1963); Michael Lienesch, *Redeeming America: Piety and Politics in the New Christian Right* (Chapel Hill: University of North Carolina Press, 1993); Barbara A. McGraw, *Rediscovering America's Sacred Ground: Public Religion and Pursuit of the Good in a Pluralistic*

America (Albany: State University of New York Press, 2003); Brian Malley, *How the Bible Works: An Anthropological Study of Evangelical Biblicism* (Lanham, Md.: AltaMira Press, 2004); Catherine Margaret Miles, *Carnal Knowing: Female Nakedness and Religious Meaning in the Christian West* (Boston: Beacon, 1989); James Rudin, *The Baptizing of America: The Religious Right's Plans for the Rest of Us* (New York: Thunder Mouth's Press, 2006); and Elaine B. Sharp, *Morality Politics in American Cities* (Lawrence: University Press of Kansas, 2005).

17. See Marty Klein, *America's War on Sex: The Attack on Law, Lust and Liberty* (Westport, Conn.: Praeger, 2006) for numerous examples.

18. See Ann Wagner, *Adversaries of Dance: From the Puritans to the Present* (Urbana: University of Illinois Press, 1997). Also see Elizabeth Aldrich's article in this volume.

19. John Elsom, *Erotic Theatre* (New York: Taplinger, 1974); Ivor Forbes Guest, *The Romantic Ballet in Paris* (Middletown, Conn.: Wesleyan University Press, 1966); Parmenia Migel, *The Ballerinas: From the Court of Louis XIV to Pavlova* (New York: Macmillan, 1972); Lynn Matluck Brooks, ed., *Women's Work: Making Dance in Europe before 1800* (Madison: University of Wisconsin Press, 2007).

20. Jeff Pollard, *Christian Modesty and the Public Undressing of America* (San Antonio, Tex.: Vision Forum, 2004); see Jim C. Cunningham, *Nudity & Christianity* (Bloomington, Ind.: AuthorHouse, 2006), on the historical and geographical contexts of modesty and various biblical interpretations of nudity.

21. Tim LaHaye, *How to Be Happy Though Married* (Wheaton, Ill: Tyndale House, 1963).

22. Several of the many organizations that have leaders who speak out against exotic dance are: American Decency Association, American Family Association, Americans United to Preserve Marriage & American Values (formerly Family Research Council), Child Welfare Foundation, Christian Broadcasting Network, Citizens for Community Values, Concerned Women for America, Concerned Women for America's Culture and Family Institute, Coral Ridge Ministries, Eagle Forum, Family Research Council, Florida Family Association, Focus on the Family, Free Congress Foundation, National Association of Evangelicals, National Center for Law and Families, National Empowerment Television, Southern Baptist Convention, Traditional Values Coalition, and Wall Builders.

23. Hanna, "Empowerment: The Art of Seduction in Adult Entertainment Exotic Dance," in *Music, Dance and the Art of Seduction*, ed. Frank Kouwenhoven and James Kippen (Leiden, the Netherlands: Chime, 2008).

24. I identified these tactics during thirteen years of field research across the country, conducting interviews with dancers, club management, patrons, community members, government representatives; reading letters from strangers who wanted to share their stories with me; observing behavior; watching television; and reading newspapers and reports on several listservs, websites, and chatrooms dealing with sexuality in society, adult entertainment, Christianity, and civil liberties.

25. Hanna, "Review of Eric Damian Kelly and Connie Cooper, *Everything You Always Wanted to Know About Regulating Sex Businesses*," *Journal of Planning Literature* 17, no. 3 (2003): 393–94.

26. Linda Kintz, *Between Jesus and the Market: The Emotions That Matter in Right-Wing America* (Durham, N.C.: Duke University Press, 1997).

27. Len Munsil, *The Preparation and Trial of an Obscenity Case: A Guide for the Prosecuting Attorney* and *How to Legally Stop Nude Dancing in your Community* (Scottsdale, Ariz.: National Family Legal Foundation, 1988; 1994).

28. U.S. Attorney General John Ashcroft used the Patriot Act to enter the fray in "Operation G-String." Attorney General Alberto Gonzalez made war on pornography (exotic dance is erroneously placed in this category) a top priority of his office. One FBI agent anonymously said, "I guess this means we've won the war on terror. We must not need any more resources for espionage." See Barton Gellman, "Recruits Sought for Porn Squad," *Washington Post*, September 20, 2005, A21.

29. R. A. Baron, "Sexual Arousal and Physical Aggression: The Inhibiting Influence of 'Cheesecake' and Nudes," *Bulletin of the Psychonomic Society* 3 (1974): 337–39. The criminal justice system has no evidence of a correlation between watching exotic dance and raping women.

30. "Strip Club Vandals Return," *Indianapolis Star*, October 10, 2001.

31. In addition to Dance USA, Alley Theatre, Association of Performing Arts Presenters, Kathleen Chalfant, Tony Kushner, The Looking Glass Theatre Company, Terrence McNally, Oregon Shakespeare Company, Yvonne Rainer, Rachel Rosenthal, Theater Artaud, Theatre Communications Group, and the Walker Art Center also contributed to an amicus brief to the U.S. Supreme Court in *City of Erie v. Pap's A.M.*

32. This paper has focused on female dancers who perform for men and also for women, who are increasingly attending exotic dance clubs. Some clubs may have an occasional night featuring male dancers and there are a few clubs that cater to women patrons and put on all-male shows. Exotic dance regulations apply to both female and male dancers, and litigation in a 2006 case in Prince Georges County, Maryland, included clubs featuring female dancers and a club featuring male dancers.

33. Hanna, "Ballet to Exotic Dance—Under the Censorship Watch," in *Dancing in the Millennium: An International Conference; Proceedings*, Juliette Crone-Willis and Janice LaPointe-Crump, compilers (Washington, D.C.: 2000), 230–34; "Dance under the Censorship Watch," *Journal of Arts Management Law and Society* 29, no. 1 (2002): 1–13.

34. Adolf Hitler, *Mein Kampf* [My Struggle] (New York: Houghton Mifflin, 1943), 254–55.

35. World Pornography Conference, Center for Sex Research at California State University, Northridge, 1998.

The Hidden Authoritarian Roots
in Western Concert Dance

Robin Lakes

*O*ne of the great puzzles within the western concert dance world is why so many artists who create revolutionary works onstage conduct their classes and rehearsals as demagogues. Such teachers are engaged in teaching practices that replicate and reproduce in the dance studio the very power relationships they are often critiquing as unjust and inhumane in their artwork onstage. The artist-educators examined in this essay, a significant number of whom favored humanistic themes and dances with a social conscience, created some of the most exquisite choreographic works of the twentieth century. In the quest for brilliance, which was attained by the artists discussed in this essay, something has gone amiss in the daily treatment of the very dancers who contribute to making the artistic product brilliant.

Grover Dale, a former dancer and codirector with choreographer Jerome Robbins, highlights the incongruities. "Robbins's demands on dancers were common knowledge. For an artist who built entire works on 'the futility of intolerance,' he had plenty of his own to work on."[1] Dorothy Bird, an early Martha Graham Group dancer, recounts how, in 1935, an outside evaluator for a funding organization advised against financial support for the Martha Graham company on the grounds that

> her methods were in direct opposition to his strongly held convictions con-
> cerning democracy, women's rights, and human dignity. He was startled

---

This article is adapted from a more extensive piece, "The Messages behind the Methods: The Authoritarian Pedagogical Legacy in Western Concert Dance Technique Training and Rehearsals," published in *Arts Education Policy Review* 106, no. 5 (May/June 2005): 3–18.

by Martha's relationship with the members of her group, concluding that she not only ignored many people's individual rights but actually trampled on them. . . . He felt strongly that whether people worked in a factory or a mine or in the arts, . . . they should be treated with dignity and consideration. His conclusion was that he could have awarded the money to Martha on artistic merits, but hers was not a democratic organization. He went so far as to say that some members were treated as if they were slaves.[2]

The striking irony exists that authoritarian teaching methods are often utilized as a means toward the end of creating and teaching anti-authoritarian concert dances. Why is it that the onstage visions of anti-authoritarianism and social justice do not translate into reforming educational practices in the dance studio? What are the roots of the authoritarian pedagogical heritage in the concert dance world? The political, ethical, and psychological climate of the classroom affects dancers' educational and artistic processes and products. A contradiction exists between the liberating power that an arts education can provide and the continuing history of authoritarian teaching modes in this field. Although dancers have long shared whispered dressing-room complaints about authoritarian dance teacher behaviors, this "secret" of the western concert dance world could benefit from being more fully "outed" or unmasked to analyze its dangers, examine its authoritarian roots, and point the way toward reform.[3] The lay public may be amazed at the horrors inflicted in the name of dance, an art form that many associate with freedom, expressivity, passion, and abandon. Although a myriad of other subject matters now reveal the application of and yielding to the reformation of pedagogical thought, dance technique classes and rehearsals seem to remain one of the last holdouts or bastions for counterproductive teaching ideologies passed on and preserved from earlier eras.

The enabling or collusion that has sometimes allowed the thriving of teaching behaviors deemed in this essay as "abusive" is a defensive posture, perhaps tied to the fragile threads on which the concert dance world survives in many western cultures. It is almost as if there is a veneer of protectiveness within the subculture of dance that does not want fully to yield to the historical evolution of education and its current critical pedagogical analyses. Perhaps in an art form so steeped in respect for one's elders, there is hesitancy about so bluntly questioning their teaching behaviors, as if such an act would undermine one's heritage.

A thorough investigation of teaching in the world of postmodern dance technique and rehearsals is beyond the scope of this article.[4] What this study does reveal, however, is information about the heritage of teaching methods that is passed down in the dance field, about the philosophies behind this pedagogical heritage, and about the possibilities for incorporating elements of twentieth-century progressive educational thought into dance studio classes and rehearsals.

The journey that led to this investigation can be traced to a series of conferences held within recent years.[5] I noticed that a number of questions occasionally recurred at these professional educational meetings. What can dance teachers and administrators do about emotional or physical abuse that they witness in the dance technique classes or rehearsals going on in their studios or departments? How can one intervene with colleagues or "master" teachers to protect one's students from this problematic treatment? Will tyrannical teaching methods simply die out when a whole generation retires? If not, why are authoritarian teaching practices still perpetuated by some members of the new generation of postmodern choreographer-teachers?

To expose and investigate the roots of this disturbing pedagogical heritage and the philosophies that underpin it, a definition and exposition of authoritarian or destructive dance teaching behaviors are first offered. Next, an overview of how the dance community has habitually responded is presented. Finally, theories that can begin to explain the roots of this pedagogical legacy are offered. This unmasking of prevalent dance teaching philosophies and practices can, I hope, pave the way for healthier, more humane learning environments for dance students and professional dancers.

DEFINING AND EXPOSING
AUTHORITARIANISM IN DANCE CLASSES

The authoritarian personality structure harbors such characteristics as low opinion of human nature, punitiveness, fatalism, contempt for the weak, cynicism, aggression, an ironic submission to authority, intolerance for ambiguity, and projection, ascribing to another person attitudes present in oneself.[6]

Specific authoritarian teaching behaviors evidenced in dance technique classes and rehearsals range over many kinds. They can include rote imitation and repetition over time with unchanging verbal prompts from the teacher. They can escalate to humiliation of students for making errors, screaming, sarcasm, mocking, belittlement, barbed humor, and bullying. Questions are often dismissed or squelched and the questioners demeaned. Some teachers exhibit preoccupation with arbitrary behavioral control, engage in unfair or negative comparisons to other students, encourage rivalries, refer to adult students as "girls" and "boys," and use other forms of infantilization or patronization. Others employ inappropriate personal attributions not based on fact, or comments that violate privacy codes, including some shaming or denigrating comments about students' weight, build, or body type. Then there is the alternative of silence or withholding of feedback and responses or, at the least, giving only backhanded compliments. Teachers exhibit frustration and impatience if there is not immediate and continued mastery of the material presented; some ignore certain students, or storm out of the room in an exasperated rage out of disappointment or anger. Some even engage in physical abuse in the form of hitting, slapping, or punching body parts with a hand or a stick. Both physical actions and verbal attributions that seek to render the student powerless are often delivered in a demeaning fashion.

These messages can be transmitted to dance students through direct verbal language, adjunct verbal asides, and tone of voice, or through unspoken forms such as the use of silence, eye movements, and eye contact (or lack thereof). They can be transmitted through body language, as in particular kinds of posture or gesture. They can also be conveyed through the choice of classroom activities.

In rephrasing Marshall McLuhan's adage that "the medium is the message," Paul Grosswiler used "the method is the message" as a phrase in a book title.[7] In applying his concept to the realm of pedagogy, one sees that *how* a subject matter is conveyed can be more powerful than its *what*—the content. In fact, the method actually becomes part of the content of the class, and a class or rehearsal's form can convey as much as, if not more than, its content. When dance technique is taught, much more is going on in the room than just the passing on of the subject at hand. There are actually two subject matters in the classroom. Unconsciously or not, ideas about many other aspects of life, including power, gender, and equity—and about how the teacher believes learning takes place—are being conveyed in that room. No matter how liberating the subject matter may be, it can be undermined by oppressive ways of working in the classroom. Teaching behaviors and methods of the teacher teach a set of rules, beliefs, and ideologies as powerfully as does the curriculum, the syllabus, or the lesson plan.

Examples abound that make concrete some of the preceding definitions of authoritarian dance teaching.[8] What follows are brief descriptions of teaching by so-called master teachers or dancers who have worked with them followed by a deconstruction of some of the meanings embedded in their statements.

"He slashed people to pieces. Once he called someone a half-wit, but the following day he apologized, saying, 'I was wrong. You have no brain at all.' People were always hysterical crying. Sometimes they could leap from there and make progress. Other times it just destroyed them," former American Ballet Theatre dancer Enrique Martinez remarked on rehearsing with choreographer Antony Tudor.[9] The encoded or embedded pedagogical message is that the teacher can cause improvements in learning to occur by conveying to a student that he or she is unintelligent. A student who thinks he or she is stupid will learn better. Making students cry and think that they are stupid is a useful teaching approach.

Some teachers "pierce the student with the barb of self-doubt that can remain with them for the rest of their life," choreographer, teacher, and author Daniel Nagrin has said when discussing factors that potentially erode the dancer's state of mind during a performance.[10] The encoded pedagogical message is that teachers are very powerful. Their judgments can become part of a student's self-conception. Consider the following passage:

> Paul, what are you doing? I said get off [the stage]! You have had plenty of opportunities to learn the back fall on one. Even beginners know the back fall on one. Do you expect me, me, to give you special coaching on the back fall on one? Oh no, sweetie pie, you are a big boy now. I am not your mother![11]

So recalls Paul Taylor on rehearsing with Martha Graham as a member of the Martha Graham Dance Company. The encoded or embedded pedagogical message seems to be that mistakes or errors are not permissible. Trial and error elimination is disallowed as a learning mode. All learners should learn at the same rate. Perhaps the teacher thinks that labeling an adult student as a child will improve his or her learning abilities, or will shame the learner into working harder.

An example of the passing on of this pedagogical heritage follows, as when Taylor himself reflects:

> I usually don't yell, but I can become terribly threatening. I've actually hit dancers. I've bitten little fingers that stuck out too much. I've slapped wrists. I've threatened to throw people out of the window. People don't usually learn unless there's a little pain involved.
>
> When a new dancer joins the group, he feels he has to prove himself; he's somewhat insecure. So I sometimes intentionally see what a little stress and strain will do to him, at what point he's going to break; naturally each one is different. Dancers are like animals that you train. While you don't usually do it by bullying them, you don't necessarily do it by giving them little yummies, either.[12]

Here, the embedded pedagogical messages are that the teacher produces pain in the classroom so that learning will occur and that testing an insecure student to ascertain his breaking point is a useful teaching and learning tool for some unspoken end goal that the teacher has in mind. Dance students are similar to pets.

Taylor also says of his role as artistic director: "My role as surrogate father, as I begin to see it, is to help dancers through the company, molding them, not only to a special stage style but to an offstage one."[13] The encoded pedagogical message is that the teacher reigns in all aspects of a student's life. The teacher has preset molds into which he or she plans to encase the student.

Wilma Curley, long-time rehearsal assistant to Robbins, "recalled that he deliberately terrorized the dancers in the company, except for the chosen few he favored. 'Jerry would say, "They're scared shitless of me," and then he'd laugh. He did it on purpose, and he got what he wanted out of those people.'"[14] The embedded pedagogical message is that purposeful humiliation is a good teaching tool. The ends justify the means. In addition, the enjoyment of practicing intimidation is acceptable behavior on the part of a teacher. James Moore, a dancer in several of Robbins' works, recalls:

> I remember talking to him about the way he would act during rehearsal, how vicious he could be . . . and he said "You know, when I'm working, all I can see is the work, for everything else I have blinders on." Anything else was a distraction, so he just cut or lashed out at anything disturbing him or getting in his way.[15]

The embedded pedagogical message is that it is acceptable to view dancers as the raw material in dance, similar to inanimate paint. When dancers are being utilized for an artistic vision, their thoughts and feelings do not matter. Dancers' thoughts and feelings are a distraction to the artistic process of the teacher.

Cynthia Gregory, former star of the American Ballet Theatre, says the following about rehearsing with Tudor: "I was scared to death of Tudor. He was kind of a scary person. I would work with him, and he would humiliate me. I would cry. It was difficult. . . . But Tudor liked to torture you. He would look at you and immediately know your weak spots."[16] The encoded pedagogical message is that the teacher knows all and sees all. The teacher identifies weaknesses in the student and reveals them publicly to the student in cruel ways. Errors on the part of students are best corrected via humiliation. Regularly causing students to cry is an acceptable activity in a learning environment.[17]

The stories continue, with one by dance critic Deborah Jowitt who recalls being in class at the Juilliard School of Music's Dance Department:

> Among my earliest memories of Anna Sokolow is that she threw a chair at me. Well, toward me. And others. I still feel the shock in the pit of my stomach. . . . She wanted us to rush toward the front of the stage and stop at the very edge. . . . We couldn't get it right . . . so she yelled "GO!" and,

as we tore forward, she hurled the chair at us. . . . The chair didn't actually touch anyone, but it hit all of us, I think, in some very deep place. Once anger and shock subsided, we realized that her need to see bodies molded every second by passion and commitment transcended the polite transactions we were used to at rehearsals. (Anna was invited to join the Juilliard faculty the next spring.)[18]

Here, physical abuse of students is used to make a teaching point. Violent activities in the classroom replicate in real life the emotional or kinesthetic response that the teacher seeks to elicit from the student. This behavior is promoted by those in authority.

Indeed, through collusion or avoidance, leaders of dance education organizations often do not see the behavior described above as problematic. In fact, these behaviors receive a stamp of approval when the teacher is rewarded with a promotion. Many leaders do not seem to regard it as their role to protect students from emotionally unsafe environments in the dance studio. Rather, they seem to follow Graham who, according to biographer Don McDonagh, once "remarked coolly to her rehearsal pianist Robert Dunn, 'I never destroyed anyone who didn't want to be destroyed.'"[19]

EXAMINING HOW THE DANCE COMMUNITY RESPONDS

To the dance insider, these teacher behaviors will not shock or surprise. Often, they are seen as "going with the territory" of dance training and rehearsals. Though progressive university educators such as Margaret H'Doubler and, later, her student Alma Hawkins (both strongly influenced by the ideas of John Dewey[20]) put forth humanistic dance education agendas starting in the 1920s,[21] their approaches were, even in most university settings, largely bypassed in favor of the dance training methods cultivated by teachers in professional dance studio settings. What is the dancer to do in the face of authoritarian regimes in the dance classroom and rehearsal space? Although the current era begins to yield the possibilities of reform, earlier responses to charges of authoritarianism, as well as some disturbing current writing, reveal how deeply entrenched the pedagogy is.

One line of thought suggests that the dancer view teacher abuse as a compliment—that it is an honor to be attacked. The student learns to love the attention, even if it is negative attention. The perceived gift to the student of the "master" teacher's brilliance justifies the teacher's behavior. Platitudes and pardons are offered up in an attempt to correlate artistic genius with the right to be a tyrant in the studio. The student should buck up and tough it out through these rites of passage. The composer John Kander, who "witnessed the extremes of [Jerome] Robbins's behavior over time," said, "I think there was at least for a period a kind of mythologizing of that kind of behavior—well that's called 'artistic temperament.'"[22] Janet Soares, former teaching assistant to dance composition teacher Louis Horst, adds, "Being 'taken over the coals' by Horst had become the imperative first step for every modern dancer."[23]

Furthering this perspective, the author of an article in *Contact Quarterly* cherishes a memory of the "honor" of physical abuse while recounting her experiences as a fourteen-year-old taking the Martha Graham School's June course in 1952. "I could not bring enough power to the movement. I was just going through the motions. I failed to connect with the source. Martha crouched in front of me . . . 'I'm going to slap your face,' she said. The right side of my face exploded and I fell away from it to the left, spiral and contraction doing their work for real. . . . I was surprised and shaken, a little embarrassed, somewhat gratified to be singled out. But the important thing was that she had given me her movement. I now possessed a tiny bit of Martha. . . . It was the slap that gave me Martha unmediated. . . . [I] received the gift of Martha's sacred self."[24]

Other justifications for such treatment abound. To make light of cruelty and avoid the responsibility of naming verbal abuse, a dance writer can describe it as Tudor's "wicked tongue" and "rapier-sharp barbs."[25] The justification of expediency is also put forth. "Many choreographers get the reputation for being bastards. When one is fighting for his life, when one is drowning, he forgets his manners; he hasn't time to cut his nails," writes Murray Louis.[26] Finally, in some cases, the results are seen as all that matter. "The only real basis for judging a teacher is the product he or she turns out: good dancers," asserts Melissa Hayden, former New York City Ballet principal dancer.[27]

Members of the dance world can also blame the messenger for revelations about authoritarian teacher behavior. Gelsey Kirkland's autobiography (1986), in which she critiques abusive and authoritarian teacher behaviors within the New York City Ballet as well as unveils safety and health issues within the company, provoked attacks from a number of dance critics. Attempts to dismiss her on the grounds that she was overly sensitive appeared, as well as implications that she was making it all up. "She is so abristle with hypersensitive antennae attuned to hostile vibes real or imagined," wrote Harris Green.[28] In another attempt to discount the content of her revelations, the writer Ruthanna Boris described Kirkland's personality as "angry and willful" and geared toward launching a "vendetta catharsis."[29] A third dance writer, Tobi Tobias, implied that Kirkland is not really that bright and mocked her for her critiques. "The catalogue of woes continues inexorably. . . . [Artistic

Director George] Balanchine fails to understand her as the lyrical, dramatic, *thinking* artist she dreams of being."[30]

Kirkland was also accused of being ungrateful to Balanchine by two writers who seemingly could not separate their love for Balanchine's work from her critiques of his methods. "There were, of course, unpleasant facets to the man's personality. He was not always a 'nice person.' . . . But what do such gullies matter on the verdant terrain of his achievement?" asks Green.[31] Critic David Vaughan says Kirkland was "always willful and rebellious, even at the ballet school" and criticizes her for rejecting Balanchine's "modernist aesthetic."[32] Perhaps in their minds, her revelations threatened his status as a choreographer. She was not critiquing Balanchine's construction of dances, however. John Percival more accurately reads the educational politics behind Kirkland's writing:

> She upset her teachers by wanting to know why ballet pupils are supposed to shut up and do as they are told (but then we expect them to dance intelligently!) . . . The reaction of the American ballet establishment has been to gang up against her . . . . Her real crime, I feel, is that she dared suggest Balanchine was human, when everyone knows he was really a god. One day the serious questions Kirkland raises about the teaching of ballet and the running of ballet companies will have to be faced . . . . Why not now?[33]

Some advisors suggest finding another teacher if the dance student cannot "take it." "Some of the best learning is being taught by some of the worst, nastiest people in the world. Some people weather it and some people don't. . . . If you are being brutalized and you can't stand it and you can't learn, go someplace else," Nagrin suggests.[34] Such advice assumes that all dancers have someplace else to go.

A spate of dance advice books has been written in the spirit of survival guides, with the onus put on the students to cope in a harsh environment, not on the profession of dance teaching to change. Coping mechanisms, including psychological and behavior modification techniques, are advised as necessary to succeed.[35] The message is that student behavior, not pedagogical practice, will have to yield to change in this unreformable world. "Take responsibility for the conditions of your work," dancers are urged in advice on "eight ways to take charge."[36]

In a new spirit of optimism Jowitt has written, "We hope to ascertain without doubt—and spread the word—that sane and humane practices in the classroom, rehearsal hall, and the day-to-day functioning of dance companies are not antithetical to artistic excellence, but in fact promote it."[37] However, while the academic dance literature since the late 1980s is filled with calls for both curricular reconceptualization and a reexamination of teaching methods, recent mass-market dance publications reveal the authoritarian teaching tradition to be an ongoing problem. In advice columns for young dancers, the continuing harsh realities in the studio are exposed. In *Dance Magazine*, a student signing her letter "Trapped" writes,

> I feel like a wimp complaining about my mean teacher. The problem is that if she doesn't stop picking on me soon, I think I'm headed for an emotional breakdown. Every class she behaves the same way, using name-calling, shoving, and humiliation whenever a few of us dancers make a mistake.[38]

In the response to "Trapped" as well as in suggestions offered to students in a similar recent periodical, the columnists advise "talk to the director"[39] and "if the teacher's cruelty is habitual behavior, it should be reported to the administration immediately."[40] The advice to dancers now seems to have evolved from coping to empowerment. Nevertheless, what protection do young people have if the administration has no background in pedagogical reform on which to draw in making employment decisions or in offering professional development workshops for its teachers?

GETTING AT THE POSSIBLE ROOTS OF THE ONGOING PEDAGOGICAL PROBLEM

Without examination of their underpinnings, destructive teaching behaviors are fated to be perpetuated and continually replicated in the dance field. The teacher carries within him- or herself unexamined agendas and points of view, or masked awareness of what exactly is guiding his or her conduct and choices as a teacher. Tracing these roots does not justify authoritarianism in dance pedagogy but rather suggests the ideological allegiances that allow its perpetuation. Ten ideologies are briefly presented here as explanations for what may be guiding authoritarian pedagogical choices.

Culturally Derived Metaphors for Education

The politics of the classroom are reflected in part by the metaphors used to explain education in western European thought. Educational philosopher Henry Perkinson traces the metaphors through time as follows.[41] The Greeks construed education as initiation for the aristocracy into the valued culture of the time. The teacher was viewed as a guide into this culture. The role of the student was to be trained to gain entry into the culture. Seventeenth-century pedagogy constructed education as the inculcation of a predetermined body of knowledge. The teacher's role was to transmit and cause learning to occur. The student was viewed as a passive receptor. Metaphors for students such as blank slates, empty vessels, and balls of wax emanate from this era.

Beginning in the twentieth century, the purpose of education gradually began to be viewed as human growth. The teacher has increasingly been seen as a facilitator of experiences that promote growth, since growth cannot be imposed. The student is viewed as an autonomous agent who solves problems. In addition, all learners are seen as fallible, needing to perform trial-and-error experiments for learning to occur. As children, early to mid-twentieth-century dance innovators would have been products of either the first or second eras in western European pedagogy and, as unreflective teachers, many continued to replicate the teaching models imprinted from their youth.

Culturally Derived Metaphors about the Body

Metaphors for teaching and learning about movement and the body are harbored within the teacher's mental constructs. These often masked or unexamined images underpin the teacher's ideology and become pedagogical guides for the teaching choices that are made in the classroom. Laban educator Carol Lynn Moore's brilliant analysis of body metaphors, as interpreted by writer Judith A. Gray, reminds us that the teacher's symbolic projection of metaphoric views of the body—how the teacher views the body—colors all his or her pedagogical choices and defines the power relationships constructed between teacher and student.[42]

Moore's theories prompt the following questions: Is the body viewed as a lazy and willful beast of burden that needs to be broken and whipped into shape in order to perform its assigned tasks? Is the body seen as a well-oiled machine constructed to produce preset molds, operated efficiently by a neutral technician for exact duplication in production, and capable of mechanistic motion without emotion? Is the body a visually beautiful, sculptural external object of art, as defined by the teacher who uses the iconic forms of modeling and posing of her own body as the teaching mode? Is the body viewed as a free, unfettered child—imprinted with a "naturalness" that resists cultural codes, imprints, and conventions?

Is the body regarded as a lump of clay waiting to be imprinted by the teacher as sculptor? In the western visual arts, the raw materials do not need supportiveness; they don't need emotional responsiveness. The creator does not need a psychological relationship with her inanimate materials. Is the body seen as a computer into which can be fed all necessary data, which can then be stored and accessed at will in exactly replicated, errorless form when prompted by the "programmer" (the teacher)? In dance, all these metaphors diminish the totality and complexity of the human learner, whose learning process results from the interplay of affective, cognitive, social, and sensory/kinesthetic stimuli.

The Guru

Given the often embattled status of innovative concert dance in the early and mid-twentieth century, as well as the aesthetic drive among its creators to explore their own idiosyncratic movement vocabularies, artistic innovators needed fervent dancers who would sacrifice for the cause and who could function as true believers in an ideal, upholders of an aesthetic dogma, pure interpreters, and proselytizers. Common usage of words such as *goddess*, *high priestess* or *priest*, or *master* in the dance literature reinforces the acceptance of worship of choreographers and teachers in the mindset of the dance world. Certainly there are positive and negative associations with the concept of a guru.

In its positive form, associations arise regarding respect for a wise elder, a visionary leader, a guide. The term *guru* becomes highly problematic, however, when the master teacher consciously cultivates and imposes idolatry from the students, an unfortunate reality within the pedagogical heritage of dance training. "You don't know how you are doing. Only I know how you are doing. You don't know how you are doing."[43] These words, by a former Martha Graham company lead dancer speaking to her students in a recent technique class, assert that the teacher is infallible, all-knowing, and all-seeing. The teacher is not interested in cultivating the students' abilities to self-assess or self-correct and become their own teachers. The teacher wants the students to remain dependent on her judgments.

Louis Falco, former member of the José Limón Dance Company, offers this experience:

> I grew up in a modern dance world where choreographers were gods and dancers were subservient expressions of a particular philosophy or school of thought. Years back, if you danced with one company and took a class with another company, you were a traitor. You were married to those people. It all came out of insecurity and fear, an angry, tight feeling among the whole scene that always distressed me and alienated me on a certain level. When I was dancing with José [Limón] up at Connecticut College and I'd have an hour or two free, I'd go take a Graham class or Cunningham class. He would see that and get very angry, but to me it was absurd because I had made a major commitment to him.[44]

Sadistic Behavior

For some, the "how" of teaching incorporates unquestioned brutality. Stuart Hodes, former dancer in the Martha Graham Dance Company, recounts a disturbing classroom experience: "She [Graham] was testing me. She raked her nails down the front of my chest to get me to contract more. She raked her nails across my inner thighs to get me to turn my legs out more. Later, when I was sitting on the floor in second position, she saw the marks her nails left on my thighs and said, 'I wonder what your girlfriend will think of that?'"[45]

Here, the teacher is using physical abuse to make a teaching point. Metaphorically, she is also branding the student, leaving her mark, in a display of power and ownership. In addition, the teacher considers it her right to pry into the student's private life, seeming to set up a competition between the student's allegiance to the teacher and his commitment to a significant other.

Child-Rearing and Ambivalence about the Gifted Child

In the dance world, the legacy of infantilization of dancers, continuing long after they become adults, contributes to the perpetuation of ongoing parental relationships in the dance classroom. The power dynamics are colored by how the teacher views children and their motives.

Author Joseph Mazzo makes this connection. "Both [Jerome Robbins and George Balanchine] appear to work by the dancers-are-difficult-children system and neither is a permissive parent."[46] Some of this resonates with historical tracts about rearing a gifted child.[47] The adult must make sure that the talented youth reaches her moral development because of having talent. On the other hand, the gifted child needs punishment so that he or she does not get too inflated. Elements of resentment and competition can be heightened when parenting a gifted child. Because of assuming evil intentions on the part of the child, the parent fears that the child will overtake the status of the parents. This distrust of children and the attendant belief that they are up to no good becomes the justification for physical and emotional abuse. The adult brings the child down a few notches to maintain the hierarchy. By switching the words *parent* to *teacher* and *child* to *student* above, insights into the complex power dynamics of the dance studio are highlighted.

Survival of the Fittest

Leaving aside the widespread issue of the Darwinian selection of body types in the dance world, another insidious form of "survival of the fittest" exists there. By buying into a kind of Social Darwinism that prizes emotional toughness, some technique classes and rehearsals have as a partial purpose to toughen up the dancer. They become a rite of passage, a trial by fire, to see if the dancer fits in. If the dancer can survive this, he or she can survive the dance world. To utilize this method as an evolutionary way to whittle down the number of participants in the dance field, however, seems unnecessary as well as inhumane.

The following exchange between Louis Horst and Evelyn Lohoefer, a student in his music composition classes, exemplifies this ideology. Once, Horst screamed at her, "'God damn it, when I tell you to do something, don't sit there and refuse to do it!'" Lohoefer recounts. She then got up to leave class. "He [Horst] walked over to me and kind of pushed me on the shoulder and said, 'Humph! You have got guts.' . . . He never gave me a bad time again. What he really wanted was simple reversal. The only thing that saved me was that I got mad. For him it meant, 'OK. You can stand up to me, and maybe you'll make it.'"[48] Thus, an atmosphere is created whereby the most sensitive souls (the ones who can't "take it") may exit the field, leaving only the least sensitive artists to stay in the dance world. The irony of this as a desired characteristic for an arts profession is striking. It is as though there is a correlation between being able to withstand cruel and unusual punishment and artistic excellence.

Militaristic Pedagogy

That German and Swiss gymnastic training is part of the heritage of American concert dance is well established. The pedagogy that accompanies this subject matter resembles military teaching ideology because gymnastics grew out of a form of military training. Military "drills" set the pedagogical model that became transposed onto American physical education and later influenced the teaching practices of concert dance. Like basic training in the military, the dance teacher may have as a goal to break the student down in order to build her up in a new image or to fit her into a predetermined mold.

Anne Green Gilbert, artistic director of Creative Dance Center and Kaleidoscope Dance Company in Seattle, describes characteristics of the learning environments during her dance training from 1959–1973 that suggest parallels to militaristic sports pedagogy:

> Most of my teachers, except for two, even through college, were only concerned with the physical side of dance. . . . They taught in a rote way. "Do as I do and do it NOW!" We could not communicate with our peers and we stood around in our self space or waiting in lines. There was little reflection, . . . just steps (imitate the teacher and good luck!). If you did not understand corrections, that was too bad. No one tried to say it another way or show a picture or provide a skeleton or suggest books to read.[49]

The cultivation of self-discipline, obedience to law and command, subordination of the individual, and distrust of instincts arose as meanings embedded in a gymnastics pedagogy manual from the late 1800s as examined by Jowitt.[50] Dance technique and rehearsal teaching can be viewed in a similar light by observing the dualism inherent in dance classes wherein assertive, sensual, or abandoned movement is offered up via militaristic teaching modes.

Traditional Vocational Education Training Concepts

The arts entered the realm of vocational education curricula through the doorway of crafts training derived from the European guild system of training artisans and craftsmen. Performing arts high schools later found a niche and a justification in school systems as specialty vocational education high schools. The allegiance of some segments of the dance field to a vocational education model is problematic because of the teaching ideology embedded within the vocational heritage.

As early as 1913, progressive educators such as John Dewey, who defined education as growth, opposed the creation of separate vocational schools within a statewide school system on the grounds that school curriculums should integrate both academic and practical learning.[51] This integrated model, he believed, produces a "socially meaningful educational environment," promotes democracy, and creates a mobile society that lessens stratification by economic class privileges.[52]

The limitations of vocationalism in the schools is further revealed by examining characteristics of vocational education pedagogy, including the following: a "pragmatic construction of schooling";[53] a narrowly defined set of goals and skills; utilitarian view of the subject matter that focuses on product-oriented teaching and learning modes; the replication by the apprentice of the behavior modeled by the master; the acknowledgment by the student that the master knows all the acceptable ways to perform the skill; trust that the master knows the underlying reasons for his way of performing the skill; and the inculcation of moral virtues such as "industry, perseverance, and thrift."[54]

The limitations of this ideology when applied to an education in the performing arts seem evident. A "master" teacher implies a master at the craft, not necessarily a master at teaching the craft. Therefore, the best learning environment is not ensured. Additionally, dance teachers who embrace a vision for dance training as vocationalism may unwittingly transpose craft guild models onto a subject matter that does not thrive on such an approach. Defining technique and rehearsals as existing in the realm of practical and utilitarian skill-based training misses the complexity of the subject matter and the ultimate goal of what an artist needs. Dancing and performing combine creativity, athleticism, scientific knowledge, multiple forms of intelligence, multisensory perception, musical intelligence, and affective and cognitive responses.

Traditional Acting Technique Training

That early and middle generations of contemporary dance pioneers had exposure to Stanislavski-based acting methods has been widely established. However, some teachers applied the methods to dance with an odd skewing or a misapplication of the approach. One can only surmise that this may be due to an incomplete understanding or to their replication of acting teachers or directors who taught via this tyrannical pedagogy.

In these cases, the teacher's view of his role goes beyond simply coaching students toward sense or emotional memories or empathic, imaginative identification with another to create lived circumstances. The twist on the Stanislavski Method occurs when the teacher/artist creates circumstances in the classroom to elicit his version of emotional truth. Students' memories thus become imposed by the teacher, not self-selected by the student. Instead of teaching students tools for accessing emotion, the teacher, in his impatience for "results" and his self-appointed role as manipulator, imposes emotionally volatile classroom experiences on the students. The creation of incidents in the classroom then becomes the source material for later emotional recall.

An example is found in an interview with dancer Ze'eva Cohen, who talked of Sokolow and her tendency for harsh verbal criticism

> and physical abuse. . . . One, she stereotyped people. If you came from a middle-class well-to-do family, or if you were blonde, you were out. Immediately. . . . She was a total autocrat. . . . She had no patience so she would look at a person and if they were blonde or if they were pink-skinned. . . . She would just look at them and say, "Have you ever suffered in your life?" . . . I've seen her once, I think I've seen her saying, "Now you will," and going to tear the shirt off their back, or begin to bang on their back with her fists.[55]

Here, the suggestion is that the mentor has the power and the right to make judgments about the students' memories and to deem them as unable to be accessed except by her physical attacks. The teacher is allowed to degrade the student as a teaching activity to make up for the student not having suffered, by the teacher's standards, in real life. The implication is that a teacher is justified in causing suffering to occur in the classroom so that a dancer can replicate that suffering onstage and that quick theatrical results are possible by imposing stress on students. The approach is pedagogically dangerous because it is based on an artificially induced mode of producing emotion in students derived from manipulative abuse by an authority figure.

Lack of Self-Definition or Denial of Self as 'Teacher'

Once, Balanchine declared, "I never 'became a teacher'; no, I am a person who teaches. Bad dancers 'become teachers.'"[56] Regardless of the number of waking hours a choreographer may spend teaching, some artists exhibit a lack of respect or understanding for all that the education profession encompasses and a desire to withhold self-identification with that occupation, perhaps viewing it as lower on the career rung. Teaching is thus viewed as a default profession and the act of teaching as a nonevent (a denial that a dance class or rehearsal is an educational activity).

Teaching is a profession with its own job description, standards, and assessment methods. Since "master" dance teachers did not self-identify as teachers, there has been a lack of conscious awareness of what is involved in the process of education. This explains why locating archival statements, manifestos, or essays about teaching written by "master" teachers largely proves futile. A paucity of evidence exists that reveals any self-reflection about how these teachers conceived of education. Of course, the *how* of teaching goes on whether or not one is conscious of it, whether or not one thinks it is important, and whether or not one has ever reflected on it.

WHY THESE PRACTICES ARE PROBLEMATIC

By its routine enabling of the above-mentioned teaching behaviors, the dance field may still unwittingly foster models for dance technique and rehearsal instruction that are rooted in outmoded and indeed destructive educational philosophies. Authoritarian teaching can be challenged on a number of grounds, regardless of justifications and defensive explanations that it "works." It fosters emotionally (and sometimes physically) abusive atmospheres. Its politics upholds a template for regressive, antidemocratic relationships. It is insupportable when analyzed through the lens of reform and constructivist pedagogical thought since it does not foster deep, higher-order thinking.[57] Moreover, it flies in the face of what is now known in the realm of the learning (brain) sciences since it ignores the climate for learning necessary for the human mind to construct knowledge.[58] The effects of the "hidden" curricular agendas in authoritarian classrooms and rehearsal rooms are great. These messages have the potential to create fear, anxiety, stress, or lack of affect in dancers, which does not foster an environment where deep learning can take place. Learners who are full of fear and intimidation are less able and willing to investigate, question, play, explore, and take risks. How does this approach prepare dancers for the kinds of versatility required by the dance field in this era?

There is a risk, too, of these uncovered inequities and oppressive practices being carried on by students when they themselves become teachers. Within a mentoring system that, through modeling, transfers teaching behaviors part and parcel with the transference of the dance subject matter, young teachers can become imprinted with and reproduce an approach to teaching that they unconsciously received, never examined, and are now perpetuating, regardless of its effectiveness or value. The novice dance technique teacher may never have examined the assumptions behind how students learn and what kind of a learning environment the teacher should create. Agnes De Mille explains the problem. "When one knows the correct order, one can teach Cecchetti and earn money," she writes. "Teaching dancing is something else again. They don't trouble about this in class. . . . Where are [future dance teachers] to pick this up? By osmosis leavened with terror."[59]

Some dance educators say they are aware of teaching styles that are carried out within their dance programs that are not as educative as they could be or that carry a hidden curriculum of messages that contradict or undermine the content of the subject matter. Although frustrated by what they see going on in the dance studio, teachers are often reluctant to provide constructive advice to colleagues. A forum is not always present to provide evaluation and feedback; moreover, some faculty members are considered to be above critique. In addition, many teachers do not have the grounding in educational theory to shape a discussion about how learning takes place.

There is a danger in assuming that pedagogically unsound teaching styles will just fall away with the retirement of an older generation of dance teachers. In the case of some contemporary dance artist-teachers, the content from their original "master" teachers has been discarded, but the pedagogical methods live on. So, pedagogical methods are not tied to the specific dance techniques being taught. The continuation of authoritarian teaching philosophies should be a matter of urgent concern to the field.

NOTES

1. Grover Dale, "Remembering Robbins: A Dancer's Adventure," *Journal for Stage Directors and Choreographers* 11, no. 2 (Fall/Winter 1998): 31.

2. Dorothy Bird and Joyce Greenberg, *Bird's Eye View: Dancing with Martha Graham and on Broadway* (Pittsburgh: University of Pittsburgh Press, 1997), 105–6.

3. Some scholars suggest that authoritarian dance teaching practices are appropriate or desired in certain cultures or subcultures. See, for example: Mia Keinänen and Howard Gardner, "Vertical and Horizontal Mentoring for Creativity" in *Creativity: From Potential to Realization*, ed. Robert J. Sternberg, Elena L. Grigorenko, and Jerome L. Singer (Washington, D.C.: American Psychological Association, 2004), 169–93; Lesley A. Rex, Timothy J. Murnen, Jack Hobbs, and David McEachen, "Teachers' Pedagogical Stories and the Shaping of Classroom Participation: 'The Dancer' and 'Graveyard Shift at the 7-11'" in *American Educational Research Journal* 39, no. 3 (Fall 2002): 765–96. None of the authors referenced is a member of the dance culture(s) he or she writes about.

4. In research entitled "Examining Teaching Philosophies and Practices in Post-Modern Dance Technique Class and Rehearsal Settings," which I am preparing for publication and have presented at the 2005 "Dance and Human Rights" Congress on Research in Dance International Conference, I utilize interviews, participant-observation, and dance literature to investigate the state of pedagogy in postmodern dance technique classes and rehearsals. Preliminary findings suggest that a number of "master" teachers in this realm emulate nonproductive teaching approaches from earlier eras.

5. These include the National Association of Schools of Dance (NASD) annual conference in 1995; the Not Just Any Body global conference in 1999; the International Network for Performing and Visual Arts Schools conference in 2000; the American Educational Studies Association annual conference in 2002; and the International Association for Dance Medicine and Science (IADMS) annual conference, also in 2002.

6. Richard Christie, "Authoritarianism Re-examined," in *Studies in the Scope and Method of the Authoritarian Personality: Continuities in Social Research*, ed. Richard Christie and Marie Jahoda (Glencoe, Ill.: Free Press, 1954), 123–96.

7. Paul Grosswiler, *The Method Is the Message: Rethinking McLuhan through Critical Theory* (Montreal: Black Rose Books, 1998).

8. Source materials for this essay include dance literature, interviews, archives, and participant observation of dance classes and rehearsals.

9. Donna Perlmutter, *Shadowplay: The Life of Antony Tudor* (New York: Viking, 1991), 255–56.

10. Audiotape of Daniel Nagrin teaching the course "Acting Techniques for Dance Performance," at the American Dance Festival at Duke University, Durham, N.C., July 1982.

11. Paul Taylor, *Private Domain* (San Francisco: North Point Press, 1988), 69.

12. Tobi Tobias, "A Conversation with Paul Taylor and George Tacit," *Dance Magazine* (April 1985): 57.

13. Taylor, *Private Domain*, 255–56.

14. Greg Lawrence, *Dance with Demons: The Life of Jerome Robbins* (New York: G. P. Putnam, 2001), 264.

15. Lawrence, *Dance with Demons*, 264.

16. John Gruen, *People Who Dance: 22 Dancers Tell Their Own Stories* (Pennington, N.J.: Princeton Book Company, 1988), 55.

17. Teachers also frequently get personal in ways that may seem to cross an acceptable line. For example, dance writer Donna Perlmutter reports that Tudor said, "And what could you have been doing last night to have such a high leg extension this morning?" He would ask some poor humiliated boy or girl—both sexes were fair game. Apart from the harmlessly chiding remarks, though, were the ones he inflicted with what some say was malevolence. "What's that you're doing?" he would ask. "I thought I asked for an attitude, not an imitation of a dog lifting his leg over a fire hydrant." Perlmutter, *Shadowplay*, 233–34.

18. Deborah Jowitt, "Anna at Eighty-five," *Dance Magazine* (August 1995): 38–39.

19. Don McDonagh, *Martha Graham: A Biography* (New York: Praeger, 1973), 95.

20. H'Doubler studied with Dewey at Teachers College at Columbia University, 1916–1917. Janice Ross, *Moving Lessons: Margaret H'Doubler and the Beginning of Dance in American Education* (Madison: The University of Wisconsin Press, 2000).

21. Margaret Newell H'Doubler, *The Dance and Its Place in Education* (New York: Harcourt, Brace and Company, 1925); Alma M. Hawkins*, Modern Dance in Higher Education* (New York: Congress on Research in Dance, Inc., 1982 (reprint of text from 1954, originally published by Teachers College Press, Columbia University).

22. Lawrence, *Dance with Demons*, 275.

23. Janet Mansfield Soares, *Louis Horst: Musician in a Dancer's World* (Durham, N.C.: Duke University Press, 1992), 135.

24. Maggie Kast, "Martha's Hand," *Contact Quarterly* (Summer/Fall 1999): 54.

25. Muriel Topaz, *Undimmed Lustre: The Life of Antony Tudor* (Lanham, Md.: Scarecrow Press, 2002), 31, 196.

26. Murray Louis, *Inside Dance: Essays* (New York: St. Martins Press, 1980), 122.

27. Melissa Hayden, *Dancer to Dancer: Advice for Today's Dancer* (Garden City, N.Y.: Anchor, 1981), 33.

28. Harris Green, "Three Views of Kirkland's *Grave*," *Ballet Review* 14, no. 4 (Winter 1987): 77.

29. Green, "Three Views," 85.

30. Tobi Tobias, "Books," *New York*, October 20, 1986, 98–99.

31. Green, "Three Views," 79.

32. David Vaughan, "Media," *Ballet International* 9, no. 12 (December 1986): 88.

33. John Percival, "Back from the Living Dead," *Dance and Dancers* (February 1987): 21.

34. Daniel Nagrin, taped interview with the author, May 2002.

35. Guidelines for selecting and evaluating teachers (and avoiding certain teachers) appear in advice books, with warnings about negative teaching practices. See Ellen Jacob, *Dancing: A Guide for the Dancer You Can Be* (New York: Danceways, 1981); Marian Horosko and Judith R. F. Kupersmith, *The Dancer's Survival Manual: Everything You Need to Know about Being a Dancer . . . Except How to Dance* (New York: Harper and Row, 1987), 20–21; Daniel Nagrin, *How to Dance Forever: Surviving against the Odds* (New York: Quill-William Morrow, 1988); Linda H. Hamilton, *Advice for Dancers: Emotional Counsel and Practical Strategies* (San Francisco: Jossey-Bass, 1998), 35–53;

and Teri Loren, *The Dancer's Companion: The Indispensable Guide to Getting the Most out of Dance Classes* (New York: Dial Press, 1978).

36. Horosko and Kupersmith, *The Dancer's Survival Manual*, 222, 225.

37. Deborah Jowitt, *Not Just Any Body: Advancing Health, Well-Being and Excellence in Dance and Dancers* (Owen Sound, Ont.: Ginger Press, 2001), 3. These are conference proceedings from the Not Just Any Body conference, 1999.

38. Anonymous writer in Linda Hamilton's column, "Advice for Dancers," *Dance Magazine* (March 2002): 66.

39. Hamilton, "Advice for Dancers," 66.

40. Nicole Flender, "Every Class Has a Silver Lining," *Dance Spirit* (May/June 2003): 49.

41. Author's class notes from Henry Perkinson's course "Twentieth-Century Educational Thought," New York University, winter 1988; see also Henry J. Perkinson, *Learning from Our Mistakes: A Reinterpretation of Twentieth-Century Educational Theory* (Westport, Conn.: Greenwood Press, 1984).

42. Carol Lynn Moore's theories are discussed in Judith A. Gray, *Dance Instruction: Science Applied to the Art of Movement* (Champaign, Ill.: Human Kinetics Books, 1989), 54–60.

43. From class notes by the author based on remarks by a former Martha Graham Dance Company lead dancer, teaching in a New York City studio, June 2002.

44. Louis Falco, "Freedom," in *Further Steps: Fifteen Choreographers on Modern Dance*, ed. Connie Kreemer (New York: Harper and Row, 1987), 45, 47.

45. Stuart Hodes, interview with author, New York City, July 11, 2002.

46. Joseph H. Mazzo, *Dance Is a Contact Sport* (New York: Saturday Review Press and E. P. Dutton, 1974), 188.

47. Alice Miller, *For Your Own Good: Hidden Cruelty in Child-Rearing and the Roots of Violence* (New York: Farrar, Straus and Giroux, 1983).

48. Soares, *Louis Horst*, 150.

49. Anne Green Gilbert, e-mail interview with author, September 25, 2003.

50. Deborah Jowitt, "Nineteenth-Century Gymnastics: Beyond Strength and Health," in *Retooling the Discipline: Research and Teaching Strategies for the Twenty-First Century/Proceedings of the Society of Dance History Scholars 1994* (Riverside, Calif.: Society of Dance History Scholars, 1994), 124–25.

51. David John Hogan, *Class and Reform: School and Society in Chicago, 1880–1930* (Philadelphia: University of Pennsylvania Press, 1985), 180, 304.

52. Hogan, *Class and Reform*, 87–88, 180.

53. Henry J. Perkinson, *Two Hundred Years of American Educational Thought* (Lanham, Md.: University Press of America, 1987), 15.

54. Perkinson, *Two Hundred Years*, 177.

55. See Ze'eva Cohen, "Interview with Ze'eva Cohen," transcript of unpublished interview by Monica Moseley. Oral History Project, Dance Division, New York Public Library, Oct/Nov. 2000.

56. See Suki Schorer, *Suki Schorer on Balanchine Technique* (New York: Alfred A. Knopf, 1999), 24.

57. Two educational theorists expand on these ideas. In the essay "Strategies for Developing Flexible Learning" in *Developing Vocational Expertise: Principles and Issues in Vocational Education*, ed. John Stevenson (Crows Nest, Australia: Allen & Unwin, 2003), 219, Clive Kanes explains that constructivism is a "view of learning in which learning is characterized other than as information transfer. Rather, knowledge growth is a learner-directed process of developing, extending, modifying and reorganizing existing knowledge in order to generate purpose-built knowledge structures." The author Virginia Richardson, in *Constructivist Teacher Education: Building a World of New Understandings*, ed. Virginia Richardson (London: Falmer Press, 1997), 3, continues, "Most constructivists would also agree that the traditional approach to teaching—the transmission model—promotes neither the interaction between prior and new knowledge nor the conversations that are necessary for internalization and deep understanding."

58. In *Enriching the Brain: How to Maximize Every Learner's Potential* (San Francisco: Jossey-Bass, 2006), 183, Eric Jensen explains: "Many students experience daily stress that is over and above the healthy limits. It comes from bullying, rude teachers, overdemanding parents, and life's events. When there are unpredictable stressors, the brain's capacity to learn and remember is severely impaired. Animal studies show that behavior stress modifies and impairs a key learning structure called the hippocampus and reduces learning capacity." Jensen continues in *Teaching With the Brain in Mind* (Alexandria, Va.: Association for Supervision and Curriculum Development, 1998), 57, "It can't be repeated enough: Threats activate defense mechanisms and behaviors that are great for survival but lousy for learning. Threats carry other costs. You get predictable, knee-jerk behaviors when the brain senses any threat that induces helplessness . . . This fact has tremendous implications for learning. Learning narrows to the memorization of isolated facts."

59. Agnes de Mille, *Speak to Me, Dance with Me* (New York: Popular Library, 1973), 50.

· 9 ·

Human Rights and Dance
through an Artist's Eyes

YUNYU WANG

*E*very artist responds instinctively to the world. Art, after all, reflects the times in which it is born just as deeply as it reveals the artist who gives it life. Those of us finding artistic voice in the years following the Japanese occupation of Taiwan were both cursed and blessed by the depth of confusion and suppressed emotion in our society. As children, we felt these emotions even when we could neither understand them intellectually nor discuss them with adults too frightened to even admit the reality of events. Almost four decades of White Terror silenced our elders' voices but found resonance in the work of my generation, their children and students.[1] Today, many of my generation are just beginning to understand the legacy of those who witnessed the February 28 Incident in 1947 and then fell silent, or were silenced.[2] As an adult, I can only view my own art and those of my generation with wonder; how did we fail to read in our own work the depths of our intrinsic understanding? What gave us the drive and optimism to believe that we could somehow escape repression or just omit political ideas from our work? I hope that those jailed or disappeared in the years of White Terror will somehow know that my generation carries deep within us their unspoken ideas.

Growing up in a scholarly family, although admonished, I was allowed to read widely. I did not know the danger that I might bring to the family. Many books were banned at that time, including those about modern ballet that contained photos eulogizing the Chinese Revolution such as *The Red Detachment of Women* and *The White Haired Girl*, and dissidents were routinely jailed. My own choreography reflected the dichotomy of the times. My formal education promoted with severity and verve the new surge of Chinese culture from the motherland. Yet, like my friends, I returned home each day to parents whose native language and culture, after fifty years of occupation, was Japanese. At the same time, I found a secret fascination for native Taiwanese culture, even dancing for two years in the National Folk Dance (*minzu wudao*) Competition sponsored by the Kuomintang Government in the late 1960s.

After graduating from college in 1973, I became a lieutenant in the military performing group touring the island for five years in shows that portrayed the brilliance of the Taiwan government. I won four gold medals and became famous for military dances, moving soldiers to tears at a memorial to President Chiang. I did my work well, never questioning the inherent confusion of a culture ruled by a repressive government and burdened by contrary desires of reunification and nationalism. I didn't often even question our inability to resolve conflicts between generations now literally speaking two different languages. Like many of my generation, I accepted that these ideas were in the realm of politics and, well trained by my elders, I avoided any statements about politics. That was the role of the government.

I also joined Cloud Gate Dance Theatre, the first professional modern dance company in Taiwan as a founding member in 1973. Under the charismatic direction of Lin Hwai-min, we performed his epic masterpieces of Chinese and Taiwanese heritage. The political situation was emotional, but Mr. Lin led us with the composure of a child of political leaders and the courage of a visionary. In 1970, the United Nations ceded Diaoyu Island to Japan without the agreement of Taiwan. Seen as a betrayal by the United States, Taiwan was shocked further by the withdrawal of recognition by the United Nations in 1971 and insulted by Nixon's 1972 official visit to Beijing. The country felt betrayed by the West and orphaned by the homeland. Sympathies were divided between a nationalist view embracing Taiwanese culture and rejecting communism, and the vision of reunification with China. Many citizens felt both urges made more complex by the increasing influence of American culture.

For four years I danced and choreographed for both the military and Cloud Gate, one dedicated to cherishing the harshly repressive Kuomintang government and the other supposedly free of political trappings or control. Taiwanese themes began to emerge with Mr. Lin's 1976 *Wu Fong*, based on the culture of the aboriginal peoples of the island. One of the nine indigenous tribes, the Pan-Wan, performed with us that season, and other dances with Taiwan themes followed into the repertory. New ideas also began with Mr. Lin's encouragement of our own choreography in 1977. Although he seemed infinitely mature and self-possessed, Mr. Lin was just a young man at that time, barely five years older than I. We relied heavily on his leadership and judgment and did not fully understand the political or economic pressures that must have plagued his mind. I clearly remember the day that he expressed to us the loneliness of his life, remarkable in both its depth of feeling and my own surprise.

Lin Hwai-min left the company to study in the United States shortly after, in 1977, and charged the dancers with administering the company for the months that he was gone. It was, of course, a mixed blessing. I began presenting my own work, including *The Path of an Orphan*, based on an ancient Chinese poem and set against music by a young Taiwanese composer, Chien Nan-Chang. The solo work had many layers of meaning, each hidden in metaphor to avoid political problems. That work, and my next piece, *Fate of the Marriage*, attempted to give voice to my perspective on the complexity of Taiwanese life.

The political situation changed dramatically in the late 1970s. On December 16, 1978, the United States broke diplomatic ties with Taiwan and the country was stunned and emotionally reeling. That same evening, Cloud Gate premiered Lin Hwai-min's signature masterpiece, *Legacy*, to an audience of six thousand that overflowed the theatre in Chai-Yi, chosen for its significance as the first settlement of Chinese ancestors to Taiwan. National and ethnic pride was written on the faces of the tearful performers as they told the story of the early settlers to an audience that understood the long struggle of occupation by the Dutch, the Portuguese, and the Japanese. I was dressed in street clothes, like the other performers, as I carried the ritual incense through the audience to the offering onstage. One by one, we shed our contemporary clothing to reveal traditional peasant garments. We began the same voyage that our ancestors completed when they landed at Chai-Yi, united as one people. Forgotten for that moment was the conflict between China and Taiwan; we were one.

Political idealism was cut short by the Beautiful Island Incident on December 10, 1979. More than thirty core revolutionists, members of the Democratic Progressive Party, were jailed and convicted by a military tribunal. Political insurgency was seen by the government in every corner of the culture and artists took care to avoid statements that might destroy their careers, or their lives. Cloud Gate conveniently toured Asia and the United States that spring and, in 1981, offered an innocuous program of western modern dance, including Doris Humphrey's *Passacaglia and Fugue in C Minor*, *Shakers*, and *Water Study*, reconstructed from Labanotation by Carl Wolz. I was less savvy than Mr. Lin and, unhappy, left for the United States and for graduate school. I returned in 1987, several years after beginning a teaching career in the United States, to a Taiwan newly released from martial law. The Kuomintang allowed the Democratic Progressive Party, including those dissidents jailed in the Kaohsiung Incident, to express their opinions. With rising freedom of expression, the long-repressed citizens marched for political freedom and, in 1999, the Democratic Progressive Party rose to power. The vibrancy of exchange has given voice to a new generation of artists no longer fearful of suppression, watched over by a generation just beginning to find peace with their own fears and their own history.

NOTES

1. The "White Terror" started after the 228 Incident. Martial law was imposed on May 19, 1949, for 38 years. Thousands of Taiwanese were killed, vanished, or imprisoned.

2. The 228 Incident was an uprising on February 28, 1947, in Taipei, Taiwan. It was suppressed violently by the Kuomintang (KMT) government. The KMT forbade the discussion of the event for fifty years until 1995. The event is now commemorated as Peace Memorial Day in Taiwan.

Part Two

CHOREOGRAPHING
HUMAN RIGHTS

• 10 •

Fagaala

GERMAINE ACOGNY

*T*he second creation of the JANT-BI Company received its inspiration from one of the first books about the genocide in Rwanda: *Murambi, le livre des ossements,* by the Senegalese writer Boubacar Boris Diop (Boubacar Boris Diop, *Murambi, le livre des ossements*: Paris, Stock, 2000). The choreography is a collaboration between Kota Yamasaki, a Japanese choreographer, and myself.

I represent the telluric nature of African dance, combined with my great sensitivity and the experience of a long career. Kota is the spearhead of the young generation of Japanese choreographers. His work is based on Butoh, a dance form forged on a will of revolt, a necessity to leave tradition, and express the traumatic experience of World War II. In this creation for seven Senegalese male dancers, we worked together in order to find, through their specific gestures, a common language capable of creating powerful and touching images. A language with which to whisper and shout the human tragedy of genocide; a strong body language, voices and sounds, symbolizing suffering and hope.

So *Fagaala* is the meeting of Butoh and African dances, in order to show various deep emotions coming from the catastrophes of genocide: fear, hatred, pain, torture, murdering madness, forgiveness, love, hope.

This murdering madness has existed since the dawn of time; it will probably never completely disappear. But in order to reduce this violence, each one of us must fight against fear, hatred, and vengeance, those feelings that can easily invade us. In moments of doubt, I ask myself about the utility of the things I do. Isn't the creation of a center for educating African dancers pathetic

Pape Ibrahima N'Diaye (Kaolack) in *Fagaala,* choreography by Germaine Acogny and Kota Yamazaki, JANT-BI Company, 2004. Photo by Thomas Dorn, courtesy of JANT-BI.

if we look at all this horror? But in moments of light, I know that my only way of fighting against this fatality is *dance.*

One of the reasons I made this piece has been the necessity to answer this question: "What would I have done in the same situation?" I, like everybody, including citizens and politicians, would like to become conscious of the urgent need to find solutions for peace in order to extinguish the flames of hatred and assure that this type of event will never happen again. I have tried to find a body language inspired by all the inner distress invoked by the collective madness. The suffering, the horror, and the screaming of pain caused by this tragedy has been linked with and translated by the dancers' bodies, so as to call out to the world, and shock and disturb the bodies and spirits, but reveal, at the same time, a tiny light of hope, ready to become a ray of sun.

For me, as well as for Kota Yamasaki, the dance is a way of showing my thoughts and transmitting my messages, of exploring new forms of human relationships and community, and, at the same time, of discovering something that could change time. I would be happy if someone would see my work and feel afterwards that his or her life could never be the same as before. I am further convinced that dancing has the power to move beyond nationalities and individual barriers. *Fagaala* emphasizes the inherently common and primordial elements, which each human being has in one's possession, especially human rights.

· 11 ·

Your Fight Is Our Fight

Protest Ballets in Sweden

Cecilia Olsson

$\mathcal{I}$ am looking at an old black-and-white photo: it is a close-up of a scared, wide-open eye framed by arms formed like a swastika. Those familiar with Swedish dance history will at once recall the picture. The face belongs to dancer and choreographer Birgit Cullberg, and the well-known photo has played an important role in defining Cullberg's image as a politically committed artist. Dated 1941, the captured moment is from her short ballet *Kultur-propaganda*, an outspoken satire of the Nazis performed in a revue staged by the noted producer Karl Gerhard. Gerhard was an unequivocal anti-Nazi and antifascist, and in his revues, the Germans were challenged and mocked to the chagrin of the German delegation in Stockholm.[1] Another photo depicts an old woman in a foot-length red dress; her long hair hangs loose, and her right leg kicks high in the air, angry and energetic. The woman in this strikingly forceful full-frame picture is once again Birgit Cullberg. It is thirty-six years later, and she is dancing Mother Earth in *Soweto* (1977), a ballet by her son Mats Ek, dealing with the political situation and apartheid in South Africa.

The two pictures are important. Apart from embracing the whole of Cullberg's career, they visualize a heritage and a tradition of politically committed choreographers, that is, choreographers who take a moral stand in order to heighten awareness of injustice and encourage social change. Neither of these works has been performed in decades. Hence, the pictures become focal traces around which memories crystallize. These images are the connecting link in the pages that follow, guideposts in a narrative set within a particular Swedish political context.

Birgit Cullberg in Mats Ek's *Soweto*. Courtesy of the photographer, Lesley Leslie-Spinks.

All humans have equal rights. Still, human rights are violated every day all over the world. Despite the Universal Declaration of Human Rights, these rights are affected by political conditions and too often enjoyed by only a chosen few. Violence and oppression—political, cultural, social—have always been core focal points of both Cullberg's and Ek's work; so too have human relationships and love viewed from many perspectives. The following essay discusses the connections between human rights, the ideology of the "people's home," a phrase coined by Prime Minister Per Albin Hansson (1885–1946), and dance in Sweden during the 1970s.[2] At issue are the ballets *Rapport* (1976) by Cullberg, and *Soweto*, both seen in light of the political forces and cultural changes in Sweden and the world at large in that decade. It is crucial to grasp the sociohistorical context in understanding how these works became vital contributions to a concrete political discussion, and how they inspired genuine political engagement among audiences and critics with regard to human rights.

COMMUNITY AND SOLIDARITY

In a famous speech made in 1928, Hansson coined the celebrated phrase "the people's home" from which grew the so-called Swedish Middle Way or the Swedish Model. He proclaimed:

> The foundation of a home is the community and the feeling of together-ness. The good home does not know of any privileged or neglected, nor fa-vorites or stepchildren. There the one does not look down upon the other, there no one tries to derive advantages at the expense of others; the strong do not press down and plunder the weak. In the good home, equality, consideration, co-operation and helpfulness prevail. Applied to the grand people's- and citizen-home, this would mean the subversion of all social and economical barriers, which now divide the citizens into privileged and neglected, into sovereigns and dependents, into robbers and robbed.[3]

Many of Hansson's speeches stressed the idea of community and solidarity. Collective attitudes, involving mutual understanding instead of antagonism between citizens, were to form the basis for political actions and decisions, and shape twentieth-century Sweden. The most important and dominant political catchword was *equality* (in the beginning exclusively between classes and among men; women and children had to wait). By the late 1970s, the campaign for the "people's home" had reached its peak, and by the early 1980s the political discourse had altered.

Meanwhile, during the 1960s an economic boom, which followed in the aftermath of World War II, continued in Sweden. In 1968, the Social Democrats won a convincing victory in the election, and in the following years they accomplished a number of reforms; the constitution, the labor market, and the educational system, were all dramatically changed. However, in 1973, the party almost lost the election, and the parliament was equally split into two blocs, the left and the right, with one hundred and seventy-five members each. That year was also marked by a series of incidences that created much anxiety in Sweden, as the political arena was surrounded by domestic and international crises. Hostages were taken at a bank in central Stockholm (an incident that made famous the phrase the "Stockholm syndrome"). The RAF (Red Army Faction), ETA (Basque Homeland and Freedom), IRA (Irish Republican Army), and other terrorist organizations operated through-out Europe, and in 1975 German terrorists (commando unit Holger Meins) occupied the West Germany embassy in Stockholm, killing four and injur-ing twenty-five. Events like the coup d'état in Chile followed by the death of President Salvador Allende, the rise of the junta in Greece and other dictatorships in Europe (Spain and Portugal), the liberation of colonized African states, and the publication of Aleksandr Solzhenitsyn's *Gulag Archipelago* occupied both public and private spheres. The lack of commercial television, and only two public service channels, meant that almost everyone in Sweden followed the same news programs. Television was considered an important educating link, providing the citizens with information and critical comments on domestic and international events.

Anticapitalism, anticolonialism, and *anti-imperialism* were, not surprisingly, frequently used catchwords. Early on, Sweden took an official standpoint against the apartheid regime in South Africa. In the 1950s, renowned public figures debated, for instance, the political situation in South Africa. In 1959, Per Wästberg, a journalist, and a former missionary, Gunnar Helander, strongly influenced by the work of the Swedish National Union of Students (SFS), launched the Fund for the Victims of Oppression in South Africa. SFS was working on the government, and shortly after the start of the fund, the Swedish secretary of state brought up the situation in South Africa at the United Nations General Assembly. Olof Palme, the Swedish prime minister during 1969–1976 and 1982–1986, made sure that issues of apartheid were brought into the limelight, thereby ensuring they received public attention.[4] From the late 1960s, Sweden cooperated directly with African liberation movements. Not only was the African National Congress (ANC) supported in South Africa, but liberation movements in other countries like Angola, Zimbabwe, Mozambique, and Guinea-Bissau received substantial aid from the Swedish government as well. The right-wing conservative party was against providing assistance, but among all the other political parties (on the right as well as the left), the unions, and the so-called African Groups, which were initially local NGO solidarity groups that in the 1970s became one organization, the consensus was firm regarding the importance of supporting the fight. Even when the Social Democrats lost the election to the Liberals and Conservatives in 1976, the official support of Africa did not change. On the contrary, as Tor Sellström points out in his comprehensive study *Sweden and National Liberation in Southern Africa,* "despite internal Swedish contradictions . . . due to the massive support enjoyed by the movement the essential political, exclusive assistance to ANC in South Africa was under Carl Bildt's non-socialist government not only maintained, but for all practical purposes considerably expanded and increased."[5]

The political situation in South America was another concern for the Swedes in the 1970s. The Swedish government financially supported the Allende democratic government in Chile. After the military coup the subvention was withdrawn and transformed into humanitarian aid for the people of Chile. Just as in the case with Africa, all parties except the conservatives assembled to jointly make a statement against the new military regime and the encroachment on the former democracy.[6] In addition, solidarity groups were formed all over Sweden and from these local groups a national Chile Committee was founded in 1973, whose main goal was to spread knowledge about the current conditions in Chile.

In this cultural-political environment, works of art with a clear political message flourished. Gustav III is often mentioned as the founder of Sweden's first formal cultural policy by establishing the Swedish Academy (1786) and the National Theater (1788). Around 1800 the first parish libraries opened to the public. Cultural policy was understood as creating a national identity, later also as a main tool in educating the people. In the 1950s and 1960s the artists debated the stiff and old artistic models and methods, aiming at radically changing the literary, music, drama, and art scenes. Art institutions, like Moderna Museet in Stockholm, gave extensive exposure to that which was new and revolutionary. For instance, Merce Cunningham, John Cage, Yvonne Rainer, and Steve Paxton performed in 1964 in a program called "Five New York Evenings" at the Moderna Museet. Leif Nylén wrote in *Den öppna konsten. Happenings, instrumental teater, konkret poesi och andra gränsöverskridningar i det svenska 60-talet* (The open art. Happenings, instrumental theater, concrete poetry and other crossovers in the Swedish 60s): "What was so special regarding the sixties in Sweden was the alliance between the avant-garde, the institutions and the media. In New York the happenings took place at galleries downtown, or in semi-private environments, not at the Museum of Modern Art."[7]

In 1974 the government declared a new cultural policy aimed at the right for everyone to express themselves, as well as to take part in arts and cultural events. The idea of cultural democracy was new, meaning among other things that each ministry was obliged to take into account "culture" in a broad sense. Artists were no longer called artists; they were named "cultural workers." Independent theater groups got extensive support, and were openly political in their approach to their art form. And within the educational system, from elementary to high schools, South African and South American arts and culture were taught to reflect the parts of the world in which Sweden was politically engaged, as well as to counter dangerous commercialism.

DANCE AND POLITICS

It was against this broader backdrop that the Cullberg Ballet was founded and achieved success. Cullberg's political commitment and her company fit well into the social democratic project. The company was established in 1967 as part of Riksteatern, the Swedish National Touring Theater inaugurated in 1933. Riksteatern is a producing and touring organization currently made up of more than two hundred local and regional theater associations. Since its founding, the idea of Riksteatern was to provide all of Sweden with high quality dramatic art, one of the objectives of the Social Democrats' program. As part of Riksteatern, the Cullberg Ballet toured extensively across the country, as well as worldwide. Cullberg was its artistic director from 1967–1988; Ek started as a dancer in the company in 1973, and was artistic director 1985–1993. By being part of Riksteatern, the Cullberg Ballet connected with a large and diverse audience across Sweden, giving the company significant cultural and social status.

Cullberg's and Ek's roots are to be found in the Central European tradition; Kurt Jooss was one of Cullberg's teachers. His influence is clear in both style and choice of subject.[8] Also, before entering the dance scene, Ek had worked several years within the field of theater. As strong, dramatic dance theater, Cullberg's ballets, such as *Revolt* and *Rapport,* openly deal with war, oppression, and the fight for human rights and freedom, collectively as well as on an individual basis. Ek would follow in her footsteps in making provocative and engaging ballets on similar issues. In his work, the poor, the odd, or that which is somehow different is often the focus or a point of departure. Power relationships and human rights also play a central role. For example, in *Saint George and the Dragon* (1976) western imperialism is the topic, and *Antigone* (1978) pays homage to the Greek resistance movement. Mats Ek explains: "*Antigone* is about the conflict, which occurs when the demands of those in power run counter with the human rights of the individual. In the ballet Antigone is fighting to free her brother who is believed to be an instigator of rebellion. . . . It is not many years ago Greece suffered from dictatorship, and then, typically, Antigone was forbidden."[9]

The remainder of this essay consists of a reading of two works, which in a particular context had an enormous impact.[10] *Rapport* and *Soweto*, both in their specific ways, address questions regarding human rights, how they are violated, and what has to be done to change those circumstances. The mutual interdependency between domestic and foreign politics plays a central role in each work. Cullberg's and Ek's outspoken engagement and comments through their artistic work helped to spread the official political agenda and responded to core issues in Sweden. They are reactions to urgent international political situations—apartheid in South Africa and the conflict between the so-called First World and Third World—advocating human rights in its broadest and deepest sense, the right to freedom, equality, and independence.

Dance can be viewed as political, as has been said and written repeatedly. Yet the bonds between politics in a wide sense and dance are delicate, and many questions may be raised. What circumstances make a dance work possible? What is the difference between success and failure in terms of political concerns? *Rapport* and *Soweto* achieved political significance partly by reaching out to a large audience, partly because of the close accord between individual and community with its deep roots in the Swedish society, and partly by exploring physicality in relation to shared experiences—moving from more intimate to open questions about human conditions. Equally important was the strong, prevailing belief in the overall advantage of the Swedish "middle way" for *all*. It was an ideology concurrently deeply embedded in the cultural and social understanding of the period, driven by a wish to extend the "people's home" and its philosophy to also embrace the rest of the globe—a focal political mission. This was a time when striving for a common future—beyond differences and conflicts—was a widely shared ideal that fueled both human aspiration and political action.

DANCE AS A WEAPON: THE POWER OF ART AND ARTISTS/DANCING FOR A BETTER WORLD

> . . . defending their right to dignity, to freedom and to life.
>
> —Pablo Neruda[11]

Cullberg's *Rapport* premiered in November 1976 at the Royal Opera House in Stockholm. It was part of a triple bill, including Roland Petit's *Le jeune homme et la mort* and George Balanchine's *Allegro brillante*. The event received substantial attention in the media, as this was the first time the Royal Opera Ballet and the Cullberg Ballet Company had collaborated on a production.[12] "*Rapport* is a poetic version of a political conflict," said Cullberg in interviews. The conflict in mind (though not limited to), I suggest, was the situation in Chile at the time. Cullberg recognized Pablo Neruda, who had received the Nobel Prize in literature in 1971, as a role model. His poetry inspired her, she said, as did his devotion to human rights and his never-ceasing courage to speak for the voiceless. A poet is also the main character in the ballet. Composer Allan Pettersson's Seventh Symphony was chosen as a point of departure for the choreography, a choice that also was discussed in the media, focusing on Cullberg turning to music rather than to literature and drama as the springboard. The intensity of the score, its sensitivity, painfulness, and strong dramatics captured her, as did Pettersson as a person also being compellingly committed to social issues.[13]

In *Rapport*,[14] two groups, the Rich (the Businessman, the Girl, the Dictator, Ladies, Militaries or Officers, and Bureaucrats) and the Earth's Poor (the

Poet, the Narrators, the Searcher, the Protester, Two Men and a Dead Girl, the Woman and the Soldiers) meet. They dance inside and outside a white circle projected on the stage and forming a center for the action—a forum for the unprivileged to give their view on inequality, injustice, struggles, abuse, and poverty. A series of events is presented onstage. The Poor dance personal histories and shared experiences of strenuous, hard work for a daily living, oppression, and humiliation. Their costumes (leotards, long or short tights) are in warm reddish and reddish-brown colors, in sharp contrast to the Rich all dressed in white (the women in light airy dresses, the men in tail-coat jackets). The Poor use all parts of the body—arms, legs, torso—at all levels in space. Many of the movement sequences are built on socially established gestures supported by politically recognizable postures; there is a large dose of pathos and pride. Other movements conventionally pull away in different directions to show their struggles and longings for a better life and how the characters are trapped in circumstances. They form tight groups holding together, though within this group dynamic individualism is stressed, so as to avoid presenting them as just any anonymous group of people.

The Rich on the other hand move with stiff bodies in a very restrained manner and dance in half circles or line up in ceremonial-like processions using ballet vocabulary. The Rich seldom dance by themselves unless they have a position within the society or community they represent, like the Businessman, who is characterized by strutting movements and arrogant facial expressions. They are partly depicted as a blindfolded "mass," in contrast to the Poor whose members, as mentioned above, stand out as distinguishable individuals. The Rich have lost their capacity for compassion and love, and therefore can be considered as hibernating or unconscious, as dead, or simply not human. The white of snow and winter seems to refer to the coldness of the Rich. As if to emphasize the egocentrism of the Rich, they are not given any expressions of being notable personalities; quite the opposite, they stick out as anonymous "nobodies." Even when dancing simultaneously, the Rich display no sense of fellowship. In this way, Cullberg reverses the classical perspective in which the privileged appear as strong individuals.

Among the two groups are the Poet, the Poor's spokesperson, and the Girl, a representative of the Rich, who challenge the seemingly fixed social order. The Poet, gifted with a boundless language reaching beyond borders, and with courage to stand up against the oppressor, leads the Poor to overthrow the Dictator, whose resemblance to Pinochet or Franco is not to be mistaken. He interprets for the Poor, rearticulating what they express. He dances for them, and he turns to the audience as if to reach out and bridge the distance. The Girl is pure and innocent, not yet destroyed by greed, power, and arrogance. She breaks the barrier: she listens to the Poet, is touched, understands the poetic language, and challenges her position among the Rich by dancing a duet with the Poet. Being at once within and without their political/social communities, the Poet and the Girl induce their respective groups to sharpen their perception and to reconcile and realize that only by solidarity and working together can a dignified life and freedom be achieved—for all.

The glorifying ending of the ballet shows the Poor and the Rich leaving the stage (and the present state) walking toward a bright light in the background—all except the Poet who sits down in the middle of the stage, turned to the audience. The closing moment offers no tangible suggestions as to how to solve the political conflict. In this way, *Rapport*'s already powerful message is strengthened. Throughout the ballet Cullberg turns to the audience; the discussion on stage extends to include all. She approaches them/us, encircles their/our existence, as if to say: "You too are part of this. You too have a responsibility."

Which technique does Cullberg use in managing to both criticize the audience for passivity and at the same time engage them in the cause for equality and human rights? I suggest this is achieved through a delicate balance between accusation, without causing guilt, and empathy, without being patronizing. She is well aware of her power to evoke the spectator's self-consciousness and conscience. As a representative and a member of the Rich, the Dictator, when defeated, sits on a balcony/box—which easily could be a box in a theater—glancing at the stage, that is, the world, as if he were dissociated from it. As a spectator no one likes to be identified with the Dictator—but it is inevitable, as the spectator's physical position literally is very similar. The Poor's facial expression, when gathered in groups, shifts from slightly accusing to demanding, appealing to the audience's sense of humanity. In letting the political, psychological, and physical converge, Cullberg succeeds in bringing forth each and everyone's accountability as a human being to make human rights a matter to take seriously—urging the privileged to explore all possibilities to consolidate a new order in which equality prevails. "There the one does not look down upon the other, there no one tries to derive advantages at the expenses of others; the strong do not press down and plunder the weak," to once again quote Hansson.[15]

COMMUNAL SOLIDARITY:
MANY VOICES ARE STRONGER THAN ONE

. . . the struggle against apartheid is a legitimate and universal cause.

—Olof Palme[16]

"It is necessary to depict political issues also in ballets," says Mats Ek in an interview in *Dagens Nyheter*: "When the audience see '*Soweto*' I hope they will feel how absurd the situation is in South Africa; that the only possible solution is liberation and independence for the blacks. That is what I show in the last scene, which is a vision of the future."[17] Later in the program he states that his work is an "attempt to provide empathetic insight into the blacks' situation," knowing it to be impossible to really know, belonging to a privileged group spared from living in horror.

On June 16, 1976, hundreds of students were killed by South African police in the suburbs of Johannesburg. The casualties caused by the cold-blooded shooting in Soweto would, as Sellström writes, "dramatically bring the more fundamental political issue of physical oppression to the fore."[18] The incident focused attention on the South African cause and mobilized public support. Palme, an excellent speaker, and not then prime minister, could concentrate on his international career, which coincided with his keen dedication to South Africa. He dexterously intertwined the roots of racism in South Africa with the working-class struggle. Echoing Hansson, Palme said:

> The children of Soweto have shown that they do not want to grow up as victims of an obnoxious system. . . . What it all amounts to, when the ideological trappings are removed, is that the white authorities do not want to give up their relative prosperity and their privileged position. In order to retain these privileges they profess a vicious and anachronistic doctrine of race supremacy; they have created a legal and social structure in total contradiction of fundamental human and political rights; and they use massive violence against those who oppose or try to change the system. But the privileges of the white minorities rest on two pillars: first, the continued use of cheap labour and the economic exploitation of the African population; second, the continued support from abroad, from what the leaders of the racist regimes usually refer to as the "free world". Without these two pillars apartheid would crumble.[19]

The premiere of the work took place two days after the first anniversary of the killings in Soweto, on June 18, 1977, at a guest performance by the Cullberg Ballet at the Royal Opera.[20] As with *Rapport* the year before, *Soweto* drew the attention of the media, and received extensive press coverage. The production toured all over Sweden, and was reviewed in almost every local newspaper. The press reactions ranged from very positive to more critical points of view from an aesthetic angle, discussing its flaws as a ballet. However, regarding the subject matter and how it was handled, Ek was praised:

> Soweto is, as known, a suburb to Johannesburg, where the white South Africa in a giant ghetto keeps its worst paid workers, whose poverty is a

condition for its [white South Africa] welfare. . . . To watch "*Soweto*" is as close as one can possibly get to culture shock. This is what it is, this is how it has to be, this has to be how the blacks experience their situation in South Africa. In any case I don't know of an author or filmmaker who has succeeded in portraying the situation in South Africa as convincingly as the Cullberg Ballet in "*Soweto*."[21]

A mechanical doll, "Little Blanche," in a white Victorian dress holding a white parasol, is placed in the front left corner of the stage. She looks out into the auditorium, gazing above the heads of the audience members. Her back is turned to the group of eight dancers squatting center stage. Reminiscent of the Swedish ruling class at the turn of the twentieth century, Little Blanche is a direct reference to the history of oppression and inequality in Sweden, as well as a representation of the "ruling white upper/middle class" in South Africa.

Farther down on the right side of the stage is an old woman seated on a stool. She is the progenitor, Mother Earth—all in red, the color of revolution—the doll's opposite. At once the relation—and discord—is established. Mother Earth is the first to make a move. She turns facing the audience, opens her knees, stands up, and opens her arms in an embracing gesture toward the spectators. A hollow sound peals, and a sharp light illuminates the doll. Mother Earth looks sharply at the doll, turns her back and walks back to the stool.

As in *Rapport*, distinguishable individuals meet as a collective; again, women and men with different histories, yet all experiencing discrimination and oppression. Their current situation creates violent behavior between them. Mother Earth mediates and focuses their (at times) aggressive energy on the outside, toward causes of their present suffering, to something constructive that leads to change. She convinces them not to be victims, to acknowledge their roots and be proud and realize that they themselves can make a difference. She makes them become conscious; "liberation is to be found in the struggle and the revolt . . . to realize the whites are intruders/invaders that have stolen their land," as one critic writes.[22]

To begin, the dancers move in disparate directions, to underline their loneliness. The movements are almost always performed in diagonals. When they rise, they lift their arms like birds, as if they are trying to fly and/or flee. Ek, as was his custom, uses a collage of music dominated by western, African, and African American music. Having his mother, Birgit Cullberg, dance Mother Earth is ingenious because of her previous political engagement and straight-forwardness on stage, as well as with regard to her age; she was then sixty-nine years old. When she dances she embodies all experiences possible, not the least being how oppression gives birth to the most dangerous element of all, namely, fear, which prevents us from speaking the truth, to protest against injustice and oppression. By the end she lets loose her hair and dances the path to freedom, a new society in which equality prevails—a people's home.

Soweto is not just a distant, dutiful political comment on a world event; it turns the particular into the universal, and the universal into the particular. The values grounded in the ideology of the "people's home" were evident. As an act of solidarity, those values were easy to transfer, reflecting the working-class struggle taking place in Sweden at the turn of the twentieth century, and the politics of the 1970s.[23]

The Cullberg Ballet has always been a company of dancers from diverse national, cultural, and social backgrounds, originating from most parts of the world. They represent a multicultural world, not just one very limited community. This solid, vigorous collective is built by and reliant on equally strong individual dancers, who are never anonymous on stage—a people's home in miniature. At the same time, in terms of aesthetics, the Cullberg Ballet is strongly linked to an established European modern dance tradition, and hence is an important and valuable part of the cultural capital belonging to the well-educated middle and upper classes, traditionally conservatives and liberals, and liberal-oriented social democrats. The company's (Cullberg and Ek's) political commitment has involved touring all over the country; it has reached out to the nonhabitués, the working class, and politically active people on the left flank of the political scale, ranging from social democrats to socialists to communists. In other words, the Cullberg Ballet has attracted a socially, economically, and politically, widely diverse group. Assembled under the same roof, they have all received the same message.

In *Rapport* and *Soweto,* Cullberg and Ek practiced their inherent freedom of expression in defending rights that embrace all people. Oppression and limitations of human rights will always be here if we are not attentive to their existence. These works illuminate how fear and indifference are dangerous for all, and threaten democracy. Only through solidarity and togetherness can evil be conquered, and a "people's home" be built. The Cullberg Ballet represented simultaneously the individual and the group, firm individualism within a strong collective. As a spectator, one could agree or change one's mind. Even some who did not agree ultimately honored and supported the struggle against oppression by paying homage to the dance and the dancers. That is, by applauding the ballet and the performers, the audience indirectly supported the ideas expressed. In *Rapport* and *Soweto,* the art, the dance, and the political visions were, and remain, inseparable.[24]

NOTES

1. One of the most famous couplets by Karl Gerhard (1891–1964) was "The Notorious Trojan Horse." The text alludes to the German occupation of Denmark. The Germans protested by threatening the Swedish government that they would stop all

film imports. Karl Gerhard then hummed instead of sang the menacing lines, which could not be stopped. Karl Gerhard was heavily criticizing Swedish neutrality.

2. Per Albin Hansson was prime minister during 1932–1936 and 1939–1946.

3. Per Albin Hansson, "Folkhemstalet" speech in Second Chamber, Parliament, 1928, at angelfire.com/pe/peralbin/folkhemstalet.html (accessed March 22, 2002).

4. Palme and his actions were constantly debated by conservative forces, which supported heavy industry and capital. Palme was assassinated on February 28, 1986.

5. Tor Sellström, *Sweden and National Liberation in South Africa, Vol. 2, Solidarity and Assistance 1970–1994* (Uppsala: Nordiska Afrikainst, 2002), 836.

6. Lucy Viedma, "Chile i samlingarna" in *Världen i källaren* ["Chile in the Archives" in *The World in the Cellar*] (Stockholm: Internationellt i arkiv och samlingar, 2002).

7. Leif Nylén, *Den öppna konsten. Happenings, instrumental teater, konkret poesi och andra gränsöverskridningar i det svenska 60-talet* (Borås: Sveriges Allmänna Konstförening, 1998), 74.

8. Kurt Jooss' *The Green Table* was for many years in the Cullberg Ballet's repertory.

9. Mats Ek explains in the program "Riksteatern/Cullbergbaletten," season 1979/80.

10. The analysis relies solely on still pictures, reviews, personal notes, and memories. In neither of the cases has there been access to video recordings.

11. Pablo Neruda (1904–1973), banquet speech, City Hall, Stockholm, December 10, 1971.

12. At the time Ivo Cramér was ballet director at the Royal Opera in Stockholm. The collaboration probably was possible due to Cramér and Cullberg having worked together earlier in their careers.

13. See for instance, Lis Hellström, "Birgit Cullberg på Operan: Stor satsning på nutidsbalett" (Birgit Cullberg at the opera: Big/huge investment on contemporary ballet) in *Dagens Nyheter,* November 4, 1976.

14. *Rapport* (report) is also the name of a news program on Swedish television.

15. Hansson, at angelfire.com/pe/peralbin/folkhemstalet.html (accessed March 22, 2002).

16. Olof Palme, "Struggle against Apartheid Is a Universal Cause," speech given at the World Conference for Action against Apartheid, Lagos, August 22, 1977, at anc .org.za/ancdocs/history/solidarity/palme-c3.html.

17. Mats Ek, interview in *Dagens Nyheter,* June 17, 1977.

18. Sellström, *Solidarity and Assistance*, 549.

19. Palme, speech, Lagos, August 1977.

20. I am indebted to Allyson Way, former Cullberg Ballet dancer, for sharing her memories with me of *Soweto* during my Dance History and Theory class for repetiteurs, held fall 1998 (University College of Dance, Stockholm).

21. Bengt Karlström, "Cullbergsbaletten [sic] i Växjö: 'Soweto' som hullingar på åskådarnas hjärnor" (Cullbergbaletten in Växjö: *Soweto* as spearheads in the viewers' brains) in *Kronobergaren*, November 8, 1977.

22. Karl-H. Sandberg, "Balett—tidens ansikte. Cullberg Sandvikssucce" (Ballet—The face of our time. Cullberg success in Sandvik), in *Arbetarbladet*, October 17, 1977.

23. This was an era in Swedish politics when the country took on the mantel of being the "world's conscience." Defending international law was extremely important, being a small country squeezed between two superpowers. Hence it was important to support the United Nations. Defending other small nations equaled defending the country.

24. In February 2007 the Cullberg Ballet celebrated its fortieth anniversary. The company put together a Jubilee performance, which toured Sweden during the year. For the occasion the Cullberg Ballet dancer Alexander Ekman choreographed a short piece, an homage, to Birgit Cullberg, by using her famous appearance and dancing in Ek's *Soweto* as a point of departure.

Dancing in Paradise with
Liz Lerman on 9/11

Linda Frye Burnham

$\mathcal{A}$t 9 a.m., September 11, 2001, I was pulling up to Detroit's Hannan House senior center, ready for a Liz Lerman Dance Exchange workshop, when National Public Radio informed me a plane had crashed into the World Trade Center. I rushed into the building and found Lerman with three of her dancers huddled around a radio at the reception desk, discovering a plane had struck the Pentagon.

The four started calling home, suburban Washington. The lines were jammed. We couldn't find out much. In a display of professional resolve, the team went on with its agenda. Eventually, half a dozen older women arrived, mostly African Americans. To my dismay, they seemed focused on the task at hand, and were content to wait for a news update in a half-hour. They began to talk happily about the last time they had worked with Lerman.

"You made a lasting impression on me," said a woman named Barbara. "I have always known that I am beautiful. My daughter saw me on stage the last time Liz was here, and she said, 'Now everybody knows you're beautiful. *Ray Charles* knows you're beautiful.' I've always been a buff, but I've always been in the audience; you gave me a chance to be on the stage!" This opened a lively, relaxed exchange around the circle. I felt my blood pressure dropping to normal.

Finally, Lerman got down to the work of the day, drawing forth material for a piece called *Hallelujah: In Praise of Paradise Lost and Found*—astonishing,

Excerpted from "Everybody Say Hallelujah," commentary on the Liz Lerman Dance Exchange community performance initiative, 1998–2002, by Linda Frye Burnham for the Community Arts Network website.

considering her husband and only child were beyond her reach, out there somewhere in the turmoil in D.C. "What do you think Paradise is for you?" she asked. People conjured up sharply remembered images—peace of mind, a sunny window, a kiss in the morning. Lerman gathered the storytellers' gestures and five minutes later we had a dance—hands balanced each other, thumbs came up and traveled in a circle, arms rose, fingers touched cheeks.

An emissary from real time brought the news of the twin towers collapse and the plane crash in Pennsylvania. I felt panic return, then recede again as Lerman plunged back into the workshop: "Is anybody from Paradise Valley?" referring to a historic black Detroit neighborhood. Stories were told about the lively Black Bottom neighborhood, and the entertainment that went on there twenty-four hours a day. They recalled Billy Eckstine and Sara Vaughn, the Joe Louis Chicken Shack, and the 606 Barn. All of it was plowed under for a freeway "to get folks from the suburbs to the city quickly."

Lerman led the women toward stories of being forced to move from Paradise Valley, and they offered tough tales of growing up black in Detroit and being "raised on discrimination": "after the war we couldn't get jobs, they took the light-skinned first, and you just did the best you could," and "there were no blacks on buses in 1948–1949, white men would jump on and beat blacks up." There were sweet and funny stories, too. Finally, Barbara looked directly at Lerman and said, "We wouldn't share these stories with just any-body, you know. We trust these dance people." All the people hugged and we went out into a new world of trouble. But for a little while, Liz Lerman had us dancing in Paradise.

· 13 ·

What Was Always There

Ralph Lemon

"*You* got to come along with me. You'll never find your way back if you don't and that's the truth." We park our rental in front of the Blue Front Cafe and hop into Jimmy Holmes' white Ford F150. It's ten minutes past noon and ninety-five-year-old Mr. Walter Carter is waiting.

Without a shortcut, we drive through a tangled landscape of dirt and graveled pig trails, under a canopy of live oaks, the road shaped by that filtered sunlight, sheltered green. And then the other Deep South of bare wooden bridges, rain-fed ponds, cotton field railroad crossings. Looking out the back right passenger's seat window, I imagine that long before, and for a long time, this was only wild, fertile landscape. Then antebellum. A battleground, then Reconstruction. The Deep South. A battleground. A growing national mythology continues. The Delta, specifically, hill country. The country, a wild, fertile landscape and its old American secrets.

"Look at it! Comin' from the big city, bet you can't believe that there's still untouched country like this. And people live out here!" Jimmy drives, smiling, "Been a long while since I've been out this way."

Jimmy drives these narrow dirt roads as if not a stretch or bend has been forgotten. And, yes, people live out here, in this "untouched country." A

Editors' Note: In this excerpt from a longer article, African American choreographer Ralph Lemon uses an experience from a research trip to the American Deep South in 2002 to poetically reflect on the complex legacy of slavery and segregation. During the trip he performed impromptu "living room dances" and visited several unmarked lynching sites, which he responded to through highly personal exercises he calls "counter-memorials." He ultimately incorporated his reflections into a dance piece entitled *Come Home Charley Patton* (2004).

Walter Carter, Bentonia, Mississippi. Copyright Ralph Lemon, 2002.

giant working farm, a little lived-in shack, another little lived-in shack, another giant working farm, the unkempt hills, and dense forest delta obliterating the difference.

Mr. Walter Carter, the oldest known resident of Bentonia, Mississippi, looks like he could be in his late sixties, a small man. He's waiting outside a simple brick house, in front of his screen door, dressed for an outing. A tan Homburg, a dark blue jacket, creased tan slacks, a yellow plaid shirt, and dark-brown snakeskin cowboy boots. "Thirty-five minutes late," he barks.

After a few requisite photos in front of the house, we pile back into Jimmy's pickup and drive back to the Blue Front. Along the way, Mr. Carter gives commentary, on houses and yards of past friends and relatives, a yelling tour guide, with perfect vision and almost deaf.

"I've outlived everybody," he brightly bellows.

Not far from Yazoo City and Robert Johnson's presumed third gravesite, outside Greenwood, is the quaint but oddly trendy hamlet of Bentonia, Mississippi, official population 390. A railroad crossing. Trendy because it has one of the few remaining juke joints in the Delta, the Blue Front Cafe. It's famous on most blues maps. Hometown of Nehemiah "Skip" James, Henry "Son" Stuckey, Jack Owens, and Buddy Spires, who still lives there and holds the Bentonia blues lineage. Along with Jimmy "Duck" Holmes, who has owned the Blue Front since 1976. Yes, a real, live juke joint, alive in that it has survived and continues to function.

In the mid-fifties the Blue Front was a mini-mart. The juke in the front, and in the back of the front room, against the wall, one could buy fruit, vegetables, shoes, and clothing. In the back room was a kitchen for hot dishes, and in a room farther back was a barbershop. More recently, when Levi's filmed Jack Owens for a commercial in 1995, the director made sure all the Coke signs were removed and the soiled ceiling and half-painted walls stayed in place, making the place immaculately authentic to a history that has not stayed in place.

Jimmy's house, a white one-story ranch resting on a wide grassy lot right off Hwy 49, part of what had once been his father's sixty-acre farm, sits right next door to the original Blue Front Cafe, owned by his father. Later it became the tiny whitewashed shotgun house of Henry Stuckey.

Jimmy remembers being five or six when he first held the giant guitar that belonged to Stuckey. Later, sitting in the front room of the house, taking lessons on his bright yellow plastic guitar.

"I told him I wanted to sing like Elvis Presley but Son Stuckey, he said, 'naw, that's white folks. I want you to sing like me.' Stuckey taught me the Bentonia style, the same style he taught Skip James. You know, he had nine kids, something like that, and not a single person related to him knows a thing about his music. You talk to them and they don't remember nothing."

It is part of Jimmy's mission to explain over and over, as best he can, the difference between Stuckey and James and Owens. How Owens and James became famous and how there's not a single photograph of Stuckey anywhere that anyone knows about.

The original Blue Front is now mute and exposed. Weather-washed of color. Inside, rooms, sort of, free to the whole, with fallen clouds of yellowed insulation, and then an openness, free of critters, because it's too cold, an openness holding onto skeletons of tables and faded upholstered chairs, a sink, a tattered reproduced painting of a bouquet of flowers, still hanging on a leaning wall, barely, irreversible.

Jimmy parks. Mr. Walter Carter hops out of the truck and practically jogs to the porch of the Blue Front, anxiously waiting for Jimmy to unlock the door.

"The pulse of this town," says Jimmy. "If it weren't for this place there'd be no place, no town and that's the truth."

We enter and sit in white plastic chairs, in the foreign afternoon darkness of the Blue Front. Jimmy offers us Cokes.

"Now, you've got to yell so he can hear you," Jimmy reminds me. I had prepared a few simple questions for Mr. Carter. Sitting inches away from him, I yell so that he can hear.

I ask, "What has kept you alive all these years?"

"Don't know. All my friends are dead."

"He's got more energy than most folks I know," Jimmy shouts from behind the bar.

Mr. Carter begins again: "I don't have much appetite but I eat when I need to eat. Doctor gave me some medicine to make me hungry, cost $15 and didn't do nothin', $15 and didn't do nothin'."

I'm sorry to hear that, I say, and then I try again. "What makes you happy?"

"Bein' around people, laughin' and talkin'. Jokin'. Lookin' at the TV. The soaps. Guiding Light's my favorite."

"How 'bout before? Do you remember or did you ever see Amos and Andy?"

"That was good. I liked that show. You can't get no good ones on TV now, gotta have cable."

"Were those characters very different from the people you knew, grew up with?"

"No, not that much. I liked 'em."

"How 'bout movies, what's your favorite movie?"

"Don't watch movies. You need cable for that. All the good stuff's on cable."

"I mean in a movie theater."

"Never been to a movie theater."

"How 'bout music? What do you like to listen to?"

"Oh, I like any music."

"Did you ever play guitar?"

"Oh boy, no!"

"He played with the women," Jimmy laughs.

"Did you know Skip James? Jack Owens? Henry Stuckey?"

"Yeah, yeah, I knew Skippy James. Skippy James. He was different from most folks. He was a preacher for a while. Then he'd play music, then he'd preach. Made a couple records, two or three. Jack I knew, a musician too. He stayed right up the road here. Went across the water to play. He and I was almost the same age. Stuckey, a musician too. A fisherman, fished all the time, everyday. Used to live right off 49. He would give a juke and we'd go to his place to frolic, when I was eighteen, nineteen, stay all night. He died over there in Satartia. They was all farmers."

"Frolic?"

"Frolickin', jukin', dancin', havin' a good time."

"Jukin'?"

"Dancin'. The waltz . . . the one-step . . . two-step . . . the slow drag."

"The one step, the slow drag? Do you remember any of them?"

"I don't know, it been so long. Well . . . yeah, I reckon so."

He gradually stands, unexpected, surprising everybody. Standing still for a few seconds, outside of remembering, and then he starts to move, mostly his legs, sliding, without bending any limbs, announcing and then moving from step to step. First the one-step, then the two-step, then the slow drag. His body thin as a rail and light, stiff, shining. Arms rounded. Hat tilted to the side. His cowboy boots scratching out music on the sandy concrete floor, surprising himself. Then he stops, places his hands on his chest, coughing, then smiling, a revelation.

Jimmy says, "Did you see that? See that rhythm his feet got? I didn't know he could do that." Jimmy shouts, clapping, "That's old partner, that's old. I been knowin' him all my life and never known he could do that." We were all clapping.

I ask if he would do the slow drag again, the side step with the weird rhythm. It was remarkable. He demonstrates it again, a little puzzled this time, stepping and now forgetting. After a few seconds he stops and sits, crosses his arms, unfazed.

A train roars by, suspending the interview and time. Until Mr. Carter mentions something about a young boy in Jackson who lost his legs recently, playing too near the tracks. It confused him.

"I bet he crawled up under that thing while it wasn't runnin'," he says. Jimmy nods. The whistle seems to go on forever, a long freight; maybe five minutes goes by before I can ask my next question.

"Did you ever have any problem with white people, a long time ago?"

"No, not really. I knowed what you had to do to get along with them. You had to say 'yessir' and 'no sir.' You couldn't just say 'yes' and 'no.' You couldn't say you couldn't do what they asked. You had to try and do it."

"Was that hard for you?"

"Oh, yeah, it was hard." He laughs.

"Did you ever see a lynching or know someone that was lynched?"

"Well, hmm . . ." He pauses. And uncrosses his arms. "They hung Gary, hung him, when I was a chap. He was goin' with Miss Lilly Wallace, Gary was. Her husband was dead. Miss Taylor, her sister, stayed with her that night, with Miss Wallace and saw Gary sneakin' by the window and turned him in. Because of the rain they tracked him. Brought him over to Captain Taylor's place. Captain Taylor told Gary if he told him the truth they wouldn't bother 'im. Gary told the truth and Captain hollered, 'Come and get 'im boys!' Gary was stupid, believin' Captain Taylor like that, 'Come and get 'im boys!' They hung him from an ol' plum tree, over there cross the tracks that we chilluns used to play in. We called it gator limb, us chilluns, played up under it every-day. That's why they hung him there, I believe. Big ol' tree set over side of

Mrs. Helen Kent and Ralph Lemon in a "living room dance." Copyright Ralph Lemon, 2002.

the dirt road. They left him hangin' there till a white woman came down the road the next day, in a buggy and horse and got scared, made the black folks take him down."

"Was Lilly Wallace a white woman?"

"Yeah. She and Gary was goin' together. Secret."

"Is the tree still there, the plum tree?"

"Oh man, no! No, man, no! That was a long time ago."

"What was Gary's last name?"

"I don't remember."

Six months earlier, I had danced in the Blue Front. I'd gone South, again, this time to research what might be left of the environment of the Delta blues and to dance in the living rooms, yards, and available spaces of those surviving friends, children, and grandchildren, along a slice of Mississippi's back roads, encountering some of the haunted ones. A personal project, a counter-memorial, a meditation. I was thinking about the following in particular.

Knoxville East Tennessee News
February 3, 1921
Camillia, Ga. Feb. 1 1921, "Jim Roland, Negro, was lynched near here yesterday after shooting Jason I. Harvel, a white man, who had held a pistol on him and ordered him to dance.

> Both men were well-to-do farmers. Each was standing with friends of his own race in front of a country store. Harvel pulled out a gun and ordered the colored man to dance for the amusement of himself and his white friends. Roland grabbed for the gun and it went off, killing Harvel.
>
> Roland fled but was soon found by a posse which riddled him with bullets. Before doing so, the posse leader commanded Roland to dance. He refused."

How poetic that one seemed.

I remember, every morning I'd stretch and warm up in the narrow space between the double beds of a Days Inn or a Comfort Inn, or a Motel 8 or 6, sometimes a Hampton Inn, from Memphis to New Orleans, in preparation for an opportunity to dance for someone. Sometimes it happened; sometimes it didn't. There was magic in this spontaneity. There was also preparation for this spontaneity, making myself available for a conversation, in which both parties are saying yes.

For instance: "Here, I want to show you something that comes from the big city. And "Here, I want you to hear something from down here that you already know about that I discovered back in the big city." Or "Here, I want to give you something that is about both places and possibly beyond, up there, and down here."

And then you say, "Although, I'm not quite sure what it is you're doing here, yes, I accept. And you can even photograph this moment. Sure, why not?"

"Welcome is every organ and attribute of me," sings the *Leaves of Grass*, Whitman.

And then I say, yes, why not? I can assure you, I know a lot about creative formality, in conversing with society, and can afford to bring some artificiality to these grass-roots convergences, making the frighteningly mundane more vivid. Now, if that sounds interesting, let's get on with it.

So, Buddy Spires, of Bentonia, Mississippi, the blues harp partner of Jack Owens, told Jimmy "Duck" Holmes over the phone that if his visitors wanted to hear him blow the harmonica it would cost us $20. $5 extra to video.

Jimmy pointed out Buddy Spires's yellow shotgun house from the Blue Front, across the railroad tracks, told us we had to pick him up and bring him back to the Blue Front.

Buddy Spires was sitting in the draped late afternoon darkness of his front room, wearing huge black sunglasses, putting on pomade and greasing his hair back with a comb. Once finished, he neatly placed the comb on a side table, next to the jar of pomade and put on a white Royal Crown baseball cap with a purple brim.

"How long you been playing the harp, Buddy?"

"Since I was five, a gift from Santa. I got a harp and a BB gun, that's all I wanted. Harps didn't cost but a quarter. You could buy 'em at the drugstore. BB guns was five or six dollars. Things are expensive now. But I ain't bought a harp in a long while, tourist folk come round and give me harps for free. Guess I don't know if there's anything to miss about them ol' days."

"Do you miss Jack Owens?"

"God yes. We had such good times, so many experiences together. Been two years. I try to keep my mind in the present but then I'll start to think about him and. . . . Didn't think what we was doin' all those years was anything, but people come around and wanted to hear us play. We been to California, twice, New York, once, Chicago, once, and where is it where it's really cold? Not Iowa, been there, once. Iowa weather is cool, not too cold."

"Minnesota? Wisconsin? Canada?"

"Nope, been to those places, all once. I can't remember where, but Jack and I arrived in short-sleeved shirts and it was so cold the producer had to buy us some coats."

Buddy still finds this incident funny and laughs. Buddy will tell this story over and over. Being blind, he doesn't have to remember a face, voices come and go, and it seems handshakes don't count. Doesn't matter to him who's heard it once or twice or three times. It's a good story.

I asked if there was anything special about Bentonia harp music and he said no. Said he trained himself and just happened to be living in Bentonia, in that way his music had a Bentonia style. Later he mentioned, as though it weren't very important, his awesome father, Arthur "Big Boy" Spires, who lived and played the blues in Chicago, excluding him from a Bentonia style altogether and making him famous.

We drove Buddy back to the Blue Front. I bought him a beer and he sat and waited, telling jokes about preachers, the devil, and rabbits, while Jimmy plugged in his electric guitar and a couple of microphones. (Jimmy prefers the acoustic guitar, his "Baby," but it was missing a string. Jimmy, who was a student of Jack Owens, said Owens only played acoustic. Owens did at times play an amplified guitar. But I knew what Jimmy meant.)

"After Son Stuckey, Jack was my guru," Jimmy announced. "Whenever anyone asked Jack where his blues came from he'd say from working in the cotton fields or behind a mule. 'What else you'd expect a man would think about, workin' like that?' he'd say. You know, the most amazing thing about the old blues musicians? Something no one ever talks about? They were all illiterate. Couldn't read or write a lick! Would make their songs up in their heads, in cotton fields, behind mules, sometimes before going to bed and the next morning they'd have the song. Ready to play."

Bentonia blues, open E, high wailing. "Nobody knows how the tuning got this way, but this is what makes Bentonia style so compelling," Jimmy continued, almost ready to play. (Actually, I'd read that Stuckey discovered the open E minor tuning while a soldier in France during World War I, from soldiers he took to be Bahamians.) A baleful sound. Startling, in how it refuses to entertain. And then that high-pitched singing: James had it, Owens had it, and Jimmy replicates it.

Jimmy said, "Son Stuckey, too, had a real tenor voice, you had to, no amplifiers in those days."

Buddy just blows the harp, a precise and muddy rage, without style, in complete love, in between beers.

Between trying to decipher a music that I could not decode, practically stomping my feet, and restoring Buddy's empty beer bottles, I sat, if one could call this sitting, and waited for something fast, upbeat. It never came. What's left of the environment of the blues. What was always there. So I waited and then said fuck it, and didn't wait for an opportunity, for the music to say, yes, come join us.

I did anyway, got up from my plastic chair and began to move, for a song, a boisterous dirge, like the rest of the music. A dance that had no steps or shape, like the music. No longer research. I disappeared, rhythmically, without discrimination. But not in the way I had dreamed. I danced, with bended knees. An intelligent moving body breaking down into a very hard floor as Jimmy and Buddy played "Hard Time Killin' Floor Blues," oblivious to my dancing, while the onlookers, smiling, sitting around tables that propped up untidy ash trays and cans of Budweiser, watched and nodded, acknowledging how my body was losing an opinion, in the bottomless soul of this place.

I stopped, sat down, no one clapped, no one said yes, nothing became more vivid, the music continued. And I was the only one surprised.

I remembered something Jimmy said. "Once, when those folks were shooting the Levi's commercial, one of the camera crew, a boy from England, somewhere like that, walked in to the place and fell to his knees and wept, howling, that he'd heard of juke joints all his life but never thought he'd ever see a real one."

A few days later, I thought how presumptuous I had been, dancing there, trying to experience something, trying to make something happen, forcing a complex event, even though private, there, in a place where there was absolutely no reason for obscurity, no discernable reason. Instead, what I found was perfect absence, a screaming dumb blankness, a complete refusal to occupy a space I could never understand, because it keeps changing.

Very unpoetic, this realization. And a perversity of fate, I yell. Like Gary's story, whose last name Mr. Walter Carter couldn't remember, or maybe never knew. (Gary is now just Gary, and in the end that is his history.)

Mr. Carter, arms crossed, legs outstretched and crossed, continues to listen, if now showing a little exhaustion.

I then try to explain the particular absence I had experienced, without once using the word *history*. I also leave out the words *dancing* and *dying*, in an attempt to make a more spiritual point. Ultimately, Mr. Carter doesn't understand, or doesn't hear my queries, has nothing to say. He doesn't ask me to dance again, so that he can see for himself.

And I have no more questions for him. We sit facing one another in silence, listening, like the rest of the Blue Front community, to R&B music from a jukebox that now blasts through the juke joint, until Mr. Carter falls asleep.

The pulse of the town? 6 a.m. to 10 p.m., normal hours, modern hours, and no dirt floor, not this time. The whole town does seem to wander in and out of the Blue Front, kids, teenagers, adult men, women, and seniors. All black, but for the occasional European or Japanese. This is not an all-black town, by the way, absolutely not.

After a few minutes Mr. Carter wakes and suddenly shares a story, as if he thinks I've asked another question, or as though it were a dream he just had, about a big black buzzard-like bird, a prophecy bird, that flew over his house when he was a small boy, a bird he'd never seen before and never saw again, and how the next day his uncle was murdered, had his brains blown out with a shotgun.

Mr. Carter, wide awake now, then boasts about how he doesn't need a "stick," at ninety-five and how amazing that is. Says before he retired he was a gardener, for a long time. Says he's been retired for a long time. Says he has to jog around his house every night, right before bed, otherwise he can't sleep.

• *14* •

Cambodian Dance
and the Individual Artist

Sophiline Cheam Shapiro

$\mathcal{I}$ am a child of war and terror. Yet, beginning in 1980, as a thirteen-year-old survivor of Pol Pot's killing fields, I was able to rebuild my life and help rebuild my culture by studying the thousand-year-old art of *robam kbach boran* (classical dance). Within a few years, I, along with a whole generation of newly trained traditional performing artists, was touring my war-ravaged country, attempting to heal its deep wounds and reminding it that Cambodian culture has more to offer than genocide. We were also working for the government, which was eager to convince a restive population of its legitimacy. *Robam kbach boran* has always been a possession of the powerful—in the Hindu temples of Angkor, the royal palace, the Ministry of Culture—and its stories have supported their power. But as the result of my unique situation, I have claimed "ownership" of my art, choreographing new work that speaks, not of the greatness of princes and the harmony of the heavens, but of the conditions of the world as I see it and the state of the Cambodian spirit.

I began to develop new work in 1998 when I returned to Cambodia to collaborate with my former colleagues on the faculty of the Royal University of Fine Arts, adapting Shakespeare's *Othello* as a concert-length dance drama, which I have named *Samritechak*. Through the piece I offer my fellow Cambodians a difficult proposal: Take responsibility for your sins. Surviving members of the Khmer Rouge today never say they were responsible for killing millions of innocent people. In fact, the powerful in Cambodia almost never accept responsibility for their misdeeds. Othello, despite being a prominent general, punishes himself for killing his innocent wife. And in *Samritechak*, Othello's last words are "Punish me."

166

While exploring ways to create a sense of drama within a primarily aesthetic form in *Samritechak*, I also became interested in exploring the dance's capacity to express emotion. So, following the 1999 assassination of a close friend, I began to experiment with ways of using classical dance to reenact my friend's sense of doom during the days before she was killed. (Her diaries suggested that she had been having an affair with a powerful man. Many people believe that his wife hired the gunmen who opened fire on her in the middle of a crowded Phnom Penh market, though this has never been proved.) This crime led to a solo piece, *The Glass Box*, in which I use the imprisoned, agonized spirit of a Cambodian woman to expose the harsh laws and social pressures that protect abusive husbands and that turn women against each other.

Sophiline Cheam Shapiro performing her work *The Glass Box*, 2003. Photo by Jerry Gorman, courtesy of the Khmer Arts Academy.

Being American and Cambodian, I have access to resources and opportunities that most Cambodian dancers do not have. But my hope is that they too will find a way to own their art and use it to speak of the human condition. I am eager to hear what they have to say.

Dancing against Burning Grounds

Notes on From Sita: Lament, Fury, and a Plea for Peace

ANANYA CHATTERJEA

I had grown up with an impression of India and Indians as being on the whole committed to a policy of nonviolence, only ruptured at shocking moments with the shooting death of Gandhi by Nathuram Godse, and later, of course, of Prime Ministers Indira Gandhi and Rajiv Gandhi. Still, my growing up was nourished by stories of the noncooperation movements, of nonviolent civil disobedience, which I heard again and again, sitting in my father's lap. I was happy to believe that, despite grossly unfair systematization of gender and class, the Indian government's slogan of "unity in diversity"—many religions, cultures, and languages coexisting—was not so far from the truth. I was content, for that time, to dance the classical dance I was learning, pieces that articulated human longing for the divine, and reflected the harmony of artistic creations with the cosmic rhythm.

All of that myth was shattered terribly with the unprecedented rise of Hindu fundamentalism as a powerful force in Indian politics during the 1990s.[1] Indeed, one of the greatest threats in South Asia generally, and India particularly, seems to be the rise of American-style militarism, with an emphasis on the accumulation of nuclear power. The issues are wrapped up with the mounting forces of religious fundamentalisms and concomitant intolerances, and the destruction of principles of secularism.[2] Manipulating popular sentiment on issues of cultural ownership seems to have become a prime ploy of politicians to divert attention from deeper failures in government management. The violation of human rights here assumes redoubled proportions. There is first of all the miscarriage of the faith vested in the democratically elected government by communities, because instead of leading them in negotiating the tensions between them, the governing bodies have actually played a leading role in fanning differences, sharpening hegemonies, and pitting these communities in violent conflict with each other. Secondly, the government, in supposed retaliation, has unleashed violence on these communities, ensuring devastation of huge proportions. The destructive 2002 Hindu-Muslim riots in Gujarat are exactly an instance of such political posturing and power play, based on reactionary notions of religio-national belonging.[3]

Women's groups in India, which have worked on a totally different model from the Euro-American women's movement, have often been at the forefront of struggles against the violation of human rights in India—movements for literacy, economic reform, or about prohibition policies, censorship, police corruption, environmental concerns, land controls—largely because they recognize the intersection of these issues with the violence that dogs their lives. And many of these women's groups have used cultural performances as highly effective modes of resistance and consciousness-raising: street plays, songs, artwork in the form of posters, and procession-based performances. Environmental activist Medha Patkar, writer Arundhati Roy, dancer/choreographer Mallika Sarabhai, for instance, along with many other women, have been important leaders in the resistance against the government's failure to control the Hindu-Muslim violence in Gujarat. Choreographers like Chandralekha have also worked for many years with women's groups exclusively, creating images that encourage the dismantling of sociopolitical inequities.[4]

Such artists have been instrumental in my coming to question the limiting of "serious" dance to concert performances. Indeed, it was artists such as these whose work pointed me toward examining the effective neutralization of politics in some categories of art-making, for instance, in classical concert dance. I realized that the emphasis on philosophical explanations and metaphoric interpretations often allowed for the aestheticization of real violences and suppressions. I gradually moved away from my training in Indian classical dance, particularly in terms of content and theme, which in turn necessitated an investigation into and stretching of form. I felt a dissonance between what my artistic aspirations were and what the performance of the classical forms said for me. I wanted to work with form and content that, while rooted in the cultural and aesthetic specificities of South Asian performance traditions, would still allow for the interpretation of historical inheritances from a contemporary perspective.

While stories of politicians inciting religious fanaticism are as old as politics, the recent escalation in the violation of human rights in the wake of religious fundamentalisms and political inequities, and in the forms of retaliation in the name of justice globally, has positioned artists in critical and precarious positions. What can I dance about in this context? How can I dance so that rhythm will not seem gratuitous in the face of tragedies of such proportions? How can I dance in a way that refuses to aestheticize, and thereby soften, the harsh edges of some brutal realities? I want to think through some of these questions in this essay because I also realize that, given the volatile global situation, these are vital considerations for many artists across the world.

When I had moved away from a career as an exponent of classical dance, I knew that I no longer wanted to dance about the love of the mythological and popular Radha and Krishna or about the feats of goddess Durga.[5] I wanted to create work celebrating lives of women whose history of resistance was inspiring, not idealized women whose larger-than-life images and powers were difficult to connect with. However, I could not, and indeed did not want to, dissociate myself from some of the mythical women in South Asian history and legends, women who continue to inhabit our personal histories and move in our bodies. These are women whose legacies would be with us for time to come, and I felt that we had to understand their lives, their minds, and their actions in terms of their contemporary relevance. These are also women who resonate with the contemporary issues that are the stuff of our daily struggles, and our visions for social change.[6]

In pondering the possibilities of creating political performance, and the choreographic interventions I could make, I have also been aware that contemporary avant-garde performance from nonwestern cultures has also often been read as "western-influenced." This, of course, is a not-uncommon by-product of the domination of Eurocentric historiography in which the radical edge in culture or politics seems to belong inevitably to the West. Because of this it was important to work with indigenous cultural practices, innovating upon them and extending them, to signify differently, and to connect to local histories of resistance. This meant a broadening of the "traditional" practices that I looked upon as the resources that were available for me to work with. These included classical and folk dance and movement forms from India, as well as connecting to the little-publicized history of women's resistance to violations of human rights in India, and the performative modes deployed by them as part of their activist agenda, such as barricading the house of a wife-batterer (*gherao*), singing songs about him, forcing upon him the public humiliation of trying to make his way through the lines of hostile women every time he leaves or enters the house.

I want to reexamine one of my pieces, *From Sita: Lament, Fury, and a Plea for Peace,* in this context. It is my hope that articulating the thoughts behind the creation and performance of this piece will allow me an opportunity to consider what its implications might be. Specifically, I want to explore some of the complex questions that I was addressing in creating a piece about Sita, the central female figure in the Indian epic, the Ramayana.[7] For when I performed it in Delhi in July 2003, I had to revisit several of the issues that I was grappling with at the original time of its creation in 1998. Intensely heightened communal violence and the violation of dignified citizenship, and women's activism in the face of such aggression, formed both the backdrop that inspired the creation of the piece, and against which I considered its revival.

Sita, at least as she is understood in contemporary popular culture, poses a particularly difficult challenge for those working out of a women-centered and politicized orientation, and I agonized over my decision to create a piece about her. How can we reconceptualize our relationships to these women like Sita, whose stories are made to loom large as idealized role models and make us police ourselves into an oppressive conformity, in ways that still allow for progressive politics? Yet because Sita is an icon that is manipulated and simultaneously silenced in the problematic politics of Hindu fundamentalism, it was imperative to reclaim her voice.

There exists much literature on the many versions of the Ramayana in folk and rural oral culture as well as texts such as the Adbhuta Ramayana, in which Sita's story has been retold in different ways. What I wish to highlight is how, at this point in time, pressures toward presenting a uniform, dominant culture, sealed with nationalist and state approval, have created a master narrative that seeks to flatten out variations. Further, seeking performative resistances to monolithic representations presents a difficult set of questions, one quite different from those in a literary project. In order to contextualize this discussion, I will give what is indeed a simplistic synopsis of the basic narrative line of the Ramayana, focusing on some parts that significantly concern Sita.

Sita, the princess of Mithila, given as daughter to King Janak by Earth, is married to Ram, crown prince of Ayodhya. The politics of an extended royal family are complicated and Ram comes to be banished to the forest for fourteen years by the machinations of his stepmother, who wants her son to be heir-elect to the throne. Ram is accompanied on this long sojourn by his half-brother Lakshman, and Sita, on their insistence. They encounter several difficult situations and adventures, and ultimately settle down in the forest. Ram's political rival Ravan, King of Lanka, abducts Sita through a clever maneuver and keeps her prisoner in a garden, the Ashokavatika, in Lanka. Ram, accompanied by Lakshman, Hanuman the monkey god, and other allies and their armies, travel to Lanka and wage war against Ravan. Ultimately, Lanka falls. But public opinion, apparently, keeps Ram from taking Sita back as his wife after she has lived, perforce, with another man and she has to walk through fire to prove her "purity." Though Sita emerges unscathed, this proves to be insufficient ultimately, and she is repeatedly asked to give evidence of her unblemished sexuality. As Madhu Kishwar has argued convincingly, this "testing" of Sita's chastity remains an embarrassment in the Indian popular psyche.[8]

Finally, in utter disgust, Sita requests her mother Earth to split and take her in; her wish is fulfilled and she disappears into the fold of the earth.

I have acknowledged my own initial deep-seated resistance to creating a piece about Sita. Almost immediately, however, I realized that since my misgivings were a reaction to the typecasting of Sita as the all-suffering, ever-patient, and devoted wife, which has been thrust upon many Hindu women as an ideal to be emulated, it was necessary to counterpoint this reading by a very different one. While it is obvious that Sita also presented an amazing model of courage and fortitude in other ways—bringing up her two children in the forest by herself, a single parent after being forsaken by her husband, and refusing ultimately to go through yet another "chastity test" for him, for instance—these aspects of her character seem to be overshadowed by the insistent focus on her idealized suffering.

Most of all, I wanted to steer away from the pathetic victim image of Sita that has currently become popularized through media portrayals, which are complicit as much in the strengthening of overarching patriarchal and fundamentalist structures as in the micropolitics of subjection. These are images made widely available for popular consumption through a media industry driven by global capital, through film magazines, paper articles in local languages and in English, and through videocassettes, all accessible in general stores in India, and in the "Asia Imports" or "India bazaar"-type "Indian stores" in major diaspora locations.[9]

In creating a piece on Sita, and in trying to understand her legacy to us, there were several possible choreographic directions to take, even in the tried-and-tested repertoires of various performance genres. But I was not going to dance the traditionally performed events in Sita's life, such as her *swayamvar* or betrothal ceremony, in which only Ram succeeds in lifting up the magnificent bow of Shiva and stringing it, and consequently winning her hand in marriage; or the *sitaharan* episode, in which she sends Ram to get her the golden deer she has spied in the forest and is ultimately abducted by Ravan. These pieces that retell the stories of her life always focus on incidents that are prior to the moment of that disappearance, and abide by the characterizations of women in these classical performance traditions. But I realized that it was important to focus on precisely that point of disappearance, for it is as much a gesture of utter frustration as of decided protest.[10] It also marks her exit from the texts of the Ramayana. In this culmination in silence then, the protest is diminished: Sita, whose sons Luv and Kush are now teenagers and are asking difficult questions of their father, is allowed only such dissent that snuffs itself out. This also happens at precisely that point in time when Sita's social status as mother of two grown sons might have allowed her more voice in a patriarchal society in which she has previously been seen primarily as young bride, adoring wife, wronged woman, and mother in sequence. Also, I was interested in seeing her in the now, and the problem that I repeatedly came up with was: how does one reimagine, re-embody, and perform a disappeared body precisely after that dissolution?[11] Another difficult question revolved around ways to recast the story of Sita so that it could align with a progressive, not just liberal, politics.

Unavoidably, my rethinking of Sita resonated deeply with the political scene in India in the early twenty-first century, laboring under the frictions created by the maneuvering of popular sentiments by politicians, and the murderous hatreds unleashed by religious fundamentalist ideologies. In particular, for Hindu religious fundamentalists, the attempt to recreate India as a Hindu state was birthed in the concept of saving Ayodhya, the home of Ram and Sita. Ayodhya is also the site of the very well-known Babri Masjid, which was destroyed on December 6, 1992, in a violent religious feud. Ram and Sita are inseparable in the Indian psyche, invoked as always already together, as in the saying, "Jai Siya Ram, Jai Jai Siya Ram" (Glory to Sita-Ram, Glory glory to Sita-Ram). Hence, Sita is embroiled in this violence, unwillingly, in my image of her, because through the different textual accounts, one could always read her as a woman who argues for peace and against violence.[12]

It struck me that since, according to all versions of the Ramayana text, Sita can clearly be described as a pacifist, or at least as someone who has always sought to maintain peace, she must be horrified and upset by the violence with which she has been associated. In fact her horror, like the violence she continues to experience, must occur at several levels: within the text of the Ramayana and the war leading to the destruction of Lanka, and in her life thereafter, cast as an icon of Hindu womanhood in the face of increasing violence against "other" religious groups. However, I believe spaces can be carved out within that very restricted notion of Hindu womanhood, from which to signify possibilities for more resistive reinterpretations.

Indeed, several Indian feminists have talked about the ways in which Indian, specifically Hindu, women have found it empowering to hold onto religious practices, and use them obliquely to gain certain ends that are otherwise denied them. For instance, "religious rituals like the *karvachauth* (an annual fast that married women keep for the health and well-being of their husbands) meant that she had a day off once a year and a new sari at the end of it!"[13] Muslim women too have been able to use the burqua (veil covering face and body), for instance, to create an anonymity that is ultimately helpful in protecting themselves and creating access to places that might otherwise be difficult to reach. In such situations, in which the unobvious conflation of religious and cultural practice can be made to allow for resistive spaces of a kind, the complete rejection of religion as oppressive practice can be problematic.[14] At the same time, in performing her as a speaking and moving subject,

Collage of images of Ananya Chatterjea in her work *From Sita: Lament, Fury, and a Plea for Peace*, 2001, collage design by Pramila Vasudevan. Photos by Eric Saulitis, courtesy of Ananya Dance Theatre.

advocating for peace, while conforming to the dominant image of women's participation in political movements in India, I also tried to position her in protest to the women leaders of the fundamentalist movement who openly espouse violence against "other," specifically Muslim, religious groups.[15]

I want to invoke the possibility of creating alternative images in talking about my revisioning of Sita and link it to a discussion of shifting religious/mythological symbols and modes. If religiosity and mythology are sometimes distorted in order to be fitted to current political gain and circulated anew, then why not twist these co-opted signs one more time and create images that resist that very co-optation?

However, while I did not want to claim for her a transcendental ahistorical consciousness, it was important, I felt, to move away from the more patriarchal readings of Sita that existed both in given texts and in current political practice, and wonder how she might have thought and felt, how she might have reacted from a culturally contextualized, women-centered perspective. I was inspired by regional characterizations of Sita, as known through work songs, *jatra* (a particular folk theatre tradition in Eastern India), and other theatrical traditions that, more often than not, color her differently from the way most textual versions do. Here she is sometimes angry, sometimes sad, sometimes upset at what has come to pass, and generally suffers less silently than the classical texts would have us believe.[16]

I had also decided that I was going to reimagine Sita from the pictures of her that existed in popular consciousness, concentrating largely on what I had learnt about her from the tales my mother and my grandmother told me as they tied my hair; from the songs Renu, the woman who cleaned the houses in our neighborhood, sang as she scrubbed the floor; and, generally, on the impressions of Sita I had gathered from conversations with other people, mostly nonacademic, while growing up in Calcutta. I would not remain with scholarly research on textualized perspectives on Sita because it was vital to understand her in the context of our lived lives, and to reimagine her in terms of the issues for which we wage our battles daily. This is significant because it is precisely the reiteration and reinterpretations of the epical text in the popular consciousness through these "domestic" modes of dissemination that make the Ramayana story seem to represent the social norm. Further, the most vital sources of my inspiration, women's retelling of the Ramayana story in work songs and folklore, are written mostly from the perspective of Sita and often change the story in important ways.

I began my process by exploring the idea of Sita's lament, her anguish. I focused on that infamous incident in the Lankakanda section of the Ramayana, in which Hanuman is sent by Ram as messenger to get news of Sita. I will briefly recount that section as I remember it being narrated by the women in my family and my own reading of the Ramayana in my school days.

To evade the guards at the city gates, Hanuman uses his magical powers to reduce his size, slips into the city, and enters the Ashokavatika where Sita is sitting alone. Proving to Sita that he is indeed an emissary from Ram, and paying his respects to her, he is about to return to Ram with the assurance that all is well with Sita, when he asks Sita if he can eat some of the fruit hanging from the trees in the garden to satisfy his hunger. As he eats the fruit, he is suddenly seized by a desire to draw the attention of Ravan to his presence and condemn Ravan's actions publicly, particularly for keeping Sita a prisoner. Hanuman now increases his size manifold, and ravages the garden, making sure that he is noticed. Soon thereafter, the guards of Lanka capture him and take him before Ravan, and Hanuman severely upbraids Ravan in that king's court. Enraged though he is, Ravan heeds the advice of his brothers and ministers who remind him that Hanuman is a messenger, who has entered enemy territory not with the intention of attacking, but on behalf of another, and so, according to the rules of honorable combat, he should not be killed. Ravan then orders his guards to set Hanuman's tail on fire as punishment. In burning pain, Hanuman decides to plunge his tail in the ocean surrounding Lanka, but as he does, he deliberately drags his flaming tail over the city, setting much of it on fire.

For me, this became a focal point for the piece. Generally, since Hanuman is revered as a divine figure, the ideal and true devotee of Lord Ram, and Ravan, dark-skinned and from across the waters (Sri Lanka), is seen as barbaric and monstrous, the sympathies in this situation usually go with Hanuman. But if Sita is always one who has desired peace and abhorred violence, then I could imagine her as truly outraged and distressed at this incident—outraged at the violence enacted on both sides, but also utterly distressed at the unthinking and unnecessary cruelty of Hanuman's action, ruthlessly disrupting the lives of so many innocent citizens of Lanka. In my imagination, Sita then becomes someone who is horrified at what she witnesses as the aftermath of Hanuman's action: the destruction of homes, the loss of life, injury, the helplessness of people caught completely unprepared in the midst of military crossfire. The picture of the destruction at which Sita stares in utter horror also seemed more and more to draw past and present, mythical time and lived reality, together for me, for, if anything, this picture of destruction echoed the experience during the riots following the uprooting of the Babri Masjid. Anyway, from my perspective, the more Sita thinks about this, the more strongly the truth stares her in the eye: in the minds of people who have lost so much, she is inevitably associated with their pain. Indeed, though she is not directly the cause, she is indissoluble from it, for it is apparently a protest against her misery that has led to violence and the suffering of so many unnamed individuals, uninvolved in large political battles. Her name has been, and will be, invoked in these contexts—Hanuman's anger at the fact that "Mother Sita" could be kept captive, away from her beloved husband, causes him to spark off the exchange between him and Ravan. Now, it has been the claim of the Hindu fundamentalist party that the welfare and sanctity of Ram and Sita in their homeland were endangered, and that this ultimately led to the attack on the Babri Masjid. Sita realizes that she has become entangled in the homelessness, injury, pain, and suffering of so many people. This then became another point of exploration in the piece; for Sita, who had always advocated peace, to be so embroiled in senseless violence perpetuated and sustained by others must be a source of pain as well as anger.[17] Could she have needed, in desperation, to condemn these acts and to try to dissociate herself from them repeatedly? In my mind, this also must have been compounded by the fact that, since many of the women in the royal court at Lanka had befriended her, she must have developed personal, comforting, and nurturing relationships with them.

I see Sita as endlessly going over the events of her life and of that day in retrospect, insistently articulating her very different reading of them, intersecting her narrative with questions and laments. She calls on Hanuman, the wise one, reminding him that he indeed had provoked the violence that day: "You hurt Ravan indeed by sending his golden city up in flames, but what did you have to gain by destroying the homes, the lives of so many innocent people?" As she goes on to recount the scene of the fiery destruction, in my new work, she relives the horror of those moments when she could but stand and watch:

> Suddenly from where I sat at a distance, I saw raging flames set the sky ablaze and black swirls of smoke billowing up. . . . As my hands filled with black ashes pouring down from the sky (*staring at my hands, disbelieving, knees folding underneath me as if giving way to the deluge of ashes, allowing my body to pull me to the ground*), my ears were deafened with the relentless cries for help (*rushing to the downstage left corner*), the cries of old people trodden over in the rush to escape (*rushing to the upstage right corner*), the panicked screams of children separated from their parents (*rushing, rushing, and then stopping dead in my tracks, always arriving late*), the laments of men who had rushed to their homes only to find ruins in their stead, the chilling screams of mothers whose babies had slipped from their grasp . . . oh, the horror, the horror of those moments, each stretching to an eternity . . . and the shriek of that one little girl for her dead mother standing in front of her burning home ringing in my ears forever (*rushing my hands to my eyes, my ears, to my ears, to my ears, unable to shut out the visions and the sounds, winding my arms around my face and upper body, my body cringing*) . . . aaaah!
>
> And then . . . (*looking from one side to the other, running to that corner, running back, hiding my face, looking down, eyes fighting to stay open, shifting as if from face to face, cowering from the harshness of the glances that seem to close in upon me*) . . . the inevitable turning of all gazes toward me, silent, but accusing, angry, broken. It was not enough to say that I abhorred violence, that I condemned such meaningless brutality. . . . I could only stammer out my dissociation from this act, I dissociate myself, dissociate myself, dissociate myself (*brushing my chest with my hands as if pushing off a load, stepping back, brushing my chest to push my hands out, stepping back, brushing my chest, stepping back*) . . . but it was not enough, it was not enough . . .

As she recalls those dreaded moments, the looks in the faces of men, women, and children who had lost their homes and each other in the fire, fixing her with their silently accusatory stares, and remembers her frustration at her implication in this ravage, she is flooded with anger. A series of movements that take her crouching low to the floor, somehow covering her eyes, her ears, trying to block out sights and sounds unbearably painful, she begins to dance in anger. One fist, then both, one foot after another, are flung out from her tightly knotted-up body on the floor, building up to larger and larger explosive movements, dancing out a fury and a resentment that is justified—more so, in the current context, where once more, her name has become associated with the project of "saving" Ramjanambhumi and the ensuing violence. Dancing to percussive drumming, feet stamping irregular rhythms that cut through possibilities of any uniform rhythmic structure, arms slicing through the air, whirling around with fisted palms thrusting up into the air and out to all sides, hands reaching deep down to rush upwards as the torso curves into the body and unfurls up with force. Legs that swing out from hips and whip the body around slice the air, as the arms batter the air with punches on the alternate beats of the rhythmic cycle of the music. The limbs plunge the body into a series of falls forward, backward, and sideways, from which she recovers with reckless precariousness, pivoting upward from a low fall, propelling the body into a diagonal rise and run.

Here, however, as she creates images of volcanic outburst and rupture, is a vital moment, a turning point in the piece: Sita realizes in shock that, in her anger, she is on the way to a similar kind of violence and destruction that she had just condemned. Suddenly, in the midst of her furious spinning around, she reels to a halt. She stands in profile, the image of stillness. One hand rushes out to restrain the other, which was about to punch the empty air. Her neck falls back, her eyes searching the sky for peace, for understanding.

> Even now, when I recall that day, I am seized by a fury so strong that I feel like belching up the molten lava from under the earth, pounding on the stable ground till it cracks under your steps, uprooting your homes with violent earthquakes . . . till I hear the shriek of that little girl for her dead mother, ringing in my ears forever! . . . aaah! I must dissolve this destructive rage, for violence breeds violence, breeds violence, breeds violence . . .

I had started off thinking about my resistance to the image of Sita as passive and docile. In the final phase of the development of the piece, I returned to thinking about this and to questioning whether there could not be other readings, particularly of her last act of returning to the folds of her earth mother. For even while Sita's final act of calling on the earth to split and make way for her, and her exit underground, could immediately be read as an act of resistance, I felt I needed a slightly different understanding of it, especially one that did not see that exit as a final one. It is important to acknowledge here that this need is very much located in the politics of the contemporary context. Both in terms of the national framework, in which the reigning political philosophy glorifies specific masculinist nationalist histories while submerging certain others, and in terms of the international framework, in which overarching racism tends to cast Third World cultures as not-so-civilized, lacking notions of women's rights and human rights, populated by men who suppress their silent women, it seemed urgent to posit a history of women's resistance and foreground strong role models of South Asian women. I wanted to see Sita, not as someone who had been swallowed up by the earth, albeit willingly, and was silent thereafter, but as someone who has continued to raise her voice even from the depths of the earth. There would be nothing passive about my Sita, I decided. She would be an underground activist, advocating tirelessly against violence and for peace, reminding us through earthquakes, through rumblings and tremors of the ground on which we tread, that violence would only lead to further violence, and always to the suffering of endless innocent and uninvolved peoples.

Thus the piece exists as an interlude—as some moments in Sita's voluntary resurfacing—in the time she takes amidst her work underground to speak to us. It begins with the sound of knockings on the ground. Still in darkness, Sita speaks, her words intercut with the scraping of bangles on the floor as wrists begin to pound the earth:

> Can you hear me? It is I, Sita, Sita from the underworld. It is I, Sita, speaking to you from the depths of the earth, speaking to you through the rumblings of the earth under your feet, reminding you to look for the peace in the midst of the madness, to say NO! Can you hear me? It is I, Sita, once princess of Mithila, once wife of Ram, mother of Luv and Kush, and always daughter of the warm, brown earth. I speak to you from the depths of the ground where I made my abode one day in final protest and outrage at the incessant and unreasonable demands you have made upon me.

It was important for me to recall, in that beginning, the way in which Sita identifies herself at the last moments of her life in the traditional texts—not only through the web of familially defined relationships, but as someone who had emerged from the earth, and who is now making an active choice to move away from her present life through its folds.

While realizing the dangers of the woman-earth identification, I want to point out how this integral connection of Sita with land, invariable in all versions of the Ramayana text, and very much a part of rural culture, has a very specific valence in this context. At a presentation at the Asia Society, Gayatri Chakravorty Spivak and Madhu Kishwar talked about the reimagination of Sita in aboriginal, tribal, and even rural cultures, in which Sita is deeply associated with land and her name is repeatedly invoked in projects dealing with the recovery of land. While Spivak talked about Sita being invoked in rural undertakings to promote agriculture without chemical fertilizers, Kishwar talked about the Stree Shakti Sanghatana's Lakshmimukti campaign, where the men would willingly transfer the ownership of land to the women of their households, in order to set right the historical wrong done to Sita, and to free

the village from her curse. These images also emphasized the continuing valid-
ity of the legacy of Sita, reimagined in different ways by different groups of
peoples, and the collaging of past and present, mythical and experienced, time
and space, in understandings of her. Thus, the ancient wrong done to Sita,
her abandonment by Ram during her pregnancy, her potential homelessness
at that point, her difficult life as a single parent of two sons, is sought to be
rectified/avenged even now, as if the memory of that pain has remained en-
graved in popular consciousness through time.

In the dance piece, Sita, the earth-born, as I imagined her, explores her
relationship with the earth three times, using a similar repertoire of movements performed and recreated through three entirely different modalities and
energies. In actuality, the performance of the differential relationships with
land signals Sita's emotional transformation, and marks the dramatic movement of the piece. And even though I have constantly guarded against any
woman-nature identification, I have deliberately choreographed the earth as
absent partner in Sita's dance in the tradition of movements like Chipko,[18]
which have created a symbiotic relationship of women with land and its resources, a historically, socially, and economically vital factor in a culture that
is still primarily agricultural.

In the early moments of the piece, caught in the throes of her lament
for burning Lanka, Sita descends to the ground slowly from standing, one leg
stretching out, the torso caving forward as she sinks, sinks, all the time digging,
digging the earth in front of her, digging the earth to the side, as if to bring
the soil over her head to cover her ears and eyes, arms reach down and round
up above the head, covering herself, submerging herself below the ground so
she can no longer see or hear or smell the raging fire, and the agony of the
people trying to escape its flames. The body lowers, as if trying to flatten itself
to the level of the earth, hidden under it, indistinguishable from it, away from
the angry stares of the people whose homes had been destroyed. Rising, she
steps back, reaching her leg long. The torso bends low as the arms curve up
from reaching to touch the ground only to fall on her body as if lamenting
the anguished history of war and destruction ingrained in every particle of the
soil that her fingers feel. Earth is cover here, while its destruction is the cause
of Sita's deep anguish. Most of all, it is the only retreat Sita seeks in her agony
at being associated with the burning of Lanka.

As she realizes her inseparability in the minds of the people of Lanka from
the destruction of their homes, her anger mounts: The same curvilinearity
in the arms and upper body, this time rent with fury, moving out from her
body instead of moving in, is shot through with fisted hands, which punch
holes through the layers of Earth under which Sita now lives. Now both
arms together reach from down upward, curving out forcefully like volcanic

eruptions. The feet move rapidly in irregular rhythmic structures, marking moments of heightened anger with explosive stamping intersected with jumps on flexed feet that meet loudly with the floor on landing. Repeatedly the arms thrust out from the body, swinging her body sharply from one side to another, slicing through the air as they move. The earth here is the ground of her dance, sustaining her fury. Her movements invoke the outpouring of volcanic lava, and she pounds on the floor with her feet as if to will the earth to erupt with anger as she has.

Yet, the anger catches itself; Sita will not, even in her justified fury, even in reflection only, repeat the violence and destruction that she so abhors. The very earth, whose potentially destructive energies were previously coursing through her limbs, now seems to remind her of its power of growth, nurture, and fulfillment. This time the arms curve to reach down and out, and down and out again; rising from the ground, the hands sprout in *mukula hasta* (a gesture signifying buds), as if willing growth and fertility to return to the ground. Full curves ripple through the arms and torso, the expansive curves of her hands carry her across space, punctuated with rhythmic footwork. Here Earth becomes her mode of action and activism, and as she reacquaints herself with it, she returns again and again to say No! to the madness of violence. Grounded in a deep *chauka mandala* (wide-stanced, knee-bent, body position), the feet skim the surface of the earth to move forward continuously, arms circling out while palms flex up in a typical gesture of arrest. Finally, in the end, Sita knocks on the earth floor with her hands, while her feet sound the floor for emphasis, in rhythms of two, six, three, to remind of her continued existence underground championing the cause of peace, urging an end to the frenzy whipped up in her name, in the name of religion, of honor, of justice.

Finally, the last section of the dance casts, or recasts, Sita as the untiring activist, working from the underground in her quest for peace. Evoking images of cultivation, growth, harvest, and celebration, and using the harmony of rhythm and music to structure the movements, Sita dances, punctuating her dance with movements that remind the audience of her initial knocking on the ground from under it, and asking them to look for the peace in the midst of madness, and say NO!

> But when you hear knockings of the earth under your feet, when you feel strange rumblings of the rocks that line your paths, remember it is me, reminding you to look for the peace in the midst of madness, say NO! Find the peace in the midst of madness, say NO! Find the peace in the midst of madness, say NO! Say no! Say no! Say no!

The last moments of the piece find Sita returning slowly to the depths of the earth, deepening lower and lower, closer to the floor, with arms raised overhead as if still tapping on the earth floor above her with her fists. Sita continues to live then, as an advocate of peace and human rights—this, for me, is her legacy. This legacy is what I tried to choreograph and embody with deepest resonance in this piece. And through dancing her fury and her indignation, her search for peace and activism, I tried to humanize her and resist associations with the Bharatmata/Mother India image, which is again open to co-optation by different nationalist agendas.[19]

I have tried to arrive at an understanding of Sita from the perspective of rural and tribal imaginations, as a woman whose spiritual practices and rituals fall in between the fault lines of organized religion, whose culturally specific images and mythologies are associated with the specificity of socioeconomic conditions, the labor of agriculture, for instance. Further, I felt what was most important about even textual conceptions of Sita to me was her possible alignment with South Asian women's histories of protest. Moving away as much as possible from specifically Hindu markers of the text, I focused on the specific horror that any kind of fundamentalism and hierarchical structures like patriarchal aggression reap: I wanted to leave Sita's religious affiliation in the moment of the piece unclear, and her specific identity as Hindu princess and queen is stated in the nature of a "once-" (once princess of Mithila), in the past. This, I felt, allowed me more complexity in addressing what a secular, yet culturally specific, politics might look like.

Again, while it was important to me to imagine her as working on her own initiative, undefined by her relationships with her husband and her sons, I felt it was vital to respect the web of relationships that is the working context of most women, certainly South Asian women's lives. These relationships invoke a sense of community that specifically includes the other—the child whose cry rings in Sita's ears and moves her from lament to fury to shock is a child of the "other" community—in ways that are not about tokenized or marginalized presences.

I want to end with this quote from Uma Narayan in which she talks about daughters retelling the stories of their "mothers," iconic figures deeply invested with cultural capital, which resonates profoundly with my own experience in creating and performing this piece.

> [F]eminist daughters often have accounts of their mother-cultures that differ in significant ways from the culture's own dominant account of itself. . . . Re-telling the story of a mother-culture in feminist terms . . . is a political enterprise. It is an attempt to, publicly and in concert with others, challenge and revise an account that is neither the account of an individual nor an account "of the culture as a whole," but an account of some who have power within that culture. It is a challenge to other political accounts that distort, misrepresent, and often intentionally fail to account for the

problems and contributions of many inhabitants of that context. It is a political attempt to tell a counter-story that contests dominant narratives that would claim the entire edifice of "our Culture" and "our Nation" for themselves, converting them into a peculiar form of property, and excluding the voices, concerns, and contributions of many who are members of the national and political community.[20]

I did not want to dance the traditional narratives of Sita that one learns as part of the repertoire of the classical dance forms, nor did I want to embody her with movements that have to do mostly with gentleness and traditional images of "femininity." In creating the picture of Sita I ended up with, I inflected her with much more of my own imaginings about her than can be supported by strictly textualized analyses of the Ramayana. But, just like those "traditional" accounts and performance pieces about her, my retelling of her story is a political venture, though it differs significantly from the ways in which the dominant culture tells its own narrative. It is through retelling these stories and remaking these histories for ourselves that we resist the submerging of our voices in metanarratives about our communities, and recreate our histories and worlds in ways meaningful to us.

NOTES

1. Some of the prime vehicles for the Hindu fundamentalist movement are the VHP and the RSS organizations and the BJP party. The Vishwa Hindu Parishad (VHP) or the World Hindu Council was registered in July 8, 1966, in India, with the acknowledged objective of consolidating, strengthening, and making invincible "global Hindu fraternity by following the eternal and universal life values based on Sanatan Dharma and work for total welfare of humanity on the basis of the unique cultural ethos of Bharatvarsha," (at vhp.org/englishsite/b-objectives/aim_object.htm). The Rashtriya Swayamsevak Sangh (RSS) or National Volunteers Society was founded in 1925 and developed under the direction of well-known leaders such as Madhavrao Sadashivrao Golwalkar. Initially framed as a cultural organization devoted to regenerating Hindu society, it is currently best described as "a mass, fascistic organization" (Keith Jones, "India: the BJP-RSS nexus," Newsletter of the World Socialist Web Site, at wsws. org/news/1998/jun1998/bjp-j20.shtml). The BJP, or the Bharatiya Janata Party (Indian People's Party), was the dominant party in the coalition government of India. It was created in 1958, in its earlier incarnation as the Bharatiya Jana Party, as the political wing of the RSS. These latter two organizations, along with some others, together compose the Sangh Parivar, the group/family of organizations that form the leadership of the Hindutva, or Hindu fundamentalist movement. The religious engineering and newly evolving symbols "included, among many other things, a proliferation of jagarans around mother-cults like Jai Mata Di in places more or less without such

cults so far; a media-invented goddess like Santoshi Ma; devotional pop music; a rush to modern 'hi-tech' pilgrimages for the upper middle classes, like Vaishno Devi; and charismatic gurus or god-men, each with a distinct interpretation of Hindutva and salvation strategies for well-defined clienteles," Tapan Basu and others, *Khaki Shorts and Saffron Flags* (New Delhi: Orient Longman, 1993), 111. The party was defeated in the 2004 elections by the Congress Party and its United Progressive Alliance, but continues to be an important nexus of power in Indian politics.

2. Tapan Basu, Pradip Datta, Sumit Sarkar, Tanika Sarkar, and Sambuddha Sen, academics and political commentators analyzing Hindu fundamentalist politics, talk about the sudden burgeoning of new forms of religiosity that coincided with the growing popularity of the specifically Hindu councils and cultural organizations, new modes of worship and sacred symbols that are as communally driven as dictated by political convenience. It is these politically spawned, vitally altered forms of Hindu religious practice that prepared the way for a much more aggressive, lands-and-boundaries-centered, inherently militant communalism.

3. For instance, on February 27, 2002, the Sabarmati Express train was set on fire in the town of Godhra in Gujarat. The passengers inside the train, primarily Hindus, were mostly burnt to death. Terrible Hindu-Muslim riots ensued during which countless people were killed and injured, homes were destroyed, and cities ravaged. While Hindus blamed Muslims for starting the fire, Muslims reported that they were reacting to prior provocation, and recent findings have suggested that the fire might have been started from within the train. Riots and violence continued well into a year after that in Gujarat, with government often openly supporting the destruction of Muslim households.

4. There have been artists, like theater directors and playwrights such as Badal Sircar and Safdar Hashmi, who have consistently created work highlighting both state-sanctioned and socially entrenched atrocities and demonstrations against them; poets such as Faiz Ahmad Faiz, who protested the coercive politics of the Pakistani bureaucracy and restructured the Urdu ghazal, the format traditionally used to create love poetry, to write protest lyrics.

5. Admittedly the stories of Radha and Krishna have much to offer even though they operate under the overarching metaphor of heterosexual love, which is understood to be a reflection of human love for the divine. This is a tradition in which sexuality and physical play figure largely as an expression of love, and thus allow for an understanding of the body as the site of this human-divine union. And though the feminization of the devotee who serves and the masculinization of the divine who blesses with presence is nothing new, it is true that Krishna can be quite the playful god, full of mischief. The love stories, however, are always told from the point of view of male desire. The gods in fact are humanlike in the ways in which they play, are enraged, take revenge, forgive, and run the entire gamut of human emotions, and in this their interactions reflect the problematic hierarchies that organize society in general. Again, the amazing powers of the goddess Durga and her many manifestations can be seen as part of that empowering tradition of *devi-puja*, or goddess-worship, in which the goddess is responsible for saving the world at a time when all gods have failed. This of course does not preclude a patriarchal imaginary and Durga is as much wife and

mother as goddess. As protector of society, she is the universal deified mother. The respect that is accorded to goddesses such as Durga, Kali, Lakshmi, and Saraswati does not of course translate to a respect of women at large, though the role of the matriarch-figure who is the center of the household is often a powerful one.

6. I recognize that this is a deeply personal project, but I do want to work through the images that, as a dancer and choreographer, have formulated my body. I also want to rewrite them in ways that allow me to share stories with my daughter, who, growing up in America, asks about "traditional" stories from her culture. I additionally want to observe that in attempting to rewrite this story, there are many traditional perspectives that I was aware of, growing up in India: there is the anxiety over fundamentalist politics; there is also the apparent Aryan-Dravidian split resulting in North Indian dominance and the imagining of the people across the waters, in Lanka, as demons; and there is the rewriting of the Sita story in several parts of South India where Sita is not abducted by Ravan, but leaves willingly with him. In trying to carve from it a politics that I could live with, I had to grapple with the many strands and layers that complicate the reception of this narrative, and ask who the audience for such work might be. In the end, I valued the process of working with a narrative that, though still flawed, allowed me to struggle with questions of how I, born a Hindu, might work with my daughter and other children, not in a silencing through guilt, but by both admitting the cultural specificity and location of being born a Hindu, and working towards a more secular, inclusive community.

7. This solo piece, which I choreographed and performed, integrates text, movement, music, and dance, and was premiered during the Sita symposium held at Columbia University in summer 1998.

8. In a talk presented at the Asia Society in conjunction with the Sita Symposium, "Reforming Sitas vs. Reforming Rams," on April 30, 1998, Madhu Kishwar argued eloquently about the remaining popular sense of urgency to undo the wrong done to Sita.

9. Interestingly, while the overwhelming majority of India's population cannot afford personal television sets, in 1987–1988 people gathered in locations equipped with one—others' homes, shops—in order to watch the telecast of the fifty-two-part Ramayana series directed by Bombay filmmaker Ramanand Sagar, which heralded a resurgence of interest in this story. The images from this film had a powerful impact on the popular consciousness. For more on this, see Arvind Rajagopal, *Politics after Television* (Cambridge: Cambridge University Press, 2001).

10. In reading her point of disappearance as an act of disobedience, and continuing to perform her through powerful movement imagery, I have placed her in a tradition of protest and activism that is a vital part of South Asian women's histories. In this, and in analyzing my own intentions in taking up this project, I am reminded of Gayatri Chakravorty Spivak's reflections on the particular responsibilities that third-world feminists who work in international frames strain under. She points out that they must "keep up their precarious position within a divided loyalty: being a woman and being in the nation, without allowing the West to save them. . . . Women . . . have an immense historical potential . . . of knowing in their gendering, that nation and identity are commodities in the strictest sense: something made for exchange. And they are

the medium of that exchange," Mahasweta Devi and Gayatri Chakravorty Spivak, *Imaginary Maps: Three Stories* (New York: Routledge, 1995), 180. Spivak's comments push me deeper to reflect on the politics inherent in this project, my own politics, and difficulties of performing deconstructing centralized narratives while attempting to create personal mythologies.

11. Also, how does one invoke a continuity of presence through an art known precisely for its tracelessness? Performance has been spoken of continuously as the form that presents particular difficulties for analysis and theorizing because, once the performance is over, there are no traces left of this once-vital happening. The performative text in fact resides in the bodies of those embodying it, and is continuously reinvented or resurrected every time it is staged. And this is not just in the perception of audience, or conditions of staging, but also because the dynamics of the different bodies on stage often make for subtle changes in the choreography. What better mode for Sita in which to reclaim her voice and herself as expressive subject?

12. In imagining Sita as recognizing that she is repeating a kind of violence that she has experienced, I am locating her in the tradition of a women's movement that is heedful of interlocking cycles of violence. I am also placing her in a historical context in which small communities of women, whether urban or rural, literate or illiterate, have worked hard to eke out means of resistance that work through nonviolent means. This also echoes the Gandhian tradition of nonviolent civil disobedience that characterized much of the struggle for independence, and which allowed women to enter the movement in large numbers. However, in casting Sita's anger as a reaction to the violence, I also want to place emphasis on the fact that she has been subjected to violence of several kinds, which include but are not limited to the emotional abuse in the cruel and repeated rejections by Ram, and the epistemic violence in the current fundamentalist appropriation of her as a willing partner in a gory politics of hatred.

13. Urvashi Butalia, in *Women and Right-Wing Movements: Indian Experiences*, ed. Tanika Sarkar and U. Butalia (London: Zed Books, 1966), 106.

14. The story of rebel-saint Mira, whose devotion to Lord Krishna and religious fervor earned her social sanctions whereby she could defy the restrictions placed on her, as woman, as queen, and as widow, is a case in point. Cases in counterpoint are examples of women leaders such as Vijayraje Scindia, Sadhvi Rithambara, and Uma Bharati from the Hindu fundamentalist party, who have used their status as *sanyasin* (holy women, and therefore by necessity celibate) and their dedication to "Hindutva" to earn themselves vital positions of leadership within a political party that is deeply conservative and reactionary.

15. In this I am also seizing upon the obvious discomfiture that the right-wing movements seem to have with Sita despite their occasional invocation of her as role model for Hindu women. For large though her figure looms in the popular imagination, her abduction by another male, her life as a single mother, her ultimate defiance even according to the dominant accounts, make it difficult to manipulate her as an iconic figure in the same way that goddess figures like Durga can be. Specifically, her final act of disobedience—the refusal to testify the "purity" of her body—is when Sita falls silent, and to the bottom of our consciousnesses.

16. Detailed research on this has been done by several scholars, primary among whom is Dr. Nabaneeta Dev Sen, former professor of comparative literature at

Jadavpur University, Calcutta. See, for instance, her paper, "Lady Sings the Blues: When Women Retell the Ramayana," in *Proceedings from the Sita Symposium* (New York: Dharam Hinduja Indic Research Center at Columbia University, 1998).

17. Indeed it is true that in the Aranya Kanda section, Sita questions Ram about his apparent propensity toward violence and whether this vitiates his dedication to Dharma or duty. I quote from Sita's words to Ram: "The moment your eyes light on a rakshasa, your fingers itch to kill him, and to you, to think is to act. . . . Unless provoked to do so, it is not right for you to kill anyone, even if he is a rakshasa," Kamala Subramaniam, *Ramayana* (Bombay: Bharatiya Vidya Bhavan, 1981), 230. On the other hand, Sita has been, in some lesser-known versions, such as the Adbhuta Ramayana, portrayed interchangeably with Kali, and cast in the *raudra rasa*, the furious mood. She is very much the warrior here and picks up Siva's bow when Ram passes out in combat and kills Ravan. Interesting as this is, it would be problematic, even in intertextual reading, to see this as a popular or even somewhat-known version of the story. For details, see Thomas B. Coburn's article, "Sita Fights While Rama Swoons," *Manushi* 90 (Sept.–Oct. 1995): 5–16.

18. The Chipko Movement of 1973 occurred in the area of Uttarkhand in Uttar Pradesh. The women of these rural areas were the first to recognize the link between excessive deforestation and the depletion of social and environmental resources. Protesting the government's program of incessantly logging forests, these village women embraced the trees even as the contractors arrived at the site, positioning themselves between the contractors' axes and the trees. Hence the movement was named *chipko*, which means embrace.

19. One of the criticisms leveled against the Indian women's movement is that, despite the resistance to hegemonic Hinduism, the models of strength—Shakti figures, warrior queens such as Rani of Jhansi—have still been overwhelmingly Hindu. The attempts to secularize Sita, to bring her in conversation with Sri Lankan women whose reactions cause her to experience herself as betrayer and violator, and finally her recuperation as the earth-spirit from tribal accounts, are part of the endeavor to work with Sita's legacy from locations that are the "other" of Brahmanical Hinduism. There were many conversations I had with friends and colleagues about the possibility of casting her as a Muslim woman, but I felt the vital point was to cast her as being opposed to structures of organized religion per se, which have inherent possibilities for rigidity and fundamentalist deployment. I want to thank my colleague and friend, Jigna Desai, who spent many hours arguing with me about this point and for pushing me to articulate the differences between an antifundamentalist position and a secular one. While her suggestion was to recast the mythology totally to make Sita Muslim, I felt that I still wanted to stay away from organized religions and from the possible side-effects of assigning "good" and "bad" values to any one religious or cultural group. I also felt that this approach would free the Sita story from being a Hindu story specifically, and that the inclusion of various religious practices would not necessarily make for "secularism" in the long run. I also realize that in thinking through these issues, I may have reached but a flawed reimagining of Sita.

20. Uma Narayan, *Dislocating Culture* (London: Routledge, 1997), 9–10.

Human Rights Issues in the Work of Barro Rojo Arte Escénico

CÉSAR DELGADO MARTÍNEZ
TRANSLATED AND EDITED BY NANCY LEE RUYTER

$\mathcal{A}$ red dusk. . . . As much on the stage of the Palace of Fine Arts of Mexico City as on a dusty street in the state of Guerrero, Barro Rojo Arte Escénico (BRAE) has spent its twenty years of existence developing a high-profile presence in the cultural life of Mexico.[1]

In 1982, Barro Rojo (its original name) was established in the city of Chilpancingo as a project of the Autonomous University of Guerrero. At that time, the university was supporting various kinds of work with marginalized sectors of the society, and the company began its life participating in marches and meetings. Barro Rojo's founders were the contemporary dance artists Arturo Garrido of Ecuador, Daniela Heridia of El Salvador, and Serafín Aponte, a native of the state of Guerrero. The dancers rehearsed in the pavilion of the city's park because there was no studio available. The color of red clay (*barro rojo*) evokes the image of blood, and from the beginning the group's members shared a commitment to use their dance to address aspects of what was going on in Latin America, lacerated as much of it was by war, bloodshed, and a constant violation of human rights.

THE PATHS OF LIBERTY

The first work that Barro Rojo presented was *El camino* (The path or road) by Arturo Garrido (1982). The piece addressed the fight for liberty by people of El Salvador.[2] The harshness of the war under which they were suffering was "narrated" in recorded testimonies by members of the population who told

El camino, choreographed by Arturo Garrido and performed at the Campo de refugiados, El Salvador, 1988. Photo courtesy of Jorge Izquierdo.

how their houses were being destroyed, their fields burned, and their loved ones assassinated. While the voices of the hopeless Salvadorans were heard from the loudspeakers, a dancer under a spotlight began to move, extending his long legs and his slender arms. Dressed in trousers of coarse cloth and with his torso nude, Arturo Garrido began a dance of desolation, helplessness, and hatred—a dance about the destruction that does not respect men, women, children, or old people living in a war zone. As he threw an excruciating gaze to the public, the chorus appeared, representing the people—frightened men and women jumping from one place to another on the stage, fleeing from the bombs that were being dropped from planes that could be heard clearly over the loudspeakers. The heart cringed; hope wilted; sadness flowered. Meanwhile the music of Adrian Guyzeta and his experimental group supported the dancers in their action of unbridled rushing to reach a place where they could protect themselves from torture—both physical and psychological.

Garrido presented *El camino* in plazas and on the streets, places not usually considered hospitable to dance performance. Although the company had had no experience on formal stages, the dancers jumped into the adventure of traveling to Mexico City in 1982 to participate in the annual dance competition for the *Premio Nacional de Danza* (National Prize for Dance). The experience was frightening: the stage lights blinded the dancers, the stage area was spatially disorienting, and the demands of the rehearsals exasperated this group that was not yet used to working within professional time limits. The result, however, was that they won the prize. From that moment on, the reputation of Barro Rojo began to grow within the many strands of the Mexican dance world.

THE POLITICAL PRISONERS

In 1984 Barro Rojo changed its location to Mexico City, leaving behind university support and embarking on a path of independence.[3] In 1987 Laura Rocha[4] premiered *Crujía H* (Ward H) in which she addressed the theme of political prisoners, an ongoing phenomenon in Latin America, as well as in many other parts of the world. The dancers, Francisco Illescas[5] and Jorge Alberto (Beto) Pérez, enclosed in a space delimited by the imagination, suffered torture from those charged with punishing the prisoners. The performance of the dancers was blood curdling: they beat themselves; they shook; they writhed from pain, appearing to be torn apart without any mercy. This short work managed at times to move the public in an astounding way; tears appeared on the contorted faces of those in the audience, and they had no power to stop them.

THE EXILE

After a change in the administration of Barro Rojo, in which Serafín Aponte replaced Arturo Garrido as director, the group significantly changed its manner of approaching thematic material, most of which, however, was still related to various human rights issues. The company began to incorporate dramatic structure into its choreographies, using that as a scaffold to support the pieces.

An early work in this vein was *Vientos de espera* (Winds of waiting) directed by the Peruvian Óscar Naters (1990). It was one hour in length—longer than any of the company's previous works—and was divided into eight parts variously choreographed by Naters, Rocha, Aponte, and Illescas. The piece was an homage to those who had been exiled, but did not tell anyone's particular story.[6] Rather, it focused on the loneliness, nostalgia, distress, and bitterness that results from leaving the land where one was born—and on the challenge of constructing, despite the sorrows, a new life in which memories weigh heavily. With an impressive poetic charge and dazzling beauty (although that seems paradoxical), scenes depicted the torment of men and women who had to abandon their country because life was no longer possible for them there. One scene showed a woman being tortured by two men who kept dunking her head into a tub of water; in another, the bodies of two nude dancers were hanging from ropes. *Vientos de espera* alluded to those who had fled from the dictatorships of places such as Argentina, Uruguay, and Chile, but it was constructed in a way that transcended time and place. It could also refer to the similar tragic circumstances in Palestine or Sarajevo.

By this time (1990), with eight years of experience that included both successes and failures, Barro Rojo was beginning to establish itself as one of the foremost dance companies in Mexico. *Vientos de espera* highlighted the dance artistry of Rocha, Pérez, Ponte, and Illescas, all of whom demonstrated high technical and interpretive levels. They were developing as dance artists and gaining maturity.

THE ANGEL SOBS SUSPENDED FROM A TREE

> Poets don't invent poems
> The poem is somewhere behind
> It's been there for a long, long time
> The poet merely discovers it
>
> —Jan Skacel[7]

In 1991, Barro Rojo premiered *Tierno abril nocturno (De la vida de los hombres infames)* (Tender April nocturne [Of the life of infamous men]) by Laura Rocha and Francisco Illescas. This work stands out in the history of contemporary Mexican dance for its thematic approach, its choreographic engineering, the strength of its five dancers, and also for its having drawn on the works of three European writers—Milan Kundera, Michel Foucault, and Jean Genet.

The structure of *Tierno abril nocturno* had its origin in Kundera's *The Art of the Novel.* After much experimentation, Rocha and Illescas began to see a close relationship between novels and choreography. For them, the latter is as complex as the former—particularly in a dance piece seventy-five minutes long. From Kundera, the choreographers drew the idea of developing the dance work along several lines, appropriating the idea of polyphony. Kundera writes:

> Polyphony in music is the *simultaneous* presentation of two or more voices (melodic lines) that are perfectly bound together but still keep their relative independence. And polyphony in the novel? First let's set out its opposite: *unilinear* composition. Now, since its very beginnings, the novel

has always tried to escape the unilinear, to open rifts in the continuous narration of a story.[8]

Working with this concept of polyphony, Rocha and Illescas constructed a dance that refers to imprisoned men but can imply the lack of liberty in other contexts as well—in places such as orphanages, mental hospitals, boarding schools, and even military camps and religious seminaries. The story does not emerge in a linear manner but is presented in seven parts, each with its own independence. At the same time, the parts could be assembled in different ways.

The theme of irreverence in the works of French playwright and poet Jean Genet and French philosopher Michel Foucault struck the choreographers, inspiring them to aesthetically explore a quality of ugliness that eventually became a fundamental element in *Tierno abril nocturno*. In that piece, Rocha and Illescas depict transgressive sexuality in the choreography as Genet does in his works, and they draw on Foucault's writing on torture and imprisonment in his *Discipline and Punish: The Birth of the Prison*.[9] As Illescas comments, "If, with Genet, we draw the characters with an obvious sexuality, with Foucault, we find their habitat, we contextualize them."[10] In their development of *Tierno abril nocturno*, Rocha and Illescas used words or phrases from Genet and Foucault as motivation for the dancer/actors. (It should be noted that Barro Rojo has always worked as a collective, meaning that, while there are designated choreographers, each piece is developed through group work.) Wanting above all to avoid the performers falling into a kind of commonplace expression, they worked to transform Genet's poetry (such as the following passages) into dance. These excerpts are from "The Man Condemned to Death."[11]

> The wind that rolls a heart on the pavement of courtyards,
> An angel who sobs enhooked in a tree,
> The column of azure that enwraps the marble
> Make open in my night the gates of rescue (p. 15)

> O come my heaven of rose, o my blond basket!
> Visit in his night your condemned-to-death.
> Tear away your own flesh, kill, climb, bite,
> But come! Place your cheek against my round head (p. 25)

> And the ancient murderers hastening for the rite
> Crouched in the evening draw from a dry stick
> A little fire which the little punk, active, steals
> More moving and pure than a moving prick (p. 29)

For *Tierno abril nocturno*, Rocha and Illescas decided to work with a vision of society in a negative flow that had nothing to do with beauty. It was as if they were digging into the trash heaps of history. They made their own words of Foucault such as the following:

> In each culture there exists, without a doubt, a coherent series of dividing lines, for example: the prohibition of incest, the definition of insanity, and possibly some religious exclusions. The function of these acts of demarcation is ambiguous in the strict sense of the term; from the moment in which the limits were determined, they opened the space for an always possible transgression. This space, at the same time circumscribed and open, possesses its own configuration and its laws, in characteristic form for each epoch, what could be termed a "system of transgression."[12]

Integrated into Rocha and Illescas' conception of the life of imprisoned men were their own personal histories and those of the performers of the piece. They drew upon their own memories. As Illescas noted, "All Mexican men have suffered during tragic years in primary school where they were regularly assaulted. I believe that most of us men have suffered from the brutality of older students during our school years."[13]

Regarding the dance language used in this piece, Rocha and Illescas believed they had to use strong, fast, and violent movement, and that the best source for the quality they sought was in the techniques of acrobatics. Therefore the five dancer/actors trained in that as well as in theater techniques. The scenic elements of *Tierno abril nocturno* consisted of seven boxes that were used in the development of the work. During the piece, the dancers placed them in different configurations and moved within, over, and under them. The costumes of the dancers were grotesque, with the trousers too large, distorting the dancers' bodies; there was also some nudity.

The spectators see five men in prison who suffer insults, violence, and bad treatment, but at the same time, there flourishes among them friendship, love, and play. Like the Genet texts, this piece scandalized and provoked rejection from some of the public—whether in the Palacio de Bellas Artes in Mexico City or in smaller cities such as Mazatlán, Culiacán, Ensenada, or San Luis Potosí. The negative response was to scenes that included nudity or depicted men in the act of love. It is interesting that some people are more scandalized by nudity than by violence. People are more accustomed to (and accepting of) seeing two men fight than make love with one another since the latter is an offense in male chauvinist society. But there were other reactions of the public as well. Among those who accepted it, *Tierno abril nocturno* seemed to touch men more than women. There were cases in which more than one man left the function crying. Apparently, for some men, seeing themselves reflected in a violent situation might have elicited memories of attacks from their childhood or youth.

The choreographers applied to their own work the orientation that Milan Kundera has expressed in relation to poetry. Poetic creation, he argues, means "breaking through a wall behind which something immutable . . . lies hidden in darkness. That's why (because of this surprising and sudden unveiling) 'the poem' [the dance] strikes us first as a dazzlement." Kundera goes on, comparing poetry and history: "In the eyes of the poet, strange as it may seem, History is in a position similar to the poet's own: History does not invent, it discovers. Through new situations, History reveals what man is, what has been in him 'for a long long time,' what his possibilities are."[14] Rocha and Illescas did not consider that they were inventing movement expression, but rather discovering it.

Their exploration of an innovative approach to dance that distances itself from past practices, such as those of the ballet or theatricalized folklore performances, places Rocha and Illescas in the vanguard of dance dramaturgy in Mexico. In *Tierno abril nocturno*, what these choreographers did was to subscribe also to these words of Milan Kundera: "Indeed, if instead of seeking 'the poem' hidden 'somewhere behind,' the poet 'engages' himself to the service of a truth known from the outset (which comes forward on its own and is 'out in front'), he has renounced the mission of poetry."[15] And even though Rocha and Illescas address a theme difficult to express with the body (human rights in a particular context), they don't renounce the mystery of the construction of a choreographic poem.[16]

THE WOMEN WALK BEARING THE CROSS ON THEIR BACKS

> There is a way that you can make me completely happy, my love: die.
>
> —Jaime Sabines[17]

Just as Rocha and Illescas have addressed the situation of imprisoned men, so too have they embarked on an exploration of the reality of women's lives. The result was the 1992 work *Mujeres en luna creciente (La vida está en otra parte)* (Women in the crescent moon [The life is elsewhere]). The central theme of *Mujeres* is pregnancy and all that is said or left unspoken about it. The piece traces different stages or experiences through which some women live—from childhood with its innocent games to abortion. The choreography develops on three planes—those of single women, female children, and wives. The atmosphere is poetic and at the same time extremely raw. The work has moments of irony that some have judged as irreverent. *Mujeres* contains some scenes of family violence and suggests what that imposes on the society.[18] At the same time, the work has an extraordinary beauty that causes us to remember that dance functions as a visual art.

The work dismisses the idea that the pregnant woman loses her sensuality and sexuality, as many suppose. It presents women who love fully, who remember their men through the odor of the shirts they wash, who suffer abandonment, who are mistreated, segregated, minimized. It shows women who suffer continually the negation of their personal rights precisely because they live in a society in which the men still have the last word and take for granted their power over women.

THE AMOROUS ANTIPATHY

> Sex is subversive; it ignores the classes and the hierarchies, the arts and the sciences, the day and the night. It sleeps and only awakens to fornicate and return to sleep.
>
> —Octavio Paz[19]

It is the 1940s. In a dance hall, a couple performs a dance with passion. The public—like a voyeur—watches through the keyhole everything that happens inside that space (loaded as it is with smoke, music, alcohol, and desire). Laura Rocha (by then director of the company) and Francisco Illescas surprised the audience in 1996 with *Del amor y otras perversiones* (Of love and other perversions). The theme of this work comprises all the possibilities of love and its opposite. While a range of specific topics is addressed, underlying the discourse is violence—which can appear whenever two or more persons love each other. From a caress to a blow. From a kiss to bodily mistreatment. From the illusion of mutual love to disdainful rejection. From the desire expressed through a glance to the loathing of enemies. From the loving embrace to the desperate struggle. Carlos Ocampo wrote about this piece, "Fragment after fragment, the spectator is pulled into reconstructing his own memories of the moments when desire takes over his body. In the radiation of erotic energy is rooted the power that moves the entire scenic machine. There the men and women find each other and lose each other; they fondle each other under the folds of the clothing."[20]

SETTLING OF ACCOUNTS

By 1997 Barro Rojo Arte Escénico had been active for fifteen years and enjoyed high status and regard in the context of the national cultural scene. To celebrate this anniversary, the company premiered *Ajuste de cuentas (El recurso del miedo)* (Settling of accounts [The return to fear]), choreographed by Rocha and Illescas. In a conference devoted to BRAE and its work over the years (held at UNAM, the National Autonomous University of Mexico), dance writer Albert Hijar noted, "The work of BRAE is not limited to issues of dance and discussion of the many tendencies within that particular field; rather it forms a significant part of what must be seen as a radical reply to the horror of the end of the millennium."[21]

After *Tierno abril nocturno*, Rocha and Illescas returned to the theme of violence in their piece *Ajuste de cuentas*—what occurs everyday in public and private places; what keeps men and women from the most fundamental enjoyment of life; what powerfully injures those who have nothing to do with the cause of wars; what we inhabitants of great cities suffer and endure; what remains openly exposed but unpunished with the help of corrupt systems of justice; what promotes kidnapping, torture, and the shameless violation of human rights.

In *Ajuste de cuentas* the stage is peopled with those who destroy all, who annihilate, who insult what came before, who strike those who only desire to live. Through all this, the spectator's mind can relate what is being portrayed on stage to what has been prevalent in the offstage world. The massacred body. The days and nights full of danger. The murderers of the defenders of human rights, as in the internationally known case of Digna Ochoa. The assaults. The political persecutions. The raids on homosexuals in the Cuauhtémoc neighborhood. The kidnapping of Nellie Campobello. The slaughter of Acteal in Chiapas. The official line that resolves nothing. The sadness in the eyes of Rosario Ibarra because of the disappearance of her son twenty-four years ago.[22]

With a shattering performance by the dancers, the work's discourse developed in the display of blows, symbolic rapes, sacrifice of the body as a vehicle for punishment—and in the penetrating gaze of an angel who all the time was walking around the stage as if his kingdom lay outside this world. *Ajuste de cuentas* assaulted the spectator without mercy, shook him, aiming to make him uncomfortable. It put forward—without concessions or concealing make-up—a vision of something that affects us all. On the stage were containers, oil drums of two hundred liters, which were manipulated by the dancers as the choreography evolved. There were nine dancers in the work, all performing with a high degree of technical and interpretive skill. Their bodies conveyed sensations and emotions and demonstrated that to "discipline and punish" can be converted into something common and everyday. The tortured and the torturers are united in the dance, which can refer to many situations such as those that have occurred in Mexico City, Barranquilla, Caracas, or Chiapas.

This complex work can be interpreted in various ways: The villain kills the angel and then commits suicide. Does this show that evil triumphs over good? Does it imply hopelessness—in all its glory? Is the allusion to the world having reached a dead end? Whatever one's interpretation, Barro Rojo Arte Escénico—even with its new generation of dancers—is still committed to the themes—so often tragic—of human life and human rights in their choreography. They confront and present lived realities.

LORCA THAT I LOVE YOU LORCA

It is a fear of something, of anything, of all.

—Jaime Sabines

To commemorate its eighteenth anniversary in 2001, BRAE premiered *Vientos de Lorca* (Winds of Lorca) by Rocha and Illescas. The piece "speaks" of the life and work of the Spanish poet and dramatist Federico García Lorca and does not stop at the smell of blood, or at the spilling of blood of the man who was riddled with bullets because of his political position, or at the innocents assassinated by Spain's *Guardia Civil*. In the midst of the Lorca memories, in which allusion is made to the music and dance of Gypsies, the poet would die in the war that destroyed the hope of many men and women. Again, in the luxuriousness of a tree, where birds sing to life, human rights violations appear. The theme is present on the stage. From the beginning of the work one is constantly aware of the death that surrounds the poet.

Vile death! Treacherous death! Death that attacks without any piety! Death to ideas! Death to human values! Death that smells of death!

AT THE END OF THE TUNNEL . . .

A light that shows the exit. While in the world the violation of human rights continues, BRAE continues presenting its dance (sometimes carrying hope) on diverse stages: a stony street, a theater in Barranquilla, or in New York . . .

NOTES

1. The *Palacio de Bellas Artes* is the major venue for the presentation of Mexican and international artists in dance, music, and drama.

2. El Salvador had been in turmoil from at least the 1950s and suffered successive repressive regimes. By the 1970s there had developed increasing violence between the government forces on the one hand, and peasant and church organizations on the other. A military coup in 1979 plunged El Salvador into a civil war that lasted into the 1990s.

3. There is significant difference in Mexico between dance groups supported by the government or other institutions (which may involve a measure of control) and those that are independent. The latter lead a much more precarious existence and have to earn or solicit the resources needed to produce their art.

4. Laura Rocha (b. Mexico City 1962), dancer, choreographer, and teacher, holds the degree of Licenciada in Artistic Education with specialization in dance from INBA (*Instituto Nacional de Bellas Artes*—National Institute of Fine Arts) and also trained at other institutes in Mexico and in New York. She joined Barro Rojo in 1986 and has served as director and choreographer as well as dancer.

5. Francisco Illescas (b. Guadalajara 1959) trained in dance at various institutions in Mexico and earned from INBA both the Licenciado in Artistic Education with specialization in dance and the Maestría in Artistic Education and Research. He also studied in New York. He joined Barro Rojo in 1983 and has served as both choreographer and dancer. He is now working independently.

6. Latin America, as other parts of the world, has seen many cases of the exile of those who dare to oppose whatever party is in power. While preferable to death, exile can make of one a refugee who is homeless faced with trying to establish a new life in unfamiliar and perhaps unfriendly surroundings.

7. Jan Skacel (Czech poet), translated from the French by Linda Asher in Milan Kundera, *The Art of the Novel* (New York: Grove Press, 1988), 99.

8. Kundera, *Art of the Novel*, 73–74.

9. Michel Foucault, *Discipline and Punish: The Birth of the Prison*, trans. Alan Sheridan (New York: Vintage Books, 1995). First French edition 1975.

10. Francisco Illescas, quoted in César Delgado Martínez, "Tierno abril nocturno: entre Kundera, Foucault y Genet," *Blanca Movil* 67 (1995): 8 [Editor's translation from Spanish to English].

11. Jean Genet, *The Complete Poems of Jean Genet*, in *ManRoot* 12, trans. David Fisher et al. (South San Francisco: ManRoot, 1981), 14–37.

12. Kundera, quoted in Delgado Martínez, "Tierno abril nocturno," 9.

13. Illescas, quoted in Delgado Martínez, "Tierno abril nocturno," 9.

14. Kundera, *Art of the Novel*, 115–16.

15. Kundera, *Art of the Novel*, 117.

16. For this work, the choreographers embarked on a process of research and discovery in relation to both thematic concerns and movement vocabulary. The creators do not, therefore, present a black-and-white picture of evil abuse in opposition to some ideal situation.

17. Jaime Sabines (1926–1999) is a well-known Mexican poet; from his *Antología poética* (México: Fondo de Cultura Económica, 1985), 187.

18. Family violence is a frequent occurrence in Mexican society. It is taken for granted in some circles that a man has the right to beat his wife or children if they

displease him. As in the United States, there are those who work to free or protect victims from domestic violence.

19. Octavio Paz (b. 1914), Mexico's most respected poet and essayist, from *Lo mejor de Octavio Paz. El fuego de cada día* (México: Seix Barral, 1989), 189.

20. Carlos Ocampo (1954–2001), one of Mexico's major dance critics and writers. From his *Cuerpos en vilo* (México: Consejo Nacional para la Cultura y las Artes [CONACULTA], 2001), 83.

21. Albert Hijar, "Barro Rojo en el terror del siglo XX," Mesa Redonda: Sala Miguel Covarrubias, Mexico (October 23, 1997). Unpublished transcription by Angélica Del Angel Magro, 1.

22. Digna Ochoa was a dedicated human rights lawyer who received many threats against her life and was finally, in 2001, assassinated in her Mexico City office. Nellie Campobello was one of the leading dance innovators in Mexico in the early part of the twentieth century. She was born around 1913 and disappeared in the 1980s. It turned out she had been kidnapped and efforts on the part of the dance community and others to find her, or what had happened to her, were continually thwarted. The town of Acteal was the scene in 1997 of a paramilitary massacre of forty-five Tzotzil Indians while they were worshiping in their church. Rosario Ibarra's son was detained in 1975 and remains "disappeared" to the present day. Ibarra has continued to fight for information about her son with substantial support from Amnesty International. She has also been active in working for a peaceful solution to the conflict in Chiapas.

· *17* ·

Requiem

LEMI PONIFASIO

LIFE, DEATH, NEW BEGINNINGS

I thought about the village where I was born. This is the village of the sunset. A golden ball of light always sits on the ocean. We would chant naughty songs to the sun of where he is going that night. Then we go inside and pray. I thought about the Kiribati village called *Taratai*—meaning "look to the sun." I thought about my three-year-old son, Le Manaia, wanting to go to the Mysterious Beyond—supposedly where dinosaurs go to if they misbehave. He says Steve Irwin is not dead; he is walking in the muddy water.

As a little boy, one of my most important tasks was to strike the bell three times a day for the Angelus Domini. This Angelus Bell was a gas cylinder hanging from a mango tree. I never knew it was a gas cylinder. I always imagined hitting a bomb. I remembered looking underneath low-flying DC-10s for falling cylinders. Looking underneath was also a way to work out whether a plane was a male or female. Anyway, a chorus of birds would always accompany the silence after the bell. I had a faithful dog, named Jealous, who always howled in tune. One evening a car hit him. I kept watch over him until he died at dawn. I wept. Then at sunrise I went out, dug a grave, and buried him.

Editors' note: Lemi Ponifasio was commissioned to create a work for the New Crowned Hope Festival in Vienna in 2006, a festival celebrating the 250th anniversary of Mozart's birth. *Requiem* is the new work he created; this essay is a reflection on the piece and on its creation. It was originally published in Peter Sellars [artistic director], *New Crowned Hope Festival* (Vienna: Folio Publishing, 2006), 39–41.

My family had a special role in the village. I remembered the calls to attend countless burials and administration of last rites. I remembered the arrival of death to a person, usually when a final prayer is being said or a song is being sung. My father died the same way. I remembered tears falling from his eyes as we sang a good-bye song at his hospital bed. He then took a quiet breath and departed. I remembered giving him his last shave minutes later. I remembered it was a gorgeous mourning. My father is buried in front of our doorstep. We always say hello and good night to him.

I remembered the faces of people minutes before the bombs at the Liverpool Street station. I remembered the moving escalator while everyone stood in silence. I remembered the emptiness of London streets. I remembered walking quietly days after, wanting to place angels all over the stations. Then I thought about the hopelessness of the Angel of History and the terrifying Angel of Rilke. I felt sad. I remembered sitting in an eerily empty 747 on my way back to New Zealand. I felt I was inside an angel above the clouds and closer to the gods.

I remembered a writer who asked me why do I laugh while talking about death.

Then I thought about the laughter of children that whole day. I thought about the Kahui twins.[1] Did someone hear them laugh? I thought about children in mass graves. I thought about Whina Cooper holding her *mokopuna's* hand walking toward the future.[2] Then I remembered why my parents let us children eat first.

When I started to create *Requiem*, I thought we should build a house so that we can see in or be in the inside. I always wanted to be in the House of Night and Day. Of Immensity and Space. I thought I must invite the ancestors for *Requiem* from the beginning of time. They are the whole reason why I have this human existence. Hawaiki is not a mythical land but a state of being. In Albert Wendt's words—

> Inside me the dead
> Woven into my flesh like the music of bone flutes[3]

I am thankful for the gift of dance. It is a miraculous spirit that activates our kinship with the world, the living, the dead, the river, stone, sky, and all sentient beings. In *Requiem* the voices of song have been composed by ancestors and sung by the living. The music has been created from the sound of this land with stones, bones, insects, water, and birds. I hope in the play of shadows we feel the light. In the quiver of the dancer's body we sail in this memorial vessel carrying our ancestors. I hope *Requiem* is more than making poetry. I hope for a community occasion, a *powhiri*, a *kava* ceremony, a Biblical psalm, a meeting, a preparation, a pilgrimage, purification, remembrance, and hope.

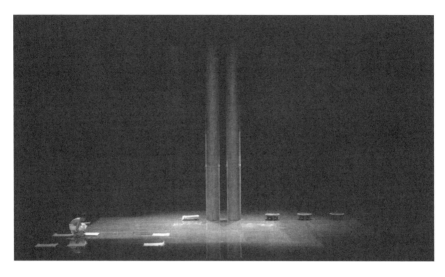

Requiem, by Lemi Ponifasio, performed by MAU, New Crowned Hope, Vienna, 2006. Photo by Armin Bardel, courtesy of MAU.

NOTES

1. The three-month-old Kahui twins died from their injuries in 2006 in what appeared to be a case of domestic abuse within a Maori family.

2. Dame Whina Cooper (1895–1994), honoured as Mother of the Nation, was a Maori community and political activist. At the age of eighty, she led a protest march the length of New Zealand's North Island. A *mokopuna* is a grandchild.

3. From Albert Wendt's "Inside Us the Dead," in *Lali: A Pacific Anthology*, ed. Albert Wendt (Auckland: Longman Paul, 1980), at abc.net.au/arts/ocean/s1/s1_pom.htm.

Sardono

Dialogues with Humankind and Nature

SAL MURGIYANTO

LETTER TO A DANCER: AN INTRODUCTION

Dear Pak Sardono:

We have seen the soaring smoke from a distance since February 1983. The sky has become gray, the sun overcast. We are preparing ourselves by digging a ditch encircling our village. We cut the bushes and clean everything flammable within eight miles of our village, Tanjungmanis. But, fire burns almost everything. Hard as it is for us to believe, this fire burns the ground and approaches our village from all directions, faster than we expected. It bakes our dry fields and turns our huts into ashes.

Five years ago, Pak Sardono's students brought us clove-seedlings. We have grown them with care. We were to have our first harvest in two years. This crop is now destroyed. Our plan to stop moving from one forest area to another and to settle has vanished.

For months we have been living in hell. We lack food and sleep. Men, women, old, and young fight the approaching fire. But the nearby river has become shallow and using only bamboo water-pumps, we can't do much. Once in a while, fire flares violently up into the skies. One day, the roof of a house at the edge of our village came in contact with the fire. We worked hard to keep the house from being destroyed. We were exhausted, worn out and scared.

City people call it a "forest fire." For us, it is our source of life: trees, vegetation, and water sources are burnt. Wild animals come out of the forest. Their claws are peeling; they must have run for miles on the burning ground. Mountain boars, mouse deer, and monkeys that usually run away and hide when they sniff human beings now come to us. In a normal situation, we would have had a big feast. Now looking at them is like see-ing a member of our family in agony. Their suffering is ours. It is almost impossible to kill them. But, we are starving to death. Their meats, though, taste bitter. We feel our Doomsday is near.[1]

BUILDING FRIENDSHIP AND UNDERSTANDING

This letter was written by Ngang Bilung in June 1983. He is head of the Tauw clan of Kenyah, a subdivision of the Dayak, the indigenous people of Kalimantan. The forest fire caused by mismanaged logging undertaken by the Indonesian government in cooperation with timber companies for the sake of "progress" and economic wealth was neither the first nor the last. Again and again it has been occurring during severe dry seasons in different parts of Indonesia's rainforest. As such, the indigenous people of the Kenyah Tauw clan of the Dayak have repeatedly become victims of progress.

In early September 1987, another forest fire occurred. Hearing of this in Jakarta, Sardono W. Kusumo reread the above letter to recall his experiences with the Kenyah Dayak. Sardono had met Ngang in 1978 when he came to Tanjungmanis, a Tauw Kenyah village on the bank of Kelinjau, a tributary of the Mahakam River in East Kalimantan. Sardono was to supervise a group of students from the Jakarta Institute of the Arts (Institut Kesenian Jakarta, IKJ) led by Deddy Luthan, a dance major.[2] These students were doing fieldwork in the area for eight months. But when Sardono's students asked the Kenyah to dance, Ngang gave an unexpected answer: "You want us to dance? I don't think it is the right time. We have come a long way to begin a new life. Many things still need to be done in the field, otherwise we will starve this year. We will dance only after completing all this work."[3] Surprised, Sardono's students had learned their first lesson. They had come a long way from Jakarta to Tan-jungmanis to learn the dance of the Kenyah. The Kenyah had also come a long way to make a better life, but they faced a bitter reality. It took more then ten years for this group of forty families to move from Long Uro, Apo Kayan (the plateau at the headwaters of the Kayan River), in the high interior of central Borneo, to Tanjungmanis. They rowed down rapids, walked through rainforests, planted and harvested on their way, and built not only shelters but also canoes to take them downstream. In 1973, they arrived in Tanjungmanis and settled. They chose the place because it is "close" to (about a nine- to ten-hour boat ride from) the nearest coastal city of Tenggarong where they can get salt, soap, sugar, and kerosene and send their children to high school. They also assumed that they would be able to cultivate a dry field for their food quite easily.

Sardono and his students decided to stay and help the Tauw Kenyah do their work. It was a pleasant surprise for the Tauw Kenyah. For the first time in their lives, eight educated city people were willing to stay and help them work in the field. Later, these students also brought them 7,500 clove and pepper seedlings, and sent Ngang to Bogor, West Java, to learn how to grow these crops. Since then, Sardono and his students have become reliable friends of the Tauw Kenyah. During this stay with them in 1978, Sardono learned how peacefully they lived with nature and how well they preserved their environment. The Tauw Kenyah understand the ecosystem through practice and feeling. This encounter aroused Sardono's interest in ecology. In 1979 his *Meta ekologi* was performed outdoors in mud to create an awareness of earth and water and emphasize the importance of the interdependence of human and natural ecologies.

In November 1981, Sardono went back to Tanjungmanis with two former students of IKJ, Gotot Prakosa (cinematographer and photographer) and Seno Gunira Adjidarma (journalist). They did preliminary research to trace the route of Tauw Kenyah migration. This task, however, required a lot of preparation and proper timing. They went back to Jakarta and had to wait until November 1982 to trace just a small part of the migration route, guided by Ngang. For several days, they traveled from Long Apung to Lebusan in the

Icang Zaini in *Meta ekologi* by Sardono W. Kusumo, performed outdoors at the Jakarta Arts Center, 1979. Copyright Jakarta Arts Council.

Apo Kayan highlands by walking along the forest paths and rowing a canoe on the Kayan River. This adventurous trip almost cost them their lives. Their canoe capsized in rapids and in order to save themselves, they had to let their cameras sink to the bottom of the river.

To pursue a better life and education for their children, Ngang Bilung and his people had to sacrifice their beliefs, longhouses, and traditional medicines to come to Tanjungmanis. Before they realized it, domestic and foreign logging companies controlled the forest around Tanjungmanis. Cutting trees without properly rejuvenating them, they destroyed the ecosystem. Plants, animals, and the people living in the forest suffered. The forest fire in 1983, which destroyed 3,500,000 acres of land, was the biggest forest fire in the history of the country. For three months, Ngang Bilung and his people were surrounded by fire. Ironically, these logging companies were greatly supported by the central New Order government in the name of progress and economic wealth for the people. The rainy season saved the lives of Ngang Bilung and the others.

To combat the 1987 forest fire, the national government chartered a flight (for $2,600 US per hour) to drop water bombs. Once more, rain that fell two hours later extinguished the fire. The Kenyah's problems continued. Government officials claimed their swidden cultivation of dry rice, commonly referred to as "slash and burn" agriculture, was the cause of the fire.

Sardono flared up. He lit his own "fire" in Jakarta to gather funds, forces, and friends. He planned to show city people how the poor and powerless Kenyah had become the victims, not the cause, of the forest fire. Accompanied by Deddy Luthan, Gotot Prakosa, Rio Helmi (photographer), and three journalists, Sardono went to Tanjungmanis to observe the fire closely.

VOICING THE UNHEARD, SHOWING THE UNSEEN

Later, in Jakarta, Sardono organized an event that focused on the Kalimantan forest fire tragedy called *Kerudung asap di Kalimantan* (A veil of smoke over Kalimantan), which took place over nine days (November 24 to December 2, 1987) at Taman Ismail Marzuki Arts Center (TIM), Jakarta.

Gotot Prakosa prepared a photo exhibition and video showing what he had seen in East Kalimantan. Sardono contacted ecologists and various environmental organizations to arrange a discussion on Kalimantan ecology. Sardono himself choreographed a multimedia piece, *Hutan yang merintih* (The lamenting forest), featuring fifteen dancers from the Jakarta Institute of the Arts and eleven Dayak artists (six males and five females) to sing, dance, and play their traditional music. As a choreographer, Sardono is interested in more than theatrical performance. Sardono is a thinker, an intellectual, who is concerned with the lives of real people and their social problems and culture. His choreographic approach is also worth noticing: instead of creating a dance for the Dayaks, Sardono let them perform their own dances. Sardono told me:

> I am very careful in working with the Dayak. They are so . . . unpreten-
> tious. Unlike us, their concept of performance is not theatrical. I could
> not work against their concept. So I simply put it in a frame by creating
> the beginning and the ending. The mid-section of the piece is fully theirs.
> My main concern is how to make the beginning and the ending integrated
> with the rest.
>   This frame helped a city audience to focus their attention on my message,
> which is the ecological damage, the forest fire tragedy in East Kalimantan.[4]

The Lamenting Forest opened with a seven-minute slide show on Kalimantan's virgin forest by human ecologist Herwasono Soedjito. Sardono explained,

> I used slides, video, and film because they communicate effectively with the
> city audience I wanted to reach. The Kalimantan forest fire was not caused
> by the Dayak, who have been living in the Kalimantan forest for hundreds
> of years, but rather by city people, who have mistreated and spoiled Ka-
> limantan ecology. Through *The Lamenting Forest*, I wanted to make them
> aware of this problem.
>   The Dayak, alone, won't be able to solve their problem. They need our
> help. We must be concerned about the environment and, in this matter,
> we can learn a lot from them.[5]

Following the illustrated lecture, the eleven Dayaks (nine Kenyahs and two Modangs) gathered at center stage. They sat on the floor encircled by a strong, red spotlight, as if they were spending their evening in a longhouse in Apo Kayan. Then, one of the women began a song of lament (*ngendau letau*), telling her story of the forest fire. At the end of each line, the rest of the Dayaks repeated it. In the background, a recording of various sounds of nature (water rapids, birds, other animals) from the Kalimantan forest was played.

The lament slowly faded. Tony Prabowo's music loop[6] accompanied the entrance of fifteen IKJ dancers (eight females and seven males), who dressed in traditional Kenyah costumes. In unison they walked in a circle, single file. Their arms described the wing movements of flying hornbills, feathers adorning their hands. Sardono recreated their movements from traditional Kenyah dance steps. After completing one circle, these dancers joined the Dayaks sitting on the floor to form a larger circle. Throughout most of the performance all of these dancers remained on stage.

When the music loop stopped, a Dayak musician played a long-bodied lute with three strings (*sampe*). Then, one Kenyah woman stood up and put on the splendid headdress called *bluko*. She performed a solo (*Kanjet temengan*) accompanied by *Dot Diot*, a piece on the lute. Her dance was centered in a narrow floor area. Her wrists led the graceful movements of the hands, which manipulated the hornbill feathers. The dance ended, but the *sampe* lute kept on playing. Another Kenyah woman stood up to lead the IKJ female dancers in a group dance, the *Datun julut*. Every dancer held a bundle of feathers in each hand. They advanced in a single file with slow steps, rhythmically stomping their right feet. In the background, slides of the Kalimantan rainforest appeared continuously on the three screens even after the dancers and the lute player had finished.

Later, two male dancers with swords (*mandaus*) in their right hands and long wooden shields (*kelambits*) in their left hands performed *Kanjet pepatai*, a dance that simulated a head hunting fight. Each dancer moved slowly and kept his legs bent, almost always in a closed position. Occasionally, the dancers bumped their shields against their swords.

At the end, seven IKJ male dancers entered to perform the masked dance *hudok*, led by a dancer of the Modang Dayak (a neighboring subgroup of the Kenyah). This dance was accompanied by three long, giant drums (*tewung*) and gongs that were placed under the slide screens against the back wall. The dancers wore wooden animal masks representing the rat, boar, bird, crocodile, and monkey. Costumes of bark cloth and fringed banana leaves covered their entire bodies. They wore rattan hats adorned with black and white feathers. The rest of the dancers slowly withdrew from the stage.

The *hudok* dancers moved in a circle, jumping up and down to the drum and gong beats. Slides of the Kalimantan forest fire flashed on the screen. Dressed as a Kenyah warrior, Sardono entered. He danced under a spotlight with a sword and wooden shield in his hands. While scenes of the Kalimantan forest fire continued to appear on the left and right screens, the center screen featured a 2,000-watt spotlight and moving slides of flames. The fire effect and the continuous beating of the giant drums and gongs dramatically intensified the atmosphere. Rusli, well-known painter and member of the Academy of Jakarta, told me:

> The last scene of *The Lamenting Forest* sent shivers down my spine. Sardono had done an impossible task by integrating tribal dancing, his own dance, and audio-visual images in such a way that made me believe what I saw was the real thing.
>
> Dancers, wearing animal masks, danced joyfully only to be swallowed by the ferocious fire. Sardono, dressed as a Kenyah warrior, beautifully fought with sword and shield. He, too, was scourged by fire.[7]

The stage was empty. The drums and gongs had stopped. For a moment, there was only silence. Gradually, Tony's music of the Dayak lament was replayed.

Sardono W. Kusumo, Yola Yulfianti, Dillianti, and Danang Pamungkas in *Sunken Sea*, by Sardono W. Kusumo, Selasar Sunaryo Art Space, Bandung, Indonesia, 2006, from the stage installation *The Mountain of Wind* by Sunaryo. Photo by Adi Rahmatullah, courtesy of Selasar Sunaryo Art Space.

The fire images were replaced by a film of a logging company's workers cutting down hundreds of huge trees with sophisticated chainsaws and scenes of the aftermath of the fire—burning trees and acres of dried, abandoned land along the Kelinjau river.

Onstage, the sounds of the Kenyah's lament continued for another four minutes to end the performance.

Sardono's activities have inspired many artists and strengthened the commitment of scholars and environmentalists to empower the Dayak and promote their life, culture, and arts. In 1987, H. Zailani Idris, an alumna of IKJ's dance department from Tenggarong, East Kalimantan, with the support from the regent of Tenggarong, initiated the establishment of the Institute for the Development of Culture in Kutai (*Lembaga Pembinaan Kebudayaan Kutai*, LPKK), Tenggarong, to preserve and develop the arts and cultures of the Malay and Dayak. Sardono himself continues to explore dialogues between humankind and nature. His *Sunken Sea* reflects on the tragedies of the 2004 tsunami and 2006 earthquake in Indonesia.

NOTES

1. Ngang Bilung quoted in Sal Murgiyanto, "Moving between Unity and Diversity: Four Indonesian Choreographers," PhD dissertation, New York University, 1991 (Ann Arbor, Mich.: University Microfilms), 317–22. Sardono W. Kusumo was one of the four choreographers I investigated for my doctoral research in 1988. To trace his works and creative activities, I had to travel into the tropical rainforest of East Kalimantan to interview Ngang Bilung and his people about what Sardono had done with them. My investigation of Sardono's *Lamenting Forest* inspired my first interaction with the Kenyah Dayak along the Kelinjau River in 1988.

2. Among the results of this fieldwork was Deddy Luthan's collaborative dance piece *Petutung Pekah* (1978), choreographed and performed along with Dayak Kenyah and Dayak Modang artists in Jakarta for the completion of his study at the dance department, Jakarta Institute of the Arts.

3. Sardono W. Kusumo, personal communication, July 23, 1988, in Murgiyanto, "Moving between Unity and Diversity," 318.

4. Sardono W. Kusumo, personal communication, June 1, 1988, in Murgiyanto, "Moving between Unity and Diversity," 338.

5. Kusumo, in Murgiyanto, "Moving between Unity and Diversity," 329.

6. After witnessing and recording Sardono's rehearsals, composer Tony Prabowo did an experiment. He cut his *ngendau* (the melodious and melancholic story-telling song) tape into phrases and, using a recording device, he put them into a music-loop that repeated the lament over and over. Sardono liked Tony's composition and incorporated it into *The Lamenting Forest.*

7. Rusli, personal communication, December 6, 1988, in Murgiyanto, "Moving between Unity and Diversities," 336.

· 19 ·

Adib's Dance

Gaby Aldor

$\mathcal{I}$t was in the early afternoon when Naomi came in. We were in the middle of the rehearsal, but when we realized she had brought someone along with her, we stopped and took a break to meet him. We were rehearsing *The Lane of White Chairs*, a movement theater production based on short stories written by me, inspired by my neighborhood, a cul-de-sac lane in the old city of Jaffa, Israel. Local inhabitants are a mixture of many races and religions, including Israeli Arabs of Muslim belief; Christians; Jews coming from Arabic countries, the United States, or Europe; and Armenians, all of varied social standing, from the most miserable delinquents to bourgeois patriarchs, single mother families, and celebrated bohemian artists.

The work was based on movement emanating from visual and verbal images, and it told the forbidden story of two young Arab lovers, whose families sustain an old enmity, and the return of Taher, the former Palestinian owner of one of the houses, to the place where he was born, revisiting his childhood.

Naomi introduced her guest, Adib, a Jordanian citizen whose Palestinian parents fled Israel during the 1948 war. (We produced this play in 1997, after the peace treaty with Jordan was signed.) He was a trained actor, a graduate of an American university, and he played together with Naomi Ackreman, one of our actresses, in the Palestinian-Israeli-American theater group sponsored by the peace-seeking organization Seeds of Peace.

We welcomed Adib, prepared some coffee, and were eager to hear his story. I felt we might benefit from such firsthand evidence, to incorporate into our piece. But Adib didn't have such memories—he was a smiling, handsome young man, eager to pursue his budding career. He told us, though, that there were varied tales of exile circulating among his rather affluent parents' friends, and that his parents didn't dwell on past events, as bitter as they may have been. His father used to brush the memory away, smiling and thanking God for his good fortune, while others were lamenting their fate. In their stories, Jaffa, the rather run-down ancient port town, where the theater is located, became the lost paradise of their past. He indicated it was a matter of temperament and choice whether to burden your life with memories of painful times, or to go on living the best you can, leaving your past behind.

But we were not satisfied, we wanted to have some story, some memory, some verification of what we believed would be going on in the mind of a returning refugee. Adib looked around and said, "It is a great place you have here, congratulations." The space given to us by the Tel Aviv Jaffa municipality and Udi Ilan, the general manager of a housing project erected on the grounds, to use for rehearsal and later as our theater, used to be, it seems, an old stable for horses and carriages. It was vast, deserted for many years and later used as a warehouse. It had wooden poles scattered in two rows, and we used its spaciousness to experiment with the performer-spectator relationship, unconventional stage proportions, and seating.

"My father used to have stables and horses," he said suddenly. We looked around. "It could have been your father's," one of the actors said. "Maybe," Adib said softly. We all laughed. Being Israeli Jews and Arabs we are used to these sudden turns of ownership, seeing your home from the outside, not ever to return to it. Our parents lost their home in Europe, as did my family in Vienna during World War II, as did my Iraqi neighbors in the early 1950s, as did many in the Arabic countries, and never talked about it. The Arab actors in our company lived not too far from where their families had been banished.

We pressed on. I was looking for something without knowing exactly what to search for. And then Adib said, "All I can remember is my father telling how little time they had to pack and get away," and he stood up and made this gesture with his arms of collecting and grabbing things, and then opening the arms as if throwing them, whispering, "You have five minutes to go, five minutes," as his movement of collecting and holding in his arms, his back bent, got faster and faster until he stopped and said, "That's all I remember, this gesture."

We proceeded with our rehearsal. There was an improvisation in progress, in which the performers would elaborate on a given theme. The performers were holding wide, shallow bowls filled with rice, shaking the grains of rice so as to clean them. The rhythmic shaking of the rice in the big aluminum trays had a pleasant sound. It became a musical instrument in their hands, expressing joy or suspense, or aggression, the actors making it fly above their heads in long transparent arches, as a blessing, or repenting, attacking with it, caressing with it, as if making love.

Suhil Khadad, the actor who was playing Taher, the Palestinian who returns, was missing from rehearsal that day. In the spur of the moment I signaled to Adib, who was sitting and watching, to join in the improvisation. Hesitating at first, but not resisting the temptation to be a part of a moving group, he joined in.

Adib was an accomplished dancer, grasping the way the other performers moved in an instant; he was better trained than some of them, and he plunged himself into the improvisation with a sudden seriousness and commitment. The group kept on moving, incorporating his unique body language into their hidden stories and experiments. He was moving fast, his body becoming tense, as if holding back a lot of energy and emotion. He used small quick steps. There was something fierce about the way he danced, changing directions abruptly, his face becoming more and more hard. Samer Azar, the drummer, who has the talent to detect undercurrents of emotion before others, became even more intense on his percussion set. And slowly I realized, we all realized, that Adib was telling us something even he wasn't aware of. The other performers were highly tuned in to him. He was dancing what seemed to be fear, and they tried to reassure him, offering him their bowls of rice, accepting his anger, trying to go along with him. But he wouldn't comply—he isolated himself, turning away from the soft gestures, from the silent pleading of the group. He didn't want any solace, wasn't to be comforted. His fear subdued, he went on with the frenzy of isolation.

The scene went on and on, relentless. The openness of the group, the insistent accepting, didn't falter. It seems that this strange, fascinating dance could spill over into the street, envelop us all in its truth and unspoken pain. There seemed to be no resolution to the scene. After what seemed to be a very long time, I resumed my position as director, together with Ygal Ezrati, the codirector, who was as spellbound as me. Covering my excitement with a matter-of-fact direction, I attempted to find the right moment to lead the improvisation to a halt. And then, Iris, who in the love story plays the mother of the bewildered groom, began to sing. She has this amazing voice, but she didn't sing alone. The performers' voices became a chorus, a prayer, and a hymn of compassion. And then it stopped.

There was a long silence, and then a lot of hugging. Adib couldn't be seen; so many arms were around him. Now that his dance was over, still a bit shaken, he again smiled. We incorporated his story, his memory, into the work. Khadad, the actor who plays Said, is repeating this frenzied gesture of collecting things in the scene where his memories overwhelm him and he is trying to seize the little boxes, which are the stages' miniature version of houses.

We learned from Adib his hidden fear and anger. Maybe he learned ours. I hope we gave him our understanding and compassion in return.

Part Three

HEALING, ACCESS, AND THE EXPERIENCE OF YOUTH

Japanese Butoh and My Right to Heal

Judith Kajiwara

$\mathscr{B}$ecause of its eerie visual impact, the artistry of Japanese butoh has a very powerful effect upon both performer and audience. Performed with extremely slow, improvised movement, it elevates consciousness, gently opening up untapped dimensions of clarity, creativity, and insight. As time, space, and reality are altered, boundaries dissipate and a connectedness with self and others is experienced. By seeing from a higher perspective, the potential for healing is created. This potential is the primary focus of my work as a butoh solo artist and teacher.

Butoh first appeared in Tokyo in 1959 and was labeled "Ankoku Butoh," the "dance of darkness." Tatsumi Hijikata (1928–1986), considered the "father of butoh," chose this name because of the form's bizarre, ugly gestures, mixed with its labored, slow-motion pacing, reflective of the shocking aftermath of postwar Japan following the bombings of Hiroshima and Nagasaki. Hijikata, along with other disgruntled, young Japanese artists, had begun to explore new modalities of expression. Butoh rebelled against what they saw as both the refined, elitist demeanor of Japanese dance, and the empty, superficial beauty of western ballet and modern dance. Believing that the Japanese body and spirit differed from western sensibilities, Hijikata sought to reverse this aesthetic. Before performing butoh, the entire body was splotched in white powder. Grotesque, disfigured, nude, and seemingly inhuman, his intent was to rebirth the physical body into a spirit yearning to release its pain. Expression was raw and disturbing—with an uncensored honesty that acknowledged hidden wounds that needed to be healed.

Decades later, butoh has spread throughout the world and is still performed as a nonmainstream, counter-culture dance form.

I was born three years after the end of World War II and am a Sansei (third-generation Japanese, born in America) who grew up on a farm in central California. During the war, because my grandparents and parents were Japanese, they were incarcerated for three years in an internment camp in Amache, Colorado.[1] As a child, I absorbed an intangible awareness of humiliation, pain, and anger. These feelings shadowed my parents long after the war, and also shadowed me.

My parents' generation, the Nisei (second-generation Japanese, born in America), compensated for and sedated their postwar feelings by becoming "good" Americans, committed to following the "American Dream." I was a child of that "American Dream." Many Nisei, still needing to prove their loyalty as Americans, denied their children the beauty of Japanese culture and language, fearing they would be "less" American. Their ultimate hope was that their children would never experience the pain of racism as they had.

I always felt isolated from white America. To me, white Americans exuded a physical, intellectual, and verbal superiority. Growing up, I was sensitive and bashful, awkward and unable to understand where I fit. I cherished the times I spent at my all-Japanese church where I could escape into the joyful spirit of our community—the only place I felt truly alive and fulfilled! Other Sansei in my community seemed to eagerly merge into white society, many eventually living a life of class and privilege. Their belief that racism did not exist was unspoken. This denial contradicted and further confused my own reality; and, decades later, childhood remembrances still pulse heavily through my blood.

Though dance was always a part of my life, finding a style that truly personified my cultural and spiritual identity was a prolonged, meandering chase. Butoh, with its rebellious Japanese roots, seemed to flawlessly mirror my Japanese American experience. Its intense, controlled movement style could be misunderstood as a reticence, often interpreted as weakness, of Japanese Americans to express themselves. Yet, because it deemphasizes the aesthetics of the body, its physical confinement and inward concentration encourage the release of self-imposed limitations, freeing us from the haunting syndrome of *enryo* (to hesitate out of politeness). In this way, butoh is a bridge between my life as an American and my displaced spirit as a Japanese woman. Like a kindred spirit, it kept calling me, inviting me to seek refuge within its wisdom.

Reprising my childhood joy as a member of my church community, early in my career, I entirely dedicated myself to teaching dance in San Francisco's Nihonmachi (Japantown). To dance with each other was the key to freedom of expression and finally finding our voice. Not surprisingly, other Japanese

Judith Kajiwara in her work *AD: The Final Fantasy*, 2007, a tribute to her mother's ten-year struggle with Alzheimer's. Courtesy of the photographer, Edmund T. Coppinger.

Americans had also experienced suppressed feelings, and a lack of confidence in expressing themselves. I realized that my students encompassed the same pain, fear, and anger that I had; and given a safe, supportive, noncompetitive atmosphere, their dances magically flourished.

Concurrently, the Japanese American internment became the centerpiece for my performances and workshops. Because of its meditative pace with movement that is improvisational and minimalist, butoh is an ideal dance for anyone, regardless of age or ability. For example, walking in slow motion across a room with a group of people, eyes focused straight ahead, is a simple movement exercise. Yet it evokes a powerful inner vision of what it was like, or may have been like, to be a Japanese American internee forced to move en masse. Butoh breaks down barriers between people, opening up uncomfortable feelings that have been repressed for many, many years.

Similarly, in performance, by crafting stories told through butoh, a spiritual and emotional web is woven between performer and audience. Butoh, with its disturbing intimacy, can provide an experiential pathway for audience members to find their stories or relive a memory. Many have quietly wept while watching butoh.

Two examples of my full-length solo butoh pieces on the Japanese American experience are *The Ballad of Machiko* and *Samishii*. *The Ballad of Machiko* is based on a true story, told to me by my mother, of an Issei (first-generation) picture bride² who travels from Japan to live on a farm. Because her husband resents her lack of outer beauty, she is physically abused and mercilessly forced to work. *Machiko* pays homage to the countless young pioneer women who, over a century ago, endured challenging and difficult lives to start a new community of Japanese in America.

Samishii (to be lonely), based on a story by Sansei writer Ronald Phillip Tanaka, explores the cultural dilemmas of a Sansei man living within the ambiguity of American society. He is torn between his Japanese values and those of America, struggling with issues of loneliness, drug use, relationships, masculinity, and personal worthiness.

Woven into each of these pieces is the remembrance of the incarceration of Japanese Americans. The indelible struggle between pride and shame—experienced directly by the Issei and Nisei, and passed down to the Sansei—continues to dissipate with each subsequent generation. Yet we are forever reminded of this chapter in our history by the Japanese word *gaman*—to persevere, to endure pain, and to suffer with dignity. In creating *Machiko* and *Samishii*, it was important that the characters in these stories convey the feeling of *gaman* to the audience. In spite of a history of racism, struggle, and injustice, Japanese Americans share with other Americans a common dream for a better world. Along the way, we have experienced blockages and have fallen into many dark nights. Our inner power, and those of our ancestors, could have diminished many times. It is only now, in beginning to heal, that we are able to speak out and support our collective struggles with communities throughout the world. This in itself is empowering, bringing closure to open wounds, and breaking through the fragile walls that had falsely protected us.

Today, when despair can easily consume our spirit, I am grateful to share the artistry of butoh with others. Though many artists consider butoh a privileged, esoteric art form—often presenting it as too ugly and intense for a general audience—I believe butoh must be rebirthed to a new level beyond what some consider a strange art form. Its potential—as an accessible dance expression for those who are ready to become visible—is yet to be uncovered.

Butoh is a daily part of my life, and through it, my personal and cultural legacies continue to heal. Valuing my own story encourages stories from others still reticent. By learning from each other, our interconnectedness is strengthened and our spirits are renewed. Butoh is my promise that our healing grants us the opportunity to move forward toward our dreams.

NOTES

1. In February 1942, President Franklin D. Roosevelt signed Executive Order 9066 calling for the immediate mass evacuation of 120,000 people of Japanese ancestry living on the west coast. Sixty-two percent were American citizens. They were incarcerated in ten internment camps composed of hastily built barracks located in the remotest areas of Arkansas, California, Arizona, Utah, New Mexico, Wyoming, and Colorado. Each person was allowed to bring only what he or she could carry. They were released an average of three and a half years later.

2. A picture bride marriage refers to an arranged marriage between a Japanese woman still living in Japan and a Japanese man who had immigrated to America. The couple was introduced through photographs. Many times the man would send his potential bride a younger picture of himself, or one of a much more dashing man. Sadly, many of these brides—who were often twenty years younger than their husbands—led lonely, unhappy lives.

Dancing in our Blood

Dance/Movement Therapy with Street Children and Victims of Organized Violence in Haiti

Amber Elizabeth Lynn Gray

*T*he fields of psychology and humanitarian assistance are merging with increasing intensity as the incidence and prevalence of violence in the world grows. Post-traumatic stress disorder, diagnosed after the Vietnam War and succinctly defined in the *Diagnostic and Statistical Manual of Mental Disorders* (*DSM-IV*), has illustrated the need for mental health professionals to pay more attention to the disturbing effects of war and other forms of organized and systemic violence on individuals and communities.[1] This attention, however, has at times focused on the pathological components of traumatic experience, reducing the experience of a human being at any point in his or her life to that of the trauma. Where trauma exists, especially in areas of ongoing social trauma, resiliency also lives, and the social forces that contribute to individual and collective resiliency can be garnered in support of meaningful healing processes.

In many areas of the world, long-standing civil unrest, conflict, poverty, and oppression create conditions of stress and violence in everyday living that are less newsworthy than war, and therefore often forgotten. These situations can be equally as disturbing to the human psyche and collective experience. Haiti, a country often known only for its poverty and filth, continues to suffer from the ongoing trauma of slavery-related oppression that is an integral part of its history. Haiti's past is a complex and unique web of colonization, slavery, cruelty, resistance, resilience, and liberation, and its recent past includes intense periods of extreme violence and instability, including kidnapping, torture, and rape as an act of war.

Formerly an island inhabited by the indigenous Arawak-Tainos people, and the Ciboneys and the Caribs who came from the southern mainland, Haiti was first a Spanish and then a French colony. Christopher Columbus, thinking he had discovered India, called the original inhabitants of the island "Indians." These native peoples were slaughtered during colonialism and Africans were imported as part of the slave trade as early as 1502 and up until 1789. It was, historically, one of the more brutal places to serve as a slave, and many died from extreme conditions, disease, and torture. Eventually the Spanish and the French fought over control of the island and its resources, and Hispaniola, named by the Spanish, was divided into two countries: the French controlled the western half and renamed it Saint Domingue (now Haiti), and the eastern half, remaining under the control of the Spanish, is now the Dominican Republic. Haiti, renamed by the former slaves who eventually took control of Saint Domingue, is an Arawak word for "mountainous land."

What is unique to Haiti is its status as the first independent black nation in the western hemisphere. On August 14, 1791, while Saint Domingue was controlled and the slaves were brutally oppressed by the French, a socially and spiritually charged gathering took place. This meeting of slaves and escaped slaves from the many different tribes (over twenty-one ethnic groups compose the population or peoples who now call themselves Haitians) who had been forcibly brought to the island provided the impetus for dynamic social change in Haiti.[2] The slaves had retained their spiritual connections, practices, and beliefs despite colonial attempts to suppress them, and this gathering became both a meeting and a spiritual call to action. An all-night ceremony took place, and the revolutionary leader Boukman appeared. The rhythms, dances, and rituals of rage and action, known as *Petwo*, or *Petro*, were born.[3] From this night of fiery rhythms and dances grew a long fight for freedom. The general slave revolt began on August 21, 1791, and on December 31, 1804, the formerly enslaved peoples of Haiti declared independence.

VODOU AND DANCE/MOVEMENT THERAPY

The amalgam of spiritual beliefs and practices that evolved from the fusion of many tribes gave rise to the tradition of communal gatherings, rituals, rhythms, drumming, dancing, and healing rites that are known in Haiti as *Vodun*, *Vodou*, or *Vaudu* (referred to in this chapter as Vodou) and in the United States as Voodoo. The years of civil unrest and conflict, coups and political instability, and violence in the streets, in addition to conditions of extreme poverty, contribute to the ongoing and current trauma and suffering in Haiti, and to the survival of Vodou. Haiti's history of extreme conditions was, and is, matched by a spiritual force that fostered resiliency and the ability to endure. Vodou not only cultivated the strength and resiliency to organize a rebellion and revolution, and endure hundreds of years of political and social upheaval; it continues to permeate everyday life. Haiti is an artistic culture with a strong spiritual cosmology; the rituals and traditions of Vodou infuse life with healing, faith, and a strong sense of family, community, and social responsibility.

Vodou has at its core a central belief that its longevity and integrity as a spiritual practice and a way of life are determined in large part by the health and well-being of its practitioners. Vodou is a familial, ancestral, human-centered cosmology and a danced religion.[4] It is maintained through familial connections, and it is through this hereditary continuum that it manages to survive periods of intense oppression and silencing. For instance, during the occupation of Haiti by the United States Marines from 1915–1934 when drumming was outlawed and vast numbers of drums were initially destroyed by the occupying forces, practitioners or sevitos, as they are known, continued their traditions in more remote areas of the islands, and whatever drums could be saved were guarded in hidden places. (Eventually, it is said that the Marines ended up assisting practitioners to preserve their drums and, therefore, traditions.[5]) In earlier times of occupation and ongoing colonial rule, when drums were burned and destroyed, the slaves created alternative instruments using basic materials found in nature. These "racine" or roots instruments (*tambou marengwen*) include holes in the ground of varying depths covered by large leaves and tree bark of varying tensions, strings or twine of varying tension tied between branches, and other creative percussive instruments, which could be played less loudly than drums and then easily hidden or dismantled.

Deep ancestral respect is an integral aspect of Vodou, and the ancestors are venerated in the form of *lwa*, the spirits who inhabit through possession the sevitos of Vodou. The ancestors also continue and maintain the legacy of Vodou as aspects of the *gwo bon ange* (big good angel, or collective soul) described later. Of its humanocentrism, Fleurant writes: "Vodou recognizes one transcendental spiritual entity whose work is reflected through his/her creation, in the totality of the universe. . . . This, Vodou, as a religious system and as a way of life for the Haitian people, summarizes in its teaching the limitless potential of Homo sapiens for realizing their ontological vocation, the attainment of spiritual freedom in this life."[6]

I began to work as a dance/movement therapist in Haiti ten years ago. I was drawn to Haiti first because of the dance. As a movement therapist I became curious how the dance- and rhythm-based rituals and traditions of Haiti and the practice of Vodou fit into the concept of therapy. Initially I imagined that dance/movement therapy, a somatic and creative arts psychotherapy with roots in ancient healing traditions from around the world, would be a perfect and well-suited healing modality for working with children who suffer from the multiple forms of ongoing violence and abuse that contribute to conditions of social trauma in Haiti. Dance/movement therapy has its roots in the rituals and traditional healing practices of indigenous cultures around the world.[7] This is one important reason it can be an appropriate therapy for clients who come from different countries and cultures.[8] In addition, because dance/movement therapy focuses therapeutic work directly on the body and its movement, it provides a uniquely targeted therapy modality for survivors of extreme and ongoing stress and violence, albeit one that must be modified to be culturally congruent and noninvasive. In my ongoing work with street children (of which there are an estimated 2,500 in Port au Prince alone),[9] child survivors of the prisons (and often torture), and abandoned children who are also mentally and physically challenged, and adult and child survivors of organized violence, I have learned how a western psychotherapeutic practice, even one that integrates seemingly "cutting edge" therapies such as dance/movement therapy must undergo its own transmutation from being theoretically and conceptually a psychotherapy, to support the type of communal practice that is integral to the cosmology and practice of Haitian tradition.

Theoretically, dance/movement therapy is holistic; the individual is viewed as an integrated unity with mind and body reflecting and affecting each other.[10] Inherent in this integration is the premise that muscle tone, or a balance between relaxed and tense states, affects the psychic attitude and vice versa. Dance/movement therapy theory posits that the health–dysfunction continuum is reflected somatically, in the body. The theoretical foundation of dance/movement therapy is influenced by several perspectives from the field of psychology: somatic, psychodynamic, transpersonal, and interpersonal perspectives. For the purposes of this article, these are briefly explained here, along with their relevance to work with survivors of trauma.

From a somatic perspective, the integrated unity of an individual is the result of healthy development, broadly defined as the successful sequencing of the basic neurological actions that make up our earliest developmental movements.[11] Viewed in relationship to the environment, humans develop in an organized, sequential manner. Each phase in this developmental process has somatic and physiological elements as well as psychosocial aspects.[12] The successful and satisfactory completion of each of the phases supports healthy development and a state of health that is reflected in the body. This perspective is an important one in the treatment of trauma survivors because of the disruption to their ability to sequence experience.[13]

The psychodynamic perspective began its influence on dance/movement therapy at the earliest stages of its development as psychotherapy. Wilhelm Reich, who paid close attention to the expressive movements of his patients and posited "defenses were rooted in the body as muscular tension," was developing his work around the same time that Marian Chace, who is considered the pioneer of dance/movement therapy, was developing hers. The psychoanalytic influences of the period supported similar theories in their respective works.[14] Fran Levy writes, "Both were experimenting with psychomotor therapeutic intervention as a way to unlock the thoughts, ideas, and feelings they believed were held in the musculature in the form of rigidity."[15] A focus of dance/movement therapy is to foster movement patterns that begin to mobilize and release the tensions of chronically tight areas, thereby supporting the expression of "repressed excitation and affect."[16] There is relevance in this theoretical underpinning to clinical work with survivors of trauma, and in particular, trauma that involves physical abuse to the body such as child abuse, sexual abuse, and human rights abuses related to war, civil violence, and torture. These abuses are a direct attack to the physical human structure, and to one's humanity. The emotions and excitations, or arousal and fear, that this attack produces are often necessarily repressed as a means to survive, and can sometimes safely be expressed through dance and movement, given the appropriate context. This phenomenon is described by Judith Hanna as cathartic and as having the potential to reduce depression, accumulated psychic stresses, and to safely restore "more enduring personality patterns."[17]

Under the umbrella of the psychodynamic perspective it is also important to consider the interpersonal perspective. From this perspective, dance/movement therapy is viewed "as a process of resocialization vis-à-vis the interactive process."[18] Such a view takes into account that healthy human development requires a communicational relationship between an infant and his or her caregiver. This early foundational relationship is "carried out primarily through mutual sensori-motor engagement."[19] That the earliest form of communication is movement has implications for clinical work with survivors of extreme social and/or relational trauma from other countries and cultures, for there is often a verbal language barrier between client and therapist, and many cultures, as in Haiti, emphasize family and community bonds and commitments over individual needs. Movement—the primary means of expression in dance/movement therapy—is behavior that is experienced by all people, everywhere, to some extent, especially in the early part of life.

Object relations theories also influence the interpersonal aspects of dance/movement therapy; the internal representation of early relationships is often present in the therapeutic relationship. In dance/movement therapy, such representations are frequently invoked through sensation and motoric activity, as well as through images and memories. The rehabilitation of a survivor of human-induced trauma will always depend on the ability to build healthy relationships. For relational trauma, the importance of relationship in the healing process cannot be overemphasized. The extreme state of dependency created by the physical and human rights abuses can create an uncanny bond between the perpetrator and the survivor, or the governing body that abuses power and the community. In the course of therapy for the survivor, this bond can appear as an internal representation or experience of the perpetrator. The manifestation of this in the physical structure of many clients I've seen is a withdrawal into a subservient or fetallike posture, a somatic expression of helplessness.

From a transpersonal perspective, being human can be described as a creative and a sacred act. Dance is an ancient form of worship in many cultures, and the use of dance in rituals of mourning, celebration, and divination is frequently cited. "What is made sensorily perceptible in dance, such as anxiety and fear, is thereby made accessible to purposive action by individuals or groups."[20] Dance is both art and sacred experience, and in the joyful, ecstatic, and often painful states expressed by many forms of ancient and contemporary dance, the body is the medium for expression and divination. Trudi Schoop, whose work focused extensively on the use of improvisational movements as "free association" and planned movement formulation as ego function, believed that any form of man-made art draws on the creative forces of the "UR." She describes the UR as "endless space and/or endless time that continues with no apparent reason."[21] A healthy body creatively and freely opens to our connection to this universal force, or life energy, and the act of healing can be seen as restoring a sense of awareness of, and connectedness to, what Lewis calls "the universal pool of knowing."[22] With regards to the experience of physical abuse, an act of unspeakable terror, the words of Claire Schmais best describe the significance of the transpersonal perspective: "By virtue of the nonliteral or apparently nonrational aspects of the creative act, deep feelings that defy words can be symbolically represented."[23]

In fact, it is the transpersonal perspective that most strongly provides a rationale for the application of dance/movement therapy to work with survivors of trauma and human rights abuses whose culture, language, and cosmology are different from that of the therapist or facilitator. This transpersonal perspective supports the integration of the customs, rituals, and traditions familiar to the culture into the healing process or therapeutic form. And because of its emphasis on movement, nonverbal communication, and the holistic continuum of body-mind-spirit, dance/movement therapy is an effective medium for this type of integration to occur.

Dance is an integral part of ritual practice that has carved the ontological path of human development and human "beingness." Dance, as a human phenomenon, differs from the ritualized dances of animals in that humans can make meaning from, and assign value to, the culturally sanctioned, nonverbal movement patterns that emerge, either spontaneously or in choreographed dances. Dance is a reflection of the human ability to extend beyond preprogrammed motoric sequences necessary to the survival of our species, and to engage in a creative act that supports a transformative process. Vodou is a danced religion that recognizes and celebrates all these aspects: in my work in Haiti as both a dance/movement therapist and an initiate, I have learned that the dance *is* the healing and expresses the continuum that exists between the spiritual world and the world of humans. Maya Deren, the anthropologist who spent many years studying Vodou and became an initiate herself, writes, "To dance was at once to worship and to pray. . . . To dance is to take part in the cosmic control of the world." As ritual dancing, the dances and ac-companying rhythms and drumming of Vodou (which are truly inseparable) have as their intent "to affect the participant, the means by which the physical act creates a specific psychic state are refined and developed." Deren describes ritual, in the context of ritual dance, as an "exemplary demonstration of prin-ciple in action, so that the actual dance is, itself, principled."[24] In my own experience, dance, song, rhythm, and spirit are central to the preparation, ceremony, and post-ceremony activities in every traditional *lakou* (spiritual gathering place), and the body is the site and source of everything from the mundane to the divine.

When I began my work with children in Haiti, and later with adult sur-vivors of a massacre on the massacre site, I was quickly schooled in the basics of group facilitation from the perspective of their culture and cosmology.[25] In Vodou, the facilitator does not assume a unilateral or linear leadership role; he or she initiates the group activity or ritual, and an oscillation between lead-ing and following occurs. My work as a group facilitator or therapist evolved from that of a traditional dance/movement therapist to that of a facilitator of communal gatherings that integrated the rituals of Haitian tradition and Vodou. My subsequent initiation and ongoing work as a sevito further guides my work so that my facilitation skills are the correct balance between relaxed or open, and tense or directive, leadership states—like that of healthy muscle tone. In other words (the words of my spiritual teacher), I learned to "show up, shut up, and get what's going on." I quickly learned that the children were my teachers, and that dance/movement therapy was best suited to group pro-cess as a response to, and integration of, their cultural and spiritual practices. I also discovered that many of the principles of dance/movement therapy appear to share similarities with principles of Vodou, a fact that has more relevance, perhaps, for the author than for the children I worked with. It is my belief as I continue to work at least once a year in Haiti that the rituals and practices of Vodou provide essential developmental, social, historical, and cultural progres-sions and landmarks that are healing in their own right.

In classical dance/movement therapy, based on the work of Chace, group therapy is usually done in a circle. The circle creates a safe container for group expression, process, and healing. In Vodou, the ceremonial dances are also done in a circle, around a clearly delineated center within the peristyle (ceremonial space), called the *poteau mitan*. This *poteau mitan* represents the intersection of the vertical and horizontal dimensions. It is also the point where the physical world and the spiritual world meet. Dance/movement therapists work with the concept that horizontal, vertical, and sagittal dimensions of movement are milestones in human development that are visible in individual and collective movement. They observe movement gestures and patterns, and mirror observations back to participants in an act of reflection and witnessing. The therapeutic relationship depends on this kinesthetic empathy, which is communicated nonverbally, through mirroring and attunement, and verbally, through reflective and descriptive dialogue.

In Vodou, as in dance/movement therapy, the mirror is an important concept; it is believed that those who have died exist in a world, *Guinee*, on the other side of the ocean. *Guinee* is the ancestral home of the Haitians. The ocean serves as the mirror through which ancestors reflect the actions of our individual and collective lives back to us. Each human life has a *ti bon ange* (little good angel), the part of the soul directly associated with the individual, and a *gros bon ange* (big good angel), the life force that all sentient beings share. At the time of birth it enters the individual, and when death occurs, returns to the universal source of life force, God. This principle of collective experience informs a strong sense of responsibility to both the ancestors and to all those with whom life is shared, and appears to be similar, albeit more broadly based, to the Jungian concept of collective unconscious or the dance/movement therapy concept of UR.

Vodou as a way of life embodies the ongoing human relationship with the natural, ancestral, and spiritual world, and imbues life with meaning derived from its rituals. Both the individual and the collective body are tools for divination and prayer. Healing in Vodou occurs in community. The community is always present in the traditional gatherings and rituals of healing to support and witness. There are always observers to the dancers and drummers in ritual, who literally and metaphorically "hold the space." This communal aspect is similar to the dance/movement therapy practice of authentic movement, pioneered by Mary Whitehouse, in which there is always a mover and a witness (and sometimes, several movers and witnesses).[26] The form relies on the integral and inseparable relationship between movers and witnesses as reflections of one another for its function.

Finally, in its impressive attempt to survive colonialism and long periods of occupation, Vodou integrates many of the saints and symbols of Catholicism. They are included in altars, ceremonies, and religious rites and are as much a part of the practice as the African-derived symbols and spirits. This integration helped the tradition of Vodou to survive by "evolving" it to include more current religious elements that dominated the colonial societies and culture. In fact, Vodou is described as an always evolving religion. Integration is also one of the principal healing processes of group dance/movement therapy.[27] The group experience is seen as an opportunity to integrate the individual issues and actions of group members into a communal healing group process.

WORKING WITH STREET CHILDREN IN HAITI

The problem of street children is a global one that grows daily. Street children may be children who truly live on the streets, sleeping where they can and forced to eke out an existence.[28] Such a life can often include prostitution, sexual slavery, drug dealing, and crime. Some of the street children go home at night, but they often face unbearable abuse in their homes, caused by the oppressive and impoverished environment in which the family lives. Many children in rural Haiti are sold to wealthier Haitians in the cities to be used as *restaveks*, and while at times they are treated respectfully as household help, this position can also mean sexual slavery, extreme neglect, and abuse. Torture is prevalent in the jails in Haiti and, more recently, in the frequent cases of kidnapping occurring in Port au Prince. Many street children are jailed, repeatedly, by law enforcement officials and sometimes by their own parents, simply for being on the streets or because their families cannot provide adequate care for them. Kidnapping affects adults and children alike on almost a daily basis.

Haiti is, for all practical purposes, a low-intensity conflict zone; the years of colonial rule, slavery, and oppression have created social conditions that contribute to ongoing street and civil violence, and continue to plague the social well-being and health of the Haitian people. The period of 2003 to the present has been plagued with violence and danger, and Haiti is, as of this writing, currently occupied by United Nations Peacekeeping Forces. Corruption in the government and a severe depletion of resources contribute to ongoing starvation, poverty, and distress, which impacts almost every Haitian's life. At times, even the wealthy endure frequent power, water, and petroleum shortages, and ongoing civil unrest and violence. The use of weapons, and specifically guns, is increasing in street violence, especially among the ever-growing numbers of gangs. Despite, or perhaps due to, these deplorable social conditions, Vodou continues as a response and powerful intervention to transform the energy of extremely challenging social conditions in Haiti.

To work in Haiti, I prepared myself with tapes of varying rhythms and musical styles, and ideas for group activities. The children who participated in one of several programs I have worked with, CODEHA, were part of a

simple education program run from its founders' backyard, adjacent to a gar-
bage dump (other programs include St. Josephs Home for Boys and Wings of
Hope in Cap Haitien, and project Pierre Toussaint in Cap Haitien; children
are all male and aged six to twenty-one). In one early group session I led, they
quickly abandoned my recorded music, and several of them began to drum.
They drummed the rhythms of Vodou, and initially only acknowledged the
rhythms as such. After several more sessions, they began to name and describe
the rhythms to me, sharing the names and meaning of the *lwa* for whom the
rhythms were played, and demonstrating some of the dance movements that
accompanied these rhythms. The children who were not drumming began
to move in and out of the center of the circle, one at a time, taking turns
leading, being followed, and following. As each child created a movement
phrase in the center, he or she turned toward each child in the outer or witness circle, and they mirrored movements to one another. No child skipped
being witnessed by each member of the group. It was made clear to me that
each person had to spend time in the center, to lead or initiate movement, to
be seen, and then to offer back to each mover in the center the mirroring of
his/her movement. This practice is similar to the tradition of the solo circle
that exists in many African dances and rituals, and somewhat similar to the
traditional dance/movement therapy circle, although rarely in the traditional
psychotherapeutic group setting have I seen group participants so consciously
seek the center of the circle, and the opportunity to be seen and to have their
experience reflected back to them.

The dances they shared displayed a wide repertoire of movement styles.
Yanvalou, danced in supplication at the beginning of all ceremonies, consists
of graceful, fluid snakelike movements that honor Damballah and Aida Wedo,
the snake *lwa*. They have been described to me as the *lwa* who represent
creation, and they are perhaps the most widely known *lwa* in Haiti.[29] The
children also taught me some of the movements associated with the dances for
the *Guede*, the entities of life and death. One of these dances, *Banda*, contains
movements that depict our sensual and sexual nature as human beings, and the
dance, in my experience, is one that pokes fun at human folly and therefore
contains elements of humor and trickster energy. This dance and rhythm is
usually found toward the end of a ceremony. They also shared the strong, war-
riorlike movements danced in *Nago* for the *Ogoun* (warrior) family of *lwa*.

As our work together progressed, an exchange between the children and
myself occurred. Although they were aware of the roots of their Vodou traditions, rhythms, and dances as being African, they complained that they did
not know any "real African dances," and wanted to learn them. Thus began
an exchange in which each child would teach me a movement from a social
or sacred dance associated with *Rara* (the rural equivalent of Mardi Gras) or

the Vodou ceremony, and I would reciprocate with a movement from a West African dance.[30] In this exchange we taught one another about the histories and meaning of the dances, as we knew them, and discussed the collective history of Africa and Haiti.

The children also taught me to cocreate with them and incorporate rituals to begin and end each session that we eventually integrated into every session. They instructed me that ritual was the way to integrate the meaning of our work together into daily and ongoing life. One we created consisted of a simple cleansing ritual using water, to clear the space and to retain the "freshness" and "newness" of the dance after clearing the soul of excess energy and burden. The children stressed the importance of my understanding that healing only occurs when there is community-endorsed movement into and out of the spirit world through ritual and that this is how we make connection with the ancestors, ask for assistance and support, and integrate what we have learned and what we must do to take right action into our daily lives.

The dances of Vodou are dances that both celebrate life and initiate the essential processes and experiences of life, as they relate to the continuum of existence we are all part of. These dances, embedded in a meaningful and historical philosophy of the existence of all life, are core to the healing of children in Haiti. Individuals express and process suffering in the presence of community, and the community builds resilience through a creative, collective process that mirrors and honors the very roots of Haitian culture.

CONCLUSION

As mentioned previously, the strongly transpersonal nature of dance/movement therapy and of dance itself as a creative force lends it to the discovery of a historically common language for the deeper expressions of the soul that is likely inherent in dance/movement therapy and in the healing rituals of not only Vodou but of many of the healing rituals and traditions to be found in indigenous cultures worldwide. The use of indigenous healing for war-affected children in Africa has been documented as demonstrating that the practices of traditional healers may be just as effective as any western psychotherapy introduced to another culture if it is "embedded within social and cultural specificities."[31] David Read Johnson, a psychologist who incorporates the creative arts therapies and ritual into his work with survivors of trauma and has worked extensively with combat veterans, describes the importance of ritual and ceremony to reestablish social connection after individual or collective traumatic experience.[32] Ceremony can "re-contextualize the experience of trauma," and communal ritual can "encourage identification and attachment with the group and its system of defense, alleviating pressure on the individual."[33] Dance/movement therapy, a somatic and a creative arts psychotherapy with a strong emphasis in group psychotherapy, may indeed be a psychotherapeutic vehicle to create these social and cultural specificities, albeit one that must also break free of some of its western psychotherapeutic origins that can become cultural limitations.

While all western psychotherapeutic practice has merit as one aspect of response or intervention to trauma caused by war, violence, or human rights abuse, dance/movement therapy is perhaps one that merits further exploration as the need grows for countries such as the U.S. to respond to the increasing number of civil and political conflicts, wars, genocide, and acts of terrorism around the globe. The flexibility and fluidity inherent in the practice and application of dance/movement therapy create a medium in which the cultural and social practices essential to recovery from extreme stress, even if the individuals or social structures that carry them are disrupted or in part destroyed by the acts of violence, can be cultivated and integrated into a larger-scale healing process.

NOTES

1. American Psychiatric Association, *Diagnostic and Statistical Manual of Mental Disorders DSM-IV* (Washington, D.C.: American Psychiatric Association, 1994).

2. Gerdes Fleurant, *Dancing Spirits: Rhythms and Rituals of Haitian Vodun, the Rada Rite* (Westport, Conn.: Greenwood Press, 1996), 2; and Mano Brignol, personal interview, February 27, 2003.

3. The *Petwo*, or *Petro*, rhythms and dances are uniquely Haitian. The tradition of Vodou continues to honor and pay tribute to the various tribal rhythms and dances that came over from Africa (i.e., Nago, Congo, Rada, Ibo), and these are woven into all traditional ceremonies. The *Petwo* spirits who are said in spoken legend to have been "birthed" on August 14, 1791, are considered to be some of the fieriest and most dangerous spirits, and are treated with utmost respect and only called upon in specific circumstances. One does not call them or speak of them without sufficient preparation.

4. Fleurant, *Dancing Spirits*, 2.

5. Odette Weiner (Mambo), interview May 31, 1999.

6. Fleurant, *Dancing Spirits*, 9.

7. Irmgard Bartenieff, "Dance Therapy: A New Profession or a Rediscovery of an Ancient Role of the Dance?" *Dance Scope* 7, no. 1 (1972/3): 6–18.

8. It is commonly cited that dance/movement therapy has its deepest roots in ancient traditions of healing; these are not necessarily specifically elucidated in the early work. However, as an example, the Minianka tribe of Mali has always healed through

rhythm. Health is restored by leading an individual back into a state of alignment with the rhythms appropriate to his/her professional role and personal identity. Their healers make use of what physics calls the principle of resonance or entrainment. Entrainment causes two similar but slightly different rhythms to gradually fall into unison if they are placed in close proximity. A disturbed person's rhythmic patterns will shift according to the rhythms of the drums. In their use of rhythm as a tool for social integration, harmony, and cohesiveness, tribal societies show an intuitive understanding of entrainment. Also, "repetitive, rhythmic movement was thought essential [in many cultures] to build up the movement of ecstatic union with the deity, like rhythmic sensual movements and orgasm. Rhythm is medicine for both the individual and the community, and communal drumming and dancing unite celebration and healing." See Jalaja Bonheim, *The Serpent and the Wave* (Berkeley, Calif.: Celestial Arts, 1992), 154.

9. Amber Gray, "Dancing in Our Blood: Dance/Movement Therapy Voodoo and Social Trauma with Street Children in Haiti" (master's thesis, Naropa University, 1999), 30; UNICEF, at unicef.org/index.php (2007).

10. Penny Lewis, "A Holistic Frame of Reference in Dance-Movement Therapy," in *Theoretical Approaches in Dance-Movement Therapy,* vol. I (Dubuque, IA: Kendall/Hunt, 1986), 279–89.

11. Susan Aposhyan, *Natural Intelligence: Body-Mind Integration and Human Development* (Baltimore: Williams and Wilkins, 1999); Bonnie Bainbridge-Cohen, *Sensing, Feeling and Action* (Northampton, Mass.: Contact Editions, 1993).

12. Penny Lewis, "A Holistic Frame of Reference," 1986.

13. For example, while in Haiti I worked with a seventeen-year-old boy who was severely undersized from malnutrition and abuse. His body posture was fixated in the position he was found and tortured in—he was tightly bound in a twisted fetal position on the floor, and always faced the wall with his head turned to the right. He responded to only one invitation: if he were approached from his left side he would grab the outreached hand and push hard into the person approaching him. This single-armed pushing pattern (homologous push) was a very early developmental movement that appeared to be truncated at a fixated, frozen shoulder. Through our sessions his upper body began to relax and he was able to develop more relational behavior and begin to increase emotional expression. See Amber Gray, "The Body Remembers: Dance/Movement Therapy with an Adult Survivor of Torture," *Journal of Dance Therapy* 23, no. 1 (2001): 32; "Healing the Relational Wounds of Torture through Dance Movement Therapy," *Dialogus* 5, no. 1 (2001): 1–4; and "Dance Movement Therapy with a Child Survivor: A Case Study," *Dialogus* 6, no. 1 (2001): 8–12.

14. Claire Schmais, "Dance Therapy in Perspective," in *Focus on Dance VII*, ed. K. Mason (Washington, D.C.: AAHPER, 1977), 9. Marian Chace is considered the mother of dance/movement therapy, having created an extensive body of work that is still the foundation of education in dance/movement therapy in the United States. Her work, which developed around the same time as Wilhelm Reich's, displays the strong psychodynamic influences of the time, and all the pioneers of dance/movement therapy demonstrate influences from the psychotherapies of the time as well as concepts developed in the dance world (i.e., Rudolf Laban's efforts).

15. Fran Levy, *Dance/Movement Therapy: A Healing Art* (Reston, Va.: American Alliance for Health, 1988), 25.

16. Claire Schmais, "Dance Therapy in Perspective," 9.

17. Judith Hanna, *To Dance Is Human: A Theory of Nonverbal Communication* (Austin: University of Texas Press, 1979), 68.

18. Claire Schmais, "Dance Therapy in Perspective," 9.

19. Penny Lewis, "A Holistic Frame of Reference," 289.

20. Judith Hanna, *To Dance Is Human*, 68.

21. Fran Levy, *Dance/Movement Therapy*, 77.

22. Penny Lewis, "A Holistic Frame of Reference," 280.

23. Claire Schmais, "Dance Therapy in Perspective," 9.

24. Maya Deren, *Divine Horsemen: The Voodoo Gods of Haiti* (London: Thames and Hudson, 1953), 240–41.

25. The children, who participated in programs described later in this chapter, did not tolerate my showing leadership of the group process until I had been there enough times to earn their respect and confidence. Initially this group dynamic appeared to me to be resistance, but eventually I learned that the children, who were strongly bonded in their community of street children, had adapted what I later came to know, through Vodou, as interactive facilitation (my description). In Vodou, the Mambo (female) or Houngan (male) is a spiritual, medicinal, and social leader, and as such, is imbued with certain authorities, education, and powers. It is their responsibility to be familiar with the sequence of songs, prayers, and rhythms that compose a proper ceremony, based on the purpose, timing, and meaning of the ceremony. Similar to the role of the witness or mover in authentic movement or many other forms of therapy or dance, their role is to be the presence that "creates and holds the space," be it creative, healing, or ceremonial space. Other than keeping the group and ceremonial activities on track, the facilitator does not interfere, interpret, or judge; only in cases in which a participant needs assistance that the community cannot provide will the Mambo or Houngan intervene. Abuses in this power are not tolerated. Hence, the Mambo or Houngan is both leader and in service to spirit. Community or neighborhood leaders in Haiti perform a similar role for their communities.

26. Authentic Movement is a movement form in which the therapist, facilitator, or witness observes the client, or mover, in silence. Jungian psychology influenced the development of this work, and while the therapist, or witness, may be applying any of the above-described theoretical foundations of dance/movement therapy to the mover's practice, this is not usually done aloud. The witness shares observations of the mover from the perspective of "I." For example, rather than interpret or judge a movement gesture or sequence, the witness might say, "When I saw you raise your arm, I felt my own breath move upwards in my body." For a good description of Authentic Movement, see Mary Starks Whitehouse, Janet Adler, Joan Chodorow, and Patrizia Pallaro, eds., *Authentic Movement* (London and Philadelphia: J. Kingsley Publishers, 1999).

27. Claire Schmais, "Healing Processes in Group Dance Therapy," *American Journal of Dance Therapy* 8 (1985): 17–36.

28. Amber Gray, "Dancing in Our Blood."

29. Odette Weiner, interview, May 31, 1999.

30. Gerdes Fleurant, *Dancing Spirits*, 13. As a dancer I have been involved with several troupes that perform West African and Afro-Caribbean dance. The foundation of African dance and drumming, and drum circles, is the call and response: the drums and dancers are in a constant state of interaction with one another—drumming responds to the movements of the dancers, and movement responds to the rhythm of the drum. One of the dances I frequently teach, for example, is a West African (Guinea) Harvest Dance (also called "Kakelambi"), whose movements symbolize and mimic gestures associated with the important act of harvesting (planting, sifting, sowing, and picking crops). Another dance, *Funga*, from Nigeria, is a dance of welcome, in which the movement itself gestures from the heart upwards to the sky, downwards to the earth, and directly out (sagittally) toward other people in the area.

31. Edward Green and Alcinda Honwana, "Indigenous Healing of War-Affected Children in Africa," *IK Notes*, no. 10 (July 1999): 2.

32. David R. Johnson, "The Role of the Creative Arts Therapies in the Diagnosis and Treatment of Psychological Trauma," *The Arts in Psychotherapy* 14 (1987): 7–13.

33. David R. Johnson, "The Therapeutic Use of Ritual and Ceremony in the Treatment of Post-Traumatic Stress Disorder," *Journal of Traumatic Stress* 8, no. 2 (1995): 286.

Interactions between Movement and Dance, Visual Images, *Etno*, and Physical Environments

Psychosocial Work with War-Affected Refugee and Internally Displaced Children and Adults (Serbia 2001–2002)

ALLISON JANE SINGER

𝒯his article suggests that there is a fluidity of interaction between movement, visual images, *etno*, and physical environments that plays an important role in psychosocial work with war-affected refugee and internally displaced children and adults.[1] This interaction between different media is of particular significance in the building of relationships between refugee and internally displaced people and locals, and between these individuals and their physical, social, and cultural environments, contributing to and enabling processes of rehabilitation, resettlement, and integration.

During fieldwork in Serbia, from September 2001 until September 2002, I participated in the work of a Serbian nongovernmental organization (NGO) called *Zdravo da ste* (Hi Neighbor). *Zdravo da ste* was founded in 1991, at the beginning of the war in former Yugoslavia, by a group of Serbian psychologists. *Zdravo da ste*'s practical work with refugee and internally displaced children and adults was facilitated by local psychologists and teachers, some of whom had themselves been Serbian refugees from other regions of former Yugoslavia. All interviews were conducted in confidentiality, and the names of the interviewees are withheld by mutual agreement.

The ideas of the Russian psychologist Lev Vygotsky have been a central influence on *Zdravo da ste*'s approach.[2] This approach both incorporates and challenge theories and methods derived from psychology, international development, education, and the creative and performing arts. While *Zdravo da ste* were very clear with me that their aim was not therapy, they nonetheless accepted my participation with them as a dance movement therapist. Although not an arts organization, creative media and processes appeared to be central aspects of *Zdravo da ste*'s work. This article discusses *Zdravo da ste*'s use of creative and performing arts media and processes and their place within *Zdravo da ste*'s approach to psychosocial work with war-affected refugee and internally displaced children and adults. It also discusses the role of *etno*, a term further elaborated below, which was used by my informants to describe regional dance, song, music, and art forms from the former Yugoslavia.

METHODOLOGY

My methodology integrated dance ethnography incorporating participant observation, and dance movement therapy (DMT). Participant observation included participation in and later cofacilitation of workshops facilitated by *Zdravo da ste* with preschool and school-age children in Belgrade and surrounding areas, and at a ten-day summer camp in Montenegro; undertaking intensive Serbian language training both in the United Kingdom and in Belgrade; conducting formal and informal interviews; and documenting the fieldwork through field notes, video, and photography.

I chose six workshop contexts to form the basis of my analysis. These included weekly preschool workshops at one of *Zdravo da ste*'s offices in central Belgrade; preschool workshops at Kalamegdan Park in central Belgrade; children's workshops at refugee camps (called collective centers in Serbia) close to Belgrade; large intergenerational workshops at galleries, cultural centers, and the Ethnographic Museum in Belgrade that also integrated children from different collective centers and, on occasion, local children; workshops that formed part of *etno* exhibitions in local cultural centers in towns close to Belgrade; and workshops that formed part of the annual summer camp in Bijela, Montenegro. Within these workshops, I used my skills and training as a dance movement therapist to interact with the children and the workshop facilitators. My dual status as dance researcher and dance movement therapist, although giving me access to the community, created an ongoing tension particularly in terms of the development of relationships, roles, and responsibilities in the field. This was because each role had its own responsibilities that sometimes conflicted with the other position. For example, as an ethnographic researcher my role was to understand *Zdravo da ste*'s approach to their work and the decision-making processes that informed this work; as a DMT practitioner my purpose was to work directly with the children and adults as and when needed and to share my skills and knowledge with members of *Zdravo da ste*.

THE FIELD

The "field" was both postwar Serbia or, more specifically, Belgrade during 2001–2002, and the processes and conceptions of becoming and surviving as a refugee. The latter includes notions of ethnic identity, refugee consciousness, integration, and resettlement in the context of war. Graça Machel, an expert appointed by the United Nations (UN) in June 1994 to make a study on the impact of armed conflict on children, proposed:

> War violates every right of a child—the right to life, the right to be with family and community, the right to health, the right to the development of the personality and the right to be nurtured and protected. Many of today's conflicts last the length of a "childhood," meaning that from birth to early adulthood, children will experience multiple and accumulative assaults. Disrupting the social networks and primary relationships that support children's physical, emotional, moral, cognitive and social development in this way, and for this duration, can have profound physical and psychological implications.[3]

The effects of war on children and the way that they and their families and communities respond to these effects are not universal, but are shaped by differences in culture and belief systems, as well as actual experiences and choices. One effect of war is trauma, which psychologist Arthur Janov suggests becomes imprinted on the body and creates a splitting within the person between what is hidden and what is felt.[4] The traumas experienced by refugee children and families do not lie solely in the realm of mental health, but also include social, economic, political, and cultural factors.

In relation to the war, *Zdravo da ste* insisted on acknowledging the reality of the situation, refusing to label or treat as "other" the children and families displaced by the war, and worked from the basis of people's relationships to life in the present, rather than the past or the future. The coordinator of the children's team described the work of *Zdravo da ste* as "a philosophy of living and building or rebuilding again the social frame for living."[5] It was this emphasis on building and rebuilding relationships that underlay the work, and facilitated the development of the organization's programs.

Members of *Zdravo da ste* described some of the children with whom they worked as being frozen and unable to play in response to their experiences of war. A preschool teacher and member of *Zdravo da ste*'s Belgrade team suggested that one aim of *Zdravo da ste* was to activate parts of the individual that had become frozen or locked and in this way stimulate a "renewal of communication which includes [the] human soul."[6] Through their participation in the workshops, including dance and movement activities, informants described the children as opening. As the children grew older, this experience was remembered and could be used as a resource in their lives. Several members of *Zdravo da ste* described children as "initiators of change" and many of the children's workshops were used as a basis for workshops with other members of the refugee and internally displaced people's community.

In order to facilitate this change, *Zdravo da ste* used physical, visual, and narrative images in the context of the workshops. Not only were these images used as responses to the activities in the workshops, they also created the opportunity for the children to express memories, experiences, and ideas, and to use these memories to further understand themselves and their relations with others and the world of which they were a part. *Zdravo da ste* also employed visual and aural images to represent their organization and to create a focus around which participants and facilitators could feel a sense of belonging in this new context; they also considered the physical environments in which the workshops occurred.

PHYSICAL ENVIRONMENTS

The physical environments in which the workshops occurred were carefully selected by *Zdravo da ste*. For example, in the preschool program the children had their own room in which to work; over the year this became full of the visual images they created during the workshops. The preschool children also occasionally attended workshops described as "eco" or ecological workshops in Kalemegdan Park. In the workshops at the Ethnographic Museum and at the opening of *etno* exhibitions, *Zdravo da ste* created environments using the *etno* products made by the participants. In the summer camp, an eco workshop was held at Zjanica, an island close to the point where Kotorska Bay opens to the Adriatic Sea. In this workshop the children's first activity involved making movements and loud and quiet sounds reflecting a relationship with the surrounding natural environment. They then divided into smaller groups and walked through the environment collecting different objects that caught their attention while also recording sounds onto a dictating machine. The objects were later used to create small group collages, which were taken back to the hotel and added to the environments the children had created in the hotel lobby areas outside their rooms, using found objects and objects created in other workshops.

The ways in which *Zdravo da ste* facilitated interaction with the various locations where the workshops took place gave the children an opportunity to see that they could construct new relationships with a geographical place. This was important in the context of the children being displaced, forcibly removed from a familiar home environment to a new country or an area where they were considered outsiders.

In contemporary writings from archaeology and anthropology, the term *landscape* is used to refer "both to an environment, generally shaped by human interaction and to a representation (particularly a painting) which signifies the meanings attributed to such a setting."[7] Landscape is conceived of as "socially constructed and hence subject to continuous reinterpretation"[8] and "ideologically constructed."[9] Folklorist Mihaly Hoppal suggests that space, like spoken language, "mediates a value system," and the use of space follows "culturally defined patterns" that contribute to "marking out value norms for the individual."[10] Developing a relationship with a new environment and realizing the potential to create new relationships with known environments develops the opportunity to change the relationship with the past, creating new possibilities in the present and for the future.[11] These new relationships were explored in the workshops using movement, images, and creativity. Defining the relationship between a person and his or her environment and exploring this through movement are also an important part of the therapeutic process in DMT.

MOVEMENT, VISUAL IMAGES, AND CREATIVITY

The founder of *Zdravo da ste* considered movement and dance to be two of a number of "human potentials for expression," tools that could be "discovered and actualised" and used alongside other media to find and develop the hidden potential within each person, and the "voices of the future."[12] Furthermore, she considered these potentials to be fundamental to human nature and indestructible.

In DMT it is assumed that there is a relationship between "motion and emotion."[13] Exploration of movement in a creative context and a safe and contained environment facilitates the expression and transformation of emotion through understanding and relationship. The body, as well as body movement, is conceived of as both experience and a locus of change. Dance anthropologist Deidre Sklar suggests that the body itself can be understood as:

> a process, one that organizes as it apprehends and becomes what it organizes. . . . The body does not hold experience; rather, it is experience, a process rather than an object. Somatic understandings emerge as a process of incorporating and configuring information into the body one is always in process of becoming.[14]

Dance and movement have the potential to become an "interface between the conscious and unconscious."[15] In the context of war-affected refugee children, dance and movement thus become a place in which children can be given an opportunity to understand, integrate, and transform their experience of war. Conscious understanding, however, may be delayed, surfacing at a later stage as part of an ongoing developmental process, as observed by the founder of *Zdravo da ste*.

In the workshops, movement was used in several ways. For example, simple stretches were sometimes combined with games at the beginning of a workshop in order to prepare the children for the main activity of the workshop. Games, well known to the workshop participants, were sometimes used as a theme for a workshop as a way to stimulate social interactions in intergenerational workshops, for example, or workshops with children from a different collective center. Motifs from *etno* dance emerged in some of the integrated workshops and workshops with adults, including specific foot patterns, clapping rhythms, or physical formations such as chains, spirals, and circles. Movement was also used as a form of embodiment of visual images or stories created in a workshop, or of previous experiences such as a recent summer camp. For example, in one workshop for about forty children at an isolated collective center about two hours' drive from Belgrade, the facilitators worked with the theme of water with the children in order to remember the summer camp they had participated in two months before. The children were asked to find different ways of moving like water, in both small and large groups. They were then invited to create individual pictures using paints. Toward the end of the workshop the pictures were placed together in the center of the room for all to see and the children were asked to say the words that came to their mind as they looked at the pictures. The words were written down and the pictures collected to be used in a follow-up workshop as the basis of a story.

Physical images at the end of some workshops helped children reinforce the experience of the workshop as they shared these images with other participants. Movement was also used to facilitate the development of skills in reading and writing in preschool workshops, by embodying the shapes of letters while simultaneously sounding them out.

Work with memories and embodiment of memories through movement and visual images allow people to experience themselves in relation to memory, the space they are in, as well as to other people, thus potentially leading to new understandings and awareness. When images are used in order to provoke memory recall, they also take on a symbolic significance. As psychologists Beverly Roskos-Ewoldson, Margaret Inton-Peterson, and Rita Anderson suggest, "Images are often produced with intention for some purpose. As such, images tend to be inherently meaningful."[16] This implies a direct relationship between image formation and emotions, in which the emotion is the impulse behind the intention of the image formation, and may also be the result of this formation.[17] Roskos-Ewoldson and colleagues further suggest that the importance of the image determines the extent to which it is maintained in the memory.[18] Interpretation of the image and the motivations behind this interpretation determine what is considered good or bad, and in this way form the basis of the individual and cultural value of the image. Images are open to manipulation and are themselves representational both in what they show and in what they hide. Thus through their observations and responses to the images produced by the children, members of *Zdravo da ste* could interact with the children's psychological processes through the processes themselves.

Vygotsky describes young children as "eidetic" in that they are able to recall visual images and experiences with incredible accuracy.[19] He points out, however, that this faculty disappears as the child begins to think in concepts, with the onset of puberty. From this perspective, working with visual images with children complements their way of perceiving and experiencing the world. Vygotsky further suggests that for very young children, memory "appears in active perception, in recognizing"; however, as a child reaches school age, thinking becomes increasingly "depend[ent] on past experience."[20] The interaction with the creative elements used in the workshops allowed possibilities for the children of different ages to recognize and remember. Furthermore, Vygotsky proposes that awareness includes "reorganization" as well as "expression or . . . evocation."[21] This suggests that creating physical and visual images in response to memories and experiences, in the context of psychosocial work with war-affected refugee children, has the potential to allow the children to reorganize their experiences and reframe them in the present.

The coordinator of the children's team stressed that dance and movement were only two of many creative elements or media that were applied in the workshops as part of a "social frame . . . [or] social happening"; other media included voice, story, painting, and collage.[22] Creativity itself was considered to be an inevitable part of the work. The founder of *Zdravo da ste* described creativity in the following way: "I see creativity as life. It's not a means, it's not a tool, it's life and the people have such a capacity to create, an endless capacity to create. That's the life, to be creative. To create means to be alive."[23] A member of the children's team described these creative elements as bridges to connect people in "mutual action," in order to facilitate the development of social, cultural, and environmental relationships.[24] They offered people the means to harness resources inside themselves and apply them to their new situation. For a child made a refugee because of war, working creatively gave him/her the opportunity to rearm. As Luria and Vygotsky suggest, "In the process of development the child not only matures, but is re-armed. It is this 're-arming' that accounts for a great deal of the development and changes we can observe as we follow the transition from child to civilized adult."[25] For refugee children, this rearming can be considered a trigger for developmental processes in the new context of being part of a displaced community. It gives them tools for their survival and participation in the world in which they find themselves, and the future world to which their daily actions contribute. The example given below illustrates the interaction between different arts media within a workshop context at a summer camp held in Bijela in Montenegro in August 2002.

Four hundred children attended the summer camp from Serbia and Republika Srpska. During the summer camp a visit was arranged to the old Roman and medieval walled town of Kotor.[26] The initial visit was followed by three workshops at the hotel using material gathered during and after the visit. The primary media within the Kotor workshops were photography, movement and sound, and performance and collage.

Once the group arrived in Kotor they were divided into the groups of twenty children that had been formed at the beginning of the summer camp. Two teachers, one from Serbia and the other from Republika Srpska, were responsible for each group of children. The teachers gave each child a map, and each group a camera to record their experience of Kotor. As they journeyed, each child chose and photographed one image and the group as a whole chose several. Teachers told the children historical facts and stories regarding particular features in the town; one teacher also told her group about the story of Sveti Luka church. The church of Sveti Luka (Saint Luke) was a Romanic church built in A.D. 1195. It miraculously survived a series of earthquakes, the last of which was in 1979. One young boy in this teacher's group was called Luka and he identified it as his favorite place in Kotor. The story appeared to provide a metaphor for him, possibly for his life. The children used some of these stories and anecdotes in the follow-up workshops.

In the afternoon, after their return to the hotel, the children participated in a workshop on the terrace of the hotel. The group began by forming a large circle and the teacher who facilitated the workshop introduced a clapping game frequently used in workshop contexts.[27] The small groups reformed to prepare presentations based on their experience of Kotor. Each group showed its presentation to the other groups using movement and sound, and freezing when they had finished, creating a tableau to signal the end of their presentation. Within this tableau Luka's group showed a group of children falling to the floor while Luka remained standing to show the church that survived the earthquake. The individual presentations were repeated simultaneously, creating a moving representation of Kotor through which individual groups walked. The whole group was then asked to freeze to create a final still collective image of Kotor. To end the workshop the teacher asked the participants to find a way to say good-bye to Kotor. One teacher told me that the aim of the second Kotor workshop and of the performance was to consolidate the experience of Kotor.

All four hundred participants in the summer camp joined the evening workshops and each group made a presentation of their day's activities, using movement and sound. These short impromptu performances gave the participants a chance to reflect and give meaning to their experiences in the workshops and to share these with others, thus facilitating communication and integration of the experience. The performances also allowed each participant to become visible both within the smaller groups and the larger group. Luka's group repeated some of the movement images they had created earlier in the day.

Over the next few days, the photographs were developed and each group participated in a third small workshop with their respective teachers. The aim of this workshop was for the children to use the photos to create a collage. When the collages were completed, they were placed on the floors of the foyer areas on each level of the hotel where the children stayed. As I noted earlier in this article, these foyer areas and the areas outside the children's bedrooms became informal galleries of both the artwork produced during the summer camp and the objects found by the children. They also became a meeting place where the children could make new relationships and reflect on their experience of the summer camp in their own time. At one of the final evening workshops during the summer camp, all the Kotor collages were arranged on the stage area of the terrace of the hotel for everyone to see. Each group then collected its respective collage and formed an informal procession to carry the collages back into the hotel.

Within the Kotor workshops, performance was combined with photography, movement, sound, collage, and drawings. During their tour of Kotor the children chose their route and what to photograph. The teachers encouraged the children to take responsibility for their journey through the town and the photographs allowed them to develop their own relationships. In the group of the coordinator of the children's team, as one specific example, new social relationships began to be formed during the creation of the photomontage, relationships that had slowly developed through the process of the summer camp. The children and young people in this group lived in private accommodation, did not necessarily know one another, had not participated in a *Zdravo da ste* workshop before the summer camp, and some had been reluctant to participate in the activities in the summer camp. Through the process of the summer camp and the activities in the workshops, the children began to develop relationships with one another and expressed a desire to participate in future *Zdravo da ste* workshops.

The facilitators often participated alongside the children within an activity, talking with them and listening to them as they all created together. In this way the meanings and intentions behind the images were gathered from the process of the unfolding of the activities and, in some ways, can be considered as negotiated between members of *Zdravo da ste* and the children, in a way similar to the process of gathering ethnographic data. Images that seemed to be particularly poignant, for example, the recurrent theme of water or the use of images from fairytales, were often developed in subsequent workshops, and the activities that had created these responses were then applied in other workshop contexts. In this way, new workshop activities and creative elements grew out of the participants' interactions with initial processes. Underpinning this work with movement, visual images, story, and physical environments was *Zdravo da ste*'s notion of *etno*.

ETNO

Etno is Serbian for the word *ethno*—a prefix derived from the Greek language that means "people." Members of *Zdravo da ste* used the term *etno* to describe regional dance, music, and craft forms, including embroidery and carpentry, considered as arts of the people of former Yugoslavia, or Yugoslav folk arts. In the Ethnographic Museum in Belgrade, *etno* objects were identified regionally in terms of the different types of climate and soil of the regions. Clothes and architecture reflected the geographical regions from which they came. The term *etno* was also used to designate folk arts from other countries.

Etno references folk arts and practices of specific regions of former Yugoslavia, recognized through particular visual motifs, rhythms, costumes, or dance forms. Members of *Zdravo da ste* explained, for example, how the complex rhythms in Macedonian music gave it its beauty, and praised the dancing skills of the Roma women, purportedly the best dancers in former Yugoslavia. *Etno* dances from former Yugoslavia have specific structures. The open or closed circle, for example, is a popular form within Serbian dances in which *kolo* means "circle." Examples of these dance forms include *Cacak* or *Cacak Kolo*, named after a type of dancing shoe and associated with the region of Cacak,[28] *Dorcolka Kolo*, named after the Dorcol region of central Belgrade,[29] and *Malo Kolo* from the Vojvodina region of Serbia.[30] In *etno* dance performances, costumes are also used to represent the region from which the dance originates. I have given an example below of the use of *etno* dance and song by participants at the opening of an *etno* exhibition.

Informants and scholars have differing notions of *etno* or folk arts and their relationship to the community and individuals from which they are derived.

Ethnochoreologist Anca Giurchescu stresses, for example, that many scholars perceive folklore as "an ideological concept that was created simultaneously with the rise of national consciousness" toward the end of the nineteenth century. Its role is to demonstrate the homogeneity of individual nations, represented through language, history, worldview, and ways of living. She argues that folklore was used as a political tool in central and southeastern Europe in order to "symbolize the nation-state and to strengthen national awareness."[31] The founder of *Zdravo da ste* identified *etno* as "a tradition, a history, as cultural heritage . . . these are ancient rituals." Another founding member of *Zdravo da ste* described *etno* as follows:

> *Etno* is a dimension, like any other we have in our life it is an active incorporation of traditional into modern . . . sometimes our existence has been based on tradition, the message we got from our grand, grand, grand mothers and fathers, this is *etno*. *Etno* is history, but history is nothing if you don't live it and *etno* is life, but life is nothing if you don't live it.[32]

One of the preschool teachers who facilitated the workshops with children felt that *etno* was important in terms of the war in former Yugoslavia because it allowed the refugee people "not to forget their roots, not to forget their former life."[33] On the other hand, one of the founding members of *Zdravo da ste* said that *etno* implied something superficial "like an ornament." She preferred the word *culture*, which she considered to be "inevitable; it is an inherent part of life. It is the way I live, it is my tools for living, it is my context for living."[34] A member of the children's team pointed out that the younger generations were not necessarily interested in *etno*, because they "do not like to be connected with traditional things"; yet "these traditional things jump out."[35] A member of the Danish Red Cross understood *etno* to be a means by which people from different countries and regions could be identified; in this way *etno* represented people's "different cultural backgrounds." This person suggested that working with *etno* with children was inappropriate because *etno* divided people into "them and us," although *etno* dance and song could be useful in work with elderly people, because of the memories it provoked.[36] A Serbian child psychiatrist based in Belgrade found that many of the children and mothers with whom she worked did not know very much about the traditions of their country. She said they celebrated some of the festivals but did not necessarily know with what the festival was concerned. The psychiatrist identified *etno* with culture and suggested there was a relationship between culture and mental health. This link, however, was based on how a particular group of people responded to experiences in life such as grief or happiness.[37] The relationship between these different views of *etno* informs the discussion below in relation to the application of *etno* within *Zdravo da ste*'s workshops.

Etno was considered by my informants to belong to everybody; it was seen as a communal resource, part of a constantly changing living tradition passed within families and communities, through the generations. The founder of *Zdravo da ste* suggested that when the war began in the former Yugoslavia, *etno* became a "treasure" that could be exchanged between the refugees, internally displaced persons (IDP), and local people; and because the refugees and IDPs also had something to give and share, a balance of power was created.[38]

Members of *Zdravo da ste* realized that life in the collective centers created a passivity in many people because these people had limited access to basic resources for living, including work, transport, food, and medicines, and were thus dependent on donations. The coordinator of the children's team explained that it was not enough to undertake only psychological workshops but that "people also need to do something."[39] Members of *Zdravo da ste* watched what was happening within the social groups at the collective centers and through these observations created new activities for the workshops. They noticed that many people told stories about their customs and lives before the war and that working with *etno* was a way in which these stories could be brought to life in the present. For example, one informant suggested that through the making of handmade *etno* products the activity could be brought inside the person. The storytelling using words, the creation of *etno* objects, and dance and song allowed the people living in the collective centers to reaffirm their identity, open possibilities for building new relationships, develop existing relationships, and place their experience within the wider context of their culture. These personal and collective stories and objects, symbols in their own rights, were thus placed in "another social frame, not how it was, but how it is now."[40] *Zdravo da ste* also encouraged the people in the collective centers to make *etno* objects such as embroidered tablecloths and clothes that could be sold at *etno* exhibitions to generate income, and help them work toward financial independence.

At the openings of exhibitions, *etno* dance and song sometimes emerged out of the activities. For example, toward the end of one exhibition, a group of adults and older people gathered in the exhibition room as they finished their food. Amid the conversation, one woman began to sing a song and other people joined in the singing or came to listen. A member of *Zdravo da ste* told me that the songs were *etno* songs from Kosovo and Croatia. The participants accompanied the songs with small side-to-side steps, echoing dance steps used within *etno* dance. Many of the participants recognized the songs and were familiar with the dance steps that belonged to them, regardless of whether the songs were from Kosovo or Croatia. One song followed on from another, creating a warmth and commonality that held and gently rocked the people. Tears and smiles accompanied the songs. For a short while the participants shared the memory of former Yugoslavia on a winter evening; then the songs began to fade and the guests said their good-byes and trickled into the night, leaving the echo of their coming together within the fabrics, colors, and air of the exhibition.

When they did surface, dance and song were often interlinked, one medium providing inspiration and accompaniment for the other. The coordinator of the children's team suggested that dance could not be separated from other aspects of *etno* because it was part of the "whole social frame," part of the way in which people organized and responded to their lives.[41]

CONCLUSION

Children are both the most vulnerable in war, and yet also the most able to adapt and change. In this way they can become a hope for the future. Machel suggests,

> In a world of diversity and disparity, children are a unifying force capable of bringing people to common ethical grounds. Children's needs and aspirations cut across all ideologies and cultures. . . . Children are both one reason to struggle to eliminate the worst aspects of warfare, and our best hopes for succeeding at it.[42]

Feminist scholar Carmen Raff points out that a fundamental change is occurring in development practices, in which refugees have begun to "simply refuse to consider themselves as victims."[43] Refugees have opinions about their situation and their future and can utilize their choices in how they respond to and work with the situations in which they are placed. With so many people now finding themselves as refugees, integration may not be so much a matter of integration with a host community, but the beginning of a redefinition of home and relationships between people as part of a global community that is complex and multidimensional in the way that it can both incorporate and acknowledge difference. Movement and traditional dance and song practices may serve to construct bridges between these differences, and to root people with a sense of belonging.

In *Zdravo da ste*'s workshops, participants, including members of *Zdravo da ste*, had the opportunity to create new relationships with one another, and with aspects of their culture and physical locales, through participating in interactions between movement and dance, visual images, story, *etno*, and physical environments. One of the fundamental philosophical perspectives of *Zdravo da ste* was "Now is always tomorrow, tomorrow, the future is now."[44]

In this maxim, the future is created by the actions in the present. By changing relationships to other people, culture, environment, and the past, through engagement with the workshop activities, new possibilities for the future were being created, in which the past was acknowledged as a resource for the future, and sharing and integration between different people from former Yugoslavia and outside former Yugoslavia was also a resource and a place for exchange and learning. As David Lowenthal suggests, "Every act of recognition alters survivals from the past."[45] Within this work, movement and dance, visual images, *etno,* physical environments, and the interactions between them created links with the past and the possibility to have continuity between the past, present, and future. It also gave people the opportunity to participate in a shared activity. They could thus begin to engage and reassess their "collective history,"[46] a history that had been manipulated by the governments of the former Yugoslavia to incite and justify the war.[47]

NOTES

1. This article discusses interactions between movement and dance, visual images, story, *etno,* and physical environments within psychosocial work with war-affected refugee children and adults and internally displaced peoples in Serbia. It is drawn from my doctoral research in dance ethnography at De Montfort University in Leicester, U.K., between January 2001 and May 2007, which incorporates methods from dance ethnography and dance movement therapy (DMT). The interaction between these two methods and perspectives has been central to the development of the research.

2. Alexander R. Luria and Lev S. Vygotsky, *Ape, Primitive Man, and Child: Essays in the History of Behavior* (New York: Harvester Wheatsheaf, 1992 [1930]); Lev S. Vygotsky, *Child Psychology,* vol. 5 in *The Collected Works of L. S. Vygotsky,* ed. Robert W. Rieber (London: Kluwer Academic/Plenum Publishers, 1998).

3. Graça Machel, *Impact of Armed Conflict on Children* (New York: UNICEF and the UN Dept. of Public Information, 1996), II:30, 10, at bibpurl.oclc.org/web/14845.

4. Arthur Janov, *The New Primal Scream—Primal Therapy Twenty Years On* (London: Time Warner Books, 1991).

5. Interview, Belgrade, March 2002.

6. Interview, Belgrade, November 2001.

7. Peter J. Ucko and Robert Layton, "Introduction: Gazing on the Landscape and Encountering the Environment," in *The Archaeology and Anthropology of Landscape—Shaping your Landscape,* ed. Peter J. Ucko and Robert Layton (London: Routledge, 1999), 1.

8. Peter G. Stone and Brian Molyneaux, *The Presented Past: Heritage, Museums and Education,* One World Archaeology, 25 (London: Routledge in association with English Heritage, 1994).

9. J. McGlade, "Archaeology and the Evolution of Cultural Landscapes: Towards an Interdisciplinary Research Agenda," in *The Archaeology and Anthropology of Landscape—Shaping your Landscape,* ed. Peter J. Ucko and Robert Layton (London: Routledge, 1999), 459.

10. Mihaly Hoppal, "Tradition, Value Systems and Identity: Notes on Local Cultures," in *Authenticity: Whose Tradition?* ed. Laszlo Felfoldi and Theresa Buckland (Budapest: European Folklore Institute, 2002), 9.

11. J. McGlade, "Archaeology and the Evolution of Cultural landscapes," 459.

12. Interview, Belgrade, November 2001.

13. Helen Payne, *Dance Movement Therapy: Theory and Practice* (London: Tavistock/Routledge, 1992), 4.

14. Deidre Sklar, *Dancing with the Virgin—Body and Faith in the Fiesta of Tortugas, New Mexico* (Berkeley: University of California Press, 2001), 193.

15. Gregory Bateson, *Steps to an Ecology of Mind* (Chicago: University of Chicago Press, 2000 [1972]), 110.

16. Beverly Roskos-Ewoldson, Margaret Inton-Peterson, and Rita Anderson, eds., *Imagery, Creativity, and Discovery: A Cognitive Perspective* (Amsterdam and New York: Elsevier North-Holland, 1993), 317.

17. Kieran Egan, *Imagination in Teaching and Learning—Ages 8–15* (London: Routledge, 1992), 43.

18. Roskos-Ewoldson et al., *Imagery, Creativity, and Discovery,* 318.

19. Vygotsky, *Child Psychology,* vol. 5, 155.

20. Vygotsky, *Child Psychology,* vol. 5, 264.

21. Vygotsky, *Child Psychology,* vol. 5, 43.

22. Interview, Belgrade, March 2002.

23. Interview, Belgrade, March 2002.

24. Interview, Belgrade, March 2002.

25. Luria and Vygotsky, *Ape, Primitive Man,* 110–11.

26. Kotor is situated at the northern end of Boka Kotorska (Kotor Bay) in Montenegro and is a UNESCO World Heritage Site. Kotor is an important town in Montenegro because of its links with shipping and trading. Between the tenth and twentieth centuries there were many changes of power within Kotor, including control by Croatia, Serbia, Italy, the Ottoman Empire, Hungary, and the Austrian empire. Montenegrins think of themselves as a separate group of people to the Serbs, although they have been linked with former Yugoslavia, and more recently Serbia, throughout much of the twentieth century. Since May 2006, Montenegro has been recognized as an independent state. The workshop at Kotor was repeated several times to allow all children to participate.

27. The teacher initiated a clap, and one by one the participants took up the clap; the teacher then initiated slapping the knees and one by one the participants took up this activity. Stamping and then clicking fingers followed.

28. Dick Oakes, 2003, at phantomranch.net/folkdanc/dances/cacak.htm (accessed 5 April 2006).

29. Dick Oakes, 2003, at phantomranch.net/folkdanc/dances/dorcolka.htm (accessed 5 April 2006).

30. Dick Oakes, 2003, at phantomranch.net/folkdanc/dances/malokolo.htm (accessed 5 April 2006).

31. Anca Giurchescu, "The Power of Dance and Its Social and Political Uses," in *Yearbook for Traditional Music*, vol. 33 (Canberra: International Council for Traditional Music, 2001), 115–16.

32. Interview, Belgrade, December 2001.

33. Interview, Belgrade, November 2001.

34. Interview, Belgrade, December 2001.

35. Interview, Belgrade, August 2002.

36. Interview, Kraljevo, July 2002.

37. Interview, Belgrade, June 2002.

38. Interview, Belgrade, November 2001.

39. Interview, Belgrade, March 2002.

40. Interview, Belgrade, March 2002.

41. Interview, Belgrade, March 2002.

42. Machel, *Impact of Armed Conflict on Children*, Article I. A.6.

43. Carmen Raff, "The Logic of Economics vs. the Dynamics of Culture: Daring to (Re)Invent the Common Future," in *Feminist Perspectives on Sustainable Development*, ed. Wendy Harcourt (London and Atlantic Highlands, N.J.: Zed Books in Association with the Society for International Development, Rome, 1994), 71.

44. Interview with founder of *Zdravo da ste*, Belgrade, November 2001.

45. David Lowenthal, *The Past Is a Foreign Country* (Cambridge: Cambridge University Press, 1985), 263.

46. Richard Kearney, *The Wake of Imagination—Ideas of Creativity in Western Culture* (London: Hutchinson, 1988), 396.

47. For further information regarding the causes of the war and break-up of former Yugoslavia in the 1990s, see Misha Glenny, *The Balkans 1804–1999: Nationalism, War and the Great Powers* (London: Grant Books, 1999); Misha Glenny, *The Fall of Yugoslavia* (London: Penguin, 1996 [1992]); A. J. P. Taylor, *The Struggle for Mastery in Europe, 1848–1914* (Oxford: Oxford University Press, 1980); Laura Silber and Allan Little, *The Death of Yugoslavia* (London: Penguin, 1996); Tom Gjelten, *Sarajevo Daily: A City and Its Newspaper Under Siege* (New York: Harper Collins, 1995); The Ministry of Defence, *The Death of Yugoslavia* [Composite video] (London, U.K.: British Broadcasting Corporation, 1999); Office of the United Nations High Commissioner for Refugees, *Refugees—Kosovo: One Last Chance*, vol. 3, no. 116 (Geneva, Switzerland: United Nations High Commissioner for Refugees, 1999); and *Refugees—The Balkans: What Next?* vol. 3, no. 124 (Geneva, Switzerland: United Nations High Commissioner for Refugees, 2001).

Sudanese Youth

Dance as Mobilization in the Aftermath of War

DAVID ALAN HARRIS

In a world beset by such human-wrought calamities as "ethnic cleansing," "low-intensity conflict," and "scorched earth tactics," how can dance play a part in the recovery process for survivors of brutality and war? With the body itself at the center of discourse on human rights and the integrity of the person, this question may prove a surprising gateway to meaningful investigations.

For the dance/movement therapist, the integration of mind and body is fundamental to theory and practice, particularly in a fragmented and fragmenting world. The ethics of this therapeutic modality as a means of socially inflected, collective transformation mirror those of community development. Mobilizing and rebuilding communities affected by war and organized violence invariably involve recognition that the afflicted population is made up of active agents capable of self-determination and change. Like an effective community organizer, the dance therapist works to join clients on their own terms, respecting their autonomy, encouraging their self-esteem, and empowering them to trust in a body—or a community—that likely carries within it what is needed to ensure integrity of self.

On an exceptionally hot autumn afternoon for a southeastern Pennsylvania village, some two dozen southern Sudanese youth have gathered in a graciously cool Mennonite church to celebrate the launching of the Dinka Initiative to Empower and Restore, or DIER (meaning "dance" in Dinka, their tribal language). It is a month to the day since the crashing of hijacked airliners on 9/11 and the collapse of things heretofore presumed invincible by many in the United States and beyond—events cruelly reminiscent, for these young people, of the late 1980s when "holy war" ripped them as children from their homes and families. As unaccompanied minors, some thirty thousand such children—90 percent of them male—then set out alone, or in groups, on a journey that led them to Ethiopia, back to the Sudan, and eventually to Kakuma, a refugee camp in northern Kenya. Along the way thousands were slain by soldiers or taken as wild animals' prey; many died of starvation or disease. Among those who survived the thousand-mile ordeal and nearly a decade following in Kakuma, approximately 3,500 were resettled as refugees in the United States in late 2000 and 2001.

Of these, seventy adolescents under age eighteen, and about thirty "majors" up to age twenty-four, have found themselves in Philadelphia or its vicinity, all with sponsorship by the local Lutheran Children and Family Service. It is through LCFS that I have founded DIER.

Song and dance, like initiation rites and cattle herding, are pivotal to traditional Dinka culture. The twenty young men and four young women who have joined me, as facilitator, for DIER's inaugural event are all fully committing their bodies, their energy, to the dancing and drumming. No one is excluded; no one merges with the wallpaper. Smiles and laughter all around speak of the contentment of reclaiming the familiar in a foreign land, of the safety born of reviving a form that is older than their "grandfather's grandfather's grandfather," as a former southern Sudanese client described a sacred dance he taught me in the course of our individual therapy process. For me, all these dances now are new, yet the circling procession draws me in without judgment. Gently progressing in hopping steps forward, it seems for a suspended moment that, one behind another, we have always belonged here together in this eternal present. The circle holds us, provides what we therapists, echoing psychoanalyst D. W. Winnicott, refer to as a "container"—resilient enough to accommodate the emotions that these, my young teachers, may have carried in their bones for a thousand miles and more. A young woman, her joy in moving evident even in the uplift in her brow and the tiniest reverberation of her head, tells me she has not danced since Kakuma: She has found again a kind of home.

Several young men form dyads, partnering one another in a rhythmic clapping game on a repeating four-count. A cheerful fifteen-year-old calmly teaches me the sequence, and soon we share an exuberant intimacy that comes with a pair of linked palms and a pulse that has us slapping the free hand over our heart every fourth beat. Performing this with hands raised high, we form a wall by joining shoulder-to-shoulder with other facing pairs. The architecture of our arms creates a roof, under which runs first one pair, then the next, of the dissolving and reassembling fortress. My partner pulls me through, and emerging quickly we reset to resume our part in sustaining this simple chapel of clapped rhythm.

As this accordion-like structure serpentines around the church's fellow-ship hall, a published report of a very similar game, called The Tunnel, comes to mind. Mirroring the gross motor activities facilitated by dance therapists in the West in their interventions with young trauma survivors, The Tunnel afforded the boys playing it—all between nine and sixteen, and recently de-mobilized soldiers in Sierra Leone—a means of revisiting human connection and hope. At a UNICEF-sponsored camp in a country that like the Sudan has been torn asunder by a seemingly interminable civil war, these youngsters were said to rebuild trust by dancing together and joining in energetic, orga-nized games. The facility, exemplifying perhaps the best in international efforts to respond to the needs of children of war, nonetheless, itself succumbed to a resurgence of hostilities. In the wake of the camp's demise, the correspondent describing their play, reveling still in the boys' enthusiasm, did not say what had become of them.

For the resilient young Dinka exile—resettled in a comfortable bedroom community amid the rolling Pennsylvania hills, and immersed now in an an-cient rhythm, linked to a vibrant community of peers—hope is aplenty. With dance as a potent tool for sustaining group cohesion and the ritual order of things, there is every reason to anticipate fulfillment of the twin themes of our therapeutic intervention. Through this initiative, and the reliance on the collective that traditions of dancing and drumming can support, these young refugees surely will find rekindling in themselves the ancestral spirit that both empowers and restores.

Community Dance

Dance Arizona Repertory Theatre as a Vehicle for Cultural Emancipation

Mary Fitzgerald

THE EMERGENCE OF COMMUNITY ARTS IDEALS

$\mathscr{A}$rticle 27 of the Universal Declaration of Human Rights states, "Everyone has the right to freely participate in the cultural life of the community, to enjoy the arts and to share in scientific advancement and benefits."[1] This statement—with its emphasis on cultural participation and access—lies at the heart of many community arts programs in existence today. Although it is difficult to pinpoint an exact definition of the rich mosaic that comprises the field of community arts, author Mayro Gard Ewell's description resonates with the quote mentioned above. In her article, "Some Historical Threads of the Community Arts Story (And Why They Are Important)," she writes, "Community arts is about employing creative and artistic means to further humankind's search for a society that is meaningful and inclusive."[2] Ewell goes on to say that community artists today are called upon to examine the meaning of citizenship in a democracy, and struggle with some of the biggest questions facing human beings, societies, and life.

A complete history of community arts is far beyond the scope of this article; however, several movements in the past century highlight the emergence of the field's ideals. During the Industrial Revolution, for example, the prevailing Romantic notion that artists are "suffering geniuses," somewhat removed from the society at large, was challenged by the belief that artists need to have more useful roles in culture. The most notable advocate for this view was William Morris, the founder of the Arts and Crafts Movement in England. Morris supported artisanship that produced both *beautiful* and *functional* objects.

He believed that art should counter the disharmonies of industrialism, and reconnect us to each other, as well as to the natural world.[3]

This focus on connection and integration also can be traced to the Settlement House Movement of the late nineteenth century, which provided immigrants entering the United States with basic social services, education, and arts programs—such as drama and visual art. The most famous of these establishments was the Jane Addams Hull House of Chicago. Though criticized later for imposing a dominant middle-class culture, rather than truly integrating the unique practices of multiple cultures, the Hull House did contribute to the establishment of the National Guild of Community Schools of the Arts. The membership pledge of the Guild stated that no person would be turned away due to an inability to pay, or lack of so-called "talent"—a credo echoed by many contemporary community arts organizations.[4]

Paralleling the Settlement Movement, during the first half of the twentieth century, several universities set up extension programs that provided educational and cultural resources to rural areas. Some of the most prominent figures of this initiative include Frederick Koch at the University of North Carolina and Robert Gard from the University of Wisconsin-Madison, both of whom established grassroots theatre organizations that featured community members. The ideology driving such programs highlighted local issues, and used art as a means to develop democracy and "strengthen American culture as a whole."[5]

The Works Progress Administration (WPA) of Roosevelt's New Deal also significantly influenced the evolution of community arts ideals. As part of an effort to stimulate the economy during the Great Depression, the WPA employed various sectors of the workforce, from farmers and factory workers to artists, in public programs. Muralists, playwrights, and oral historians were subsidized to create work that beautified public spaces, and centered on community concerns. The WPA was one of the first programs to truly value artists as a public good, and, as a result, helped to recentralize the arts in mainstream culture. Even today, this initiative serves as a model for community arts organizations and, in the 1970s, directly influenced the strategies of CETA (Comprehensive Employment and Training Act), which employed artists during the recession.

Up until the 1960s and 1970s, dance did not play as prominent a role as other disciplines in the field of community arts as a whole. However, the sociopolitical movements of that era—civil rights, women's liberation, environmental protection, and peace—inspired several pioneers in the community dance field. African American activist Eleo Pomare, for instance, was instrumental in founding the Dancemobile in the late 1960s, a series of dance concerts presented on flat-bed trailer trucks that traveled to inner-city neighborhoods throughout New York City.[6] Liz Lerman, meanwhile, began to reconceptualize the position of dance in American culture in the mid-1970s. Unlike many of her contemporaries, who were influenced by Merce Cunningham's concern with form and abstraction, Lerman looked at dance's multiple roles in society, from therapy to spirituality to politics and social work.[7] For her, community dance provided an ideal vehicle to reunite "these incredible functions of dance and reinterpret them into art."[8]

Since the mid-1970s and 1980s, countless community dance companies have been established all over the world—both regionally and nationally, with a notable proliferation in the United States, Britain, Canada, and Australia. In the U.S., some of the most renowned organizations include the Liz Lerman Dance Exchange, David Dorfman Dance, Urban Bush Women, Pat Graney and Dancers, and AXIS (a company for dancers with and without disabilities). Although an enormous range of practices exists in the community dance field, one model tends to predominate: a professional dance company whose members represent diverse abilities, ages, and cultural backgrounds that performs both concert dance repertory, and collaborative pieces with community groups. The collaborative projects tend to be theme-based in nature, and may be structured as intensive residencies (two to three weeks) or as long-term projects (one or more years). Participants in community dance projects come from all walks of life, and often involve at-risk youth, people with disabilities, refugees, incarcerated citizens, and/or seniors. In an attempt to make it more accessible and resonant to the public, community dance is presented in every imaginable venue, including theatres, museums, prisons, living rooms, shipyards, and parks. These practices reflect a desire to use art as a means to promote an integrated and inclusive society. Like their community art predecessors, community dance artists share a set of ideals that emphasize collaboration, diversity, and participation—all essential to a society that truly values democracy and fundamental human rights.

DANCE ARIZONA REPERTORY THEATRE (DART)

Using professional community arts organizations as a model, Dance Arizona Repertory Theatre (DART), the community dance company housed in the department of dance at Arizona State University (ASU) between 1998 and 2007, also sought ways to further humanistic ideals. Similar to other traditional university companies, DART performed a range of repertory that developed the artistic skills of graduate and undergraduate students. What made the company unique, however, was that it also cultivated the students' "civic skills" by providing extensive opportunities to engage with communities. In so doing, DART united communities in artistic and culturally meaningful relationships that resonated on multiple aesthetic and ethical levels.

Under the direction of faculty members Mary Fitzgerald and Jennifer Tsukayama, DART established long-term partnerships with several youth organizations in the Phoenix metropolitan area, including the Silvestre Herrera School, The Thomas J. Pappas School for Homeless and Migrant Youth, and the Boys and Girls Clubs of the East Valley and Greater Scottsdale. These partnerships evolved out of a mutual desire to connect diverse communities and provide movement arts programs in under-resourced sectors of each of these communities.

As in the community arts movements discussed above, DART embraced a set of values that allowed diverse populations to assert a presence in the arts, and, ultimately, the culture at large. These values included a belief that cultural expression can serve as a means to emancipation from the socioeconomic constraints of such aspects as gender, race, poverty, physical ability, sexual orientation, and age, and that culture itself is a dynamic and ever-changing whole. DART operated under the premise that the boundaries typically constructed in culture—such as the dichotomies of white/black, high vs. low art, rich/poor, and so on—are artificial and of little value. Exchanging knowledge through dance allows new relationships to form within society, and some of the borders that normally exist between different communities begin to blur, allowing for an expansion and redefinition of personal worlds, as well as of the overall cultural fabric. By joining the creative forces of youth (ages six through fourteen) with college-aged students (ages eighteen through thirty) for intensive workshops each year, DART served as a vehicle for artistic expression and participation in the society as a whole. The different cultural and socioeconomic backgrounds of the students, as well as the wide range of movement skills, contributed to a unique environment for choreographic, intellectual, and interpersonal exploration.

In any type of collaborative relationship, the participants learn the skills of negotiation, cooperation, and improvisation, and to some degree, compromise. Uniting students of such diverse backgrounds through the innovative art of making dances requires that these skills develop to an unusually high degree. All the groups involved in the collaborations came away from the projects with a sense of pride in their work and, perhaps more importantly, felt that they bonded socially on meaningful levels.

In addition to shifting social networks, the very personal connections developed between two groups that normally have such little contact added a different dimension to the dances that were created. Each piece that the students choreographed spoke of their newly formed relationships as much as they did about movement concepts. And this was possibly the most inspiring aspect of the collaborative work: by exploring, shaping, and expressing together through the language of dance, the students told us about their individual histories and future dreams, as well as the stories they shared by diligently coming together for several months throughout the year in an artistic process.

Approach

During each academic year, DART met with each of its partners for approximately fifteen to twenty-five one and one-half hour sessions. Most of the sessions involved exploring improvisational concepts, collaborating on choreography, and/or working with guest choreographers. All the programs had long histories—three to seven years—which each year grew in depth and scope. In the spring of each year, we presented the results of the collaborative work in community showcases in a downtown venue in Phoenix, and at Arizona State University. In addition to the collaborative pieces, the community concerts included repertory created by guest choreographers such as Deborah Hay, Marlies Yearby, Arthur Aviles, and Pablo Cornejo for the DART-Herrera partnership. The content of the guest artists' pieces tended to explore themes of identity, togetherness, and spirituality, and highlighted the individuality of the cast members.

In Deborah Hay's elegant piece *Exit*, for example, which was set on a cast of twenty-five DART and Herrera students in 2001, the performers walk contemplatively along a diagonal in the space, improvising with minimal gestures to a score composed by Samuel Barber. These highly personal gestures are based on the concept of leaving and entering different phases of one's life, and, though sparse and simple, can be profoundly moving. Initially, Hay was reluctant to cast the Herrera youth in this piece due to what she assumed would be their "lack of life experience"; however, she quickly realized that even at thirteen or fourteen years of age, many of these students had endured significant, life-changing events that enriched the piece spiritually and emotionally. Also, since the dancers contributed their own personal movement to the work, each had an opportunity to stand out as an individual in the piece and contribute a distinct artistic voice to the overall ensemble.

Hay's piece illustrates how DART offered a tangible vehicle in which typically disparate communities came forward—at least temporarily, as a unique presence in the culture at large. Working with the guest artists challenged the participants—regardless of their backgrounds—to invest fully in their creative potential, and, ultimately, in the way that they defined themselves as individual members of society. For example, in the work that Marlies Yearby created for Herrera and DART in 2004, entitled *A Pulse, a Moment, a*

State of Being, a Breath, and Emotion, Beat, the students had to push themselves to new levels technically.

From the very first rehearsal, Yearby expected the performers to memorize complex phrases and embody them fully—with strong lines, spatial clarity, musicality, and dynamics. By no means did she "dumb down" the material for the partners—in fact, she encouraged them to execute difficult partnering sequences with the DART students, polish the work with a professional attitude, and equally contribute their ideas to the creative process. Yearby's ability to draw upon the students' personal histories, as well as her demanding yet nurturing manner, resulted in an intricate work that empowered the entire cast. Both the Herrera students and the DART members excelled in this process and grew exponentially as creative dance artists.

Although, ultimately, an enormous disparity often existed among the technical movement skills of the casts in the community projects, the depth of life experience, investment, and sense of freedom that the partners brought to the collaborative pieces became far more meaningful than virtuosity. Historically, community-based art works have been criticized for emphasizing content at the expense of formal concerns;[9] however, as community dances continue to move to the fore, drawing from sociopolitical and personal issues, artists are becoming increasingly adept at inventing sophisticated choreographic devices for a different type of medium. This medium, as Christine Lomas writes in *Art and the Community: Breaking the Aesthetic of Disempowerment*, is one "where dance may truly be a means by which individual creativity and expression occur, where celebration occurs, and where the sharing of individuals instead of material wealth occurs.[10]

The Participants

Two of the claims in the Preamble of the *International Covenant on Economic, Social and Cultural Rights* are:

> Recognizing that, in accordance with the Universal Declaration of Human Rights, the ideal of free human beings enjoying freedom from fear and want can only be achieved if conditions are created whereby everyone may enjoy his economic, social and cultural rights, as well as his civil and political rights. . . . Realizing that the individual, having duties to other individuals and to the community to which he belongs, is under a responsibility to strive for the promotion and observance of the rights recognized in the present Covenant.[11]

As a community dance organization, DART attempted to address both assertions of this covenant in that the artistic projects promoted the economic, social, and cultural rights of the participants, while developing their sense of civic responsibility. DART's primary community partners and artistic collaborators were middle-school youth from the inner city of Phoenix. Typically they lived in very low-income neighborhoods or shelters, and were from culturally diverse backgrounds, representing African, Anglo, Native and Mexican American communities. Many students had histories of living on the street, and witnessed far more violence and crime in their short lifetimes than the adults working with them. At the Herrera School, more than half of the twenty participants were boys (thirteen to fourteen years of age) from South Phoenix, whose life experiences contributed to their amazing abilities as improvisers and athletic movers.

In collaborating with the partners, I frequently discovered that young people who come from unstable home lives, which may include unemployed family members, parents in prison, constantly changing residences, and so on, develop remarkable adaptive skills. They are accustomed to change, movement, and unpredictability. They learn to be creative out of a need to adjust and "make do." Though these skills are often essential to their survival in unpredictable "real-world" environments, in dance, such abilities allow them to act quickly and spontaneously in the creative process.

The Herrera students typically generated movement material for our collaborative projects very quickly, and took physical risks in their movement that the DART members sometimes shied away from. They never hesitated to hurl themselves at each other in dangerous lifts, or find unusual pathways of inverting, and diving into and off the floor. Though some of these impulses come from the abandon of youth itself (as well as the guidance of their highly imaginative teacher, Susan Bendix), I also believe that for many of the students, the instability of their life circumstances gave them a fearless and beautiful edge in the physical realm.

The Pappas students also brought this quality to our creative work; however, this partnership had a shorter history than the Herrera program, and included fewer boys. Over seventy Pappas students were often interested in enrolling in DART, but participation was based on a reward system and limited to twenty-five students, of which 90 percent were girls. At the Boys and Girls Clubs, DART usually worked with a range of approximately twenty boys and girls, ages six to fourteen.

Although DART planned sessions for each of the projects with the partners, much of the activities involved creating collaborative dances in teams, or groups, which naturally required that the students negotiate their own terms. At the Pappas School, we began by teaching the students set movement phrases; however, even on the first day, we asked that they break into smaller groups and vary the material that they learned. Most of the students took to

Students of the Dance Arizona Repertory Theatre rehearsing their collaborative piece at the Silvestre Herrera School. Courtesy of the photographer, Tim Trumble.

this process readily, and quickly established a creative "voice" of leadership in the classroom.

The collaborative activities also brought forward the students' very rich movement languages from vernacular culture, such as the intricate footwork from stepping and hip-hop, as well as acrobatic movement inspired by martial arts and break dance. When fused with contemporary dance, these forms often took the choreography into unexpected and fresh territory. The students' vocabularies also expressed an open honesty or authenticity that highly trained dancers can spend lifetimes trying to recapture. As one of the DART students with more traditional training in dance observed:

> Through working with DART, I learned that living a human life is itself training to be a dancer. Techniques like ballet, modern, jazz, while good tools, are not the only movement languages available through which to express oneself. A current Herrera student stood out to me because of the influence martial arts has on the way he moves. He carves the space with his fingers and arms, crouches low to the ground, and moves in slow motion before finding a moment of silence. He does not know what a plié is, but he has taken his life experience and filtered it to create a movement style.[12]

A large component of the classroom sessions did emphasize the creation of an artistic *product* as part of the culminating experience, which I believe is extremely valuable to the evolution of community dance as an art form in and of itself. The end product also provides the students with an important sense of completion and accomplishment. However, at the same time, the *processes* that the participants experienced were equally significant. The relationships formed between the students, the self-discovery that took place, and the sense of inclusion created among the partners were some of the highlights of our work together. The fact that DART showed up consistently week after week at the Pappas School had as much, if not more, meaning to the students than the actual dances that we made together. Since many of the Pappas youth constantly change their shelter or hotel residences, the structure of the DART program often served as an essential anchor in their daily lives. In all of our partnerships, the intimate nature of dance and the collaborative process allowed us to build trusting relationships quickly. And, in the performances, these unique connections between the partners created a true sense of community that radiated into the choreography.

When creating the collaborative works, DART and the partners rehearsed at both ASU and the community sites. At the Herrera School and Boys and Girls Clubs, twenty-five to thirty students packed into very intimate studio spaces (three to four hundred square feet) to create intensely physical dances for the entire ensemble. At Pappas, each week we converted a cafeteria with a linoleum floor and ten-foot ceilings into our dance studio. Although these environments were not ideal for our activities, knowing more about each other's worlds—histories, communities, and cultures on a tangible level—was essential to the development of meaningful interactions. In addition to the site exchanges, DART cultivated social relationships with the students through an e-mail buddy system, whereby weekly correspondence occurred about topics related to the creative projects and individual academic issues.

Several times during each semester, students from Herrera and Pappas also came to the ASU campus, where they shadowed members of DART throughout their daily schedules, observing classes and college life. These mentoring practices inspired several youth to seriously consider attending the university, and, on many levels, contributed to the expansion of their personal life goals, and the way that they located themselves in the culture at large. Each year, more of our partners inquired about college admission policies and scholarship availability, a strong indicator that familiarity with college life at least impacts their perspectives about pursuing higher education. Of course, in order for them to actually attend college, they have a number of other educational, socioeconomic, and familial barriers to overcome.

In addition to the very real and positive impact that I believe community art can have on the participants' access to broader social and cultural engagement, as a codirector of DART for nine years, I observed some profound changes in the mindsets of the company members. Typically, ASU students enter the program with traditional career goals in performance, choreography, and education. However, after a year or more of working with the community, these goals underwent some major revisions. Collaborating with the partners caused many students to expand their notions about dance education and art making, and begin to view it as a socially transforming experience. As one former DART member stated:

> I think that working with DART and the community members taught me that dance is about community and stepping over lines into uncomfortable territory and finding out who we are and our purpose. DART/community partners have really showed me how important process is. Dance is not about product, for me anyway. I feel alive every minute because of dance. Mostly DART and community members helped me to become a better person.[13]

This change in perspective also manifested itself in the students' ways of problem solving, and thinking about the world. Researchers in the community cultural development field define this as a type of integrative thinking, whereby practitioners seek knowledge from non-arts fields in an effort to find new models, languages, and resources to enhance their own work.[14] Such fusions and intersections of thought promote different ways of approaching social issues and allow for changes in fundamental cultural paradigms. A member of DART, who worked with the company for three years, and was exposed to a range of partnership models, expanded her career goals to a twofold process. She writes:

> I am still working to be an arts administrator, but I have added a commitment to bringing dance to underserved populations, which is just about everybody. Currently, I am interested in the Teach for America program, which is a two-year commitment to a low-income school in the U.S.[15]

For me, witnessing the transformations of college students is another very heartening aspect of the program, as it reaffirms my belief in the power of community art. Beyond teaching pedagogical skills, community arts practices encourage students to participate fully in the world around them, and develop the passion and knowledge that are essential to a democratic society. By creating specific conditions, such as the collaborative projects, performances, site visit exchanges, and mentoring practices, all the participants learn about different layers of culture and humanity. Such experiences empower both sides of the partnerships—the university students and the youth—to assert a larger presence in the society as a whole.

REFLECTIONS

Despite the many positive and often profound effects that I have observed on the partnerships, as well as on the state of contemporary dance itself, several problems persist regarding community arts programs housed in higher education. Not surprisingly, all these issues are related to a difference in value systems and fundamental philosophies about the importance of the community arts field as a whole.

Many university administrators, colleagues, sponsors, and dance critics continue to separate the various functions of community art, and view it primarily as a type of social service, rather than a rich cultural and artistic exchange. Although the trend toward civic engagement activities in higher education is stronger now than at any other time in recent history,[16] the notion that the practice of such work is a form of "charity" is difficult to eradicate in the hierarchical structure of the university, where individual achievement typically receives higher acclaim than collective efforts. As a result, community arts programs continue to be intellectually marginalized and fiscally unstable.

This hierarchical mindset also carries over into views about community art forms themselves. As mentioned above, a common criticism of community dance is that the difference in abilities of the performers detracts from the overall artistic caliber of the choreography. However, as many of the DART students have observed, skill discrepancy between performers does not automatically preclude the creation of high-quality work, and, in fact, can add interesting aesthetic dimensions. Also, the much-maligned process-oriented nature of community work not only offers a vehicle for cultural expression and emancipation, but often allows for major breakthroughs in artistic approaches, and can propel choreographers in groundbreaking directions. Adherence to such artificial divisions between "high" and "low art" in the university climate prevents community programs from realizing their full potential, and, ultimately, from contributing to the fulfillment of democratic ideals.

Another common criticism of community arts programs is their commitment to long-term versus short-term partnerships. Again, this reflects a major difference in philosophies between the practitioners and the sponsors. Funding agencies and university administrators often measure the quality of a community arts program by the *number* of people exposed to the work, rather than the level of involvement of the participants. Since its inception as a community dance company in 1998, DART was committed to a philosophy that valued lasting partnerships with the community, which had the opportunity to evolve on an in-depth level.

Each year that we worked with our most long-term partner, the Herrera School, we designed a new aspect to the program, such as e-mail exchanges, poetry-movement workshops, and campus visits, which allowed for the growth of the relationships between the students, and contributed to the shaping of their career goals and lifelong dreams. Although I believe that short-term workshops or "one-shot" performances have the potential to change a person's life significantly, ultimately, I question if they have as much meaning to the participants, and benefit to the culture as a whole, as the long-term collaborations.

Finally, I also frequently ask myself about the futures of our community partners. Beyond the campus/community programs, how do we continue to honor diversity in all aspects of the culture? Though we adeptly train students in the community arts fields, are we really changing fundamental perspectives about diversity and human rights in the university setting itself? As George Sanchez writes in his article, "Crossing Figueroa: The Tangled Web of Diversity and Democracy," "Engagement must begin by making our own universities more open, more diverse, and more flexible."[17] In order to build an effective learning environment, faculty and student bodies in the universities need to reflect the diversity of our communities. I think that we could start by reshaping university policies—such as admission, financial aid, and recruitment efforts—to support our partner youth in transitioning successfully into higher education and the professional job market.

It is my belief that as community arts practitioners who truly collaborate and unite with diverse communities, we can transform and collectively reimagine the society that we share into a more democratic ideal. However, we also need to reexamine some of the biases remaining in higher education, the dance world itself, and the culture at large about the aesthetic significance and social value of community art. As has been noted by other practitioners in the field, "community-based art is in an intense stage of research and development."[18] We are still mining for languages and assessment tools that accurately represent the depth and far-reaching impact of our practices. Yet this search for definition and articulation needs to occur on all sides—by the practitioners, administrators, critics, and sponsors. Perhaps we can begin by expanding our limited definitions of contemporary dance itself, and returning to a celebration of its multiple roles in society, one of which is to be an inclusive art form that accurately represents our cultural richness and emancipates the lives of its participants.

NOTES

1. UN General Assembly, Universal Declaration of Human Rights, Resolution 217 A (III), December 10, 1948, at un.org/Overview/rights.htm.

2. Maryo Gard Ewell, "Some Historical Threads in the Community Arts Story (And Why They Are Important)," *CAN/API*, July 2002, 1–10, at communityarts .net/readingroom/archivefiles/2002/07/some_historical.php.

3. Don Adams and Arlene Goldbard, eds., *Creative Community: The Art of Cultural Development* (New York: Rockefeller Foundation, 2001), 40; Patricia Shifferd and Dorothy Lagerroos, "Converging Streams: The Community Arts and Sustainable Community Movements," *CAN/API*, November 2006, 2, at communityarts.net/ readingroom/archivefiles/2006/11/converging_stre.php.

4. Adams and Goldbard, *Creative Community*, 42; Ewell, "Some Historical Threads," 6.

5. Ewell, "Some Historical Threads," 3–5.

6. In 1967, Katherine Dunham, another pioneer in community dance programming, opened the Performing Arts Training Center in East St. Louis for neighborhood children and youth (and later senior citizens), with programs in dance, drama, martial arts, and humanities.

7. Adams and Goldbard, *Creative Community*, 41. For more information about Liz Lerman, see her "Art and Community: Feeding the Artist, Feeding the Art," in *Community, Culture and Globalization*, ed. Don Adams and Arlene Goldbard (New York:

Rockefeller Foundation, 2002), 55–69; and her "Dancing in Community: Its Roots in Art," *CAN/API*, September 2002, 1–7, at communityarts.net/readingroom/archivefiles/2002/09/dancing_in_comm.php.

8. Linda Frye Burnham, "The Cutting Edge Is Enormous: Liz Lerman and Richard Owen Geer," *High Performance* 67, no. 3 (1994): 3.

9. Adams and Goldbard, *Creative Community*, 51.

10. Christine M. Lomas, "Art and the Community: Breaking the Aesthetic of Disempowerment," in *Dance, Power, and Difference: Critical and Feminist Perspectives on Dance Education*, ed. Sherry B. Shapiro (Champaign, Ill.: Human Kinetics, 1998), 159.

11. Office of the High Commission on Human Rights, *International Covenant on Economic, Social and Cultural Rights*, December 1966, at unhchr.ch/html/menu3/b/a_cescr.htm (accessed October 1, 2005).

12. From a written interview (2004) with a former DART member for my paper, "Expanding the Boundaries of Art and Life," presented at the Congress on Research in Dance (CORD) Spring 2005 Conference, Tallahassee, Fla., March 3–6, 2005.

13. Written interview with a former DART member, 2004.

14. Linda Frye Burnham, S. Durland, and Mary Gard Ewell, "The CAN Report: The State of the Field of Community Cultural Development; Something New Emerges," *Art in the Public Interest*, July 2004: 1.

15. Written interview with a former DART member, 2004.

16. John Saltmarsh, "The Civic Promise of Service Learning," *Liberal Education* 91, no. 2 (2005): 50, at aacu.org/liberaleducation/le-sp05/le-sp05perspective2.cfm (accessed October 10, 2005).

17. George Sanchez, "Crossing Figueroa: The Tangled Web of Diversity and Democracy," *Foreseeable Futures*, no. 4 (2005): 15.

18. Burnham et al., "The CAN Report," 1.

Doing Time

Dance in Prison

Janice Ross

$\mathscr{I}$t is ironic that one of the places where human rights are most circumscribed, prison, is also a place where an activity most about self-expression, the arts, is flourishing. The surprise and irony deepen when one discovers that an art form getting special attention in the prisons is dance, a practice emblematic of bodily freedom, sensorial discovery, and unfettered personal display. Beginning with an overview of the theoretical underpinnings of realities and ambitions for dance and prison life, this examination will offer parallel interrogations of the social and human rights dimensions of dance, prisons, rehabilitation, and bodily expression and control.

THE BODY IN PRISON

Prison is commonly assumed to be a place where one loses oneself and corporeal control is forcibly relinquished, whereas dance is often regarded as a practice that hones tools of autonomy and the gaining of physical and emotional control over oneself. The curtailment of the body's physical freedom and control of its actions are the first levels at which imprisonment is "performed." Obedience in the prisons is registered through docile bodies, through the institutionalization and assignment of physical control to an external force or person. Some theatrical dance forms, like classical ballet, also seem to foster tractable bodies, but this physical and psychological tractability and pliability is in the service of an ultimate *increasing* of the expressive range of the performer's medium, her body.[1]

What then is the significance of dance in the prison system? Does it reflect a lack of awareness about what the arts can do? Or perhaps a clandestine agenda for what prisons really want for inmates? Is efficacy of the arts being denigrated or are the goals of incarceration being elevated when a prison, jail, or juvenile hall sponsors a dance artist to teach dance to inmates?

Michel Foucault has argued that modern prison's main purpose has never been rehabilitation or even punishment, but rather the exercise of discipline; the management of the undisciplined.[2] On the surface this outlook could support an attraction to certain aspects of dance, particularly the discipline-intensive genres of the art form, but at the same time it makes all the more surprising the inclusion of dance programs in the prisons that do not have generic discipline as a prime element.

All three of the dance-in-prison programs this essay discusses allowed the dance to become a more or less porous medium that swiftly grew into a forum for the kind of physical and emotional expression the inmates wanted. In Ehud Krauss's juvenile hall class, for example, this meant that an initial ensemble jazz class became instead a gently competitive personalized hip-hop jam. For Rhodessa Jones' incarcerated women, dance became a platform for releasing rage, and for Pat Graney's Gig Harbor Washington female inmates, their dance became a forum for momentarily letting down the tough front needed for survival on the street and inside prison.

Looking back, dance in America has a curious history of making chameleon changes in order to fit within different institutional constraints. In the early history of dance in American education, for example, performing was deliberately excluded as part of the curriculum, but the students in the studio classes inevitably pushed for it until a model for "educational" dance concerts, Orchesis, was born.[3] Initially, the acceptance of interpretive dance into the first American university to offer it, the University of Wisconsin at Madison in 1917, carried with it the understanding that this would be a recreational and personal development activity, and not a path to the stage. Accordingly, the structure, emphasis, and end result of dance training in the university was reshaped to be a nontheatrical experience. Initially at the University of Wisconsin, these bodies studying dance were female, hence the horror of the stage and the obsessive emphasis on maintaining chaste and healthy bodies rather than bodies that would go on display to members of the paying public, following mainstream public mores of the day.

Prisons, similar to universities, are institutions that have certain constraining conceptions of the body. The very action of putting someone in jail represents a clear delimiting of physical mobility and an imposing of physical control over an individual's body. Similarly, admitting someone into a university carries with it another set of restraints on gendered and bodily behavior. Prisons then are also institutions designed to control activity and access: access to the social world outside the individual and also, indirectly, to the imaginative and affective world within. As Foucault has noted in *Discipline and Punish*, in the chapter "Docile Bodies," there can be competing tensions between these institutional goals and their implementation on an individual, social, private, and coercive bodily level: "While jurists or philosophers were seeking . . . a primal model for the construction or reconstruction of the social body, the soldiers and with them the technicians of discipline were elaborating procedures for the individual and collective coercion of bodies."[4]

Although discipline is present in both dance and prison, its ends are significantly different in each of those arenas. Discipline in dance is often regarded as a path toward freedom, whereas discipline in prison is a mechanism for maintaining control over individual bodies. Dancing has a distinctive set of implications and associations linked to its discipline. Work sets one free in dance; particularly, the work of drilling the body in movement exercises makes it more resilient and more expressive in discovering movement. Customarily one learns through the study of dance technique how to be a sentient, yet silent, medium for another choreographer or for oneself. Strength and obedience are cultivated in equal order. Yet, like the use of discipline in prison, it too connects with the practice of surveillance. As Foucault has argued about modern culture, one of the things that drives the prison system is less an appetite for the spectacle of punishment and more a belief and desire for the surveillance and interrogation of the incarcerated. Dance can operate at both ends of this range, that of process and performance—of providing a spectacle, or of facilitating personal growth. Yet, just as equally, it can offer the guards and probation officers the opportunity to interrogate the inmates visually as they study how one is being expressive through movement. For in the prison setting, the most private and least observed part of dance for the outside world, the learning phase in the classroom, is subject to continual surveillance.

In both juvenile halls where Ehud Krauss teaches, probation officers often line the walls of the cement exercise yard that serves as the dance studio for the male inmates who take the jazz class. They watch skeptically, sometimes making jeering remarks, as the youths perform the delicate balance of being cool and just attentive enough. They try to "sag" their regulation jail gym shorts and inject gang hand semiotics into the dance steps while being careful not to stray so far into disobedience that they get removed from class. The tensions between these two performance states are particularly acute when one considers the capstone event of the "juvie" year, namely, performances at the annual Christmas show for the staff and inmates. On the surface it is the boys who are most obedient in this show. They are the ones who can be expected to show up and perform, while many of the girls often suddenly refuse to get up on the stage the day of the juvenile hall-wide performance.

On one occasion, the boys, however, used this literal stage, and the ambiguity of the performance frame, figuratively, as a place to reclaim one aspect of their suspended rights—the right to display their prowess and sexuality. They did this by suddenly breaking rank and dancing right up to the women inmates in the audience while the flustered probation officers tried to calmly regain control and lead them back to their seats. As performance theorist Peggy Phelan has noted of performance, "[I]t rehearses and repeats the disappearance of the subject who longs to be remembered."[5] These tensions between seeing, memory, and disappearance are etched with special urgency in the lives of these incarcerated teen dancers, many of whom say they don't expect to live past their twenty-first birthdays. Performance for them has both a heightened sense of meaning and recovery, for in their accelerated lives the performing moment may seem as real as the elaborately coded body semiotics of their street behaviors. Their living bodies are the most tangible reality they have in jail, and for many this is true outside as well. Dance reinforces what Phelan has called an "experience of value," which creates an acute, if momentary, feeling of worthiness. "Performance honors the idea that a limited number of people in a specific time/space frame can have an experience of value which leaves no visible trace afterward,"[6] she says.

When one considers the practice of teaching dance to children, it seems a natural pairing, an amplification of their reality, and a physical way to demonstrate and expand the freedom of their imaginations. The "discipline" of the body that happens in a creative children's dance class is therefore about calming the little performers down so that they can notice choices and, as a result, develop more physical options. In prison, however, obedience is always to an outside force. It is about answering to another individual. In dance the disciplined individual obeys the dynamics of the moving body and the aesthetic vision of the choreographer. As Foucault noted, the more obedient the body historically, the more useful it became in the context of vassalage submission and obedience to others: "A 'political anatomy' which was also a 'mechanics of power,' was being born; it defined how one may have a hold over others' bodies, not only so that they may do what one wishes, but so that they may operate as one wishes, with the techniques, the speed and the efficiency that one determines. Thus discipline produces subjected and practiced bodies, 'docile' bodies."[7]

How the dancing body then is "read" and controlled in prison as docile by the guards and officers and yet rebelliously independent by the dance teacher and student can be a complex process. On the surface, offering dance to inmates might look like another form of control or, in the instance of female inmates, another form of coerced display. However, the internal experience for the inmate may in fact be just the opposite. It may be one of expansive new freedom and, at the same time, the beginning of discovering psychological privacy, a secure place for one's core self identity. Extremes of emotional states are not always readily apparent on the body. Just as Elaine Scarry has remarked that the body in pain can be invisible in its suffering, the body in the grip of the imaginative expansion of dance does not necessarily perform its pleasure to outsiders either. If one thinks about dance in prison as being on a continuum of corporeal control, with observable physical torture on one end and subtle prohibitions of internal rules wherein the body being disciplined is touched as little as possible on the other, then Foucault's observation about punishment moving from "an art of unbearable sensations" to "an economy of suspended rights" offers a provocative context for viewing the new use of dance in prisons as a human rights practice.[8] Is its introduction a reinforcement of or a challenge to these suspended rights and "unbearable sensations"?

All three of the dance-in-prison programs this article describes serve female populations, two of them exclusively. This is a situation that compounds the complexities of rehabilitation and bodily expression at the nexus of dance in prison with an additional narrative of gender. In May 2001, an article in *The New York Review of Books* reported that "the number of women in U.S. jails and prisons has more than tripled during the past fifteen years, from about 39,000 in 1985 to close to 150,000 today and with that increase has come a sharp rise in reported incidents of sexual harassment and assault."[9] The female body in prison is charged and contested terrain even before the woman starts to move.

In 1999 Amnesty International published a report, "Not Part of My Sentence: Violations of the Human Rights of Women in Custody," that detailed custodial sexual misconduct around the treatment of incarcerated women in jails across the U.S.[10] This report listed six key concerns around custodial sexual misconduct, each one of which involved the prevalence of physical, often sexual, abuse of women inmates by correctional staff. In this way the bodies of inmates were being treated as sites of domination where submission becomes a repeated physical act of relinquishing one's control over her own body. The explicit and implicit rules of power in jail and prison thus revolve around someone else's control of an inmate's rights, body, and physical actions, and they are inscribed continuously.

Among the prison practices human rights activists are most distressed about is the "routine use of restraints on pregnant women, particularly on women in labor."[11] Graphically underlining the tensions around bodily control and authority in jails, the woman inmate in labor is a female body in an acute state of un-control. Hence she becomes a site where some of the most severe acts of control have been imposed. Amnesty International's survey documented 33 state and Washington, D.C., departments of corrections that permit, and in some instances require, restraints (shackles, handcuffs, and leg irons) on pregnant women during transportation to the hospital and during labor, childbirth, and postpartum. The regard for dance is understandably charged in a climate where the issue of who controls the inmate's body is so complicated and so systematically thorough. In one of the most extreme examples of this, the June 10, 2002 *New York Times* contained a front page report from Seoul, South Korea, about forced abortions and murders of newborn babies in North Korean prisons. "[T]he prohibitions on pregnancy in North Korean prisons dates back at least to the 1980s," the story reports, "and forced abortions or infanticide were the rule."[12]

Curiously for male inmates, this exercise of bodily control in the prisons can take the form of increasing physical actions and heightening spectatorship. Human rights welfare researcher Michael Bochenek has reported that in the Baltimore City Detention Center there are accounts that guards encourage fights between rival incarcerated youths (usually male), a practice they satirically call "the square dance." Really little more than condoned fights, a "square dance" began, according to reports by detainees, "when a guard would ask the youths if any of them had any scores to settle. If so, the other detainees would be locked in their cells and the fight would be held in an 8-square-foot area on one of the tiers of cells."[13] In this instance, having the inmates "square dance" reinforces the jail's absolute control over their bodies. They might think they are exercising free choice to fight, but an outside force in fact controls even this gesture of self-defense. The label "square dance" cloaks their hostile exchange with a sneering veneer of social etiquette and it also, perhaps, reveals something about common homophobic associations by prison staff as to what dance signifies, what it means when men dance, and what constitutes a dance. "Square dance" conjures up wholesome, middle-class, heterosexual Americans do-si-doing in a courteous social rite of greeting and parting—a practice far removed from this combative and violent exchange between males.

In educational and therapeutic circles, dance has long been acknowledged as a vehicle of self-insight and change. This becomes more complex in prisons where the long- and short-term goals of incarceration and punitively mandated change are often at odds with this art, and even this educational, agenda. Having the act of change forced and external is more of the traditional prison model. In addition, for these three programs, having the uncontrolled bodies of women and youths moving within the prisons challenges this traditional balance of social control.

EHUD KRAUSS'S "JUVIE" JAZZ CLASSES

Dance is generally imagined to be a humanizing rite, and one of the realities of prison is that it is customarily a site of dehumanizing practices. Jazz dance teacher Krauss works with incarcerated teens in the San Jose and San Mateo juvenile halls by using hip-hop to rewrite body coding away from gang semiotics and toward a more neutral, or at least malleable, social stance. On average, minor juvenile offenders are kept in these two northern California juvenile halls, where Krauss teaches several classes a week, for ten days to two weeks, so the population continually changes. However, for the male convicted felons (ninety percent of the juvenile hall population studied), two or three years in juvenile hall is more the average until they turn eighteen and are moved to adult jail where they finish out sentences that can stretch for years or decades. Since 1995 Krauss has taught two forty-five minute jazz dance classes a week with twelve incarcerated thirteen- to seventeen-year-old males and forty-eight females of the ages thirteen to seventeen, in these county juvenile hall facilities in San Jose and, more recently, San Mateo. Occasionally, an offender as young as nine or ten is incarcerated, although this is rare. There is a sad irony here, since usually the better the dancer the more classes he has taken in "juvie," but also the longer he has been in juvenile hall and thus the more serious his crime.

The dance classes, primarily jazz technique with some street dance and hip-hop influence, are offered twice a week for forty-five weeks a year. The ethnic make-up of the teens in these classes is generally 65% Latino, 15% African American, 10% Pacific Islander, 5% Asian, and 5% White. Many of these teens are not English proficient, although the dance class is taught completely in English. Participation is voluntary, but the alternative is not very appealing, as it usually means remaining confined in one's small cement cell. The physical restrictions on the youths in juvie are extreme: whenever they walk down the halls they must be accompanied by a guard, and they are required to always hold their hands locked behind their backs with hands grasping elbows; if a visitor approaches they must stand still on a line painted on the floor until the visitor passes. Bathrooms are open spaces with sinks and showers exposed and partial walls screening the toilets. Running is prohibited, and walking outside the inmate's "unit" is forbidden unless accompanied by a probation officer or guard. The guards and probation officers are stationed at a central desk and closed-circuit cameras are in evidence throughout the building.

Dance in the prison in Krauss's classes works back from the comparatively docile prison façade, through a layered presentation of self created for the streets, to a reconceived individual identity of the "rehabilitated" inmate. In prison dance, the body showcases the opposite of the spectacle of deviance that is rewarded outside. Here it is the spectacle of social *obedience*, compliance, and following the rules that wins points from the staff. Any human rights discussion of the uses of dance in prison also has to engage with cultural discourses that posit the body as a surface onto which both the subsets and controlling mainstream society inscribe their political and social ideologies.[14]

The first level of human rights instruction in these classes began before a single step was made. The simple presence of Krauss, Jones, and Graney was a critical starting point for the success of each of their dance projects. They are each strong, independent, charismatic individuals, and they responded to the inmates as student dancers, a redefinition that proved to be crucial for them.

Krauss, the teacher leading the juvenile hall classes, seems at once to be teaching dance, and at the same time defining himself in dance as an impressive and formidable presence by virtue of how he moves and conducts himself physically. So dance, and the specific genre of jazz with its emphasis on coolness and smooth moves, becomes both the medium and content of the exchange between Krauss and his incarcerated students. Krauss's jazz dance is contemporary, incorporating some hip-hop and street dance moves. In addition, the music compact discs Krauss uses to accompany his classes are the most current ones the youths like, but with lyrics the prison approves as "clean."

Ehud Krauss teaching at Santa Clara County Juvenile Hall, San Jose. Photo by Sam Forencich, courtesy of Zohar Dance Company.

The result is a structured movement experience that may at first feel more like a party than school, particularly compared to the other remedial math, English, and history classes the students in the juvenile hall are taking. However, rather than trivializing dance, this similarity to personal leisure activities actually accomplishes the reverse. It offers a model of how feeling good about oneself, taking small social risks, and pushing for mastery of one's physical self can give a sense of accomplishment with serious and important benefits. The larger lesson and human rights resonance here is that dance is one of many forums in which we operate that offers the possibility to do this. For example, in dance certain aspects of one's physical identity and presence are rendered malleable in a way that parallels the conscious manipulation of self-presentation that concerns so many adolescents and especially gang members. Learning how to perform using the body as an artistic medium suggests an equal freedom in choosing how to be *off* stage.

As in sports, there are demands, structures, and expectations in this dance class, yet most of them are expressed and responded to on a purely physical level that invites personal expression rather than obedience to a set of regulations and overseers. For example, a typical command in a jazz class might be: "Do this fast crossing side step and end at this spot on the final beat, facing the audience triumphantly in this direction." The fact that the genre of dance Krauss teaches in prison is jazz made the bridge from the art form of dance to the interests of his audience easier. The nature of Krauss's presence as a dance instructor is built in significant measure on the qualities jazz dance both articulates and highlights. Krauss embodies coolness and power as a male dancer in a manner that is clearly very attractive to the youths he teaches. A physically big and powerful man who works out at the gym daily, Krauss demonstrates a rich paradox of physical skills and social ways of being a dancer, being male, and being caring, when he teaches dance.

When one learns dance phrases and patterns, they are almost always learned by the student closely observing the teacher's body moving before him. Unlike most other art forms, learning dance technique demands a perceptual acuity toward one's own body and others' bodies as well. Physical demonstration of authority, strength, power, flexibility, grace, and smoothness are attributes of a good dancer that are particularly seductive when they are demonstrated on a six-foot-tall, muscular male. Then the "I can do that" and the "I want to look like that" drive takes over.

Students are absorbing the content knowledge of specific dance phrases and movements within the jazz and hip-hop styles, but, again, they are also learning how fluid and consciously shaped physical identities can be. In turn there are emotional and psychological shifts in one's sense of self that continued engagement with physical actions, postures, and manners can impart to the practitioner. It is the nature of dance that with a ready instrument students can build on whatever life skills they already have in their body that make it, and them, unique.

Comments from several of the juvenile hall dance students reinforced this observation. Marie T. and Fran E., fifteen- and sixteen-year-old females in the girls unit, credit the dance classes with giving them confidence, helping them overcome their shyness, and releasing stress. "My confidence is the biggest surprise I've felt from these dance classes," Marie T. said. "The teacher taught us how not to give up if we miss a step. I think this will help me keep my self-control so I'll get off probation this time when I'm finally out." Fran E. concurred about the positive socializing influence of these dance classes. "There are people in here I don't like, but when I'm dancing with them I forget about it. If you keep in mind how things went with them dancing then the differences don't seem so important." As a first lesson in human rights, this idea that compassion for another human outweighs personal dislikes is an important place to begin with these teens.

RHODESSA JONES AND THE MEDEA PROJECT

Rhodessa Jones's Medea Project and Pat Graney's "Keeping the Faith Prison Project Performance" both focus very deliberately on the reclaiming of some basic human rights among the women participants as a starting point. The Medea Project blends art and activism, prompting the incarcerated women in the San Francisco County Jail to reflect on the problems that landed them in jail and then to take a first step toward remaking themselves through the collaborative creation of an original group dance/drama. Unlike Krauss whose dance background was in mainstream modern dance and classical ballet technique, Jones's primary dance background comes from Tumbleweed, a renegade post-modern feminist dance collective based in San Francisco that Jones belonged to in the late 1970s and early 1980s. So the model she draws on with her prison group is this style of improvisatory, confessional, highly personal, and only slightly mediated, performed female identity.

Rena Fraden, in writing about Jones, has noted that in every performance of the Medea Project, the women perform a "Kicking dance," an advancing line of swaggering women.[15] On cue they suddenly snap into gestures of rage, punching, kicking, and slapping at the air that lies between them and the audience. In performance they customarily do this sequence twice, often verbalizing their anger as they continue to face the viewers, their bodies a whir of blistering gestures of hatred. "The dance was about rage," Jones said, "so

The Medea Project: Theatre for Incarcerated Women's performance of *Buried Fire,* 1996. Photo by Speyer/Capparell, courtesy of Rhodessa Jones.

many of the stories that they told in the quiet of rehearsal were about looking for love in all the wrong places. . . . I wanted to make a dance that dealt with rage but that internally focused it more. I wanted them to kick ass, to fight back, to find a safe way to fight back."[16]

While this is a choreographic directive, it can also easily be read as an assertiveness training exercise, a physical and then emotional trying on of a more self-assured confident manner. For inmates to engage in the emotionally risky territory of participating in dance in jail, participation needs to offer intrinsic rewards beyond simply pleasing an authority figure. While the connection between building self-identity and following orders may be more nebulous in Krauss's work with adolescents, in his classes for teens he opens a corresponding arena of possibility and a place for reassembling personal rights. Particularly for his adolescent males, how *not* to be menacing and fierce and instead to show a softer and less combative side to other males is the risky territory this dance class invites them to explore.

In contrast, Jones's work is unusual for the women because it is so aggressively physical. Nancy Johnson, who worked with Jones on the Medea Project, has commented on this, noting that there is little opportunity to be physical inside the jail. "I think that showing that side of womanhood and showing that anger and the fact that women do fight is really important. . . . [But] People get really intimidated by being that real. That's one of the recurring themes. That's one of the things the Medea Project demands: people who look at and get close to that are very scary."[17] Jones is tapping into a part of performance's long history as a therapeutic agent for people. At the same time she also seems to be working contrary to the customary ameliorative practice of having individuals constructively act out as a way of dissipating destructive behaviors, because at first glance Jones's theatre exercises seem to be *constructing* destruction. After a pause, however, it is clear that in fact dissipating destructive behavior is precisely what Jones is doing; passivity and bottled rage for the women are their destructive behavior just as continual macho posturing is the juvenile teen boys' liability. Dance permits both groups to learn how to move to the other side through increasing instead of decreasing freedom.

PAT GRANEY: KEEPING THE FAITH

Although Seattle choreographer Pat Graney and San Francisco-based Jones have never worked together, there are strong parallels in the larger agenda of how their use of dance for jailed women helps these inmates begin to recover from the rights abuses they suffer in their lives outside and inside prison. Ramon Gordon, in writing about drama therapy for prison inmates, observes (in a statement that is equally true for dance in prison) that the success of theatre for

Participants in the Pat Graney Company arts residency program, *Keeping the Faith: The Prison Project*, Mission Creek Corrections Center for Women, Belfair, Washington, 2007. Photo by Michel Hansmire/Sparkworks Media, courtesy of the choreographer.

inmates relies on the process being fun, exciting, interesting, and, most importantly, *indirect* as therapy.[18] "The offender resists direct, formal therapy in which he is a subjective patient. In training as an actor, he is in the role of student. Although dealing with his person and identity, criticism and evaluation is directed through him toward an entity outside himself: the exercise, scene or play. That way it seems less personal; the onus of patient is removed."[19]

Choreographer Pat Graney, who works with female inmates in Seattle, has found her work generating results that take not only the prison officials, but the inmates themselves, by surprise. Like Jones, Graney uses simple improvisatory movement exercises to loosen up the women she has been working with since 1995 at the Washington Corrections Center for Women in Gig Harbor, Washington. Instead of having to create a new language and new frame of reference, as happens in traditional psychotherapy, the inmates in these prison dance programs are able to use the immediate physical and gestural language, experiences, and circumstances of their lives to deal with their problems. Dance in this context is gently and almost invisibly educational and therapeutic. In Graney's 1999 performance of "Keeping the Faith," fifty women signed up for and completed the program and the dance performance, a public disclosure for an audience of 600 people of some of the issues that led to the initial incarceration of these fifty women. Graney uses street dance and personal gestures, readings of autobiographical writings, and singing and rapping by the inmates as the core of their performances, which, like Jones's and Krauss's dance theatre, turn out to be inescapably autobiographical.

CONCLUSION

Empirically, a number of interesting things that point toward rich potential uses of dance as human rights activity can be seen to be happening through these prison programs. On the surface the choice to take a movement class might look like a simple escape from boredom for inmates, but dance in the prisons can in fact mask a much more complex exchange.

It's at the point of losing themselves that those doing dance in prison, in fact, come closer to finding themselves. This is one of the key dynamics of dance; it can create a distance from the outside so it becomes safe to sense and explore the psychological inside. This is partly how one acquires control of oneself. In the process, valuable new insights about the nature of dance as a social practice and a human right are also revealed. In all three programs the major challenge is to make a place for a presence rare in prison, the discovery of the "soft body." With this comes the realization that a soft body is not necessarily a weak one, but it is one that is open to vulnerabilities and to emotional expression.

The politics here are reminiscent of those in disability dance in which the practice of art by those not expected to have access to it can itself be seen as a subtle critique of power and the status quo in America. Similarly, Gina Gibney Dance, a New York-based dance company, has developed a specialized dance program for domestic violence survivors. For these women the epiphany of their dance experience is the discovery that there is no wrong movement: "The dancers really make us feel comfortable. Nobody did anything that could be wrong in any way. You could express [what you felt] in any way. We will take all of this with us to the next level. In the past I felt that I was stupid, I was dumb, and I did the wrong thing. Now I am in school and realize that I can't be wrong if I don't know how."[20]

Since prison signifies the cultural antithesis of the liberated, openly expressive body, interesting things happen when incarcerated people move into this role of dancer, a role historically reserved for the glorification of a tuned, free body. It's not just who can dance and where dance can happen that is being investigated and extended through the presence of dance-in-prison programs. More importantly, the tacit driving question is, what kind of human rights agenda can dance have for the incarcerated? A first step toward attending to human rights for the incarcerated is to humanize them. For the participant as well as the attentive spectator, these dance programs hold the promise of doing just that. It may well be that these small breaths of freedom extended to the least free bodies in our society can show not just inmates, but the larger society, the deeply humanizing capacities of dance and the deeply *de*humanizing effects of the severe spatial and bodily containment of incarceration.

NOTES

1. I am using the term "tractable" here in the sense of easily managed, malleable, and pliant.

2. Michel Foucault, *Discipline and Punish: The Birth of the Prison* (New York: Random House, 1977).

3. Janice Ross, *Moving Lessons: Margaret H'Doubler and the Beginning of Dance in American Education* (Madison: University of Wisconsin Press, 2000).

4. Foucault, *Discipline and Punish*, 169.

5. Peggy Phelan, *Unmarked: The Politics of Performance* (London: Routledge, 1993), 147.

6. Phelan, *Unmarked*, 149.

7. Foucault, *Discipline and Punish*, 138.

8. Foucault, *Discipline and Punish*, 11.

9. William F. Schulz, "Women in Prison," *The New York Review of Books,* 31 (May 2001): 32–33.

10. "Abuse of Women in Custody: Sexual Misconduct and Shackling of Pregnant Women," Amnesty International, 2001, at amnestyusa.org/women/womeninprison .html (accessed November 2007).

11. "Abuse of Women in Custody," Amnesty International, 2001.

12. James Brooke, "Defectors from North Korea Tell of Prison Baby Killings," *New York Times*, June 10, 2002, 1, 6.

13. Michael Bochenek, "Police Baltimore's Jail," *Baltimore Sun*, November 1, 2000, 1.

14. Susan L. Foster, "Dancing Bodies," in *Meaning in Motion*, ed. Jane C. Desmond (Durham, N.C.: Duke University Press, 1997); Sally Banes, *Dancing Women: Female Bodies on Stage* (London: Routledge, 1998); Ann Cooper Albright, *Choreographing Difference: The Body and Identity in Contemporary Dance* (Middletown, Conn.: Wesleyan University Press, 1997).

15. Rena Fraden, *Imagining Medea: Rhodessa Jones and Theater for Incarcerated Women* (Chapel Hill: University of North Carolina Press, 2001), 95.

16. Fraden, *Imagining Medea*, 97.

17. Fraden, *Imagining Medea*, 98.

18. Richard Courtney and Gertrude Schattner, eds., *Drama in Therapy* (New York: Drama Book Specialists, 1981), 312.

19. Courtney and Schattner, *Drama in Therapy*, 312.

20. Gina Gibney, "An Open Letter from the Women of Gina Gibney Dance, Gina Gibney Dance, 2004, at ginagibneydance.org/community/open_letter.html (accessed November 2007)

Balance and Freedom

Dancing in from the Margins of Disability

WYATT BESSING

$\mathcal{A}t$ my first Dance Access class with AXIS Dance Company, I wasn't ready to come out of my shell. There have always been aspects of myself I want to keep hidden, even from myself. I felt most anxious at having to interact with others with disabilities, at seeing myself reflected in them.

I'm more comfortable around those without visible physical differences, afraid to face the part of myself I see as less acceptable within society. I have always seen my "unnatural" gait pushing me toward the outside of social groups, limiting my influence. I worried that I would further distance myself by joining AXIS's "physically integrated" dance company in Oakland, California, but I was comforted somewhat in knowing that the class would include people with and without disabilities. I could separate myself from "them" if necessary. New to the area and lonely, I had decided it was time to face this part of my being, at least obliquely.

I was born with spina bifida, a prenatal condition in which the spine forms improperly, damaging nerve tissue and the spinal cord. This causes partial paralysis and loss of sensation in the areas below the damaged vertebrae. I have an unstable, shifting walk, moving my legs by lifting from the thigh. In my braces, movement to me had come to mean a slow, mechanical plodding, oddly off-kilter and heavy, like a clock still running though its inner mechanisms have been thrown out of whack and now clatter incessantly against themselves. The metal and plastic carapace encasing my legs had become an entrapping device, a second layer of skin hidden under my clothes, not quite a part of me and yet forever attached.

I couldn't remember the last time I had taken off my shoes and braces in front of others. It's not that I can't walk or stand without them; I can, though my feet turn out and roll more severely, making straight, long-distance travel more tiring. Rather, I avoid this public disclosure because I know the "correct" way to stand, straight and stable. When I stand with braces I can almost "pass," and when I walk my gait will be slightly closer to normal. Removing my supporting devices feels like a violation of decency, displaying to the world something embarrassing and hideous, like vomit or excrement, things that should remain hidden.

But steadiness comes at the price of freedom. While I could stand steadily strapped into them, I couldn't match the fluidity, the softness I saw in others' improvisational dance movements. I was using only a part of the movement vocabulary I knew to be available to me. I wanted to be able to glide across the floor in quick or abrupt steps, interact with others in the flow of movement. In one exercise, as we moved across the floor maintaining contact with others in some way, touching hands or legs or other parts, I instead found most of my energy going to ensuring that I didn't step on and crush my partners' fingers or arms.

Through interactive exercises and prompting to look about the room and at other dancers, I began to lose my self-consciousness. I started using my sight and other senses more fully, expanding my awareness beyond myself to the music and those around me. Where before movement had always felt to me like an absurd yelling rant I would try futilely to muffle and stifle within myself, I was now using this feared part of myself in cooperative effort, creating something new and exciting. In allowing my body to interact with theirs and letting them play off me, I was helping to create a fluid dialog I had not imagined possible.

Over the course of the season, this dialog of dance would allow the lab members to form a close bond, becoming in many ways closer than friends. We knew that we were creating a particular set of movements and interactions never before conceived. We came to care for each other's welfare outside class as well, letting our pre-dance discussions spill over into our movement creations. While a group based purely on discussion might have allowed an exchange of ideas, development of friendships, and perhaps greater understanding between those with and without disabilities, placing our expression within the form and context of dance truly opened the dialog. Through dance, those with disabilities created more vivid, personal expressions of their lived experience than would words alone. Moreover, I found that refiguring the abject part of myself as a vital part of the creative process allowed me to bring myself fully into the collaboration. Suddenly, my unabridged identity joined in the play of ideas touching the lives of my classmates and growing beyond us into the world outside the studio. Dance and movement allowed me to join in the creation of culture as a full participant.

When I pulled off my shell at the second week's class, I found myself having to reinvent my conception of movement as a creative process within myself and, importantly, as a collaborative dialectic. I knew what I could (and couldn't) do within the braces, but I had to rediscover my capabilities without. My movements became an improvised riff, an internal struggle of continual reaction to changes in balance and position. Standing without the support of braces is like balancing on a beach ball rolling over a sagging mattress. I must make constant adjustments in the muscles I use to stand and in the places where my feet meet the floor. Sometimes I feel like I've lost contact with the ground completely, as if I'm floating or falling.

However, once in motion I feel most natural, letting myself move in semi-controlled collapse. I can do things I would never contemplate with braces: diving, shaking, sliding, slipping down to the ground and leaping up again. Sometimes I don't know what my legs will do next, whether I'll have to step backwards or rotate my foot slightly to the side to maintain balance. Just as I learned to watch and react to a partner in improvised dance, I began watching and slowly coming to understand my own movements, reacting spontaneously.

Near the end of that second class I found myself dancing with Nicole Richter, co-artistic and educational director of AXIS. As we pushed against each other in a mirroring exercise, I discovered a place where I could stand still without braces as I had never before. The lightest touch on her shoulder, the slightest pressure of my hand against hers, created a place of balance. Free and in control, I stood, light and lithe and "unbraced." Even pulling on her, exerting my own force with her weight as counterbalance, I could find that magical stable space and remain at rest. Within that subtlest of interaction in dance was a place where I could for the first time acknowledge my physical body as a part of me and as part of a social context.

An entire world opened up in that tiny place of balance.

Part Four

KINETIC TRANSGRESSIONS

Exposure and Concealment

NICHOLAS ROWE

The provincial isolation of my northern Australian home meant that my father only ever managed to see one of my choreographic works. He was an elderly man by then, with less than a year to live. Standing alone amidst the thronging post-performance audience, his eyes were watery and with a weakened smile he stammered, "That put a lump in my throat." He seemed to want to express more than he felt he could.

Emerging as a dancer out of a family of lawyers, I was not used to dance overwhelming words. Provoking words, reacting to words, but never overwhelming them. Verbal arguments seemed to have dominated the evolution of western ethics and philosophy for thousands of years. During the same period, physical expressions mostly sought refuge in pure beauty to survive. Pitting dance against prose in ethical debate can feel, therefore, like combating a tomahawk missile with an ornately carved wooden spear. My living room prancing generally failed to stir the kitchen jury and challenge my family's rational arguments. So, while the neighboring Aboriginal families were dancing out their ideas about life, death, responsibility, and relationships in Kulama ceremonies on the nearby beaches, I came to accept that the same ideas would only surface during oral debates over the dinner table within my Anglo-Australian family.

A sense of the connecting lines between dance, justice, and human rights remained, however, buried deep within the woven ball of ideas that shaped my world. As barely visible hairlike threads, they were often tugged upon obliviously, sometimes only becoming apparent when pulled tight in desperation.

One such moment of desperation resonates in my memory, from the night of February 1, 2001, in occupied Palestine. It was five nights before

Israeli prime minister Ariel Sharon came to power, a very odd night that ultimately highlighted for me a clear connection between dance and inequity. I was working on a new choreographic work with the Palestinian dancers Maher Shawamreh and Raed Badwan in the studio of the Popular Art Centre. The Popular Art Centre, which houses a dance studio, cinema, café, and various administrative offices, is situated in a low dip between two rises in the hills north of Jerusalem; ancient downtown Ramallah covers the western rise, and the recently installed Israeli settlement of Pisagot sits atop the eastern rise.

The cinema and snack bar were being operated by Raed and Maher, mostly so they could spend their evenings rehearsing in the dance studio in the next room. The first film of that evening had been *West Beirut*, and we began our rehearsal during the second film, *American Beauty*. There were only about twenty people in the audience, as shelling and shooting from the settlement had been getting heavier during the week. After a brief warm-up, Maher, Raed, and I started to experiment. Disentangled from the encircling intifada and cinema, we became absorbed in movement ideas. Maher and Raed were very good friends, but an odd pair in the dance studio. While Raed was very tall and solidly built, Maher was much shorter, and very inventive with what he could do with his taut and flexible body. Halfway between the two, I filled a gap. We had been working on a piece for three men and three women, but as the women were not there that evening, we just played with some new ideas, laughing as we awkwardly tried to lift and partner each other instead.

The shelling and shooting had become much worse than we had anticipated at the beginning of the night. When *American Beauty* finished and the audience began to emerge from the darkness, tracer bullets from the settlement were zipping all around the building and into the mosque across the road. Nobody could reach their cars, so we ushered everybody back into the cinema and put on an episode of the U.S. television series *Friends*, hoping a lull in the shooting would soon come.

An hour later, after the second episode, the shooting outside had subsided. We let the audience out and they scrambled to their cars and drove quickly up the hill, into the safer streets of Ramallah. As we were shutting down the projector and closing the cinema, however, the shooting began again. We stayed in the building for another hour and a half while it went on and on, sporadically yet relentlessly. By half past one in the morning we decided to run through it.

We had to cross three open sections to reach the safe streets of Ramallah at the top of the hill. First, across the road to reach the back of a mosque; second, past an open parkland and around the corner of a supermarket; and then, finally, the long road up the hill. The streets were empty but the night was clear and bright with cold, crisp air.

Fumbling with the keys, I locked the outer door of the arts center. We ran toward the mosque and around it. Between the slower heavy bulk of Raed and the shorter, darting Maher, I rounded the mosque and cowered behind its domes as a volley of bullets rang out—heavy five-hundred-millimeter bullets from a fixed automatic weapon in the settlement, with occasional luminous tracer bullets highlighting their journey's end at the mosque walls.

The next section was longer, and we mumbled a few helpless words, reminding each other that they had seen us now. Maher was very concerned about me and kept saying, "You must run fast Nicholas! You must run fast!"

As we sprinted across the next section the firing had anticipated us, and chased us to the supermarket. The rapid dull thud of the automatic weapon in the distance was preceded by the red flashes around us, and my legs dragged like soaked sponges as I tried to run faster. We crossed the medium strip, passed a pet store, two fast-food shops, and the larger supermarket, all having been shuttered closed hours before. As we finally rounded the corner, Maher ran out wide. I do not know why. He was not ten meters away when tracer bullets cut a sparkling wall between us. Raed and I ran behind the building, and he dived behind a car on the other side of the road. I screamed out to him in a whisper, and Maher called back that he was fine, then dashed across to us. We were hiding our fear in varying degrees at that point, probably me the least efficiently.

The next section up the hill was the longest. We waited for five minutes, then struck out and raced up the incline, bending close to the dark and shadowy walls. I ran hard and the air was so cold that my teeth hurt. The distant rattle continued, but no bullets traced our path. We kept running as fast as the slowest of us could, until we reached the top. At the top of the hill we moved behind the buildings, caught our breath, hid the humiliation of our fear in laughter, and separated to our homes.

Wandering alone through the back streets of Ramallah, the potential outcomes of this event rebounded in my mind with each corner. It had been an odd moment in time, inconsequential in its entirety, but sharp enough to illuminate a direct path between dance and human rights. It was a dusky path that I had been traversing for a long time, but suddenly it shone in its entirety from beginning to end, forging a very clear map in my mind.

For survival, exposure can be as essential as concealment. On reflection, it seems our greatest offense that night had been our anonymity. The rapid-firing sniper may have hesitated longer had he been with us in the dance studio earlier in the evening, and shared some moments of vulnerability and pride. Such familiarity can breed contempt, but nothing breeds a sniper's level of disdain more than complete ignorance of the victim. We had felt as insignificant as rats as we ran.

While the darkness and the distance may have incriminated us for this judge and executioner, our real status as acceptable collateral damage had been determined long before that. It may be attributed to a particular cultural paradigm that has come to consider Palestinians (or, more generally, Arabs and Muslims) as a disposable Other. By daylight, my Caucasian features might have saved me. Such exposure would probably not have protected Maher and Raed, however, and their scrambling would have been targeted through a less morally conscious lens.

This ethical distinction had become increasingly obvious to me. Every day, since the beginning of the intifada in September 2000, I had been working with a team of Palestinian dancers, actors, and musicians, traveling to the remote villages and refugee camps around the West Bank to give arts workshops for children, and every day we had to pass through a dozen military checkpoints. At these checkpoints, my Palestinian coworkers would often be humiliated, degraded, refused passage, and even physically beaten by the Israeli soldiers, while I was treated with the cautious courtesy generally offered to travelers at international airports. Sometimes I protested this discrimination. With the confident fury of my privileged political status, I demanded that my colleagues be permitted to pass. My indignant words were generally useless, however, and were responded to with other words that were parroted rather than pondered upon. Soldiers with guns do not seem in need of many words, or even their own words. The same might be said of the politicians cowering behind them. In this vacuum of personal, reflective expression, might dance communicate a more complete message?

For the last eleven years I have lived in mostly Islamic countries, working with dancers and choreographers in Turkey, Pakistan, Bosnia, and Palestine. It is a career choice that I have not regretted. When I now meet colleagues from the dance companies where I started my career in Europe and Australia, I occasionally envy the facilities at their disposal, but not the experiences. As a dancer for contemporary Muslim choreographers, and as choreographer and teacher for Muslim dancers, I have had both the artistic rewards that that entails and the sense that the day's work is more than simply for art. Refining danced expressions for presentation in the theatre often feels like an urgent surgical procedure, exposing the most vulnerable innards of a community to itself and the world, in an affirmation of that community's humanity.

The night of February 1, 2001 vividly highlighted the dangers of having that humanity concealed by ignorant and insensitive paradigms. It became an urgent reminder of how much I value the artists that I work with. It also reminded me how the very tangible, physical presence of dance can affirm human dignity, even under duress. If only those who are aiming the weapons could see such dance, instead of just the shadows of people scrambling in the dark. The verbal slogans that they so mindlessly adhere to might be over-whelmed by the image of Raed and Maysoun Rafeedie dancing in *Qamari*, a tense, romantic duet in which a young couple are connected and separated by a long piece of wood, never quite touching, never quite letting go. Or perhaps their pride in the efficiency of the military occupation might be disturbed by scenes such as *Access Denied* with Maher and Noora Baker, in which a local man is absorbed into the bureaucracy of the foreign occupying army, enforc-ing their travel restrictions on other local people. Or perhaps they would recognize the humanity of Palestinian children through *Tenth Day of Curfew*, a dance for the camera in which the brilliant young dancer Ruba Awadallah rampages through her bedroom, bounding from bookshelves to bed sets as she swings from pensive melancholy to a particularly acrobatic frustration. But should these dancers really have to entertain the foreign soldiers in order to achieve their basic human rights? Therein lies a particular ethical dilemma.

The world is pinning hopes on all sorts of diverse characters and methods for peace and justice in the Middle East. Most hopes seem to hang on verbal agreements, but over the years such words have depreciated in value through overuse. Is it possible that danced expressions might instead undermine the pathways of ignorance that have led to the current status quo? I am still plac-ing my hopes on Maher, Raed, and the other local dancers who are trying to expose themselves and their humanity more. Had he seen them dance, I think my father would have concurred, without further legal debate.

· 28 ·

The Dance of Life

Women and Human Rights in Chile

MARJORIE AGOSÍN

TRANSLATED BY JANICE MOLLOY

*D*uring the seventeen years of military dictatorship in Chile, women formed the country's most visible human rights groups.[1] In times of severe repression and censorship, many women dared to enter a forbidden zone—the streets. From this space—which was previously considered a male domain—these women demanded justice and truth concerning the fate of their loved ones who were missing due to state-sanctioned terrorism.

It is a paradox that, during the periods of worst repression in the 1970s and 1980s, Latin American women took on new roles. Accustomed to living in the confined spaces of the home and other historically female places such as markets, schools, and hospitals, through public protest women broke out of their physical isolation to transform their traditional, apolitical, passive role.

Women's language is intimate and personal, a discourse full of nurturing elements. Nevertheless, under the dictatorship in Chile, as under other dictatorships in Latin America, women transformed their language to address the political repression taking place in the country. They went out into the streets to make their voices heard, because that is where individuals become visible, movements are born, history unfolds, and authority is exercised. Women transformed the "masculine" streets through the use of uniquely female symbols, such as the handkerchiefs embroidered with the names of missing

Republished from Marjorie Agosín, *Ashes of Revolt: Essays* (Fredonia, N.Y.: White Pine Press, 1996), 143–51.

children used by the Mothers of Plaza de Mayo in Argentina. As Adriana Valdés points out, the mothers thus decontextualized and reinterpreted the languages of the street.[2]

The mothers' traditional role in society legitimized their search for an answer to the disappearance of their children. The women's unique strategy in denouncing the violation of human rights served as an opening to the public space of the street and to history. Through activities charged with a profound cultural symbolism, such as marching every Thursday afternoon in a plaza in Buenos Aires, the Mothers of Plaza de Mayo occupied the public space that was previously denied to them as women.

The authoritarian ideology paradoxically permitted them to create a collective female space and a uniquely female set of images. The women filled the physical, historical public space with a plethora of messages—the photographs of the faces of young people tied to their mothers' chests, the white embroidered kerchiefs bobbing on the women's heads in beat with their steps. Through this strategy, the Mothers of Plaza de Mayo created for themselves, as well as for those who observed them, different images and ways to unmask the oppressive military regime. They did this through and from a woman's perspective.

In the case of Chilean women, the strategy of unmasking the oppressors has also been powerful. One of these strategies has been the symbolic transformation of the *cueca*, the national dance of Chile, into the *cueca sola*—the *cueca* of solitude.

On March 8, 1983, various groups of Chilean women that were fighting Pinochet's fascism met to celebrate International Women's Day. Signs and banners filled the Caupolican Theater, located in the center of Santiago. A large sign proclaimed "Democracy in the country and in the home," underscoring that the personal is political and that domestic violence is profoundly linked to the violence in the country as a whole. The most memorable event that afternoon was the performance of the *cueca sola*, an important symbol created during Pinochet's dictatorship. Although Chile is now a democracy, women continue to dance the *cueca sola* at public demonstrations to demand justice from the government.

The *cueca* symbolizes the different stages of a romantic interlude between a man and a woman. As the guitar and harp intone the melody and hands joyously clap the rhythms, the man lifts his head, raises his large kerchief, and smiles. Face to face a few steps apart, the couple's movements unfold around an imaginary circle.[3]

The *cueca sola* is danced alone by a female member of the Association of the Detained and Disappeared. The performance suggests a strategy of revealing oneself before the oppressive power as well as appropriating the language of the body in a public space. The audience is quite familiar with the *cueca*, since it is the national dance, and appreciates the irony of the fact that it represents the same nation that has deprived the dancer of her children.

The *cueca sola* has become an important metaphor for Chilean women confronting human rights violations. Popular culture has noted and incorporated these acts of remembrance in honor of the missing, in which members of the Association of the Detained and Disappeared perform a dance of loneliness and lost love in front of an emotional crowd.[4] International music stars have been inspired to write songs about this ritual, including Sting's "They Dance Alone," and Holly Near's "*Hay una mujer desaparecida.*"

Judith Lynne Hanna, in her book *Dance, Sex and Gender*, notes that women's dances are an affirmation of their identity. Addressing the importance of female dance at the beginning of the twentieth century, she states:

> Through modern dance and its affirmation of the female body, women choose to be agent rather than object. Constrained economically as well as physically by male-imposed dress styles that distorted the body and hampered natural movement, by restricting education, and by health practices that prevented them from breathing fresh air and eating a sensible diet, some innovative women displayed their strength and their displeasure with traditional roles by breaking the rules of the rigidly codified traditional ballet. They extended the boundaries of dance with revolutionary movement vocabularies, grammars, composition techniques, themes, and costumes. Women offered new dance systems and images alongside the *danse d'ecole* developed by men. Showing their new choreography onstage invited audience admiration, empathy, and contact, perhaps relieving some women's male-imposed feelings of social and physical insignificance.
>
> The dance medium also permitted women to control and sublimate their sexuality, which had been dominated by men. To get ahead in an uncharted avant-garde, some women needed a nun-like dedication; other middle- and upper-class respectable women in dance had love affairs in and out of marriage to show their new sense of social/sexual equality.[5]

A woman who dances alone evokes in the *cueca*'s rhythm the memory of the man who is absent, and the dance changes from a pleasurable experience to a well of pain and memory. The woman's kerchief reminds the spectator of the shrouds that cover a dead body. The woman's steps take on a certain power as she moves alone through an empty stage.

As the country's official national dance, the *cueca* is full of a vast symbolism and history. The women attempt to transform and decentralize this "official" status by inverting its historical and political connection with freedom. The *cueca sola* thus becomes subversive and is reborn as a metaphor of repression and a symbol of women who fight for human rights. The dance comes to represent a denunciation of a society that makes the bodies of victims of political violence disappear, denying them a proper burial and a space to occupy, even underground, and silencing their mourners.

Through the *cueca sola*, the dancers tell a story with their solitary feet, the story of the mutilated body of the loved one. Through their movements and the guitar music, the women also recreate the pleasure of dancing with the missing person. When the women step onto the dance floor, they invoke the dead and perform a dance of life for them.

Each act of forced disappearance is a metaphor for all clandestine acts. The *cueca sola* implies a defiance of these illegal acts, but it also represents a social event in which rhythms and movements take place that wouldn't be permitted anywhere else.[6] As in the women's demonstrations in the streets, with the *cueca sola*, women take control of public spaces and languages prohibited to their gender and, in turn, reinterpret and reinvent official forms of discourse.

The women's commitment to historical and political truth is linked to their personal set of ethics. In dancing the national dance in this way, the group's members denounce the government's actions on the public space of the dance floor. By dancing the national dance of Chile alone, the women begin to emerge as historical beings with an identity of their own, defying the tradition of couples dancing together. The *cueca sola* breaks the protocol of the dominant culture in which women are prohibited from dancing by themselves and, symbolically, with their missing, dead loved ones.

In 1983, the Association of the Detained and Disappeared formed a folklore group, in which women collectively sing and compose songs about their lives as women alone.[7] Most *cuecas* deal with love and the eternal struggle of a man to win a woman's love. In the *cueca sola*, the woman is the one who searches for the affection of the missing man, who also symbolizes the mutilated and divided country.

Violeta Parra (1917–1967), one of the best-known folklore figures in Chile and throughout Latin America, is remembered and invoked by the women who write and perform the *cueca sola*. Parra sang two types of melodies that later became *cuecas* and that appealed to God and humanity to alleviate the pains of daily life.[8]

The members of the Association of the Detained and Disappeared sing *cuecas* to God, pleading for guidance in their search for the bodies of their loved ones. The women sing in the style of Violeta Parra, imitating her distinctive rustic voice and guitar. When they sing as a group, they use harps, guitars, and clapping. The *cueca's* rhythms are important; in the case of the *cueca sola*, they echo "where are they?"

Different *cuecas solas* are sung at demonstrations and memorial services, among them, "*Te he buscado tanto tiempo*" (I have searched for you for so long).

The song's theme is the search for a missing person, and the lyrics describe a long journey through the country and an accusation of the guilty.

> I have searched for you for so long
> I can't find you
> I have lost, I have cried out
> and no one wants to listen to me.[9]

The powerful chorus reveals the position the family members find themselves in as they search:

> I demand the truth
> I will search heaven and earth
> without tiring of my search
> and I will give my whole life
> and I will give my whole life
> to know where they are.[10]

The last verse of the "Song of Hope" reflects the collective search, the common consciousness in all the dancers and in all the women:

> Give me your hand, Maria
> take my hand, Rosaura
> give her your hand, Raquel
> let's affirm our hope.[11]

One of the group's members, referring to the sense of hope that the women share, tells us:

This hope is based on the strength that the struggle for life gives us. It may be that many of our family members have not survived the atrocities to which they were subjected, but according to the testimony of people who were with them, many could have remained in hidden places, and we still might be able to rescue them.[12]

The dance represents an affirmation of the life and a negation of death. In the *cueca sola*, the pleasure of dancing goes beyond the exploration of the music and the movements. Dance, and in particular this dance-remembrance, permits the body to free itself from all bonds. Through the *cueca sola* and its movements full of soft and delicate cadences, the women are representing the free body, the body that hasn't been tortured, the body that is full of life. For this reason, the folklore group is called "Song for Life." It is a life committed to politics and searching, as well as to meeting with women and hearing their individual stories. The disappearance of a loved one becomes part of the country's history, and the concept of homeland assumes a female identity; one of the slogans of the women who fight for human rights is "freedom is the name of a woman." The *cueca sola* recalls the past, the company of a partner, pleasure, desire, and the sensuality of dancing with a loved one. The dance also reflects the pain of missing a loved one:

> At one time my life was blessed
> my peaceful life filled my days
> but misfortune entered my life
> my life lost what I loved the most
> At one time my life was blessed.
>
> I constantly ask myself
> where are they keeping you
> and no one answers me
> and you don't come back.[13]

According to Leslie Gotfrit, the vision and passion that the dance inspires can be powerful in promoting social transformation.[14] As a form of resistance and denunciation of the illegal actions of dictatorship, the *cueca sola* reflects this transformational quality.

The creation of *arpilleras* by the families of the detained and disappeared during the years of military dictatorship also represents a form of resistance.[15] *Arpilleras* are small textile collages made from rags that depict daily life. During Pinochet's dictatorship, women whose relatives were kidnapped anonymously embroidered *arpilleras* that recount their personal suffering, as well as the nation's pain. In 1983, the women who created the *arpilleras* went a step further and, in addition to using their hands to embroider, they presented their whole bodies in public protests. The bodies of the persecuted came to life in the bodies of the women who invoked them with their hands, feet, and kerchiefs in the air.

Watching a woman dance the *cueca sola* has a great impact, because her steps reflect the daily trajectory of a murky national history. We again observe the incredible transformational power of the women who, from within the dominant culture and through this inherently masculine national dance, created a new, alternative cultural space. The women are truly alone, without men or a country, because this same country has taken away their men, their sons, and their husbands, as reflected in the following *cueca sola*:

> Ladies and gentlemen
> I am going to tell a story
> of all I have suffered
> and I keep it in my memory.

It is a very sad story
that I would rather not tell you
what happened in my country
where life isn't worth anything.

Children were left without parents
and mothers abandoned
life has been destroyed
the injustice doesn't end.

How sad it is for the children
when their father is missing
they are left with only
their mother's protection.

I want this to end
and that they be punished
for the crime they have committed
with "the disappeared."

And with this I say good-bye
a small piece of crystal
and those who have committed
this crime
must pay with their lives.[16]

Dancing the *cueca sola* is, then, a way for women to overcome the silence and
to remember the dead. With the movement of their bodies, they recount what
has happened to them, using their roles as mothers and wives to interpret the
male language of the street and of history through a female set of images.

The *cueca sola*, and its relationship to resistance and denunciation, is a
powerful phenomenon of Chilean popular culture. Many Chilean women
have been abused, through torture or domestic violence. The women who
dance the *cueca sola* use their bodies and the sensuality of their movements to
tell their stories to a captive and compassionate audience, transforming the
country's traditional dance into a call for freedom. Women appropriate the
symbolism of the *cueca* as they dance for independence, and through this strategy they dedicate their free, whole bodies to the cause:

Long is the absence
and throughout the land
I ask for conscience.[17]

With its powerful and moving symbolism, the *cueca sola* has become one of
the most creative and effective forms of protesting human rights violations in
Chile. For this reason, the women say as they approach the stage, "We have

created this *cueca* as testimony of what we are living and to fight so that a woman will never again have to dance the *cueca sola*."

NOTES

1. For more information about women and human rights groups in Latin America, see Jane S. Jaquette, *The Women's Movement in Latin America: Feminism and the Transition to Democracy* (Boston: Unwin Hyman, 1989).

2. See Adriana Valdés, "América Latina: mujeres entre culturas," *Revista de Crítica Cultural*, no. 1 (May 1990): 34.

3. This description of the Chilean *cueca* was given by Rodriguez Arancibia, *La cueca chilena-coreografie y significado de esta danze*, Servicio Nacional de Turismo, Santiago, Chile (1945), 42. The most complete book about the *cueca* was written by Pablo Garrido, *Historial de la cueca* (Valparaíso: Ediciones Universitarias de Valparaíso, 1979).

4. The Association of the Detained and Disappeared was created in Chile in 1974 by the *Vicaria de la Solidaridad* to investigate the fate of the detained and missing. For more information about this group's work, see the reports by the *Vicaria de la Solidaridad* for 1978 to 1984.

5. Judith Lynne Hanna, *Dance, Sex and Gender: Signs of Identity, Dominance, Defiance, and Desire* (Chicago: University of Chicago Press, 1988), 132.

6. Leslie Gotfrit, "Women Dancing Back: Disruption and the Politics of Pleasure," in *Postmodernism, Feminism and Cultural Politics: Redrawing Educational Boundaries,* ed. Henry A. Giroux (Albany: State University of New York Press, 1991), 178.

7. For more information about the folklore group created by this association, see *Agrupación de Familiares de Detenidos y Desaparecidos* (Chile), *Canto por la vida* (Santiago, Chile: La Agrupación), 1982.

8. For more information about Violeta Parra, see Marjorie Agosín and Inés Dölz Blackburn, *Violeta Parra—santa de pura greda un estudio de su obra poética* (Santiago: Planeta, 1988).

9. "*Te he buscado tanto tiempo,*" in *Canto por la vida*, 29. This *cueca* was composed by Richard Rojas.

10. *Canto por la vida*, 29.

11. "*Cancion de la esperanza,*" in *Canto por la vida*, 23.

12. *Canto por la vida*, 23.

13. "*La cueca 8018,*" collective song in *Canto por la vida*, 7.

14. See Gotfrit, "Women Dancing Back," 184.

15. For more information about the history of the Chilean *arpillera* movement, see Marjorie Agosín, *Scraps of Life: Chilean Arpilleras; Chilean Women and the Pinochet Dictatorship* (Trenton, N.J.: Red Sea Press, 1987).

16. "*Una historia,*" in *Canto por la vida*, 35.

17. From the introduction to *Canto por la vida*.

Mediating Cambodian History, the Sacred, and the Earth

Toni Shapiro-Phim

When I was in my mother's womb I moved to the rhythm of gunshots and explosions. Maybe that's where I got my love for dancing. I'm still dancing to those sounds today. . . . My parents had to run [away] then, and I've had to run, too. Dance and run and dance . . .

—eighteen-year-old dancer, Site 2
displaced persons camp, 1991[1]

$\mathcal{E}$ach morning, hundreds of girls and boys in Site 2 (a displaced persons camp for Cambodians) would gather in bamboo-and-thatch practice halls around the sprawling, dusty camp. To the accompaniment of xylophones, drums, and gongs, bodies moved in controlled grace, creating and exuding individual and collective beauty and strength in the midst of danger and despair. Inside those rehearsal huts, and on stages scattered about the camp, young Khmer people were recreating and reclaiming a cultural heritage, a way of moving, passed down by their teachers, but denied and violated by their surrounding reality, and by their immediate past.[2]

More than a quarter of a million people from Cambodia became displaced persons or refugees in the 1970s and 1980s in response to war, famine, and political oppression.[3] I aim in this essay to examine some aspects of the relationship between war, displacement, and dance for people of Cambodia, a country whose inhabitants often define themselves as both sufferers of endless war and as inheritors of a precious artistic legacy.

In the twentieth century alone, civil and international conflict touched every aspect of life in Cambodia. (For centuries before that, battles raged off

and on among contenders for the throne and between the Khmer and neighboring polities.) From the 1970s to the 1990s, the wars in and "for" Cambodia
were multidimensional: conceptual and value-laden, they encompassed battles
for control of tradition, memory, symbols, and territory.

More than two million people (or one in four) died in Cambodia
during the years of civil war in the early 1970s, under the Khmer Rouge
(1975–1979), and during the continuing war until the early 1990s. Historian
David Chandler describes the Khmer Rouge's revolution, under the leadership of Pol Pot, as "one of the fiercest and most consuming in [that] century of
revolutions."[4] It called for an elimination of class distinctions and the creation
of a uniform population of unpaid agricultural laborers answerable only to an
amorphous higher revolutionary authority. Buddhist temples were systematically destroyed, the monks disrobed; family members were separated and
children often taught to spy on and report their parents' disappointments with
the regime, considered betrayals. Starvation and disease were rampant. Forced
mass evacuations resulted in people moving to parts of the country they had
never known before. Officially there was no money. There were no stores
or markets, and no schools beyond rudimentary lessons in the alphabet—the
latter only available in some parts of the country. Almost everyone lost loved
ones to malnourishment, illness, overwork, torture, or execution. After the
Vietnamese army invaded from the east, overthrowing the Khmer Rouge in
January 1979, millions of Cambodians were on the move, searching for family and friends, for home, for a lost way of life. By the mid-1980s more than
250,000 of them were living in limbo in displaced persons camps in a war zone
on the Thai-Cambodian border.

It is the largest of these displaced persons encampments that will constitute my focus. Across and throughout the cultural-spiritual-political-military-
territorial battlefields that constituted the camps, dance was central both as
a tool of the powerful with which to claim legitimacy as (potential) leaders
of Cambodia, and as a "weapon of the weak"[5] in resisting the surrounding
destruction. Dance and dance events could perform such roles because of the
fundamental place dance occupies in the lives of the Khmer people.[6]

Dance of Cambodia has a long history interwoven with that of religions
and royalty and, more recently, modern nation-states. The dancers have variously been messengers between the monarch and the gods, integral components of village ceremonies, symbols of the independent country of Cambodia,
and entertainers. As far back as the tenth century, one creation story, inscribed
in a temple doorway, speaks of a celestial dancer who, following her union
with a wise man, became the mother of the Khmer people. Celestial dancers—*apsaras*—appeared in the thousands on the stone reliefs carved on temple
compound walls during the Khmer Empire of Angkor (ninth to fifteenth

centuries) as part of the recreation of the abode of the divine here on earth.[7] *Apsaras* remain one of the most common icons among Cambodian people anywhere, painted with spired crowns and golden jewelry on billboards, stamped on organizational letterheads, sketched on restaurant menus, and cast in cement or metal. Contemporary Cambodian dancers trace elements of their postural and gestural vocabulary, and of their costuming, to those ancient carvings. These earthly counterparts to the *apsara* "are seen as precious repositories of Cambodia's past and as such, the guarantors of her future. Dance is commonly perceived as . . . essential to the perpetuation of Cambodia as a cultural and political entity."[8]

CAMPS ON THE THAI-CAMBODIAN BORDER

Refugees from Cambodia began arriving in Thailand in 1975, after the Khmer Rouge took power. The trickle turned into a flood in 1979 and soon thereafter when, with the installation of the People's Republic of Kampuchea following Vietnam's ouster of the Khmer Rouge from Cambodia's capital, hundreds of thousands of people sought shelter, protection, and food along the country's western border with Thailand. Most of those who fled did so with the intention of going home as soon as conditions allowed.[9] Famine resulting from the Khmer Rouge's disastrous agricultural schemes as well as an international embargo, fear of the new communist regime, and apprehension that the Khmer Rouge would return to power were some of the motivating factors in people's decision to move. Others were pushed with retreating Khmer Rouge soldiers into the mountainous northwest and southwest that border Thailand.

Violent forced repatriation, military offensives followed by relocations, formal separation of camps along political/military lines, total dependency on international aid, and closing off of all prospects for resettlement abroad were the hallmarks of life on the border for the Khmer who remained there. Eventually, each border camp came under the administration of one of the three political factions that joined in 1982 to form the Coalition Government of Democratic Kampuchea whose mission was the overthrow of the Vietnamese-backed government in Phnom Penh, Cambodia's capital. The Coalition partners were the noncommunist Khmer People's National Liberation Front (KPNLF), supporters of the ousted royalty (known by the acronym FUNCINPEC), and the communist Khmer Rouge.[10] Inhabitants of each camp sometimes supported, but in any case were compelled to adhere to, the policies and programs of their leaders. The United Nations Border Relief Operation was created specifically to supervise the camps.[11] For over a decade, more than a quarter of a million Cambodians struggled to make sense of their precarious and ambiguous existence "on the border."

THE STUDY OF DISPLACEMENT AND 'SITE 2'

> Displacement is like death. One thinks it happens only to other
> people.
>
> —Mourid Barghouti, Palestinian refugee[12]

Scholars of refugee situations have invoked the concept of "liminality" in studies of the nature of life in camps.[13] Liminal periods are those in which people are separated from their immediate past before being initiated and accepted into their new roles within a given community, as in a rite of passage. This concept is helpful in so far as it points to the wrenching separation from previous identities that displaced persons suffer. However, although individuals confined to camps find themselves, as do ritual initiates, "between" statuses, the former have no idea where (to what status) they are headed, and can count on no guidance from experienced elders along the way. Many of those displaced along the Thai-Cambodian border, in this precarious state in which freedom of movement was restricted, communication with the outside was limited, and choices of where to live and what to eat proscribed, imagined and forged an identity they could share, through dance. This identity tied them to a shared (perhaps part mythic) past, and a shared homeland. Recreation of dances, and participation in dance events, were attempts by some to structure their liminal experience, and to give it meaning.[14]

In line with what Erving Goffman identifies as the experience of people in "total institutions," these "assaults upon the self . . . through which the symbolic meaning of events in the inmate's immediate presence dramatically fails to corroborate his prior conceptions of self"[15] led in extreme cases to the destruction of the self without commitment to communal or transcendental values.[16] Between nations, between political maneuverings, between the violent and the unknown, between loss and hope, Site 2 was the largest displaced persons camp on the border. The United Nations, the Royal Thai government and military, the Khmer administration of Site 2 (an arm of the resistance government-in-exile, affiliated with the Khmer People's National Liberation Front), and the international voluntary agencies created an uneasy alliance within which to oversee the situation. The majority of the 160,000 people under their "protection" or "authority" in this particular camp constituted a huge, unrecognized voice in that society. Like victims of colonialism, these men and women had to suffer the humiliation and despair of realizing that, ultimately, their very humanity—for many, all they had left—was sometimes not even protected.[17]

Dance had become a vehicle, among the Khmer, with which to somewhat override a humiliating and baneful power structure, even though the efficacy, especially long-term, of such a form of resistance to the surrounding reality can be debated.[18] Exposing the logic of the responses to confrontations between unequal parties sheds light on possibilities for embodied resistance to violent surroundings. Here I examine the logic of loss that invites a need to replace and regain, and the logic of chaos that invites a need to emphasize the idea of establishing appropriate or distinctive order, through dance.

During the Khmer Rouge years (1975–1979), dance and music as the Khmer had known and practiced them were forbidden. A revolutionary idiom was imposed.[19] Further, by the end of that regime it was estimated by surviving professional artists that between 80 to 90 percent of their colleagues, dancers included, had perished. The high death toll resulted, perhaps, from a number of factors, including their high-profile relationship with royalty and other state leaders.[20]

About six years after the ouster of the Khmer Rouge from power, in Site 2, the arts were one domain that remained independent of the management of camp international aid agencies, unlike education, sanitation, and health services, for example. In other words, these were pursuits that Cambodians in the camp decided to undertake by themselves, and continued to oversee. The pride in mastery of a subtle manipulation of energy and of intricate patterns of movement was theirs to strive for and to claim. Similar to the situation in the Nazi-created Jewish ghetto of Theresienstadt, in which "[a]rt, music, and performance transformed fear into freedom [and] [t]he act of making art suspended the collective nightmare, replac[ing] the arbitrary rules of the ghetto with individual purpose,"[21] through dance, Site 2 artists were able to realize some control over their everyday lives.

This may be viewed as a creative response to the surrounding violence, but also as one that could reach only so far. When their symbolic or concrete actions are "locked within positions of stark dependency,"[22] displaced people's opinions become insignificant and their actions ineffective beyond a limited sphere, sharply revealing their ultimate oppression. Speaking about post-World War II refugees in Europe, Hannah Arendt posits,

> Innocence, in the sense of complete lack of responsibility, was the mark of [the refugees'] rightlessness as it was the seal of their loss of political status. [Not the loss of rights but] the loss of a polity itself expels [them] from humanity.[23]

While in Site 2, some people likened themselves to animals. "We are like fish in a trap," they said, or "animals in a zoo." The analogies were invoked quite often, especially with reference to the large numbers of visitors the camp hosted fairly regularly—journalists, government or United Nations officials, and so on—who came to look, then returned immediately to lives beyond the barbed wire fences. Those living in the camp, for the most part, could not leave. They had no legal right to be in Thailand; if they were caught outside the fences, they were subject to beatings by Thai guards. Mine-strewn and war-ravaged paths were the only way back into Cambodia. They were forced to exist in what they considered the wild and dangerous *prey* (forest), with no protection from the (human) elements, becoming victims of Khmer robbers or drunken Thai soldiers at night, while U.N. and voluntary agency personnel exited safely by 5:00 p.m. each day. While dance and dance events in this camp were, in some instances, symbolic instruments of the camp's political and military elite, with performances staged at the behest of leaders for important ceremonies or visitors, they were, for the artists and their audiences, statements against the precariousness of their existence. The aesthetic, political, and spiritual potency of Khmer dance allows it a range of possible interpretations, and possible uses.

THE DANCERS

Before the war and revolution, Voan Savay would sit on the Royal Palace dance hall's tile floor each day with her eyes fixed straight ahead.[24] Back arched, shoulders down, she bent her left knee and set her foot on the floor, toes flexed upward. Resting her left elbow atop that bent knee, she raised her right leg and placed her right ankle on top of her left forearm. With her right hand she pressed the fingers of her left hand backward into a crescent, while her left elbow was pushed into hyperextension. Every muscle ached. But she dared not round her back or droop her shoulders. Insisting the energy reach her extremities and shoot beyond, she was executing just one of the many stretching exercises designed to foster the flexibility and subtleness necessary for the performance of Khmer classical dance. Savay persevered through these exhausting and demanding exercises daily in Cambodia's Royal Palace in the 1960s and early 1970s. There, she was watched, judged, and corrected by older accomplished dancers and, at times, in the 1960s, by the Queen, while surrounded by landscaped gardens. Years later, in the early 1980s, she took the same pose as described above, but on a dirt floor in a displaced persons camp, surrounded by a barbed wire fence, and watched by ragged eager novices who were trying to imitate her every breath.

At the tail end of the rainy season in 1984, a few months before the establishment of Site 2, twenty-some young Khmer dancers were performing one day in a camp called "Site 1" (located on the Cambodian side of the Thai-Cambodian border) on a makeshift stage—a bamboo platform erected in a position to catch the shade of a lone nearby tree—when thunderous booms filled the air. Artillery shells hailed from the sky, and came crashing down. The hundreds of camp residents who had gathered to watch the performance

Voan Savay (left) teaching classical dance in the Fine Arts Service building. Students dance on plastic matting that covers a raised dirt floor. Site 2 Displaced Persons Camp, Thailand, 1989. Copyright the photographer, Toni Shapiro-Phim.

scattered in the ensuing mayhem, calling to their children, not knowing where to run for protection. The dancers, also panic-stricken, looked to their teacher, Voan Savay, for guidance. Savay placed her palms together and lifted her hands before her face in a gesture of salutation and entreaty to the spirits. She quietly asked the spirits of the dance to protect her troupe of budding artists. A handful of foreign journalists, present for the performance, stayed as well, and the show continued. Meas Van Rouen, codirector of the troupe and Savay's husband, later explained, "[A]s artists, we couldn't stop until there was no audience left." The shelling was like music, but with a rhythm all its own, said some of the dancers as they recounted their tale. "At first we confused the 'booms' with the beat of the drum." When the attack ended, camp residents filtered back to see the rest of the dances.

Three years earlier, in 1981 when the then-newlyweds Van Roeun and Savay, both professional dancers, left Phnom Penh with plans to seek political asylum in a western country after journeying to Thailand, they discovered there were various camps dotting the border controlled by competing war-lords. Savay, who had been a palace-trained principal dancer with Cambodia's royal/classical dance company in the 1960s and 1970s, and Van Roeun, a graduate of the folk dance division of the University of Fine Arts in the 1970s, had become frustrated with what they perceived to be a mounting emphasis on politically inspired popular arts at the expense of the classical arts, dance in particular, in the People's Republic of Kampuchea. "We thought, where can we practice our arts under better conditions. . . . At first, we thought we would go to another country. But when we arrived at the border, our plans changed."

The camp they found was "crowded and disorganized, filled with traders taking advantage of others." Word spread that they were artists. A general in the Cambodian resistance forces gave his money and his blessing so that they could construct a fine arts center. Van Rouen recalled:

> I went to primary schools [in the camp] to select students. . . . I selected forty or so. . . . We had brought some tape cassettes of music with us. But . . . I went around to search for musicians. Camp leaders commissioned people to make instruments.

There they taught classical and folk dances. Classical (or court) dance, according to Savay, shows an ideal model of Khmer character and morals, stressing, as it does, the refined quiet grace of females and the controlled strength of males. The choreography of the dances highlights balance; stories emphasize the triumph of bravery and cleverness over treachery and buffoonery, giving people goals of control and grace and the eventual victory of justice for which to strive. The folk dances they taught in the camp added an element of fun, and an idealized (and romanticized) notion of life in Cambodia's countryside.[25]

Savay and Van Rouen's group, eventually with more than sixty students, and close to forty others on staff as costumers, musicians, and so on, began receiving material support from international aid organizations in 1983.

In 1984, at the Khmer New Year, during a downpour marking the beginning of the rainy season, artillery shells started falling along with the rain. The attack was so heavy that all the residents of their camp were evacuated. "We ran and ran. We couldn't take anything with us—no costumes, no instruments." Savay says she and Van Rouen were devastated. "The people were just beginning to understand about the arts." Upon reaching the new camp, Site 1, Khmer camp administrators offered them money to buy fabric. And they started all over again. Until the next evacuation . . .

Site 2 camp was formed in 1985 as evacuees from seven smaller encampments were brought together on a parched no-man's-land with nonarable earth and no natural source of water. Sophy and Tia, sisters who studied and performed dance with Savay and Van Rouen, were ten and fourteen, respectively, when they fled to Site 2 with their parents and three other siblings. They had started dancing because the music was enticing to them. They used to stand and watch the practices and rehearsals. Their mother agreed to

Students of Voan Savay perform a selection of folk and classical dances for a typically huge crowd of fellow Cambodians, all residents of Site 2 Displaced Persons Camp. Site 2, Thailand, 1989. Copyright the photographer, Toni Shapiro-Phim.

let them dance, believing such an endeavor would help them develop discipline, respect for elders and tradition, and a "love for the country they hardly knew."[26] Each morning in Site 2 they awoke before dawn, when it was a bit cooler, took water from a bucket that was to be rationed for that day's use, and waited beside a communal latrine. Returning home, they dusted the table or shook out the one mat in their dirt-floor home before putting some rice on to boil. Canned fish complemented the rice. They were responsible for serving and cleaning up after the meal. If their mother asked, one or the other might go to the market where they could trade some of their canned fish rations for other food. They walked over stagnant water that often rested in front of their house, abundant with flies and mosquitoes, in sarongs they had stitched into elastic-waisted skirts or in other clothes donated by international agencies, and in flip-flops, wide-brimmed straw hats protecting them from the harsh sun that they anticipated would soon be showing its heat. But they always hurried back so that they could get to the Fine Arts Service Hall in time for dance practice. (On days when one had to accompany their ailing father to a health center, or help care for a sick sibling, or help pick up their rice rations, she was late, or absent.)

They arrived at the hall where each unrolled a three-yard piece of cloth that they helped wrap around each other's waists, and twisted and pulled through their legs to make pantaloons. Tucking their shirts in, they secured this *kben*, part of the traditional Khmer dance practice outfit, with a silver belt. Sophy was studying the female roles in Khmer classical dance (that of princess or female deity) while Tia was chosen, because of a longer face and anticipated height, to study the male roles (that of prince or male deity). Some girls were studying the role of the ogre, while the boys were being trained to dance the role of the monkey, the only role in the classical tradition not reserved for women. Seated on a plastic-covered raised dirt platform, in lines divided according to these character types, the students would await a signal from their teacher, Voan Savay. Hitting the floor with a rattan rod, Savay set the session in motion. They began with arduous stretching exercises, the same ones Savay had done since she was a little girl studying in the palace. These were also the same exercises she had continued to do in Phnom Penh after the fall of the Khmer Rouge regime when she joined her surviving colleagues as they attempted to recreate their repertoire, until she decided to leave.

The musicians, seated on chairs to the side and a bit forward of the dancer's "stage," with their wooden xylophones, gong circles, drums, hand cymbals, and one quadruple-reed instrument akin to an oboe, began only when told to.[27] They didn't play for the exercises. But they did accompany the execution of the basic postures and gestures of Khmer dance known as *kbach baat*—a run-through of the vocabulary from which dances and dance-dramas are built—that lasted close to one hour. By this point, perhaps 9:00 a.m. or so, everyone would be sweating profusely. It was invariably dark in the hall, with small windows built into the thatch. This kept the glare of the sun away, but didn't allow for much air circulation. Hot and thirsty, Sophy, Tia, and the others would continue to push themselves, and brace for the prods and pinches and slaps that were hallmarks of Savay's teaching style. Khmer dance has always been handed down intimately, through the teacher's touch to the body of the student. Verbal explanations of "how" to move were rare. Rather, students were expected to watch and follow, or be molded just so, and to not forget.[28]

Following the routine of exercises and basic movements, Savay selected some students to rehearse a particular dance. Whether this was for an upcoming show at one of the stages around the camp or in their own space for special visitors (journalists, guests of aid workers, government officials, and so on), or just to expand and improve their training, girls specializing in classical dance would wait at the ready to hear what was the order of the day. Those not needed on stage went to sit by Savay's side to act as a chorus.

Whereas in Cambodia, both before and after the Khmer Rouge years, the dance world was populated with specialists in each role, and with singers, there in remote Site 2, Savay had only herself to rely upon. Though she was a star of the female role, known especially for her portrayal of an *apsara* in the dance with that same name, finding herself on her own she taught the male and ogre roles from a kinesthetic memory of how they had moved with her in rehearsal and on stage, years before. Blessed with a good voice, she also taught the youth how to accompany the dance in song. She guided a group of women in costume-making as well.

Van Rouen passed on knowledge of the folk dances he had mastered, and also taught the role of the monkey to some of the boys, even though, again, the latter task would have been reserved for a specialist in Cambodia. One of the musicians at the Fine Arts Service had been a palace artist as well, and he helped lead the other instrumentalists. In addition, whereas in Cambodia a dancer would focus on either classical or folk dance, in Site 2, they studied and performed everything regularly, even though they stated a preference for which they were judged at exam time. Students who weren't on stage or singing might form groups around the hall, together reviewing a piece, until it was their turn in front of the teacher. By 11:00 a.m. or so, everyone was dismissed, dancers and musicians and onlookers making their way home along dirt roads crowded with bicycles (one could hire a bicycle taxi if one had the means), four-wheel-drive pick-up trucks driven by aid workers, and lumbering red water trucks that had been filling up holding tanks since the morning. In the early afternoon, after yet another meal of rice and canned fish, and perhaps a short nap, students returned to the Fine Arts Service Hall, unless, of course, they needed to help collect the household's water ration or had other duties. This time they listened to a lecture about Khmer history, with a focus on temples and iconography, and about Khmer dance and music. They studied the Khmer alphabet and some basic mathematics as well. This was all part of a recreation of the University of Fine Arts program in Phnom Penh, where arts students in Cambodia, to this day, spend the mornings on their craft, and the afternoons in regular academic classes. Savay and Van Rouen's "school" was the only place in any of the camps where dance students (dance was taught and practiced in various subcamps of Site 2 and other displaced persons camps as well) could receive a diploma in the arts, which they did after taking a series of exams in both academics and in dance and singing technique following several years of study.[29]

In the late afternoon, as Sophy and Tia would head home, they might walk arm-in-arm with a fellow dancer, and perhaps stop at her house for a moment. They always made sure they were home by 5:00 p.m. when the U.N. and aid workers left and the camp was declared "closed." Yet, even in their homes, they could still be vulnerable to a hand grenade that had gone off course, tossed by someone in a domestic dispute, or to bandits or rape. And they each always had a small parcel ready to grab if they needed to evacuate once more.

HISTORY, DANCE, AND THE LAND

For the Khmer, an actual historical past has become idealized and mythologized, but this newly fashioned story affects people's perceptions of that history. The act of mythologizing is, in itself, an attempt at ordering the past.

Ordering the past, and gaining counsel from it, are ways for the Khmer, according to historian David Chandler, to try to "push back the wilderness,"[30] to encourage continuity and security amidst violence and uncertainty. Reviewing some nineteenth-century texts, he reveals that Cambodians were "continually reliving, repeating or 'restoring' what was past—in ceremonial terms, in adages, and in the agricultural cycle. Things which could not be predictably transmitted—like violence, droughts, and disease—were linked in people's minds with what was wild, and less distinctly perhaps with immoral, unremembered behavior in the past,"[31] an interpretation we can apply to the late twentieth century as well.

Traditional knowledge, knowledge of the past, and the rituals that evoke continuity reside within cultural specialists—the elders and the *kru* (teachers and spirits). The connection between past and present, for the dancers, is mediated by the *kru*, spirits of the dance, deceased teachers of the dance, deities, and living teachers. Through their relationship with the *kru*, Khmer dancers endeavor to remember (*neuk khoenh*), to acknowledge (*neuk roleuk*), and to recreate/reproduce what the teachers did before them. The student relationship with spirits and teachers is ritually acknowledged and reinforced in a Brahmanic ceremony known as *sampeah kru*, a salutation to the spirits and teachers. Each *sampeah kru* ritual ideally concludes with new possibilities opening before the participants as teachers tie cotton threads around the wrists of their students while offering blessings and advice.

Communication with the *kru* and participation in dance performances may also have provided models for ritualized resistance at the level of everyday practice under various political regimes. During the Khmer Rouge years, some dancers risked their lives, or traded invaluable grains of rice, to get incense so that they could enact secretive rituals connecting them to their *kru*, and to their pasts. As those squalid refugee camps formed on the Thai-Cambodian border, dance—its study, its rituals, including the *sampeah kru*, and its performance—was a way to push back that literal and symbolic wilderness, a way for people to locate themselves historically and physically when they were in fact the ultimate displaced and dispossessed. It was a way to try to put back together that which had been ruptured.

Khmer dance thus mediates connections between history and the sacred, as well as between history, the sacred, and the land. Throughout Cambodia, inhabitants of specific areas traditionally pay annual homage to the spirit of the founder of the village or district (their *neak ta*), through a ritual that features dance. A *neak ta* is an ancestor who provides the populace a localized historical reference through origin myths that attest to his/her existence, and who is, also, a spirit of the soil.[32]

Land, thus, must be consecrated and its spirit(s) propitiated. Only proper consecration of the land will allow those who live and build there to do so in peace. When people travel to distant, unknown territory, or to a place thought to be dangerous, they often carry a clump of land from their native village with them, wrapped and hidden, to ward off the perils.[33] Further, when Khmer soldiers feel panicked in the midst of battle, they might pick up some dirt and sprinkle it over their heads, praying for protection. The dancers of Site 2 were in a sense consecrating that untamed, dangerous land, making it somewhat habitable, somewhat ordered.

As dancers enter or leave a performance space, the choreography often traces a figure-eight pattern across the floor. In this they are marking the shape of a *naga*, the sacred serpent who inhabits both the earth and the water. Some of their hand gestures are believed to recreate elements of that mythic creature as well, the tail, for example, or its multiheaded front. The *naga* as a structural and decorative element on temple balustrades forms a bridge to the divine. And as the dancers embody the *naga*, they too link the heavens and the earth.

This link is reinforced through performance of specifically sacred dance and music. To this day, dancers perform on behalf of the monarch, as an offering and prayer to the deities and spirits, in a hallowed rite at the height of the dry season to ask for rain, and at other times to ask for the well being of the populace.[34] Enacting sacred pieces, embodying the *naga*, Khmer classical dancers have been bringing the land, the people, and the heavens together for centuries.

THE LIBERATED ZONE

When, in September 1989, Vietnam withdrew the last of its military forces from Cambodian soil, the three Cambodian political resistance factions based along the Thai-Cambodian border undertook an all-out offensive from their headquarters to capture parts of western Cambodia. The political faction controlling Site 2 (the KPNLF) secured a small area of Cambodian territory and, in early November, sent about thirty dancers, musicians, and technicians from Site 2, under military escort, into Cambodia, to the land they had just "liberated." While inside Cambodia, the artists performed a sacred danced ritual.

"We went there to ask the *tevoda* (celestial beings) to bring peace and prosperity to the people. They need the dancers for that," several artists explained upon their return to Site 2. The dancers had journeyed from the other side of the border to make a request and an offering to the deities on behalf of western Cambodia. Divine help was sought to break the cycle of war and deprivation afflicting this land and its people, "to stop the loss of life that results from incessant war." The ritual was also a means to ask that "the people of Site 2 be able to go back to Cambodia soon."

Surrounded by villagers, with musicians seated on mats to one side, having begun the rippling melodic phrases on their xylophones and gong circles, the lead dancer, visiting the "Liberated Zone" from Site 2, stepped into the performance space, dressed as a heavenly being. With a golden crown rising to a narrow point, a velvet sash over one shoulder embroidered in sequined patterns, a brocade skirt reaching to her feet, and wrists and ankles wrapped in elaborate bracelets, she resembled carved and painted images of celestial beings to whom Cambodians address some of their prayers, the *tevoda* mentioned earlier. As she balanced on one foot, lifting the bent left leg behind and up, sole of the foot facing the sky, toes flexed, she manipulated an open fan in each hand. Still on her right leg, with that knee slightly bent and her back deeply arched, she gently pulsed up and down as if she were floating through the clouds. When she stepped forward on her left leg, weight centered and low, and continued her entrance (back still arched, toes flexed even as she walked, head subtly shifting position with every step), she all the while exuded an extraordinary lightness. Eleven other dancers followed her onto the stage, moving in a figure-eight pattern across the space, recreating the shape of the *naga* (sacred serpent). Performing male and female roles, ultimately in pairs, they danced a piece from the classical repertoire, *Robam Phlet* (Fan Dance), which reflects upon the history of the Khmer, as part of their ritual prayer for peace.

The KPNLF armed forces' victory in western Cambodia gave their military and political movement a palpable boost after nearly a decade of protracted war. In order to protect their gain, the military and civilian leaders had the dancers make an arduous trek through mine fields to perform a ritual whose enactment would help to ensure a legitimate claim to the territory. They were crossing the border into Cambodia in effect to consecrate the land as Khmer.[35]

The performing body, however, can have "multiple valences,"[36] at once a symbol of the powers-that-be, a potent spiritual force, and a kinesthetic statement against surrounding chaos. Many of the Site 2 dancers spoke of not being able to imagine *not* dancing—they simply loved it, as dancers do the world over. By dancing, artists of Site 2 were, in addition to creating an enjoyable pastime, also subverting, on some level, the symbolic and physical violations of their integrity, "calling to the deities, who will respond positively if they are pleased, asking for peace," asserting a sense of continuity, community, and purpose against a backdrop of instability and cultural and physical dislocation, and reclaiming their humanity in inhumane circumstances.

EPILOGUE

Voan Savay, Meas Van Rouen, and the dancers and musicians of the Fine Arts Service of Site 2 were among the 365,000 people repatriated to Cambodia in 1992 and 1993 from the border after the signing of a peace accord by all parties. One dancer I had known committed suicide in the camp before there was an end in sight to existence there. Another saw her brother lose a foot when a grenade exploded. Eventually, Sophy and Tia joined the dance company based at Cambodia's Department of Performing Arts under the Ministry of Culture and Fine Arts. Only a handful of other dancers from the border camps did the same. Most enmeshed themselves in building new lives with their families (if they had them) throughout the country, either where they were given a small plot of land, or where they had people who would take them in. Van Rouen became director of the Phnom Penh Municipality Arts Troupe, and Savay went to work at the Ministry of Culture. Savay and Van Rouen have since moved to France.

NOTES

1. Direct quotations in this paper are taken from interviews I conducted in Site 2 camp. I worked in Baan Thad and Site 2 camps along the Thai-Cambodian border for one year (in 1989), employed by the International Rescue Committee. In Site 2, I developed and helped supervise a dance documentation program in conjunction with the dancers and musicians in residence there. In 1990, I began my PhD dissertation research on dance inside Cambodia. I made a return visit to Site 2 in 1991. While much of this chapter is based on that dissertation ("Dance and the Spirit of Cambodia," Cornell University, 1994) it is also informed by more recent research and the sad reality of new and ongoing refugee crises across the globe. It is my hope that ethnographic endeavors that pay attention to the reality "on the ground" for the uprooted might help counter reportage that glosses over that reality, and that normalizes the forces and systems that allow for or encourage such movements of people, and the unconscionable treatment they often receive, simply because they are stateless.

2. *Khmer* officially refers to the majority ethnic group of Cambodia (about 90 percent of the population), while *Cambodian* refers to any citizen of the country. In common English usage, however, the terms are often interchangeable.

3. The 1951 United Nations Convention on Refugees and the follow-up 1967 Protocol established a universal legal definition of a refugee as one who has fled his or

her country and is unable to return because of a well-founded fear of persecution. The principal protection due refugees is that against involuntary repatriation. Thailand was a signatory to *neither* the Convention nor the later Protocol. During the early years of the border encampments, forced repatriations, including over landmine-covered precipices, drew international criticism, but continued. See William Shawcross, *The Quality of Mercy* (New York: Simon and Schuster, 1984). In practice, countries of first asylum decide who does and who does not fit the definition of a refugee, and who, therefore, can be granted asylum as such. Thailand devised its own means of determining the status of asylum seekers, in this case, denying the residents of the camps along the border with Cambodia official refugee status, and the attendant protection afforded those with that designation. The border camps housed "displaced persons" as opposed to recognized "refugees."

4. David Chandler, *The Tragedy of Cambodian History* (New Haven: Yale University Press, 1991), 1. Philip Gourevitch, who has written poignantly about Rwandans, another group of people who suffered unspeakable loss and destruction, says that the reason he "look[ed] closely into Rwanda's stories is that ignoring them makes me even more uncomfortable about existence and my place in it. The horror, as horror, interests me only insofar as a precise memory of the offense is necessary to understand its legacy." Philip Gourevitch, *We Wish to Inform You That Tomorrow We Will Be Killed with Our Families* (New York: Picador, 1998), 19. The legacies of civil war, the Khmer Rouge genocide, and years in dangerous displaced persons camps are revealed in the physical, emotional, psychological, political, and cultural scars etched in Cambodia and her people.

5. See James Scott, *Weapons of the Weak: Everyday Forms of Peasant Resistance* (New Haven: Yale University Press, 1985).

6. Along with Sally Ann Ness, who wrote about dance of the Philippines in *Body, Movement, and Culture* (Philadelphia: University of Pennsylvania Press, 1992), I would like to "attempt to return bodily experience *as a form of consciousness and understanding* to a central place within the discipline of ethnographic inquiry, recognizing that to deny the interpretive potential of bodily/choreographic phenomena is to deprive ethnography of understanding an activity that may be as central to the human experience of another culture as it is marginal to that of mainstream U.S. society," 239n (emphasis in original).

7. Cambodia has been a Theravada Buddhist country since about the fourteenth century. Prior to this, Hindu/Brahman and Mahayana Buddhist beliefs and practices brought to Cambodia from India had interfaced with local, indigenous spirituality. Today the syncretic nature of the religious sphere is evident in many aspects of Khmer cultural life. As one example, Brahman, Buddhist, and animist elements are seamlessly woven into the practice of dance and its related rituals.

8. Toni Samantha Phim and Ashley Thompson, *Dance in Cambodia* (New York: Oxford University Press, 1999), 2.

9. Milton Osborne, "The Indo-Chinese Refugee Situation: A Kampuchean Case Study," in *Refugees: The Challenge of the Future*, ed. Charles Price (Canberra: Academy of the Social Sciences in Australia, 1981), 31–68.

10. The U.S. and other western governments continued to vote in favor of the Khmer Rouge holding the Cambodian seat at the United Nations throughout the 1980s, and supported the "resistance" efforts against the Vietnamese-backed government in Cambodia.

11. The United Nations High Commissioner for Refugees had authority over people in camps closer to the Thai capital of Bangkok, those recognized by Thailand as refugees. The border camp residents, however, were labeled "illegal entrants" by the Thais. These camps came under the authority of the newly established United Nations Border Relief Operation.

12. Cited in Caroline Moorehead, *Human Cargo: A Journey among Refugees* (New York: Henry Holt and Company, 2005), 27.

13. Victor Turner's explication of liminality in *The Forest of Symbols* (Ithaca, N.Y.: Cornell University Press, 1967) is referenced by Dwight Conquergood in "Health Theatre in a Hmong Refugee Camp," *The Drama Review* (Fall 1988): 174–208, and by Margaret Nowak in *Tibetan Refugees* (New Brunswick, N.J.: Rutgers University Press, 1984), as well as by others.

14. Lynellyn Long saw anomie and boredom engendered in Hmong refugee camps in northern Thailand (for those fleeing Laos) by this sustained liminality, this lack of access to productive lives, and the perceived and real lack of a future. See Lynellyn D. Long, *Ban Vinai: The Refugee Camp* (New York: Columbia University Press, 1993). In the Khmer camps, as well as those for the Hmong, seasonal cycles no longer served as focal points around which to organize lives and activities. Instead, artificial schedules imposed upon the inhabitants such as food distribution and military rotations, and the reality of never knowing when violence would strike, ruled their days.

15. Erving Goffman, *Asylums* (New York: Anchor Books, 1961), 35.

16. A study prepared for the World Federation for Mental Health and the Harvard School of Public Health found that "identifiable risk factors in Site Two [2] known to contribute to the development of serious psychiatric illness include: Prior history of severe trauma, including starvation, torture, physical abuse and the death of relatives under the Khmer Rouge . . . ; Ongoing trauma in the camp secondary to lack of physical safety and protection, including war activities, domestic and community violence; Chronic malnutrition (50 percent of Khmer children have stunting secondary to inadequate diets); Severe poverty (the majority of residents have access to minimum standards of food, clothing, shelter and other social amenities); Chronic unemployment (more than ten years) . . . ; Cultural, spiritual and moral deprivation . . . ; Extensive demoralization secondary to prior and ongoing trauma, camp confinement and the almost non-existent possibility of safe repatriation in the near future; Large numbers of head injured and physically handicapped individuals; Epidemic of domestic violence and the sexual abuse of women and children." Richard Mollica, "Communities of Confinement: An International Plan for Relieving the Mental Health Crisis in the Thai-Khmer Border Camps," *Southeast Asian Journal of Social Science* 18, no. 1 (1990): 134–35.

17. In Site 2, where inhabitants were deemed "illegal entrants," as opposed to "refugees," by the Thai authorities, protection had its own limits. In addition to armed banditry and artillery shells, people were vulnerable to the actions of the Thais guarding the camp's perimeter. Josephine Reynell's comprehensive and devastating study of life in Site 2 states that those who caught Khmer sneaking out of camp to forage for food or firewood sometimes shot (and killed) them, beat them with brass knuckles or set them up for "public humiliation . . . [by] forcing women to strip

naked and return to the camp." *Political Pawns: Refugees on the Thai-Kampuchean Border* (Oxford: Queen Elizabeth House/Refugee Studies Programme, 1987), 136. For a comprehensive review of the limits of international refugee law, see Hazel J. Lang, *Fear and Sanctuary: Burmese Refugees in Thailand* (Ithaca, N.Y.: Cornell University Southeast Asia Program, 2002).

18. In a collection of ethnographic studies of refugees from (and in) Croatia and Bosnia-Herzegovina in the 1990s, some of the authors stress that "[c]ontrary to the assumption that refugees get over their traumas in the course of consolidating their social and economic existence. . . , exile is a type of traumatic experience carved deeply in social memory, resisting the 'healing effect' of time." Renata Jambrešić Kirin and Maja Povrzanović, "Negotiating Identities: The Voices of Refugees between Experience and Representation," in *War, Exile, Everyday Life*, ed. Renata Jambrešić Kirin and Maja Povrzanović (Zagreb: Institute of Ethnology and Folklore Research, 1996), 14.

19. See Toni Shapiro-Phim, "Dance, Music, and the Nature of Terror in Democratic Kampuchea," in *Annihilating Difference: The Anthropology of Genocide*, ed. Alexander Laban Hinton (Berkeley: University of California Press, 2002), 179–93, for more on dance and music under the Khmer Rouge.

20. While there are stories of some artists killed once their identities as artists became known, many others perished because they were city dwellers or spouses or siblings of a soldier from a previous regime, all considered enemies of the revolution. It is likely that most perished along with more than a million of their compatriots from starvation and overwork, and lack of access to medical care, with nobody singling them out because of their art.

21. Anne D. Dutlinger, "Art and Artists in Theresienstadt: Questions of Survival," in *Art, Music and Education as Strategies for Survival: Theresienstadt 1941–45*, ed. Anne D. Dutlinger (New York: Herodias, 2001), 7.

22. Jean Comaroff, *Body of Power, Spirit of Resistance* (Chicago: University of Chicago Press, 1985), 251.

23. Hannah Arendt, *The Origins of Totalitarianism* (New York: Harcourt Brace Jovanovich, 1973 [1951]), 295, 297.

24. In the following sections, I have used pseudonyms for the dance students I interviewed. However, I have identified Voan Savay and Meas Van Roeun by name. Prominent in the arts community in Cambodia before and after the Khmer Rouge years, and in the border camps, and easily identified from their stories, they asked me to use their real names.

25. See Phim and Thompson, *Dance in Cambodia*, for the history and cultural context of both theatrical and ceremonial folk dances.

26. Dance teachers in all the camps I visited (some of whom learned this art as camp residents themselves) said that as opposed to the past, when classical dancers were selected on the basis of beauty, talent, and, sometimes, family/artistic lineage, anyone who wanted to, anybody dedicated enough to keep practicing, was welcome to dance in the camps. Performances, as well, were open to all.

27. The musicians, together, formed a *pin peat* ensemble, the mainly percussive orchestra that accompanies classical dance, as well as shadow puppet plays, all-male masked dance-drama, and Buddhist temple ceremonies.

28. For more on the teaching and learning of Khmer dance, see Toni Shapiro, "Dance and the Spirit of Cambodia." There are some parallels between the teacher-student relationship in classical Cambodian practice, and what Tomie Hahn explores in her wonderfully insightful (and interactive) book on the transmission of Japanese dance. Tomie Hahn, *Sensational Knowledge: Embodying Culture through Japanese Dance* (Middletown, Conn.: Wesleyan University Press, 2007).

29. In 1989, I attended these exams. Students performed a short version of the dance tradition's basic gestures and movements, a piece from either the folk or classical repertoire (depending on their specialization), and a dance they had choreographed themselves. They also had to sing.

30. David Chandler, "Songs at the Edge of the Forest: Perceptions of Order in Three Cambodian Texts," in *Moral Order and the Questions of Change: Essays on Southeast Asian Thought*, ed. D. K. Wyatt and A. Woodside (New Haven: Yale University Southeast Asian Studies Monograph Series no. 24, 1982), 60.

31. Chandler, "Songs at the Edge of the Forest," 54–55.

32. Ang Choulean, "La communauté rurale khmère du point de vue du sacré," *Journal Asiatique* 278, no. 1–2 (1990): 147–48.

33. Choulean, "La communauté rurale khmère," 147.

34. Khmer sacred dance has long been believed to have the power to effect positive change in the world. Its spirits must be respected as they, if displeased, might also wreak havoc, which people report they did when dances were performed without spiritual approval during the Khmer Rouge years. See Shapiro-Phim, "Dance, Music, and the Nature of Terror in Democratic Kampuchea." Rhoda Grauer experienced this same force in art when she went to the court of Yogyakarta in Java, Indonesia (whose dance is culturally and historically linked to that of the Khmer), to film the *Bedoyo*, a sacred dance honoring Lara Kidul, Goddess of the South Seas. When rain in the middle of the dry season threatened the project, the interpreter explained to Grauer that "it is a well-known fact that the Goddess of the South Seas is very jealous of her *Bedoyo*. This is not the first time unseasonable rain has stopped it from being recorded." A bit later, a group of women from within the court enacted a short ritual offering to the goddess. Shortly thereafter, the skies cleared. Rhoda Grauer, "Dance Matters," in *Envisioning Dance on Film and Video*, ed. Judy Mitoma (New York: Routledge, 2003), 154–55.

35. In the 1950s and 1960s, Norodom Sihanouk's travels (first as king and later, after he abdicated to become head of state, with the title "Prince"), with his entourage of palace dancers to drought-stricken areas of the country in order to oversee ceremonial performances, were a means through which the populace came to associate the royalty, dancers, and the state as one.

36. Ananya Chatterjea, *Butting Out: Reading Resistive Choreographies through Works by Jawole Willa Jo Zollar and Chandralekha* (Middletown, Conn.: Wesleyan University Press, 2004), 20.

No More Starving in the Attic

Senior Dance Artists Advocate a Canadian Artists' Heritage Resource Centre

Carol Anderson

*I*n thinking about the plight of senior dance artists, the image of the Victorian spinster—tolerated as genteel, though on an unfortunate lower echelon of society—springs horribly and vividly to mind. In recent memory, older dance artists have either been simply forgotten or expected, somehow, to quietly, inoffensively fade from view. I flash back to a memory of reading *Gormenghast*, Mervyn Peake's grim story of cruelty and power, with a pair of aging sisters locked away, far from life; when all resources are gone, they quietly starve to death.

It is far too easy to call up current, similarly chilling stories in Canada: a retired ballet teacher, for decades a seminal influence in our major national training institutions, lives a marginal existence in a tiny apartment; a sixty-something choreographer who mortgaged her house many times to support a dance series that featured the work of senior choreographers now drives a forklift truck in a big box store to earn a living; a founder of one of our key modern dance companies, his choreography warehoused, found work as a night security guard.

Too many artists have struggled with basic life issues, with indignity and impoverishment. Many of Canada's first movers, dancers, choreographers, and teachers are into their seventh or eighth decades, and their training and accomplishments most often did not include awareness of the exigencies of careful, early retirement planning. But their enormous contributions to enriching our culture deserve acknowledgment in meaningful ways. The business world, which dominates much of Canadian society, has little comprehension of the arc of an artist's life—and for the most part, artists value very different kinds of striving than those that directly relate to financial profit. As our society grows ever more brittle, what happens to the individual artist? The Canadian Status of the Artist legislation, passed in 1995, states the following:

> The Government of Canada hereby recognizes (a) the importance of the contribution of artists to the cultural, social, economic and political enrichment of Canada; (b) the importance to Canadian society of conferring on artists a status that reflects their primary role in developing and enhancing Canada's artistic and cultural life, and in sustaining Canada's quality of life; (c) the role of the artist, in particular to express the diverse nature of the Canadian way of life and the individual and collective aspirations of Canadians; (d) that artistic creativity is the engine for the growth and prosperity of dynamic cultural industries in Canada; and (e) the importance to artists that they be compensated for the use of their works, including the public lending of them.[1]

Despite the importance of the passage of such legislation, and the issues of recognition and compensation for the use of artistic work that such legislation puts forward, the fact that the lives of many artists whose efforts have had a tremendous impact on the cultural life of Canadian communities are financially precarious draws our attention to areas that must be addressed if "recognition" is to be truly valued.

Certain changes, concentrated in two related areas, do appear to be in process. One has to do with artists' life circumstances and the other concerns legacy as a means of providing greater support for, and honoring the contribution of, senior artists. One initiative that combines these areas exists in the form of a proposal for a Canadian Artists' Heritage Resource Centre (AHRC). As conceived in 2004, the proposed resource center would include assistance for seniors with issues including housing, and would also establish a fund for directing financial support to senior artists in the form of annual stipends. The center would also foster mentoring situations between older and younger artists, as a way of providing paid work for senior artists, and cultivating links among artistic generations.

Dancers have been major contributors to the plan for a heritage center. In Toronto, they have gathered at the Dancer Transition Resource Centre (DTRC), a national organization founded in 1985 that provides assistance to individual dance students and professionals at all stages of transition within and out of the field, offering academic, career, financial, legal, and personal counseling, and funding for skills courses and training through its program of Dancer Awards. Discussions initially stemmed from a desire to start a resource center for senior artists in all disciplines.

The initial motivation came from the DTRC's founding executive director, Joysanne Sidimus, who retired from the DTRC in 2006, while remaining an active dance advocate, and from Deborah Windsor of the Writers' Union, a national, not-for-profit support and advocacy group for book-published authors that was started in 1973.

International research conducted by the Writers' Union revealed that other countries have created programs to address the issues of senior artists. Countries canvassed included Ireland, Denmark, Sweden, Germany, France, Netherlands, Russia, Bulgaria, Australia, Switzerland, New Zealand, and Japan; long-term public support at about $25,000 (Canadian) per individual annually is the norm in Ireland, Sweden, and Denmark.[2] The DTRC conducted the Senior Artists Project, a national research project focused on senior dance artists in 2002, uncovering and gathering anecdotal evidence of basic socioeconomic need in Canada, along with additional needs for healthcare and emergency contingency funds.[3]

Prepared by Hill Strategies Research, the proposal for a Canadian Artists Heritage Resource Centre consolidated the various research contributions. It noted:

> If financial hardship is the rule for most artists, then it is doubly true for senior artists. Creators over 65 have made enormous contributions to the arts in Canada, and yet they are among the poorest group in the country. Most have been self-employed, have no savings or RRSPs [Registered Retirement Savings Plans, a plan that allows Canadians to defer taxation payment on savings], and few have been able to contribute independently to the Canada Pension Plan. Many face the prospect of living out their senior years on little more than Old Age Security and the Guaranteed Income Supplement.[4]

The first year of a new center was projected as an essential research year, for gathering information, including detailed statistics about levels of income and economic need among senior artists. Such statistics are necessary for case-building. For within the terms of the AHRC proposal, defining eligibility is a quandary—how to position the appeals to government so their response is not "What makes artists different from anyone else? Why not provide this support for every senior?"

The proposal goes on to outline objectives: "Upon completion of the planning stage, a Canadian Artists' Heritage Fund Endowment will be established with funds from governments, and private sources. The immediate objective will be to have enough funds to support two hundred artists at the level of $25,000 (Canadian) per annum plus up to $6,000 in demonstrated extraordinary healthcare needs not covered by provincial health insurance. An emergency fund will also be established to deal with the special needs of artists." During the second and following years, the center would be operational, with funding to be generated by private fund-raising and interest on the endowment fund.

There is an argument to be constructed, painstakingly, making reference to the past and present, projecting hope and better living conditions, and healthcare for the future. The proposal suggests that professional artists who have made a "significant" contribution to the arts will be eligible for consideration for support, and proposes that "significance" be determined by consistency of practice and time devoted to the practice of art, rather than by indicators of public profile or recognition. Age considerations include artists over sixty-five with demonstrated financial need, or over fifty with serious health issues.

Although an initial request for support for the AHRC was declined by the Department of Canadian Heritage in July 2006, the Senior Artists Steering Committee, consisting of a group of concerned representatives of the Dancer Transition Resource Centre and other arts organizations, continues to meet periodically, strategizing to identify resources and action that keep hopes for the establishment of such a resource alive. These dancers, along with others in the field, are passionate about their needs and rights, and how these relate profoundly to the insights of aging artists that should be acknowledged. Here the significance of artistic legacy comes into play.

Without memory we have no history, and without history, dance is caught in an endless cycle of reinvention. As senior artists, we owe it to our successors, to young choreographers and dancers to show them what has lived on the stage and in the hearts and minds of their predecessors, to let them know that there is vision and learning in what has come before. Mentorship offers possibilities for significant bridges between generations.

In an interview, Patricia Beatty, choreographer, teacher, and a cofounder of Toronto Dance Theatre who is now seventy-one, mused that dance looks to youth, energy, vibrancy, and potential through a lens of fear—fear of distilled, mature statements. As she perceives it, part of this is a fear of the body maturing, becoming more responsive to inner and outer realities. Full self-development of individual potential is a possibility, she observed, and should be a model rather than a threat. As a senior artist, Beatty's perspective is that connections among generations of artists need nurturing, so that younger dancers and choreographers can be guided by more seasoned artists. Creating community, she believes, will in turn create vitality.

The tone of arguments for the status of aging dancers, and the performance and preservation of works of dance has changed, and action-oriented initiatives seem to be replacing the shock of realizing we are actually growing older. Ten years ago, action on legacy matters did not seem urgent to the organized dance community, but the recent growth of activity in chronicling and documenting Canada's rich dance legacy signifies increasing stewardship within a community and an art form.[5] "Endangered Dance: A National Dance Heritage Forum" was sponsored by the Danny Grossman Dance Company on January 19 and 20, 2006. The three goals of this national conference, which took place in Toronto, were to draw attention to the need to protect Canadian dance heritage, identify the scope and location of current preservation activities, and collectively define goals for developing a strategy for protecting and promoting dance heritage.[6]

Seismic societal changes are in the works, and dancers, as ever, seem visionaries who hold up the bottom of the socioeconomic totem pole. But, a generation of dancers, now dancing strongly deep into middle age, helps make visible the shifts in ideas about the value of older people that are occurring at many levels. The province of Ontario, for example, changed its retirement laws on December 12, 2006, so that it is no longer mandatory for people to retire from the workforce at the age of sixty-five.[7] While it is too early to detail the effects of this change, which now checkerboards Canadian provinces, it is clear that the impact will be sweeping. Dancers often offer models of resilience, from juggling multiple career identities with vitality engendered by passion and physical striving that are intrinsic to their work, and they have often lived in a way that differs radically from the model of paying into the social coffers for forty years, then retiring for a few "golden" years before a socially timely death. Dance has wisdom to offer, in the broadest social context. When acknowledgment of such wisdom, and the ongoing contributions of our elders to enriching our cultural life, takes the form of real action, then, perhaps, the provision of resources such as those envisioned by the Artists' Heritage Resource Centre will move forward. Perhaps the pioneers are not going to starve quietly after all.

NOTES

1. *Status of the Artist Act, Statutes of Canada* 1992, c.33, s-19.6, at laws.justice.gc.ca/en/showtdm/cs/S-19.6.

2. Writers' Union of Canada, "Federal Funding Proposal," (internal document, n.d.).

3. DTRC, "Senior Dance Artists Report—April 2003 Draft," (internal document, n.d.). For a valuable statistical profile of professional Canadian dancers, see Kelly Hill, *A Profile of Professional Dancers in Canada*, Hill Strategies Research, February 16, 2005,

at dancecanada.net/download/Profile%20of%20Professional%20Dancers%20in%20Ca
nada%20-%20DTRC.pdf.

4. Hill Strategies Research, "Proposal for Artists' Heritage Legacy Centre," (internal document, 2005).

5. Writers in Quebec including Michele Fèbvre and Iro Tembeck have created a context for exploring the development of Quebec's extraordinary *danse-théâtre*. Tembeck's seminal 1994 work, *Dancing in Montreal: Seeds of a Choreographic History* (Madison: University of Wisconsin Press) chronicles the dance legacy that has fired and inspired Montreal's dance. Dance Collection Danse, founded by Miriam Adams and her late, visionary husband Lawrence Adams—both former dancers with the National Ballet of Canada—is Canada's dedicated dance publisher. Since 1988, when they turned their sights to publishing, Dance Collection Danse Press/es has produced a growing collection of books, encyclopedias, web exhibits, and articles, all initiatives that make accessible their archival collections and record the history of Canadian theatrical dance. See www.web.net/dancecol/.

6. "Endangered Dance: Campaign to Save Canada's Modern Dance Heritage," at endangereddance.com.

7. Ontario, Legislative Assembly, *Ending Mandatory Retirement Statute Law Amendment Act, 2005*, 38:2 Bill 211, at labour.gov.on.ca/english/news/m_mr.html.

Dance and Disability

ALITO ALESSI, WITH SARA ZOLBROD

I believe if you can breathe, you can dance. I've had the privilege of dancing with people who can't do much "more" than breathe and move their eyes, or their left pinky finger, for example, as well as trained professional dancers. Moving with such a diversity of people has taught me how universally and deeply the urge runs to dance—for people to feel, see, or even just imagine themselves expressing and creating new physical relationships. Many people I've met have either been convinced their whole lives that a) "since I have a disability, I can't dance, let alone seriously study dance and perform" or b) "I like dancing but I wouldn't enjoy dancing with people with disabilities."

I grew up poor, the son of an immigrant—more in the streets than in a nurturing home. When I was seven, my mother became a quadriplegic because of a car accident. My parents loved to swing dance, but they gave it up when she became disabled—though she still loved to boogey in her wheelchair to jitterbug music whenever it came on the radio. Because disability was so familiar to me, I learned to ignore it in a way. I didn't see her as "a woman in a wheelchair"; she was just "my Mom," a woman who loved to dance, a person with just as many quirks and just as much uniqueness as any other person. As a kid I loved dancing too, in the parking lots and street corners where my friends would gather with a ghetto blaster, or at school dances. "Strutting my stuff" helped me gain what little self-esteem I had. We kids from the inner city didn't even know that "professional" or "modern" dance existed; all I knew was that it felt good to get some attention by coming up with original ways of moving and expressing my "groove."

Fast-forwarding to many years later, I found myself still loving dance, and actually enjoying success in the contemporary dance world. I was always interested in expanding my perspective on dance, and I came across an article that really interested me, about dance teachers in England who were working with people with disabilities in institutions. One thing led to another, and my dance partner and I decided to produce a "contact improvisation" workshop for people with and without disabilities. (To oversimplify, contact improvisation is a dance form instigated in the early 1970s by Steve Paxton to explore democracy and community-building in dance through moving in relation to gravity and following a shared point of contact with a partner.) We put fliers up around town, made announcements in local newspapers, and also reached into networks of people with disabilities. It was March 10, 1987. We had no idea how many people would come.

On the morning of the workshop, people began trickling in early, and we were glad to realize the word had gotten around somewhat. Soon there were more people than we expected, but more kept coming and coming, and eventually to our complete surprise about one hundred people had gathered.

None of us had ever been in a gathering of people quite like this. There were professional dancers, contact improvisers, a blind mother with her three-year-old daughter, a guy healing from a motorcycle accident, a rodeo-rider who was injured riding a bull, and so on. One moment I remember involved two people with similar disabilities, a girl and an older man who had always been her role model. When she saw him for the first time out of his wheelchair, she quickly got out of her chair and log-rolled across the space to him. There were families, mothers and fathers with their disabled children, a boy who came with his younger sister who had a disability, all here to dance. The improvisations were so beautiful that it looked as if people had been working together for a long time, even though they had just met.

I learned that all anybody needs in order to dance is to be in a space where people are supportive, are listening to each other, and are respecting each other's limits and abilities. In talking with people afterwards, I heard that several able-bodied people had come thinking they were going to "help disabled people dance," thinking they would be in a supporting role. Instead they realized there was mutual support between them and all their dance partners, that every single person had something unique to offer, which broadened possibilities for dancing, and that each person contributed equally to the workshop. I always believed that dancing is a question more of attitude than physicality, and finally in this workshop my belief was supported and proven.

I've often wondered why I and so many "able-bodied" people I encounter find it so easy to open up and explore new movement possibilities in groups that include people with "disabilities." I think the more ways of

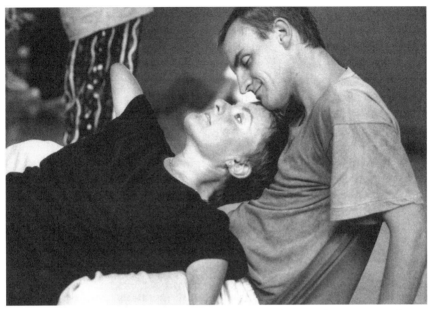

DanceAbility Workshop. Photo copyright Edis Jurcys Photography, courtesy of Joint Forces Dance/DanceAbility.

moving and thinking that we are exposed to, the more we can step out of our personal, familiar ways of doing things, and the more freedom we give ourselves to move in new ways. Also, people with disabilities may often face many obstacles and issues—physical, emotional, financial, access to transportation and buildings, lack of opportunities to dance, scarcity of representation and role models in mainstream culture, isolation, and so on—before they can even make it to a dance class. People who are liberating themselves from oppression are making a strong statement of empowerment that is infectious to everybody else in their presence.

When I first started to work with people with diverse abilities, a flood of new experiences washed away assumptions I had about dance. Mixed abilities work taught me (and continues to teach me) to listen differently and move my body differently, helping me to dissolve my old habits and patterns. As I found new shapes and forms, I opened to different feelings, and I began to respect and appreciate my body and others' bodies more, and I began to see beauty in more forms. As my movement range opened up inspired by the diversity of possibilities, my worldview began to change. When people change any of their ingrained habits, other possibilities open, be they psychological, emotional, spiritual, or perceptual. As a choreographer, this work presented me with new challenges, which forced me to discover new ways to express myself: "I can't choreograph a jump into this piece because this person can't jump, so how can I convey the same feeling?" Or, "I have to adjust my sense of timing in order to fit the range of possibilities in this group." I used to dance with able-bodied people all the time. In retrospect, this actually limited my growth as a dancer because I was only exposed to certain ways of moving that didn't include the broader spectrum of human movement potential. The ease and comfort with which I learn in mixed groups is amazing. I become less afraid of change; I learn more about improvisation here than anywhere else.

There's a little game someone played on me once. I was shown a pair of glasses and a pair of sunglasses (it can be any two objects that are somewhat similar and somewhat different), and told simply, "Compare these." The point is to notice whether a person names more similarities or more differences between the two objects. I am more inclined to see similarities rather than differences, and that is the basis of my dance work. Focusing on differences and limitations more than similarities and potentials builds barriers and contributes to oppression, both in dance and other arenas. My work isn't for people with "disabilities," it's for *all* people, based on the commitment to make dance accessible to everyone without isolating anyone. The goal of the DanceAbility method is to find the common ground in a group, and build relationships and community through dancing. As one Swiss participant of a workshop said, "We people with handicaps are not used to people loving our bodies. Normally what you learn as handicapped people is that people are looking at what is missing, what doesn't work, and nobody is looking at what *is* here and what we *can* do. This work really supports a different view: I learned to look for what is here and work with that. You give people back love for their bodies, and do that by moving, by playing and developing more possibilities to move." I don't see "disabled people" as "special," with "limits" they need to try to "overcome"; I just appreciate their unique movements as I appreciate "able-bodied" people's unique movements. I believe all people have something to contribute to their communities, and that communities are healthiest when they are able to access the resources of all their members. All bodies have both ability and disability but neither defines people's potential for relating and building a sense of self-worth and community through dance.

Monuments and Insurgencies
in the Age of AIDS

DAVID GERE

> We don't need a cultural renaissance; we need cultural practices
> actively participating in the struggle against AIDS. We don't
> need to transcend the epidemic; we need to end it.
>
> —Douglas Crimp[1]

$\mathcal{C}$ertain choreographies in the AIDS era function directly as acts of resistance
to civil authority by offering an analysis of the power structures that animate
the forces of homo- and AIDS-phobic oppression. The intent of such choreographies is to reveal the forces of oppression to the viewer, to render them
blatantly visible, thereby destabilizing them. These dances function in a realm
defined primarily by what I term *insurgency*, or, to be more exact, by the tension between monumentality and insurgency, between the status quo and the
attempt to subvert the status quo, between those who hold power and those
who, through the use of subversive tactics, contrive to alter the configuration
of power.

The importance of choreographic insurgencies in the AIDS era becomes
clear when considering the dearth of response from the United States government to the AIDS epidemic and the violation of basic human rights in relation
to prevention and treatment of the disease. Presidents Ronald Reagan, George
Bush, Bill Clinton, and George W. Bush all turned a largely blind eye upon
those who have died of AIDS. Reagan was so reticent to address the disease
that he did not speak the word *AIDS* until 1987, almost at the end of his

---

This article is a revised, shortened chapter from David Gere, *How to Make Dances in an Epidemic:
Tracking Choreography in the Age of AIDS* (Madison: University of Wisconsin Press, 2004).

two-term administration. The first George Bush was similarly quiescent, although he deserves credit for increasing funding for AIDS research and care through his support of Congress's Ryan White Act. Clinton, as a candidate, promised a response to AIDS that would rival the Manhattan Project, the intensive research initiative that had led fifty years earlier to the development of the atomic bomb, but throughout his two-term presidency he failed to appoint the powerful "AIDS czar" who would guide such a project. Indeed, no U.S. president has stepped forward to offer a commemorative speech or a transformative gesture that could be considered a sufficient response to AIDS.

In the absence of an adequate response to AIDS on the part of the U.S. government, it has fallen to gay men, lesbians, and members of other affected groups to publicly pose the most urgent questions regarding health and homophobia in the AIDS era as well as to propose solutions, all from a marginalized position outside the center of power. In the process, AIDS has been rendered public in an unabashedly tactical way. Our official addresses are not delivered by governmental leaders at major rallies—though the speeches of gay leaders at such occasions effectively mimic and sometimes parody such speeches, deriving power in the process—but rather by ordinary gay and straight citizens in their workplaces, by people with AIDS living from day to day, or by artists working in the street or on the stage. Given the heavy weight, the monumentality, of heterosexist, patriarchal, and homophobic U.S. society, such action is necessarily insurgent. That is, it signals a rising up, a revolution, a rebellion, against civil authority.

Art critic and theorist Douglas Crimp has devised a model for artistic activism that is a direct response to the AIDS epidemic, and that grows out of an analysis of stigmatization and mourning. The necessity of turning grief into public activism—and the efficacy of such activism in a time of urgent distress—is theorized with concision and sensitivity in two of his essays published two years apart. In the first, "AIDS: Cultural Analysis/Cultural Activism" (1987), Crimp puts forward an angry plea to artists in the AIDS era to do what is most important, when it is most needed. Is it enough for artists to produce lugubrious elegies? he prods. To hold benefits and raise money for AIDS research? To make art in the vague hope that the art itself will transcend our lives, and our deaths? Or, conversely, is it the responsibility of artists to save lives, responding as activists would to the AIDS epidemic? He asserts: "From the beginning my intention was to show, through discussion of these works, that there was a critical, theoretical, activist alternative to the personal, elegiac expressions that appeared to dominate the art-world response to AIDS. What seemed to me essential was a vastly expanded view of culture in relation to crisis."[2] Here, Crimp displays no patience for those artists and critics who rehearse clichés about the expressive necessity of art, specifically "the traditional idealist conception of art, which entirely divorces art from engagement in lived social life."[3]

But then, in his 1989 "Mourning and Militancy," Crimp reveals a subtle shift in his position, a shift that will allow him to come to terms with the mourning-versus-activism battle engaged in the late 1980s within the gay community.[4] (This was a battle to which he had in fact contributed with the 1987 essay.) On one side are those for whom the candlelight march or the memorial service is a moving and profoundly cathartic experience, and on the other are the activists, such as Larry Kramer, who harness their anger to accomplish crucial societal goals and who, therefore, consider mourning profoundly suspect. In attempting to articulate (and mediate) this conflict, Crimp searches for a way to understand the origins of mourning and militancy. Might these two categories, which appear on the surface to be so incompatible, actually be born of the same source?

Drawing upon the experience of his own painful grieving in response to the death of his father, Crimp ultimately locates his answer in a reading (across the grain) of Sigmund Freud's concept of melancholia, a serious pathology that, according to Freud, shares all the symptomology of mourning with the addition of drastically diminished self-esteem and the inability to return to "normal." But what is increasingly clear to Crimp is the degree to which the course of gay male mourning is systematically thwarted. The lover of the dead man sits in the back pew at the funeral, unrecognized by the family. The *New York Times* refuses to list the lover's name. (That policy was changed in 1986; "companions" are now listed.) The indignities mount up day after day. "Seldom has a society so savaged people during their hour of loss," Crimp complains, and he adds: "The violence we encounter is relentless, the violence of silence and omission almost as impossible to endure as the violence of unleashed hatred and outright murder. Because this violence also desecrates the memories of our dead, we rise in anger to vindicate them. For many of us, mourning *becomes* militancy."[5]

This theorization of the connection between mourning and militant activism—that activism is, in fact, born from mourning—runs parallel to the idea of the integral connection between the aesthetic and the political. This notion of interdependent simultaneity is crucial to any discussion of AIDS dances, because virtually every dance in this era participates polyvalently in the realms of elegy (mourning) and of activism (militancy), of aesthetics and politics. In fact, the topography of gay mourning and gay elegy is a primary component in all the activist artmaking of these times. Or, rather, it is more than a component of activism: it is its twin, its double, its ghost, its shadow.

In line with these ideas, this article considers a major "danced act of intervention" of the AIDS era: the unfurling of the NAMES Project AIDS

Quilt on the Washington Mall. This event activates choreographic sensibilities, which inherently have their political effects. It also shares a genesis in mourning with other AIDS choreographies,[6] which places these danced acts of intervention not in a soft, disempowered, or enervated condition, but rather in a dynamic insurgent relationship to oppressive monumentalities. These dances stand against the established order, against stone edifices as well as the invisible conditions of oppression.

MALL DANCE

Actions conducted in public spaces by people who have been rendered marginal or abject are necessarily rebellious, which is why the unfurling of the NAMES Project AIDS Quilt ranks as one of the great choreographic insurgencies of our time. The abjection of the lives memorialized in the quilt is made explicit in a variety of ways, ranging from male-male declarations of love inscribed on the panels to the signifying appearance of the unfurlers themselves, many of them gay men and lesbians who, through their dress, body language, and reverence for the quilt panels, publicly perform their own abjection. Moreover, the quilt is a site for abject grief, for mourning lives that, by the terms of mainstream society, are not worth much. As a ceremony intended to facilitate grieving on a mass scale, the unfurling reveals a portable graveyard attended by legions of "emotional support" volunteers; it is a site for public mourning. The unfurling ceremony that inaugurates most displays of the quilt is an AIDS dance, choreographically calculated to foment activism around AIDS.

It is Friday, October 11, 1996, 8 a.m., and large groups of white-clad performers are preparing to unfurl the NAMES Project AIDS Quilt on the Washington Mall. The physical location of the Mall forms a crucial context for the meaning-making activity of the quilt.[7] The Mall, which extends as a formal boulevard between the Capitol Building and the Washington Monument, with the White House forming a narrow triangular relationship from its position slightly to the side, affords a politicized rendering of the ceremony. The positioning of the unfurling at this site, along the base of a symbolic triangle, places the quilt in view of the nation's president, its legislators, and (rhetorically, at least) its founder and first president. The quilt display, while attracting crowds estimated to be as high as two million people, is activated by its relationship to these symbolic viewers. The spectacle is heightened by its construction as a form of speech, the quilt panels fashioned as letters meant to be intercepted and read, as statements about love and compassion for people who are living with, or who have died of, AIDS.

The AIDS Memorial Quilt displayed on the Washington Mall, 1996. Courtesy of the NAMES Project Foundation.

Just as it was for the inaugural display in 1987, the Mall has been prepared in advance by paid and volunteer NAMES Project staff, wide runners of black plastic laid out in a grid pattern to receive the large twenty-four-foot-square sections of the quilt. This bold template extends nearly a mile, from the base of the Washington Monument to the foot of the Capitol Building, transected at several points by busy roadways. The air is very cold, about forty degrees. As the sun rises higher in the sky, it sends beams of light scattering across the open Mall and toward the Washington Monument. Now and then, the sun moves behind a cloud, shrouding the scene in half-darkness.

The air seems charged with expectation. One of the organizers is calling directions into a megaphone, checking to make sure that every row of the quilt is matched with a team and a captain to guide that team. This is Youth Day, and most of the participants appear to be teenagers or their adult chaperones. Directly in front of me, a group of ten is forming: four adults and six teens. They are gathered at the sidelines, off the side of the quilt, holding hands in a circle. Their heads are bowed and it appears they are praying. A white middle-aged woman, also wearing white, stands next to me and pleasantly initiates a conversation. "These are my kids," she says. "I'm so proud of them. They're only thirteen [years old]." I ask where they are from. "Drew Freeman Middle School in Prince George's County, Maryland," she replies. Subtly pointing, she draws my attention to an African American girl in the group who recently lost someone she knew to AIDS; her mother has joined the unfurling team with her.

A voice over the loudspeaker announces that the unfurling ceremony is about to commence. At this signal, groups of eight begin forming circles around the folded sections of the quilt, each of which is situated in a space in the black plastic grid. Half the groups begin on the side where my boyfriend Peter and I are standing (the south side) with the other half beginning on the other (north) side. Far and near groups will cross and finish on sides opposite from where they began. The black plastic grid offers four rectangular openings from one side of the Mall to the other, each large enough to frame two twenty-four-foot-square quilt panels. Hence eight quilt sections are laid out like large folded flags for each group to unfurl as they progress across the quilt. The members of the group nearest me grasp hands, heads bowed, waiting for the first speaker to read the names of the dead.

The choreography involves alternate members of the group kneeling in to unfurl "petals" of the quilt—four layers of petals in all.[8] They reach down to pull back a corner of the fabric, then wait for the alternate group to do the same with the next layer. When the entire twenty-four-foot-square section is laid open, in a large diamond pattern, the unfurlers stand up and billow the fabric upward, over their heads. Simultaneously, they rotate the entire expanse a quarter turn so that the diamond shape fits the square in the grid pattern that is waiting to receive it.

The choreography is unabashedly pedestrian. As the group proceeds across the grid, opening panels in succession, some of the unfurlers remove their sneakers to avoid walking on the fabric, then put them back on again as they retreat. Onlookers run on to the grid to hold back the clear plastic that protects the quilt from the damp grass. Having laid down a section of the quilt, several unfurlers crouch and fuss with it a bit, tidying it into its location. Standing again, they walk to the next folded quilt section, grasping hands as they go, as if to participate in a form of communal protection. Their walk follows the pattern of a wide arc, the eight members of the team forming a standing circle around the next folded quilt section. The simple choreography consists of a combination of unfolding, billowing, and walking along curving pathways from one space in the grid to another. The pattern repeats eight times.

As the process continues across the breadth of the grid, the performers seem to slow down, to ease into their actions. Having completed the unfurling of all eight quilt sections in their row, the performers filter off the edges of the quilt to join hands at the perimeter. As they do this, they invite onlookers to join them. We grasp hands with the group on our side. Now the "circle" surrounds the entire expanse of fabric. This is a satisfying moment. Simple. Quiet. Contemplative. Communal. A long moment of silence offers the opportunity to gaze out on the mile-long sea of the quilt, and to absorb the symbolism of this danced action.

THE CREATION OF AN AIDS PUBLIC SPHERE

The AIDS quilt functions as a central symbol in a political movement not only to "regularize" homosexuality, to humanize gays and lesbians, to restore homosexuals from a position at the margins to a position at the center, but also, crucially, to bring governmental and public attention to bear on a health crisis of enormous proportions. A large nexus of ancillary symbols supports this assertion. The clothing of the unfurlers is white, a symbol of purity that collides with the societal signification of gayness as immoral, evil, degraded. The ceremony being enacted at the unfurling is somber and funereal, in the great tradition of military or political ceremony. The panels of the quilt are stored in a manner that evokes the triangular folds of the American flag when it is lifted off a veteran's casket. The reading of the names of the dead, often by celebrities or highly respected people, lends gravity to the occasion. The slow walk, the carrying of the fabric, the deliberateness of the actions—all these signify respect for those who have died.

The theoretical effect of the manipulation of these symbols turns out to be exactly the converse of the "silent speaking" that characterizes many AIDS dances. Here, abjection is announced, overtly signified, and rendered public, flying in the face of prevailing societal norms that call for privacy. The theatrical AIDS dance often seeks to keep its meanings at least partially obscure. The nontheatrical AIDS dance strives for the reverse. The difference between these two treatments of abjection is significant, for the very act of *announcing* abjection serves to transform the abject person into a kind of subject, however unstable. Thus, newspapers clamor to tell the stories of the dead. The unfurlers, panelmakers, and readers—all the "actors" of the ceremony—are emboldened to face their government and demand action. Abjection is foregrounded by the performance of the quilt, but then it is quickly converted into a demand for the rights of subject citizens.

This demand signals the rise of a newly configured public, a public organized to stand before its government and demand accountability in relation to direct care, research funding, and basic civil and human rights. The riots that erupted after a police action at the Stonewall Bar in New York City in 1969 have long been viewed as marking the advent of a modern gay and lesbian liberation movement. Stonewall made it possible for gays and lesbians to reveal their sexual orientations publicly, to "come out of the closet," to surmount shame with celebration. As a result of Stonewall, a gay and lesbian citizenry identified itself. I want to argue that yet another (overlapping) citizenry has now formed, in part through the symbolic valence of the AIDS quilt. Gay men, lesbians, parents, and family and friends of people with AIDS—all these citizens are standing together to demand equal rights and equal protection for people who are afflicted with HIV.

CORPOREAL FETISHES AND MOURNING

On the second day of the 1996 quilt event, I watched as a group of students from Goucher College in Towson, Maryland, learned and performed the choreography of the unfurling under the direction of Bob Pine, quilt display coordinator for the Washington, D.C., chapter of the NAMES Project. The preparations involved carrying the folded quilt sections from storage out onto the Mall. Watching people tug folded quilt sections into position is like watching pallbearers heave limp bodies out to the cemetery. The quilt is heavy, unwieldy; it resists their efforts. They do this in groups of four. I notice that the groups are quite merry as they approach the place where they are to pick up the quilt, but as they come back with the fabric in their arms, they have turned serious.

Later, I do this myself, with some of the Goucher students, and I notice how difficult it is to hold onto the quilt. It resists our grasps. In the sequence of actions, there is a particularly graphic moment when the handlers inside the storage tent heave the quilt "bodies" up to be received. In the remarkable transubstantiation of this ceremony, the fetishistic quilt panels are transformed into the flesh and bone of real dead bodies, the bodies of people we love. We carry the burden of their corpses out onto the Mall, where we touch them, view them, solace them, and grieve over them. Unlike the significations of the theatrical dance, which tend to be indirect and mediated, these fetish bodies provide a direct, unmediated signification of the AIDS dead. There is nothing abstract about the ceremony. After the quilt is unfurled, people gather next to panels that memorialize their loved ones, kneeling on the panels, offering flowers and notes. This gathering is a wake.

While waiting for the cue to begin the unfurling, the students assemble around the first section of folded quilt and join hands with Bob, who uses these last moments to explain the meaning of the quilt for him. He recounts the 1985 march to the Federal Building in San Francisco, at which the participants held pieces of paper inscribed with the names of loved ones lost to AIDS. "It looked to Cleve [Jones, NAMES Project founder] like a patchwork quilt of names. That's how the idea came to him," Bob explains. He lists the statistics—38,000 panels, 70,000 names, "and we'll read all of them." And then he asks a question that surprises me: "Ever notice which years we've done this in Washington?" One of the students answers, "Election years." "Right," says Bob. "This is what we consider to be a protest, a nonviolent protest."

So why perform AIDS? Why protest? Why mourn in a visible communal space as part of a public spectacle? Why make dances about AIDS that will be seen in national theaters? How do these activities embody the activity of a public that demands governmental response? The answers to these questions have become clear in light of the vacuum created by governmental indifference in the AIDS era. At a time of crisis, the performance of corporeality and the enactment of choreography are the most effective means available for a community to assert itself and to state its demands for action and change. Thus virtually all dances about AIDS serve to accomplish crucial cultural work, most centrally by creating a new public sphere marked by the powerful and insurgent coming together in abjection, eros, and mourning.

NOTES

1. Douglas Crimp, "AIDS: Cultural Analysis/Cultural Activism," *October* 43 (Winter 1987): 7.

2. Crimp, "AIDS: Cultural Analysis," 15.

3. Crimp, "AIDS: Cultural Analysis," 5.

4. Crimp references the fact that, at the time of his writing, activists such as Larry Kramer derided the candlelight vigil and the memorial service because the numbers of people showing up for civil disobedience were dwindling. Writes Crimp, "Activist antagonism to mourning hinges in part, on how AIDS is interpreted, or rather, where the emphasis is laid, on whether the crisis is seen to be a natural, accidental catastrophe—a disease syndrome that has simply struck at this time and in this place—or as the result of gross political negligence or mendacity—an epidemic that was allowed to happen." Douglas Crimp, "Mourning and Militancy," *October* 51 (Winter 1989): 6.

5. Crimp, "Mourning and Militancy," 8–9.

6. See for instance an analysis of choreography by the High Risk Group, a San Francisco-based dance company directed by Rick Darnell, which can be found in the original version of this article.

7. The Mall is defined here as extending from the Capitol grounds to Fourteenth Street between Constitution and Independence avenues.

8. This reconstruction is based on direct observation of the quilt ceremony, October 11–13, 1996, on the Washington Mall. In addition, I viewed a prescriptive videotape prepared by the NAMES Project. (David Thompson, director and producer, *NAMES Project Volunteer Training*, 1996. Videocassette, courtesy of the NAMES Project Foundation.)

· 33 ·

If I Survive: Yehudit Arnon's Story

As Told to Judith Brin Ingber

Yehudit Arnon was born Judith Schischa-Halevy on October 15, 1926 into an obser-
vant Jewish family, the youngest of three children, in Komarno, a small Hungarian town
on the Slovakia border. Before the war she excelled in rhythmic exercises and folk dancing.
After the liberation, she went to Budapest to look for members of her family, to no avail.
There she worked with the Ha-Shomer Ha-tzair Jewish organization to help young
survivors, and at a summer camp run by them she choreographed a pageant of victory
for 350 children. Arnon also taught orphans at a Displaced Persons camp in Aviliana
near Turin, Italy, where she met her husband. Together, they became founding members
of Kibbutz Ga'aton in Israel, where Yehudit taught dance to the kibbutz children. In
1965, Arnon convinced the kibbutz to build a professional dance studio and students
came from many of the surrounding kibbutzim for her classes. In 1970 she founded the
Kibbutz Contemporary Dance Company, which has performed extensively throughout
Israel and abroad. The Israeli government awarded her the Israel Prize in 1998 for her
lifelong achievements in the field of dance education and the performing arts.

★ ★ ★

I only studied through seventh grade, because the Nazis forbade the Jewish children to learn, and I had to sit with my mother at home. My father's
store was closed. The windows were broken in our house, and every week my
father had to report to the [Hungarian] police, because he was Austrian and a

Excerpts from interviews conducted by Judith Brin Ingber at Kibbutz Gaaton, Israel, January 5–6,
2002; in Karmiel on July 9, 2003, and telephone interviews August 17, 21, 2003.

342

Jew, and he would come back beaten. I was sent to learn sewing but I was no good. I dreamed of dance.

We knew Jews were being chased down but we didn't know about the camps. It was 1944 by the time I arrived in Auschwitz with my parents. The train car that carried us had eighty-four people and we couldn't move. An S.S. soldier raped my girlfriend in the corner. My mother tried to cover me with her clothes to shield me. It took us four days to get to Auschwitz. When the train car doors opened and we struggled out, it was totally chaotic as we were herded into lines. At the selection of who would go where, because I knew German, I said to [Josef] Mengele that I wanted to be with my mother because she was sick. He very politely answered me that because she needed treatment, I shouldn't worry, that he would take care of her, and that I should go with the other young people to work. I was falsely calm because of this for two weeks. I didn't even get to say good-bye to my father during the selection.

I was sent to Birkenau. With my shaved head and my tattooed number, I was one of one thousand women in one barrack. We slept ten to a slab, and if we wanted to turn over, all ten of us had to move. Somehow we managed to entertain each other. We talked a lot about food, and someone would tell a recipe, someone else told jokes. If someone knew how to sing, they sang; if someone knew how to tell stories, they told . . .

I remember sort of climbing on the slabs we slept on and stretching my legs into the splits. I thought that those who saw me in that moment knew I enjoyed it and I did something good. There was no pathos in it; I just loved moving. Sometimes I did a sort of pantomimed dance. I do remember one thing that was sort of a tug-of-war that I mimed with a long rope. I discovered an odd thing: my dancing could do something good for the women and it gave me strength to continue. My first audience was the movement I did for the thousand women. The splits, a bridge, jumping from place to place. Years later I participated in a program at Yad Vashem in Jerusalem [The Holocaust Martyrs' and Heroes' Remembrance Authority of Israel]. I heard that another woman survivor remembered that I pulled a boat. I only remembered the physicality of it . . .

The *Kapo* who watched over the barracks told me the Nazis were going to have a Christmas party [1944] and they wanted me to dance. I decided to say no. We all wanted to die quickly, and I thought that I would be shot—I would have a swift and good death. (For punishment Arnon was led outside, tied up, and made to stand barefoot in the snow wearing nothing but a thin, ragged dress.)

I could feel my feet freezing. I stood for hours, and I thought over and over about dance. I decided that if I would survive, I would dedicate myself to dance. Eventually I was led back into the barracks and then I was sent on to other camps.

In another camp, Plaszów-Krakow, in Poland, I had to move big stones day after day. To keep myself occupied, I would write my name on a stone, and the next day try to find it, giving myself a challenge to keep going. During the twelve-hour workday, I would also think up competitions to keep us all going while we made armaments for the Germans. However, I got sicker and sicker. We didn't know it was nearing the end of the war, and the Nazis were trying to kill us off faster by endless marching—we were marched to a different camp and many died on that death march.

In May of 1945, the Germans collected all the women that were on death marches from Freudenberg, in Moravia, and we were made to stand in front of a huge hole. I had already heard the cocking of the guns aimed at us, and in a matter of seconds I, too, would be a corpse in the pit, joining the bodies of the women who had been standing before me. Suddenly we heard screams instead of the expected gunshot. The Red Army had entered the camp and the Germans started to escape. At this critical moment between death and freedom I was in total confusion. Some of the women prisoners fell on the Nazi soldiers, but not me; I wasn't seeking revenge. Somehow I just started walking, and some of us got to the neighboring village. Me and my friends entered the first house, and it was empty, because the people had run away. The table was set and there was still food on the stove, and we just ate in silence.

Aide Memoire, with a Holocaust theme, choreographed by Rami Be'er and performed by the Kibbutz Contemporary Dance Company. Be'er was raised on Kibbutz Ga'aton and became Arnon's protégé. He is the current director of the company she founded, Kibbutz Contemporary Dance Company. Photo by Gadi Dagon, courtesy of the Kibbutz Contemporary Dance Company.

Index

Aboriginal. *See* indigenous peoples

access (to dance and the arts), xv, xxi, xxvi, xxxiin14, xxxvn25, 58, 102, 221, 256, 258, 265, 272, 283, 285, 332

Afghanistan, ix, xi, 68, 74, 78, *79*, 80, 103

African American, *xviii*, xix, xxv, 89, 150, 154, 156, 257, 337. *See also* slavery

aging. *See* senior citizens

AIDS quilt. *See* NAMES project

AIDS, xxix, 333–41

Ajuste de cuentas (*El recurso del miedo*) / Settling of accounts (The Return to fear) (Rocha and Illescas), 196

Alessi, Alito, vii, xxix, 329

America. *See* United States of America

American Ballet Theatre, *xx*, 114

American Planning Association (APA), 97, 98

Amnesty International, xxxin6, xxxiiin15, 85n53, 199n22, 274, 275

ancestors, 51, 58, 201, 224, 229

animation politique, xxiii, 51–62

Anticommunist Dance (*Fau gong vu*), 39

antidance literature, 21–31

apartheid, 140, 143, 145, 148–49

Aponte, Serafin, 188, 190

Argentina, 191, 297

Arizona, 101. *See also* Arizona State University; Dance Arizona Repertory Theatre; Phoenix

Arizona State University, ix, xiv, xxvii, 258

Arnon, Yehudit, vii, xxix, 342–44

arpilleras, 301

Asante, Kariamu Welsh, 58

Association of the Detained and Disappeared (Chile), xxvii, 298, 299, 303n4

Auschwitz, xxxiii, 343

Australia, 291, 294, 325

Authentic Movement, 229, 235n25, 235n26

authoritarianism: in dance pedagogy, 109–26

Autonomous University of Guerrero, 188

Aviles, Arthur, 260

Awadallah, Ruba, 295

AXIS Dance Company, xxviii, 258, 285, 287

Ayatollah Ruhollah Khomeini, 71–72, 77

About the Editors and Contributors

Germaine Acogny, artistic director of the Center for Traditional and Contemporary African Dances ("L'Ecole des Sables") and the JANT-BI Company in Senegal, is one of the pioneers of contemporary African dance. Collaborator of Maurice Béjart and director of his school Mudra Afrique, she created her own technique of modern African dance, which she has taught around the world. She was inspired to create *Fagaala*, a work dealing with the issue of genocide, after having read *Murambi, le livre des ossements* (Book of bones) by Senegalese writer Boubacar Boris Diop, which is the first fictionalized rendering of the Rwandan genocide. In addition to reading Diop's work, Acogny conducted personal interviews, gathering testimonies about genocide. A combination of Diop's fiction and these real-life accounts informed Acogny's perspective and creative vision.

Marjorie Agosín, human rights activist and writer, is a professor of Spanish at Wellesley College. She has written nearly twenty books of fiction, nonfiction, poetry, and essays, including *Dear Anne Frank: Poems*, a collection of bilingual poems, and *Tapestries of Hope, Threads of Love: The Arpillera Movement in Chile, 1974–1994*, which details the life of women under the Pinochet dictatorship. Agosín has won numerous awards for human rights work, including the Good Neighbor Award from the Conference of Christians and Jews and the Jeannette Rankin Award. She has also received two prestigious prizes given to Latino writers: the Letras de Oro prize and the Latino Literature Prize.

Gaby Aldor is an Israeli dance writer and critic, who lectures extensively about Israeli dance in Europe, Japan, China, and the United States. She is the contributor of the entries about Israeli dance in the Larousse *Dictionnaire de la danse,* among other international publications. She is founder and co-artistic director of the Arab-Hebrew Theater where she writes, performs, and directs plays. Her productions have won several national awards, and she is the recipient of the Rosenblum award for excellence in dance and theater. Currently she is writing a book about the Orenstein family, pioneers of modern dance in Israel.

Elizabeth Aldrich is internationally known for her work in period dance and has provided choreography for nine feature films, including *The Age of Innocence, The Remains of the Day,* and *The Haunted Mansion.* She has presented performances, workshops, and lectures throughout North and South America, Europe, and Asia and has written extensively on dance. She was responsible for the Library of Congress's American Memory Internet project, *An American Ballroom Companion, c.1490–1920,* and currently serves as curator of dance at the Library of Congress.

Alito Alessi is the artistic director of Joint Forces Dance Company (JFDC) and founder of DanceAbility. Alessi is internationally known as a pioneering teacher and choreographer of contemporary dance that is inclusive of dancers with disabilities. Alessi has received a Guggenheim Fellowship, Choreographer's Fellowship from the American National Endowment for the Arts (1992–1993 and 1995–1996), and from the Oregon Arts Commission (1991). JFDC has been in residence at the University of Oregon Dance Department since 1992. Alessi has taught and performed throughout Europe, North and South America, and Asia. He also certifies people to become teachers of DanceAbility.

Carol Anderson is a seasoned dancer, award-winning choreographer, artistic director, educator, and writer. Author of a growing body of writing on Canadian dance, dancers, and other cultural matters, her books to date include *Chasing the Tale of Contemporary Dance, Parts I and II, Reflections in a Dancing Eye: Investigating the Artist's Role in Contemporary Canada,* coauthored with Joysanne Sidimus, and *Lunch with Lady Eaton,* winner of a Toronto Heritage Award. Anderson is assistant professor of dance at York University, Toronto, from which she holds a BFA (Hons) and an MA.

Wyatt Bessing is a writer and educator. He holds an MFA in writing (Critical Studies) from the California Institute of the Arts, where he wrote his thesis on narrative approaches to the experience of disability and abjection. His work explores critical pedagogy and its connection to physical and text-based storytelling. He teaches in private practice and consults with primary and secondary schools in the areas of writing and sensory-cognitive learning strategies.

Linda Frye Burnham is codirector of Art in the Public Interest, a nonprofit organization that supports the belief that the arts are an integral part of a healthy culture, and that community-based arts provide significant value to both communities and artists.

Ananya Chatterjea envisions her work in the field of dance as a "call to action" with a particular focus on women artists of color. She is associate professor in the Department of Theater Arts and Dance and director of dance at the University of Minnesota, Minneapolis. She is also the artistic director of Ananya Dance Theatre, her dance company of women artists of color who believe in dancing to energize a future that is full of hope. Ananya believes in the integral interconnectedness of her creative and scholarly research and in the identity of her art and activism. She is the author of *Butting Out! Reading Cultural Politics in the Work of Chandralekha and Jawole Willa Jo Zollar.*

Ya-ping Chen is assistant professor in the Graduate Program of Dance Theory, Taipei National University of the Arts. She earned her PhD in performance studies from New York University, and served as the editor of *Taiwan Dance Research Journal* from 2003 to 2005. Her main research interest is in the cultural and intercultural studies of contemporary dance in Taiwan. She is a contributor to *Asian Dance: Voice of the Millennium*, *Legend: Masterpieces of Lin Hwai-min* (Chinese), and *Shifting Sands: Dance in Asia and the Pacific.*

César Delgado Martínez is a journalist, researcher, and art critic. He is the author of ten books, including *Guillermina Bravo: Historia oral*, *Raúl Flores Canelo: Arrieros somos*, and *Waldeen: La coronela de la danza Mexicana*. He is researcher at the Centro Nacional de las Artes (National Center for the Arts), where he has coordinated the forthcoming *Diccionario de la danza escénica Mexicana, Siglo XX* (Dictionary of 20th-century Mexican theatrical dance). He is president of the committee "Where Is Nellie," which has headed the search for the writer and dancer Nellie Campobello (1900–1986), who was sequestered for more than thirteen years with her death hidden. He is very involved in the study of Latin American contemporary dance and is the academic coordinator of the annual conference of Latin American Dance Critics that takes place during the International Festival of Contemporary Dance in San Luis Potosí. Mr. Delgado Martínez is one of the leading dance researchers in Mexico and Latin America with a specialization in the history of modern dance. He is also one of the major dance critics of Mexico. His strong social and political commitments are apparent in both his writing and activities.

Mary Fitzgerald has been active in the professional dance community as a performer, choreographer, teacher, and bodyworker since 1984. She was a member of Kei Takei's Moving Earth for nearly ten years, performing and teaching internationally. Currently she is an associate professor in the Department of Dance at Arizona State University, where she has received two Distinguished Teaching Awards. Ms. Fitzgerald regularly presents her own choreography, regionally and internationally. She is a winner of the 2005 Arizona Choreography Competition, and a recipient of a 2006 Artists Project Grant from the Arizona Commission on the Arts.

David Gere (PhD, University of California, Riverside) is an associate professor in the World Arts and Culture Program at UCLA. He is a coeditor of *Looking Out: Perspectives on Dance and Criticism in a Multicultural World* and *Taken by Surprise: A Dance Improvisation Reader*. His most recent book, *How to Make Dances in an Epidemic: Tracking Choreography in the Age of AIDS*, has been nominated for a Lambda Literary Award. In 2004, he lived in Bangalore, India, on a research grant from the Fulbright Association, studying the ways in which artists there are working to stop the AIDS epidemic. With funding from the Global Impact Research program of UCLA International Institute, Gere is currently leading a three-year initiative on global HIV/AIDS and the arts.

Amber Gray is an internationally known somatic psychotherapist and dance/movement therapist specializing in treatment of survivors of torture, combat, and war trauma; street children; and former and current child combatants. From 1998 to 2003 she was a senior therapist and clinical director at the Rocky Mountain Survivors Center in Denver, Colorado. In 2004–2005 she established and directed Haiti's first program for victims of organized violence and torture, and since 2001 has worked there as a dance/movement therapist with street children and child combatants. She was codirector of New Mexico's Alliance for Child Traumatic Stress, and, as director of Restorative Resources Training & Consulting, she is expanding her work to include law enforcement, combat veterans, and victims of trafficking. She has worked most recently in Indonesia (West Papua and Aceh); Darfur, Sudan; Norway; Haiti; and Australia. She is an *initiate* and *sevito* in the Fran Guinea tradition (Vodou).

Judith Lynne Hanna (PhD, anthropology, Columbia University) is a Senior Research Scholar, Dance Department, University of Maryland; dance critic; and expert court witness in cases related to free expression. Trained in various dance genres, Hanna has conducted dance research in villages and cities in Africa, and theaters, school playgrounds, classrooms, and adult entertainment exotic dance clubs in the United States. Her landmark books include *To Dance Is Human; The Performer-Audience Connection; Dance, Sex and Gender; Partnering Dance and Education;* and *Dancing for Health.* Over three hundred of her articles have appeared in publications, including *Ballet Review, Current Anthropology, Dance International, Dance Magazine, Dance Research Journal, Dancer,* the *Drama Review,* the *Washington Post,* and the *New York Times.* See www.judithhanna.com.

David Alan Harris (MA, LCAT, ADTR) is a dance/movement therapist who specializes in promoting recovery among survivors of egregious human rights abuse. In rural Sierra Leone, he supervised a team of paraprofessional trauma counselors providing therapeutic services in the aftermath of that country's brutal war. He introduced Sierra Leonean and Liberian counselors to dance/movement therapy practice—in 2005, launching the first dance/movement therapy group in West Africa; and in 2006, apparently the first dance/movement therapy group anywhere for former child combatants. His articles on these programs appear in *Torture: Journal on Rehabilitation of Torture Victims and Prevention of Torture,* and *Intervention: International Journal of Mental Health, Psychosocial Work and Counselling in Areas of Armed Conflict.*

Joan Huckstep is an independent scholar, choreographer, and educator who received her EdD in dance with a concentration in history from Temple University in 2005. Her dissertation examined the cultural and sociopolitical contexts of dance in Zaire (now the Democratic Republic of the Congo). She has been an advocate for the support of community-based dance in urban centers in the U.S., working with such organizations as Scribe Video Center, the Philadelphia Volunteer Lawyers for the Arts, and the Philadelphia Folklore Project. She has served on the boards of Rennie Harris Puremovement, Lisanga Ya Bana Kin Congolese Dance Company, and the Kulu Mele African American Dance Ensemble.

Judith Brin Ingber worked from 1972 to 1977 in Israel, where she first met Yehudit Arnon, founder of the Kibbutz Contemporary Dance Company, who has begun speaking about her experiences during the Holocaust. In addition to Brin Ingber's choreography and performance in the Voices of Sepharad ensemble, her writings include *Victory Dances—The Story of Fred Berk, a Modern Day Jewish Dancing Master,* her forthcoming book *Perspectives on Israeli and Jewish Dance,* and articles in the *Encyclopedia Judaica, Dance Research Journal, Dance Chronicle, Dance Perspectives,* and others.

Naomi Jackson received her MA in dance studies from the University of Surrey, England, and her PhD in performance studies from New York University. She has taught at the Juilliard School and Queen's College in New York, and her reviews and articles appear in such publications as *Dance Research Journal, Dance Chronicle,* and *Dance Research.* She has served as a member of the boards of the Society of Dance History Scholars and Congress on Research in Dance, and has helped to organize various conferences, including the International CORD Dance and Human Rights Conference in 2005. An associate professor in the Department of Dance at Arizona State University, her books include *Converging Movements: Modern Dance and Jewish Culture at the 92nd Street Y* and *Right to Dance: Dancing for Rights.*

Judith Kajiwara is a dancer whose parents were interned in the U.S. during World War II. She was cofounder of the Asian American Dance Collective in 1974, and founder of the Shizen Dance Theatre (1989–1995). She has taught internment healing workshops (using dance movement) to encourage Japanese Americans to further understand how the internment experience has affected their lives. In 1995, she began teaching and performing Japanese butoh as a gentle pathway to spiritual growth. She holds certifications in hypnotherapy, reiki, and crystal healing, and is a clay artist who specializes in sculpting ethnic angels. Judith lives and works in Oakland, California.

Marion Kant received her PhD from Humbolt-University in Berlin where she wrote "Romantic Ballet: An Inquiry into Gender." She has worked as a dancer, dramaturg, translator, manager, archivist, research scholar, and lecturer in Berlin, Cambridge, London, Guildford, and Philadelphia. Her publications include studies of pedagogical concepts in dance of the nineteenth and twentieth century, the ideology and aesthetic of German modern dance, and dance history in Germany, 1900–1989, the history of anti–Semitism, and antifascist exile. She is coauthor with Lilian Karina of *Hitler's Dancers: German Modern Dance and the Third Reich* and editor of *The Cambridge Companion to Ballet.*

Robin Lakes is an associate professor of dance at the University of North Texas, Department of Dance and Theatre. She holds the MFA in dance performance and choreography from New York University's Tisch School of the Arts. Her research in the realms of dance pedagogy and dance history appears in *Arts Education Policy Review, Medical Problems of Performing Artists,* the *Encyclopedia of New York State,* and *Writing across the Curriculum.* She served on the dance faculty of Northwestern University and as dance chair at the Chicago Academy for the Arts.

Ralph Lemon has been a vital force on the international dance scene since the 1980s. Since 2005, Ralph has been engaged in The Walter Project, a series of works in various art forms developed in collaboration with Walter Carter, a one-hundred-year-old African American man who has lived his entire life in Bentonia, Mississippi. The eventual inclusion of other Bentonia residents in The Walter Project has led to the creation of the Mississippi Institute, a formal structure through which local residents can participate in the development and production of interdisciplinary and experimental work. From 1996–2000 he was an Associate Artist at Yale Repertory Theatre and in 2002 was a Fellow of the Humanities Council and the program in Theater and Dance, Princeton University. He won the 2004 NYFA Prize and was a 2004 Fellow at the Bellagio Study and Conference Center in Italy. Lemon was an artist-in-residence at Temple University in Philadelphia during the 2005–2006 academic year. In 2006, Lemon was selected as one of the first of fifty artists throughout the United States to receive a United States Artists Fellowship.

Sal Murgiyanto trained in classical Javanese dance and performed with the Sendratari Ramayana Prambanan (1962–1972) and Sardono Dance Theatre (1969–1974) before making the transition into dance writing, lecturing, and festival organizing. He is presently associate professor at the Jakarta Institute of Arts in Jakarta, the graduate program of the ISI Indonesian Institute of the Arts in Solo, Java, Indonesia, and at the graduate dance program of Taipei National University of the Arts in Taipei, Taiwan. He earned his BA (1975) from ASTI National Dance Academy of Indonesia in Yogyakarta, MA (dance, 1976) from the University of Colorado, and PhD (performance studies, 1991) from New York University. He is founder and on the artistic board of the Indonesian Dance Festival (IDF, Jakarta 1992–present), a board member of the MSPI Society for the Indonesian Performing Arts, and advisor to the World Dance Alliance (WDA) Indonesia. Books (in Indonesian) include *When the Red Light Fades Out: A Dance Criticism*, *Dance Criticism: Basic Knowledge and Skills*, and *Tradition and Innovation in Indonesian Dance*.

Cecilia Olsson received her PhD at Lund University and is currently director of The Swedish Program at Stockholm University. She is writing a book on dance in Sweden from 1960–2000, and lectures regularly at various venues in Scandinavia. She has been president of the Nordic Society for Dance Research and, since 1995, dance critic at *Dagens Nyheter*, Sweden's major daily newspaper. She has been professeur associée at Département des Arts at Nice University and, among other things, worked for six years for the dance section at the National Council of the Arts.

Lemi Sala Ponifasio is one of New Zealand's leading theatre artists and a pioneer in the development of contemporary Pacific arts, dance, and theatre. Ponifasio is a High Chief of Samoa. He holds the title Sala, from the village of Leauva'a. Ponifasio founded MAU in 1995, naming it after the Samoan independence movement. *Mau* means vision, opinion, or revolution. Ponifasio travels throughout the Pacific region collaborating with master artists, musicians, orators, navigators, priests, architects, and villages. He also presents his works in major international arts festivals. His radical approach to contemporary performance is firmly rooted in the values of the Pacific, its ceremonies, and the role of the artist as a critical player in the community. His performances exist in the form of ritual and ceremony and incorporate the elements of dance, theatre, oratory, and visual arts.

Maysoun Rafeedie is a Palestinian dance artist and has worked with El-Funoun Popular Dance Troupe, Ramallah Dance Theatre, and the Popular Art Centre. A graduate of the Laban Centre London and with an MA in creative arts in education from the University of Exeter, England, Maysoun teaches dance for children through various schools and organizations in Palestine.

Janice Ross, associate professor in the Drama Department at Stanford University, is the author of *Anna Halprin: Experience as Dance*, for which she received a Guggenheim Fellowship, *San Francisco Ballet at 75*, and *Moving Lessons: Margaret H'Doubler and the Beginning of Dance in American Education*. She was staff dance critic for the *Oakland Tribune* and *Dancemagazine* and her dance writing has been published in numerous anthologies and other publications. A past president of the Dance Critics Association, she is president of the Society of Dance History Scholars.

Nicholas Rowe (PhD, London Contemporary Dance School, University of Kent at Canterbury) is a senior lecturer at the National Institute of Creative Arts and Industries, University of Auckland. His publications include the workshop manual *Art, During Siege* and the forthcoming *Raising Dust: A History of Dance and Social Change in Palestine*. Between 2000 and 2008 he resided in the Occupied Palestinian Territories working on dance projects with local artists, groups, and community centers. Prior to this he choreographed and performed with The Finnish National Ballet, Australian Ballet, Sydney Dance Company, Royal New Zealand Ballet, Nomad Dance Theatre, and Modern Dance Turkey.

Sophiline Cheam Shapiro is a dancer, educator, and choreographer whose work has been presented across three continents. She was a member of the first generation to graduate from the [Royal] University of Fine Arts, Cambodia, after the fall of Pol Pot's Khmer Rouge and was a member of the school's classical dance faculty from 1988 to 1991. She also earned a BA in dance ethnology from UCLA. Her published work includes the essay "Songs My Enemies Taught Me" in *Children of Cambodia's Killing Fields*. She is the cofounder and artistic director of the Khmer Arts Academy, which conducts dance programs in Long Beach, California, and Takhmao, Cambodia, and has received numerous honors, including Guggenheim and Irvine Dance Fellowships as well as the Nikkei Asia Prize for Culture.

Toni Shapiro-Phim is a dance ethnologist and anthropologist whose research focuses on dance and cultural/political upheaval, and gender issues, with a specialty in the arts of Cambodia. Coauthor of *Dance in Cambodia*, she received her PhD in cultural anthropology from Cornell University. She undertook three years of dissertation research in Cambodia, and spent several years working in Cambodian and Vietnamese refugee camps in Thailand and Indonesia. Her writing is included in the collection *Annihilating Difference: The Anthropology of Genocide*, as well as in *Shifting Sands: Dance in Asia and the Pacific* and *Encyclopedia of Asian Theatre*, among other publications. She has taught in the Department of South and Southeast Asian Studies at the University of California, Berkeley, and in the Department of Dance at San Jose State University, and was a research scholar at Yale University's Cambodian Genocide Program.

Anthony Shay holds a PhD in dance history and theory from the University of California, Riverside, and is the author of *Choreophobia: Solo Improvised Dance in the Iranian World*; *Choreographic Politics: State Folk Dance Companies, Representation, and Power*; *Belly Dance: Orientalism, Transnationalism, and Harem Fantasy* (coedited with Barbara Sellers-Young); *Choreographing Identities: Folk Dance, Ethnicity, and Festival in the United States and Canada*; *Balkan Dance*; and *Dancing across Borders: The American Fascination with Exotic Dances*. He is also the author of numerous articles in *Dance Research Journal*, *International Encyclopedia of Dance*, *Dance Chronicle*, *Iranian Studies Journal*, *Encyclopedia of Women in Islamic Cultures*, and the *Garland Encyclopedia of World Music*. He was a recipient of the prestigious James Irvine Foundation Choreographic Fellowship, a National Endowment for the Humanities fellowship, and received a Lifetime Achievement Award from the California Arts Council. He currently serves on the faculty of Pomona College.

Allison Singer holds a PhD in dance ethnography from De Montfort University, Leicester, England, and an MMus in ethnomusicology from the

School of Oriental and African Studies, University of London. She is also a senior registered dance movement therapist and dramatherapist. Her PhD research examined the use of and interactions between movement and dance, story, visual images, and folk arts (*etno*) in psychosocial work with war-affected refugee children and adults in postwar Serbia. Allison has held positions as the program leader and senior lecturer in the MA Dramatherapy Programme at the University of Derby, England, and lecturer in arts therapies in the MA Arts Health Programme at the University of Central Lancashire. She has extensive clinical experience as a dance movement therapist and dramatherapist with people of all ages and abilities, including refugee children and adults, adults and children with special needs, the elderly, and professionals. Her publications include a chapter in H. Payne's *Dance Movement Therapy: Theory Research and Practice*. She is currently in the process of publishing her PhD research and learning how to be a new Mum.

Yunyu Wang, professor in dance, Colorado College and visiting professor, Taipei National University of the Arts, Taiwan, is a founding dancer of Cloud Gate Dance Theater, Taiwan, performing with the company during 1973–1981. Wang received her MFA from the University of Illinois in 1983. She is a certified Labanotation teacher and reconstructor and is a Laban movement analyst. Wang has staged dances in the United States, Singapore, Hong Kong, and Taiwan. She is the vice president of World Dance Alliance–Asia Pacific and is the executive director of Chin-lin Foundation for Culture and Education in Taiwan. Among her many publications are "Taiwan's Female Choreographers: A Generation in Transition, Past and Present," in *Dialogues in Dance Discourse: Creating Dance in Asia Pacific*, Mohd Anis Md Nor, editor, "Reconstruction of Humphrey's Masterpieces in the United States and Taiwan," in a special issue of the journal *Choreography and Dance* devoted to Doris Humphrey, Naomi Mindlin, ed., as well as chapters in R. Solomon, editor, *East Meets West in Dance* and S. Friedler and S. Glazer, editors, *Dancing Female*.

Sara Zolbrod is a dancer, choreographer, writer, and actor. She has worked on and off stage for the Joint Forces Dance Company and DanceAbility since 2000. Her writings on dance, theatre, arts, and cross-cultural issues have appears in *Contact Quarterly*, *Corpus*, *New Canadian*, *Kinesis*, *Link*, and *Arthur*. She is currently coauthoring a book on the DanceAbility method.